The Language and Logic of Philosophy

The Language and Logic of Philosophy

HUBERT G. ALEXANDER

ALBUQUERQUE
University of New Mexico Press

Preface

THIS BOOK is a moderately revised and expanded version of my earlier one, *Language and Thinking*, published by D. Van Nostrand Company in 1967. The revisions have been made largely in the interest of clarity and in the updating of certain topics, especially those having to do with the theory of language and meaning.

The book was originally designed to be used in connection with a classroom introduction to philosophy. This is not to say, however, that the book is primarily a textbook. Rather, the course was designed around the material and sequence here presented in an effort to overcome some of the typical difficulties and misconceptions arising from the usual introduction to philosophy.

As its primary goal, the aim of this book is to lay a foundation for modes of philosophical thinking and many of the traditional problems of philosophy by an examination of the manner in which ideas are constructed. To this end, three basic processes of thought—abstracting, imagining, and generalizing—have been selected as the keys to concept formation. First, however, the primary mode of human expression and communication—language—has been discussed, especially in Part One, in order to help the reader and student of philosophy to become aware of the many linguistic devices which serve as indispensable clues to the processes of thought mentioned above. Part Two then deals directly with these processes, but still with attention to their symbolic formulations; and Part Three is designed to show how these processes culminate in what may be termed "the process of rational inquiry" including both science and philosophy.

For the reader already familiar with philosophy, let me say that the book presents an epistemological thesis, which so far as I can tell is somewhat novel. The emphasis in regard to this thesis is on concept formation rather than on justifications or verifications. Starting with empiricist assumptions, I am suggesting that all concepts, even those of the most imaginative sort, can be traced to experienceable roots if we add certain clearly distinguishable processes of imaginative recombination, refinement, and extrapolation, which themselves in turn are traceable to recognizable forms of perceived change. Clearly there is nothing novel in the notion that highly imaginative ideas and concepts are traceable to empirical roots. The only claim for any novelty here rests on the modes of imaginative thought which go far to explain the ways in which we construct these imaginative ideas. This thesis is nowhere explicitly stated except by implication at the beginning of Chapter IX ("Imagining"). But an examination of three basic forms of abstraction, called here "qualities," "relations," and "functions," prepares the ground for the theory of imagination outlined above. Some interesting consequences of this approach serve to clarify a number of traditional puzzles. For example, induction turns out to be that kind of imagining which has the further condition of being orderly and testable to a greater or lesser degree.

Since this book was not written primarily to proclaim a new thesis, the previously mentioned one is not made the focal point of the book. Instead, many alternative notions of concept formation (e.g., Platonic and Kantian) are indicated as alternatives, and the whole purpose of rational inquiry, including the philosophical variety, is the dominant theme. It is my hope that a clearer understanding of rational inquiry will not only increase one's ability to use it, but will gain for it greater appreciation. I hope, however, that claims for its potentialities have been adequately tempered by an awareness of its limitations.

In conclusion, I wish to thank again those friends and colleagues who have contributed so much to this work. My very special thanks are due to Dr. Archie J. Bahm for his continued encouragement and criticism. I am also much indebted to Dr. Melbourne G. Evans for his assistance on the history of the concept of the atom and also to Mr. Julius Cranston, Jr., for further aid in updating this section. I should also like to thank Dr. Charles W. Hendel, Professor Emeritus of Yale University, for his valuable suggestions in connection with this revision. Most of all, I wish to express gratitude to the many students who have "tested" this material, and whose puzzlements and challenges have constituted the most searching kind of critique.

H. G. ALEXANDER

Albuquerque

Contents

	PREFACE	v
	INTRODUCTION	1
PART ONE	SYMBOLS: INTELLECTUAL COINS	9
I	Communication	11
II	Language	33
III	Symbols	58
IV	Meaning	81
PART TWO	PROCESSES OF THINKING	105
V	Abstracting	107
VI	Qualities	129
VII	Relations	152
VIII	Functions	177
IX	Imagining	202
X	Generalizing	230
PART THREE	THE NATURE OF RATIONAL INQUIRY	257
XI	Defining	259
XII	Forming Definitions	279

XIII   Inferring   300
XIV   Systematizing   327

       BIBLIOGRAPHY   341

       INDEX   351

Introduction

FOR MANY BEGINNERS, the language of philosophy presents a formidable obstacle to the understanding and enjoyment of philosophical literature. The fault is not simply that philosophers use a technical jargon of their own, as do the scientists, although such a jargon is there to be used. More often the difficulty is that philosophical writers are fond of using ordinary words in quite unordinary senses. In this regard, the philosopher may be likened to the poet, and for much the same reason. The poet and philosopher both seek to bring about new insights by giving unusual twists of meaning to ordinary language.

The philosopher, however, is ultimately concerned with an orderly and systematic understanding of the universe and himself, and to this end his language is dominated by an urge toward logical structure and consistency. From this point of view, metaphorical twists of meaning, because of their looseness and ambiguity, may seem to be just the wrong device for the philosopher to use. There is a dilemma here which has pushed philosophical discourse in two quite opposite directions. But they are both indispensable, so that if we are to understand the language of the philosopher, we must

1

eventually discover the underlying reasons which dictate both a literal and a metaphorical language.

This question is part of a more basic issue where language and philosophy are concerned. Do our traditional languages assist or even create our understandings? Or do they simply stand in the way? Or are they perhaps neutral in this respect? To some mystics, for example, language is an impediment to be tossed aside when knowledge of the ultimate is sought. For the rationalist and scientist, on the other hand, a careful and correct use of language is essential. But how can we be sure that what appears to be a rational and correct use of language is anything more than a submission to linguistic habits and the conventions of grammar? Are these habits what we need to express to ourselves and to others our most valid insights about reality? Questions of this sort indicate the importance of a deep and primary concern with language for anyone interested in philosophical understanding.

The philosophical enterprise has had a long and illustrious tradition in the development of human cultures. The term itself is associated with the ancient Greeks, for whom it meant the quest for knowledge or "love of wisdom." Reputedly, Pythagoras (flourished c. 530 B.C.) first used the term "philosopher" in referring to himself. But it was quickly applied to the whole habit of speculation that grew up in the sixth century B.C. with the goal of giving a *rational explanation* to the universe in terms of spatial and material concepts. The philosopher was then to be distinguished from the poet, who was more involved with traditional mythic and heroic tales and with expressions of feeling. Then, with the advent of the "sophists," or self-styled experts, who in the fifth century went about teaching rather startlingly new and nonconformist doctrines concerning moral and religious matters, the term "philosopher" was taken up by Socrates (469-399 B.C.) and his disciple Plato (427-367 B.C.) to reflect their truer and more sincere love of wisdom, again devoted to a careful attention to reasoning, and especially to a theory of knowledge itself and how one really "knows."

Socrates' special style of intellectual inquiry, judging by Plato's account of it, was a method of question and answer aimed at finding the authentic natures of the virtues, like temperance and justice. The notion that there are authentic natures in some perfect or ideal form, discoverable to the human intellect, became a guiding principle for Plato also. Plato, however, extended his theory of perfect natures or ideal forms to include not only virtues but all aspects of the universe, especially in regard to human social order. And whereas Socrates, again judging by Plato's account, seems to have remained more skeptical of the possibility of earth-bound human beings coming to know the perfect natures, Plato seems to have been somewhat more optimistic—at least to the extent of believing that a few superior intellects could attain sufficient insight. To reach such understanding, however, we must follow a Socratic procedure of critical self-questioning until we finally arrive at a clarity of knowledge for which there can be no doubt.

Plato relates a "myth" based on the notion of transmigration or reincarnation of the soul as a suggestive way of supporting his notion of the possibility of acquiring a clear intellectual vision. While the soul is disembodied, says the myth, it comes to know the pure ideal forms or natures in a firsthand way. But when the soul is reborn into a new body, it loses this knowledge for the most part, so that the process of learning is that of reawakening the intellect to a knowledge it once had but no longer possesses. Learning is thus a process of recalling to mind the essential natures of the ideal forms. This figurative view, not to be taken too literally, is sometimes called Plato's "doctrine of recollection" or "reminiscence." It indicates that Plato did view with distrust any knowledge that is based merely upon simple direct sense perception of the world as we ordinarily experience it. It also indicates a belief in the existence of unchanging forms or "archetypes," which are the ultimate objects of authentic knowledge and which when properly understood will explain the facts and aspirations of this world. According to this view, for example, a particular house or tree here before my eyes is only a passing changeable imitation, more or less imperfect, of the ideal house or tree which constitutes its archetype. The same reasoning applies to human acts which more or less imitate or participate in the ideal forms of the virtues. To ge good, then, it follows that we must first know the good.

How can we be sure when we have reached the goal of an adequate intellectual vision into the nature of ideal forms? This is a difficult question for Platonism. However, Plato's general scheme along with his optimism has served as a hope and inspiration—a sort of beacon—to Western man. It tantalizes us with the possibility of some superior insights, even though these insights are not for the many. It has a strong appeal for the mathematician with his zest for grasping and exploring the implications of abstract relationships. It has encouraged the theologian in his zeal for encountering even while still on earth some inkling of perfect divine knowledge. But for the more matter-of-fact person, who prefers to trust his ordinary experiences, the answer of Aristotle has had more appeal.

Aristotle (384-322 B.C.), though undoubtedly inspired by Plato, found himself forced—probably by temperament—to reject the notion that ideal forms can have some kind of reality of their own apart from the world of experience. Instead, he thought it better to start with our normal perceptions and then to see what explanations we can make concerning them. Explanations and knowledge would result from normal human activities, such as perceiving, remembering, and organizing our recollections into general ideas so that reason can grasp their interrelations and implications. With these commonplace activities, Aristotle thought, secure truths could be reached. His confidence was thus placed upon man's native powers of reasoning. Whether we prefer Aristotle's or Plato's view of the source of ideas and knowledge, or some other, we certainly owe Aristotle a very great debt for stressing the possibility of using sensory experience as the raw material for reliable knowledge, and for initially sketching out the ways in which the human intellect can build assurances through the utilization of ordinary rational processes.

There have been other notions about the origin of knowledge. For example, some people have avowed that the important truths about man and the universe were originally revealed from on high to certain select individuals of earlier ages, to men like Moses or Mohammed. Others have felt that personal mystic insights, or perhaps dreams, are the most trustworthy sources of knowledge. But we are here mainly concerned with what might be called "the method of rational inquiry," and for this purpose the directions for attaining knowledge suggested by Aristotle seem best.

Let us end for now our excursion into the character of the philosophical enterprise with its search for understanding of a rational sort including the various ways in which knowledge may arise and return to the question of language. Language was not a primary concern for Greek philosophers, although they were certainly not oblivious to it or to its powers. Plato, for example, in his dialogue *Cratylus* specifically raised the question of the appropriateness of language to represent the objects and events that we put into words, and he suggested the possibility that some linguistic expressions have a more natural relation either phonetically or etymologically to their meanings than do other expressions. And later, in the *Sophist* (262-264), he notes that language as the expression of the mind's conversation with itself may be either true or false. Aristotle was himself heavily indebted to his linguistic analyses in discovering what appeared to him to be the basic "categories" or predicates with which our thought must work. But he seems to have regarded the various forms of expression in different languages as merely conventional differences that do not themselves greatly influence modes of thought.*

After Plato and Aristotle, the question of language and its role in the development of knowledge has recurred in some form in every generation. The philosophers of the Middle Ages, for example, were much concerned about the status of universals and whether language alone might be responsible for producing an illusory sense that universals can exist, or whether, on the other hand, language indeed expresses universal realities akin to Plato's ideal forms. Sir Francis Bacon (1561-1625) expressed alarm lest what he called "the idols of the market place," wherein vulgar understanding is governed and transmitted through common parlance, lead men astray in their understanding.† John Locke (1632-1704) was also concerned with the ways in which we may misuse language and how we can protect ourselves against these misuses.‡ But it was not until the nineteenth and twentieth centuries that the philosophical interest in language really blossomed. First with Charles S. Peirce (1839-1914), who pioneered in the field of analyzing varieties of signs and symbols, and then with Ernst Cassirer (1874-1945), who focused his attention upon the meaning

---

* See *De Interpretatione,* Ch. 1, 16a, 4-8; "Just as all men have not the same writing, so all men have not the same speech sounds, but the mental experiences which these directly symbolize are the same for all . . ." (Oxford edition, Edghill translation) .

† See *Novum Organum,* xliii and lix-lx.

‡ See *An Essay Concerning Human Understanding,* Bk. III, especially Chs. IX-XI.

of man's whole symbolizing ability, language as the primary human symbol system became a central philosophical theme.

Several schools of philosophy in the present century have offered views about language and its place in the scheme of developing knowledge. The Logical Positivists, for example, under the influence of the great logical masterpiece of Whitehead (1861-1947) and Russell (1872-1969), the *Principia Mathematica,* explored the possibility that an ideal logical language could be constructed which would afford greater precision for knowledge than the loose and vague expressions of ordinary discourse. Then the "ordinary language" philosophers of the Oxford school turned to language in its everyday usages to discover what these usages can reveal in respect to our understandings and misunderstandings of reality. In a different direction, Continental philosophy has shown a concern with the fact that language can give us an intimate and direct expression of the concrete experiences we have. Thus, for the Existentialists, language is a creative force, leading us into a sense of being.*

The foregoing sketch will suffice to indicate the fundamental interest that philosophers have had in the relation of language to human understanding. The question of the nature of this relation is a persistent and vital one. It needs a fresh look. However, this will not be our prime objective here. More modestly, we shall simply seek to lay some foundations. To this end, we can do no better than to look first at language itself, especially in regard to problems of communication, grammar and thinking, modes of symbolizing, and the nature of meaning. These concerns may at first seem out of place and trivial in an introduction to philosophical thinking, but this is by no means the case. We find very illuminating correlations between many traditional philosophical issues and the modes in which our language operates to express the nature not only of the experienced world but of the far reaches of imagination. In Part Two these correlations should become clear as we investigate abstractive and imaginative thinking. Once we grasp the underlying character of these modes of thought, together with the ways in which our language customarily expresses them,

---

* See especially Heidegger, *An Introduction to Metaphysics* (Anchor Books, 1961) , p. 145, and Sartre, *Being and Nothingness* (Philosophical Library, 1956) , p. 372.

we are well on the road to a sounder and more creative understanding of the philosophical enterprise itself. Lastly, in our concluding chapters, we shall turn to a closer look at the method of rational inquiry, involving at least a care for defining, for making inferences, both inductive and deductive, and for constructing a unified or systematized understanding. Philosophy, from this point of view, as the creation of the most highly imaginative form of rational inquiry, can then be seen as man's great achievement in reaching toward systematic understanding.

SUGGESTED READINGS

On the philosophy of language:
Alston, William P., *Philosophy of Language,* especially Ch. 1.
Dixon, Robert M. W., *What is Language?* especially Ch. 2.
Katz, Jerrold J., *The Philosophy of Language,* especially Ch. 1.

On sources of ideas for Plato and Aristotle:
Plato, *Phaedo,* especially the first third, or *Meno,* entire.
Aristotle, *Metaphysics,* Bk. I (Alpha) , Chs. 1 & 9, and XIII (Mu) Chs. 5-6.

PART ONE

Symbols: Intellectual Coins

IF REASON HELPS us to the *method* of philosophical thinking, the discussion group is its *laboratory*. In discussion we can explore with the aid of criticism some of our beliefs and their implications. Once we acquire the incentive and the knack of true dialogue, the world of ideas takes on a new dimension of possible meaning which otherwise remains closed.

Discussions sometimes fail to illuminate as they should. Perhaps what is lacking is a spirit dedicated to sincere probing for better answers; so that discussion retreats behind prejudices, dogmas, and clichés. Or perhaps communication is bad. When the trouble is communication, we encounter not only a major traditional area of philosophical inquiry—the theory of knowledge—but also the problem of language and meaning.

So, in Part One we shall examine linguistic forms and relate them to our habits of thought. Then, because the significance of language and symbols in general arises from their power to refer, we undertake to analyze the nature of meaning, with especial attention to the referential relationship.

CHAPTER I

Communication

Why concern ourselves with communication?
IN THE COMPLEX LIFE of the human community on
earth, with its nearly three billion individuals more
and more jammed together, speaking hundreds of
different languages or dialects, the problem of clearer
and more accurate communication has become extremely critical. This is especially the case in a world
in which hostilities keep man on the brink of an an-
nihilating conflict. Human beings are notoriously
touchy creatures. For example, W. J. Coughlin* suggests that a mistranslation of a Japanese word in
July 1945 may have kept Japan from surrendering at
that time. It seems that the word *mokusatsu* (literally
"silence kill") could be translated either "ignore" or
"no comment." The Japanese cabinet may have been
ready to surrender, conjectures Mr. Coughlin, but
wishing more time, it announced a policy of *moku-*

---

* *Harper's Magazine,* March 1953, pp. 31-40. This instance of
communicational failure is cited by Stuart Chase in the beginning of his book, *The Power of Words.* Mr. Chase's book, like
his earlier one, *The Tyranny of Words,* is a highly entertaining
tour through the world of semantics. Unfortunately, many
times his points break down under close scrutiny, and there is
need for caution in accepting his analyses.

satsu. Unfortunately, this word was translated "ignore" instead of "no comment at this time," making it impossible for the touchy Japanese to surrender without loss of face. If the message had read "no comment," the Japanese cabinet might have worked out surrender terms in time to prevent the atomic bombing of Hiroshima and Nagasaki.

Of course the Japanese are not the only touchy people in the world. Touchiness seems to be a fairly universal human trait, in which pride and self-esteem are closely involved. Each culture and each individual has special ways of defending its pride; and very often these ways are unintelligible to others. Even small incidents among close friends illustrate how easily touchiness can become reflected in the terms we use to communicate and cause friction. Imagine, for example, two roommates at college, George and Spencer, who are normally the best of friends. Spencer, we may suppose, tends to let his feelings get ruffled. Spencer has a car, but George has none. So George, being more popular, often borrows the car. Spencer really does not mind lending it; he knows George is a careful person. But Spencer is a trifle jealous because George is so much more in demand. Thus it happens that when George characteristically says, "Hey, Spen, how about letting me take the car this evening? I've got a date," Spencer agrees somewhat reluctantly. After George has gone and Spencer is left alone "studying," his thoughts begin to center upon the word "take." George is getting altogether too cocky. Why doesn't he ask to "borrow" the car? The more Spencer broods over the matter, the more "take" acquires a nasty possessiveness. So the next time George asks to "take" the car, it is refused for no apparent reason except a rather bitter remark about George's always *taking* the car instead of *borrowing* it. *"Take, borrow,* don't they mean the same thing?" asks George. Naturally he is annoyed, and a congenial friendship may go on the rocks.

Something like the foregoing situation is often apt to upset the pleasant calm of human relationships. To be sure, it is not words alone that cause all the difficulty. Jealousy and other forms of sensitiveness contribute their share. But the moment tensions arise, the chance of mistaken meanings or of innuendos wrongly ascribed becomes much greater. Notice, for example, how in courts of law a highly formalized terminology has grown up largely for the sake of precision, but also no doubt to fore-stall provocative utterances which in the absence of such precision might arise even more easily than they do.

To understand the social importance of communication, let us try to imagine a "society" in which no form of communication exists. Whether it is a society of human beings or of animals or of insects, one can seriously doubt whether it could even come into existence without some form of communication among its members. Pebbles on the beach do not communicate. But neither do they constitute a society, even though they may be arranged in some complex design; some interchange of messages must flow back and forth before a society is possible.* In human society communication is a basic necessity. Some few persons surfeited with human stupidity and ingratitude may enjoy the life of the hermit, but even the hermit tends to create a new society for himself peopled with the plants, birds, and animals about him, or possibly a world of heavenly hosts. Symbolic expression is sometimes taken as the essential human trait. Aristotle character-ized man both as a "political," i.e., a social, animal and as a "ra-tional" animal. It appears that these two features are closely con-nected, for in reasoning man must depend to a considerable degree upon his symbolizations, which in turn arose from his need to com-municate socially. Perhaps not every type of animal communica-tion involves "reasoning." Aristotle thought that this ability is peculiar to man; and it may very well be that human reason is the result of a wider possibility of imaginative associations than is open to other animals. In any case, extensive thinking or reasoning pre-supposes some system of signs or symbols such as arise from the need to communicate.

---

* Bees, for example, have received special attention because some form of communication plays an important role in allowing them to establish and maintain the highly complex social structure which they have. The dance of the bee on the honeycomb tells to other bees the direction and distance of food; and the scenting of food or pollen samples on the legs of returning bees indicates what to expect. This "knowledge" is spread through the beehive with amazing rapidity, samples of the food being passed from one bee to another. And not only is knowledge about food communicated but also information on the needs and condition of the queen. See Karl von Frisch, *The Language of Bees,* Smith-sonian Report, Washington, 1939; and also articles by August Krogh and Hans Kalmus in the *Scientific American* for August 1948 and July 1953.

How do human beings communicate?

Man communicates principally through language. The nature of language we shall examine in more detail in Chapters II and III, but we may observe here that it includes not only vocal or spoken forms but also pictorial, written, gesticulated, and other forms of symbolization. Presumably, speaking is man's most natural mode of communicating. Yet crude drawings have served for communicating since Paleolithic times. The story of writing, with the eventual invention of phonetic writing, is a fascinating account of one of the great human conquests. Even today, cultures such as the Chinese, which did not benefit from this invention, have suffered from the tremendous problem created by the necessity of learning so many different written symbols. Compare, for example, a Chinese typewriter with one of our own. It is impossible to put the ten thousand or so characters of traditional Chinese writing on one machine; so attempts have been made to devise typewriters with a selected minimum set of characters, say three hundred. Even this number poses a mechanical problem far beyond that of our forty-two key typewriters with their sixty-four possible characters.*

In addition to speaking and writing, man can use his arms and fingers as devices for communicating. The American Indian sign languages and the language of the deaf illustrate such methods of communication. Note that whereas the language developed for the deaf is based upon the phonetic alphabet, the Indian sign language is not. Rather it is pictorial or ideographic like primitive written symbols. Remember also the importance of facial expressions which even become formalized gestures with some peoples; for example, some American Indians point directions with their lips. Southern Europeans have the reputation of needing their hands to accompany their spoken discourse, and it is customary for most peoples to accentuate spoken language by various movements or intonations.

To supplement man's physiological tools for communicating (his voice, fingers, arms, facial expressions, etc.) he has invented a vast array of devices, especially transmitters and receivers. Some of these, such as the telegraph, require special symbol systems (e.g.,

* On Chinese typewriters, see *Popular Mechanics* for December 1947 and *Science News Letter* for September 6, 1947.

the Morse code). When we consider the variety of communication by flags, wigwags, blinking lights, and the like, to which twentieth-century man has become addicted, we can begin to appreciate a little better what an important place the need for communication plays in human affairs.

What elements are involved in communicating?

Communication may be thought of as involving four elements: (1) the communicator, or sender of the message, (2) the communicatee, or recipient of the message, (3) the transmitting and receiving devices, which in simple speaking are merely one's vocal cords and ears, and (4) the message itself. For convenience, let us designate the communicator as C_1, the communicatee as C_2, the transmitting device as Tr, and the receiving device as Rc. Then we can diagram the communicative process as in Fig. 1.

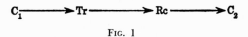

FIG. 1

But now what of the message, the fourth element mentioned above? Upon further analysis, this single element turns out to be a complex of at least four ingredients. These are (1) the *object, event, or situation* to which reference is being made; (2) the manner in which the communicator or communicatee *conceives* this object, event, or situation; (3) the set of *symbols* used to convey the communicator's concept; and (4) the *background experiences, attitudes, and knowledge* which affect the manner of conceiving on the part of either the communicator or communicatee. Let us designate these items by the letters R for the "referent" or object, event, or situation referred to; C for concept or manner of conceiving; S for symbol or set of symbols; and E for background experience, attitude, and knowledge. We can designate the relation of these ingredients schematically as in Fig. 2.

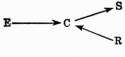

FIG. 2

The process of formulating the message is often called "encoding."* It is the communicator who encodes, and his act may be represented as in Fig. 3.

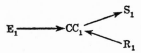

FIG. 3. *Encoding.* E_1, *the background experience, attitude, and knowledge of the communicator;* CC_1, *the concept of the communicator;* S_1, *symbol used by the communicator;* R_1, *referent as perceived or imagined by the communicator.*

The reverse process is similarly called "decoding," and is the act of the communicatee. It could be diagrammed as the reverse of the encoding process (Fig. 4).

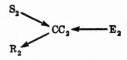

FIG. 4. *Decoding.* S_2, *symbols as understood by the communicatee;* R_2, *referent as perceived or imagined by the communicatee;* CC_2, *concept of the communicatee;* E_2, *background of the communicatee.*

For example, someone says "house." We presume there is a visible object, a house, which is his referent (R_1); and that for some reason he has formed a mental picture or idea of this house (CC_1). Further, his conception of the house has been influenced by his past familiarity with such things (E_1). And finally he has symbolized his concept with the word "house" (S_1). Now someone else hears the word "house" (S_2); in terms of his past experience (E_2)

* In the language of communication engineering, "encoding" and "decoding" may refer to the mechanical activity which takes place in the transmitter and receiver. Here, however, we shall limit these terms to the activity of the communicator and communicatee. Communication experts commonly separate the transmitting-receiving process into three stages: (1) the transmitting, (2) the channeling (or moving of the physical symbols through a medium, such as sound through the air), and (3) the receiving. "Channeling" is thus the mechanical process that goes on between the transmitter and the receiver. See George A. Miller, *Language and Communication*, pp. 7-8; or Shannon and Weaver, *The Mathematical Theory of Communication.*

he conceives the meaning of the symbol and arrives at his concept (CC_2); and then looks for the referent (R_2) which may be visible to him at the time he hears the word spoken, or it may not. The hope is that he will arrive at the same object as is referred to by the speaker, so that (if the communication is successful) R_1 will equal R_2. Or we may put it generally: communication is successful to the extent that $R_1 = R_2$.

In the above process we must not overlook the importance of the factor of background experience and resultant attitude, on the part of both communicator and communicatee. Human beings easily acquire sets of predispositions and preconceptions which tend to orient their understandings. Familiarity or lack of familiarity with certain areas of experience, for example, naturally predisposes one to view things in different ways. Constant dealing in certain affairs rather than others can produce such differences in orientation. Thus, the word "buttonholing" will have different meanings for a dressmaker and a politician.

In communication there is a better chance for success if the backgrounds and predispositions of the communicator and communicatee are similar. If the probable intentions of the speaker are well known in advance, it is easier to communicate. If, on the contrary, the speaker's attitude is unknown or has recently undergone a change, the burden of correct inference of meaning will depend upon the listener's astuteness. Suppose, for example, that two persons are hiking in the desert, when the one who is carrying the canteen hears the other mutter "Drink!" The water carrier might reasonably suppose that his companion was asking for a drink. But suppose this companion were meditating upon the sad plight of an alcoholic friend. Then his muttered "Drink!" would have quite a different and unanticipated meaning.

This whole question of the influence of background experience, attitude, and knowledge upon the parties to a communication is an intricate one. Common experience is certainly a great asset to successful communication. For example, it surprises some adults that children of different language groups, when thrown together, get on as well as they often do. In such cases, it is probable that the common interests of children serve to make communication easier, even though they speak different languages. Gesture and pantomime also frequently serve where normal language is unavailable

—but only when the intention is easily perceptible thanks to common background experiences.

We can now diagram the entire communicative process, including (1) the phase of encoding, (2) the phase of transmitting and receiving, and (3) the phase of decoding (Fig. 5). The letters in

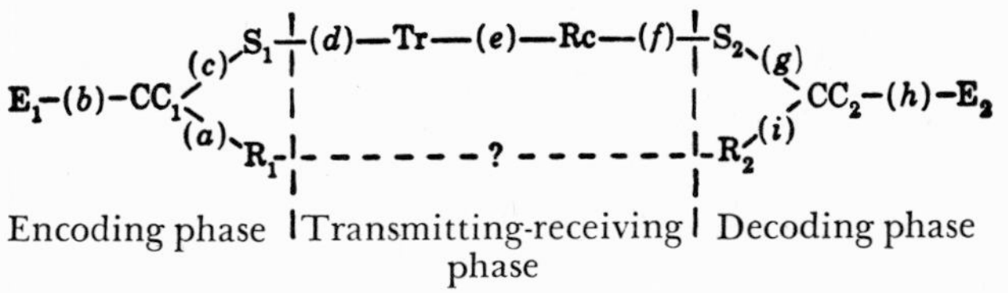

$$E_1-(b)-CC_1 \underset{(a)}{\overset{(c)}{<}} \begin{matrix} S_1-\!\!|-(d)-Tr-(e)-Rc-(f)-\!\!|-S_2 \diagdown (g) \\ | \qquad\qquad\qquad\qquad | \qquad\qquad > CC_2-(h)-E_2 \\ R_1-\!\!|------?------\!\!|-R_2 \diagup (i) \end{matrix}$$

Encoding phase |Transmitting-receiving | Decoding phase
phase

FIG. 5

parentheses designate the relations which exist between the adjacent elements of the entire process. The question mark between R_1 and R_2 indicates doubt as to whether a particular communication is successful or not. Let us turn next to the question of the success or failure of communications and investigate the possibilities in terms of the relations shown in the above diagram.

Why does communication fail?

The basic problem of communication may be taken to be the ability to reduce error to a minimum. Certain types of communication appear to have a better chance of success than others. For example, most people prefer face-to-face conversations to letter writing or even telephonic communication. Why is this so? For one thing, face-to-face conversation allows one to supplement spoken symbols with gestures and facial expressions. A textbook by itself is not so satisfactory as a textbook plus a lecturer, especially if the lecturer also answers questions. For, as Plato remarked,* once something is written down and launched on its own, it can but give back the same unvarying reply, no matter what questions the reader may wish to put to it. Written material, as he says, no longer has "a parent to protect it" and so becomes subject to many misin-

* *Phaedrus,* 275.

terpretations. On the other hand, we must not minimize the great advantage and importance of writing. Not only does writing serve better for those who have speech defects, but until the most recent times, writing alone endured, as speech could not. Cultures possessing writing have a tremendous advantage in the preservation of documents and learning, and in the freeing of time from laborious memorizing, so that in these cultures the accumulation of knowledge itself is accelerated.

Turning to Fig. 5, let us inquire into the particular varieties of error that may creep in at the various stages. We shall start with the relation (*a*) and continue on around.

(*a*) R_1 *to* CC_1. The relation indicated by (*a*) may be regarded as raising the question of the accuracy or adequacy of the communicator's concept of the referent, that is, of the object, event, or situation to which he is referring. For a simple example, consider the case of an animal running across the road in front of one's car at night. It may be difficult to form a clear and accurate picture of the object. A cat may be mistaken for a dog, or a squirrel for a rabbit. So, if a driver should say to his companion, "Hey, there went a dog!" when it was really a cat, there would be a failure because of an erroneous concept. In such a case it is possible for the communicator to use the correct symbol for his concept, but to have the wrong concept for the referent.

The primary source of the trouble here is a lack of clear perception. The communicator reports falsely because he did not perceive correctly. We must realize, however, that before a report and a communication of any kind can be made, the communicator must locate the perceived object within a set of categories already learned, and that these categories must have conventional names or symbols. What we are dealing with here, then, is a mistake in assigning a proper identification and categorization to the perceived object because of an unclear perception. If one sees an animal run across the road without seeing it clearly, and reports that it is a rabbit, when on second look it turns out to be a raccoon or something else, then one has formed the wrong concept of the animal in terms of previously learned categories of animals. This error is conceptual, but due to an unclear perception. It is therefore a *perceptual-conceptual* error. It is not yet an error in symbolizing, although the wrong symbol (e.g., "rabbit") has been used. This was the right symbol for the wrong concept, not the wrong symbol for the right concept. The trouble is with the concept, not with the selection of words.

In the above example, let it be noted, the error was due to an unclear *perception* of the referent. But the question whether all referents are perceivable should be asked. Supposing the referent is something not now perceivable, such as an old kitchen chair remembered from one's childhood, or the ratio signified by the letter π, or the shape of the earth, or democratic government, or goodness. These are all legitimate matters to which reference can be made, and therefore should be called referents, even though no one of them is directly perceivable. Of course, the old kitchen chair, though only a memory now, was once a perceivable object. The ratio π is a precisely definable relation, of which the related elements can be perceived whenever a circle is drawn with a diameter, and the diameter is imaginatively picked up and laid out around the circumference to see how many times it will go. The shape of the earth can now be perceived and photographed from a space vehicle or from the moon, but such a view of the earth only gives one side. We still need to fill in the full three-dimensional concept of the earth's shape by using our imagination. Democratic government is a concept formed from certain political ideals, on the one hand, together with certain witnessable practices, like popular voting, on the other. Such a concept, even as an ideal, becomes culturally defined, so that as a referent in one person's mind, it might or might not coincide with the accepted cultural meaning. Goodness, too, is partly a conjunction of imaginatively extended qualities and partly based on the perception of these qualities.*

There are other imaginary concepts which are probably familiar to most of us. Such, for example, are the creatures of legend and myth, such as centaurs and unicorns, which are composites of perceivable elements (e.g., human and horse parts) recombined in the imagination. The very fascinating work of the imagination will be studied in more detail in Chapter IX, but for now we are only concerned with the legitimacy of considering nonperceivable and

---

* The position here suggested will be elaborated later. Briefly, it maintains that imaginary concepts arise ultimately from perceptual data *plus the mental ability to alter abstractions* in accordance with changes also found in perceptual data.

imaginary concepts as referents. This question was forced on us by the fact that we have assumed a distinction between referent and concept, indicated at (a) in Fig. 5. If the referent were identical with the concept, there would be no relation here (except that of identity). And if there is no difference between referent and concept, how could there be an error in this relation? To answer this question, we must realize that most conceptual referents, even imaginary ones, are matters of tradition. It is not just for us to make of them whatever we will. A centaur, for example, is a well-recognized type of imaginary object, and it is as much possible to confuse a centaur with a unicorn as a cat with a dog. Similarly, the other nonperceivable referents mentioned above are subject to errors in our conception of them whenever our private notions do not coincide with the best judgment of the experts. It may be, of course, that the experts are mistaken, and that we are more nearly correct; but it is hardly for us to argue that we have the right to assert our opinions as the valid ones without having made a very thorough study of the matter.

So it appears legitimate to include nonperceivable and imaginary objects, events, or situations as referents. Referents, then, be it noted, can include at least three possible varieties: (1) those which are perceivable; (2) those which were or might be perceivable, but which are not so at the present time (e.g., the old kitchen chair); and (3) those which are never perceivable, even though they may be composed of or derived from perceivable elements (e.g., unicorns, democratic government, and the like).*

(b) E_1 to CC_1. Turning now to relation (b) in Fig. 5, we come to the influence that background experiences, previous knowledge, attitudes, and feelings may have upon the way in which we conceive or misconceive a particular referent. We all know that past experience plays a role here, and that it is difficult to formulate clear notions, even of perceivables, if we have never observed them ourselves or learned how to categorize them. Eskimos living north of the tree line, for example, have considerable difficulty in forming a proper notion of a tree. The following sketch† shows how one

* Imaginary concepts will be treated more fully in Chapters IX and XII.

† Drawing made from a photograph reproduced in the *Christian Science Monitor,* Vol. 54, #250 (Sept. 19, 1962), p. 8, and there credited to the Ministry of Northern Affairs and Natural Resources, Ottawa, Canada.

Baffin Land Eskimo imagined trees and birds, and carved them in ivory.

Here we have an example of misconception arising from lack of personal experience. Clearly, the explanations and descriptions of others were not enough to establish the proper notion of a tree, although the artist came fairly close. The carving of the trees and birds made by the Eskimo may be considered his way of communicating the notion as he conceives it.

The information we receive, from whatever source, may or may not be well understood by us, but in any case it goes to form our own body of concepts and categorizations—our "knowledge"—of the world. We rely upon this knowledge to interpret our imaginary referents, and even sometimes what we perceive. If, for example, we were disposed because of our background learning to believe in ghosts, we might take a bit of wispy fog in a graveyard to be a ghost, which of course we would not do if we were disinclined to believe in ghosts. Mistaking wispy fog for a ghost may seem similar to mistaking a rabbit for a raccoon, except that the ghost, we are assuming, is purely imaginary which the rabbit is not. The error in this case arises from a mistaken belief coming from past learning, rather than from an unclear perception.

Finally, there is another factor which may distort our understanding and cause misconceptions. This is the factor of attitudes, inclinations, and especially prejudices. For example, a person suffering from a persecution complex may see the gesture of another person as threatening when it was intended to be friendly. Because of this psychological bias the gesture is misinterpreted, and this misinterpretation may well lead to an erroneous communicative response on the part of the person suffering from the complex. This type of error causes much trouble when some concept of a complex or imaginary referent, like democracy or communism, has been surrounded with strong pro or con attitudes on the part of those from whom the nature of the concept has been learned. Thus, biases are built up within us which prevent us from forming clear dispassionate notions about these concepts. Our communications about them carry on and project this biased coloration.

In these ways, background experiences, preconceptions, and attitudes may adversely affect our understanding and cause misconceptions which in turn distort or confuse our communications. We can show this type of influence in our diagram by reversing the arrow between concept and referent, as in Fig. 6, to indicate that a

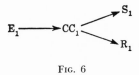

FIG. 6

given referent, whether perceived or imaginary, is being influenced by our background experience and by the concept which it has established.

All the communicational difficulties discussed so far have led to misconceptions, whether they stemmed from unclear perceptions, lack of previous experience, erroneous beliefs, or mistaken attitudes. In general, then, we might call these all "epistemic" errors, from the Greek word for knowledge, *epistēmē*. We should contrast this type of error with another type arising from misuse of the symbol system. Where the wrong symbol, such as a wrong word, is employed, whether from inadvertence or ignorance, we can call this error "semantic," from the Greek word for sign or signifying.* However, it is important to notice that knowledge of the symbol system, such as knowledge of a language, is part of our learning and part of our whole body of knowledge. We learn the symbols along with the other characteristics of the concepts we form. So, when we speak of semantic errors, we should remember that they too are in

* The term *semantic* is used in various ways. Popularly, it often means merely "terminological," as when one says, "That is just a matter of semantics," meaning "just a question of proper terminology." In modern philosophical usage, however, semantics is frequently defined as the study of the relation of signs or symbols to the objects (referents) to which they are applicable. In this sense, the entire relation of referent, concept, experience, and symbol is involved in semantics, and not merely the relation of concept to symbol alone. C. W. Morris (in *Foundations of the Theory of Signs* and in *Signs, Language, and Behavior*) contrasts semantic in this broader sense with *syntactics* (the formal study of the relations of signs), and *pragmatics* (the study of the relations of signs to their users). All three (semantics, syntactics, and pragmatics) he calls *semiotic,* or theory of signs. However, there is some justification for labeling the concept-symbol relation as principally a semantic one, since the term *semantic* focuses attention upon the function of the sign or symbol in the knowing and communicating process. The term epistemic, on the other hand, focuses upon knowing alone, without particular concern for symbolic representation.

part epistemic; but this time it is a very special kind of knowledge that is in question—simply knowledge of the meaning and application of symbols. To this type of error we turn next.

(c) CC_1 *to* S_1. Relation (c) refers to the way in which the concept is put into symbols. An error at this point would occur whenever the communicator uses an inappropriate symbol. For example, in calling a cat "dog," it may be not that one's perception is at fault, but that one uses the wrong word. Thus, if one sees a cat and thinks "cat," but says "dog," then the error is not due to an unclear perception or to lack of previous experience or improper beliefs or attitudes, but simply due to the wrong choice of words. This fault might be due either to a slip of the tongue or to unfamiliarity with the language. Or it may even be that someone intentionally uses the wrong word, either as a joke or to deceive. If the hearer catches the mistake or recognizes the joke, then there is no lasting error in the communication. But it still constitutes an initial misuse of symbols, whether accidental or intentional.

The primary problem in relation (c) is that of finding the most appropriate symbols for one's idea. Clearly a good storehouse of symbols (i.e., vocabulary in the realm of linguistic symbols) is the first requisite. But in the second place, one must have a well-developed sense of the customary and possible usages of terms; otherwise one might have an extensive storehouse of symbols, but frequently misuse them. We remember how Mrs. Malaprop in Sheridan's *Rivals* was addicted to this failure, so much so that misused words are often called malapropisms. A third requisite is a knowledge of the background and linguistic training of the person with whom one wishes to communicate. If we choose language which is likely to be unfamiliar, we make the success of the communication more difficult to achieve. The teacher, we might note, is in a difficult position when it comes to this requirement, for not only must he communicate with individuals of varied background and vocabulary, but his task includes that of introducing unfamiliar terms.

Puzzles arising out of the various specialized discourses, jargons, and slangs are too familiar to need much mention. Imagine, for example, the bewilderment of an Englishman when he reads in an American sports column: "A two-out double scoring a pair in the ninth capped a come-from-behind victory." Of course the Britisher could turn the tables on the American with the vernacular of cricket.

Oratorical and political discourse may present another problem, namely, that of reading between the lines in order to decipher the ambiguous and evasive language so often employed by those whose positions require them to be noncommittal while appearing to say something.

Poetic and philosophical discourse presents still another problem. Here words are often strangely used or strangely combined in order to give special meanings. There are perfectly justifiable reasons for these twistings of language, for often tried and time-worn ways do not adequately express one's thoughts. Thus, for example, Whitehead conveys a valuable insight in saying "religion is an ultimate craving to infuse into the insistent particularity of emotion that non-temporal generality which primarily belongs to conceptual thought alone."* Although these words are all fairly familiar ones, it takes a deal of thinking to grasp the insight which Whitehead is here expressing.

In general, then, successful communication requires the most appropriate symbols possible to express an idea and also symbols that are apt to be familiar to the prospective recipient of the message. But since in the long run there may be many recipients of a given message, appropriateness is more important than familiarity.

Symbolic systems may have a genuine and considerable influence upon concept formation. The habits of linguistic patterning channel thoughts into well-formed grooves of which we are mostly unaware. In this way, languages also help to orient us in the world. Since concepts, as we have said, color the character of referents, our linguistic symbol system can influence the ways in which we see objects. Does this mean that everything we thought we knew is influenced and changed by our language habits? Is it impossible for an American, a Russian, a Chinaman, and an Eskimo ever to see exactly the same world simply because their languages are different? That this is the case is the conclusion reached by at least one famous student of languages, the late Benjamin Whorf,† whose

---

* *Process and Reality,* p. 23.

† See Whorf, *Language, Thought, and Reality.* We shall return to Whorf's ideas in Chapter II and contrast them with the more recent proposal that there is a universal "deep structure" underlying all grammatical forms.

strong statement of this position caused something of a stir among both linguists and epistemologists. We might show the influences suggested by Whorf in our diagram by turning the arrows as in Fig. 7. Here we see represented the influence of the symbol (i.e.,

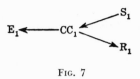

Fig. 7

language) on the concept and even on the background and the way in which the referent is viewed.

However, we must remember that the organizational schemes of the various languages have been built up through habits of conceiving. These habits in turn must to some extent arise in response to perceptual stimuli, which are, we hope, reasonably reliable indicators of the way things are. Moreover, the constant struggle to improve clarity of understanding is undoubtedly reflected in the ways in which languages are frequently changed. So let us take heart from the realization that language not only controls our thinking to some extent, but also that our thinking does shape language. We may conclude that even though orientations and attitudes embedded in language may shift surprisingly from language to language there seems to be some solid bed of common experience to which we can resort in arriving at better and better translations.

(*d*) S_1 *to Tr.* A failure in relation (*d*) would most often be *physiological* or *neurological,* caused by some inability on the part of the communicator to speak, write, or gesture adequately. Speech defects, such as those resulting from a cleft palate or a harelip, would illustrate what is meant by a physiological disability. Stuttering, on the other hand, would be a neurological defect. Similarly, writing may suffer from a physiological handicap, such as missing fingers, or from a neurological ailment, such as palsy. Slovenly speaking or writing, however, though still a failure in (*d*) would not be a physiological or neurological failure so much as a mere matter of insufficient learning or laziness.

(*e*) *Tr to Rc.* Between transmitter and receiver, failures would be of a *mechanical* nature. Telephonic communication, for example, might be interrupted by a power failure; static may interfere with radio communication; a letter may go astray. These mechanical failures are numerous and of great variety, but they are the primary concern of the engineer, not of the linguist or philosopher. By engineers they are sometimes broadly referred to as "noise," and the problem then is conceived as that of keeping such noise to a minimum.

(*f*) *Rc to* S_2. Relation (*f*) is the reverse of relation (*d*). Here the difficulty is a matter of the person receiving the message not being able adequately to *perceive* it. For example, a partially blind person would not be able to read normal written messages. As in (*d*), the difficulties here are usually physiological or neurological. The solution of the failures in this relation will rest primarily with the therapist or with the invention of aids to perception, such as Braille for the blind and hearing aids or lip reading for the deaf.

(*g*) S_2 *to* CC_2. Relation (*g*) indicates the main part of the decoding process. It involves recognizing and interpreting the symbols as received. The problem here is the reverse of that in relation (*c*), where the communicator was concerned with selecting the most appropriate symbols. Here, these symbols must be given conceptual meaning by the communicatee. A failure at this point would be due, most probably, to unfamiliarity with the symbols and their intended meanings. Whenever we listen to a person speaking an unfamiliar language, for example, we know we are listening to symbols which have meaning for some people; but for us their meanings are not interpretable. Even with a familiar language, the communicatee may understand the principal symbols, but misread some of the additional indicators of meaning. For example, if the communicator is joking or speaking ironically, it may be that the additional indicator of irony (e.g., tone of voice) escapes the notice of the hearer. Reasons for not understanding symbols are many and varied, but in general they will be traceable to an unfamiliarity with the symbol system, including its additional indicators. Failures in this relation, as in (*c*), may be considered to be semantic.

(*h*) E_2 *to* CC_2. Relation (*h*) points to the importance of the communicatee's background experiences and attitudes. Like the communicator, the recipient of the message has his own orientation and predispositions which affect his manner of conceiving. Has it ever happened to you, for example, that directions become reversed in a new location? If so, advice on how to get to a certain place, if the advice is given in terms of north, south, east, or west, would send you on the wrong course. In such cases, there is no error in communication up to the point that your own misconceptions regarding directions enter into the picture. An even more drastic example of unfamiliarity leading to misconceptions is that of the Eskimo who had never seen a tree nevertheless trying to imagine a tree. Even if a word for tree is present already in his language, or is newly introduced into his language, the Eskimo who has not seen a tree is still no better off so far as his conception goes. Failures in (h), as in (b), are failures resulting from ignorance or faulty attitudes. They are thus epistemic or emotive failures.

(i) CC_2 *to* R_2. In this final relation of our diagram, the problem is that of arriving at the correct referent from the concept formed after the symbols have been interpreted. If everything has gone well up to this point, it will not be likely that one's attention will fail to arrive at the correct referent. Yet, suppose the symbols given are all accurately and adequately interpreted, but are too general or vague to indicate the precise referent which the communicator had in mind—for example, if a person says to another, "Oh, see that mountain over there," while waving his arm in a generous and vague manner. Then it may not be possible to know precisely which mountain it is that would be the correct referent. Especially with nonperceivable referents, the symbols may be perfectly interpreted, but may be too imprecise to designate the exact referent which the communicator had in mind. For example, a reference to a "dimension" may not be correctly interpreted, not because the communicatee does not understand the word, but because the precise context in which it is being used has not been included in the message.

What checks are required for successful communication?

In the preceding section, we examined at some length the obstacles to successful communication. It may be helpful now to look at the whole question positively instead of negatively, in order to see what recommendations we can make to insure better communication.

In general, two items appear to be of outstanding importance: (1) adequate concepts and (2) a good knowledge of the symbol system being used. These two items are of importance alike for the communicator and the recipient of the message.

First, with regard to adequate concepts, there are several helpful points to remember. One is to check our perceptions wherever possible, assuming of course that the referent of our message is something perceptible. Another is to make sure that we have clarified our principal concepts as much as we can, so that we feel we have a reasonably clear meaning in mind of what it is we are talking about. This is especially important in the case of complex notions, like democracy or religion. A third important point is to look critically at our biases and prejudices, and to do what we can to counteract them. In this respect, we should remember that one of the persons in a communicational transaction, either the communicator or communicatee, may have some strong prejudice about the language being used—a prejudice that is not shared by the other person. For example, in our story about Spencer and George, the word "take" had a biased connotation for one boy which it did not have for the other. It is often very difficult for us to separate the bare uncolored referent—the object or event to which we are referring—from the fuller and richer connotational meanings including attitudes and emotional overtones connected with the language. Sex acts, for example, when referred to in a strict medical vocabulary will have quite different connotational values for most of us from what they have when referred to in the four-letter word vocabulary. For some people, however, this connotational difference may be lacking. From examples of this kind we see how important it is for the referent to be capable of being dissociated from the particular terms used lest the main point of the communication be lost in biased reactions and in vituperation over the symbols instead of the message.

Second, knowledge of the symbol system, especially languages, is of equal if not greater importance. Perhaps it seems enough to become thoroughly familiar with one's mother tongue together with some jargons or technical languages belonging to one's specialties. But in a day when the world is becoming overpopulated and the populations must learn more than ever to get along with one another, it is of the highest importance to learn the languages of other peoples. The importance of languages is not appreciated until we come to realize, as noted above, to what extent fundamental conceptual orientations are carried by languages, so that wherever a language goes, these orientations follow. Both in the basic literature of a people and even in the grammatical matrix of a language, we find subtle ways in which orientations are imposed upon thinking. We shall have more to say concerning the influence of grammar upon thought in the next chapter; but here it should be observed that these influences are so deep-seated that they normally escape our awareness. Simple translation into one's own language cannot succeed in carrying with it the grammatical orientation of the original language. So, if for no other reason than the awakening to these possible contrasts in orientation, it becomes important for everyone of us to master several languages.

But how are we to know when a communication misfires? How can we best check to see if our messages are being properly understood? Let us review here some simple tests that can be used. First, if we suspect that the communicatee's attention to our remarks has not been as sharp as it should be, we may ask him to repeat to us what we have said. This is the *parroting* method of checking. Of course, it does not really show whether the communicatee understood or not; it only indicates whether he heard. To ascertain his degree of comprehension, we may ask him to *reformulate* what we said in his own words. If these words indicate a vocabulary sufficiently close to one we ourselves might have used, then we assume he understands. This is no proof, however, and we often discover from further remarks that there is still a failure to understand. One can then only rely upon further *dialogue* which will sooner or later bring the discrepancies in understanding to light. Most often these discrepancies are the result of different conceptual structures or patterns which we, as discussants, have preestablished concerning the situation under discussion. It then behooves us to locate, if we can, the particular term or terms that are the source of the confusion, and attempt to clarify our meanings of these terms. Since most of the terms that cause this type of confusion have many alternative meanings, we can easily become impatient and peevish in our search for the common meaning. But good communication at this level requires great patience.

Let us mention again the basic rules for better communication: the communicator should

- Conceive as clearly as possible,
- Speak or write as accurately as he can,
- Use symbols which he believes ought to be within the general knowledge of the communicatee;

and the communicatee should

- Be alert and receptive,
- Use his imagination in attempting to discover the best possible meaning for each of the symbols he attempts to interpret,
- Form concepts with as clear an indication of the referent as possible.

In addition, it is helpful to carry on a dialogue, especially with regard to complex topics, until we feel reasonably confident that we have reached an understanding.

SUGGESTED READINGS

Plato, *Phaedrus* (especially from 257 to the end).
Bacon, Francis, *Novum Organum,* Aphorisms xxxviii-xliv, on the idols or false notions which beset human understanding.
Cassirer, Ernst, *An Essay on Man,* Ch. 2.
Ogden and Richards, *The Meaning of Meaning,* Ch. 1.
Wheelwright, Philip, *Metaphor and Reality,* Intro., Chs. 1-2.

CHAPTER II

Language

Why concern ourselves with language?

OUR STUDY of communication served to focus attention upon two primary areas of interest: (1) the backgrounds of understanding, including perception, structure sense, and experience—the epistemic factors; and (2) the means of communication, or symbol systems devised by man—the semantic factors. We shall leave the epistemic problem to a later section and turn our attention first to the semantic problem. In this area, language is by far the most important item. Languages are man's chief window upon an understanding of the world and of himself. Without language our complex human communications would be quite impossible. Language predominates in human communication to such an extent that we tend to think of all communication as linguistic and are led to speak of animals and insects as having languages (see p. 11). But human languages are much more sensitive and adaptable to the various demands which our intelligence imposes upon communication than are the more elementary "languages" of animals and insects. To be a human being in the full sense requires that a man have a well-developed language at his disposal. A man without a language is scarcely a man. In fact, it has been proposed that man's symbol-using capacity is his most essentially human characteristic.*

From our earliest years each one of us has been learning one or more of the traditional human languages. This is in a large way our basic educational task, for it is the doorway to all else. But in what exactly does this language learning consist? Four things stand out—pronunciation, writing, vocabulary, and grammar. The study of grammar—the structure of a language—frequently causes us the most trouble. It is a tool, a means to an end, and as with any tool, it is a nuisance to divert our gaze away from our goal while we improve the means. If we wish to saw or sew, we do not want to pause and sharpen the saw or find a better needle. Similarly with language, if we wish to communicate, we find it a nuisance to turn aside from our main purpose while we improve our knowledge of the nature of the tool. Nonetheless, improved craftsmanship requires attention to tools; and this is as much true of communication and thinking as it is of carpentry or needlework. What follows in the present chapter will serve only to outline a few major characteristics of languages in general, and the English language in particular.

Let us begin by defining language, not in that broad sense in which it could be equated with any means of communication whatsoever, but more narrowly as a formalized and traditionalized set of spoken, written, or gesticulated symbols and signs which serve to express and communicate feelings and thoughts. The word "language" itself is derived from the Latin for "tongue" (*lingua*), and referred originally to the *spoken* form; for speech seems to have been the earliest mode of communication to have been elaborated by humans. However, the written forms of communication (from pictographs to phonetic alphabets) and gesticulations (including various "sign languages") also have very primitive roots in human culture, and must be considered as much examples of language, under our normal meaning of the term, as is speech. It is tempting to extend the meaning of "language" to include all symbol systems and even all forms of human expression, such as we find in the various arts. Thus, we

---

* See especially Ernst Cassirer, *An Essay on Man,* Ch. 2.

sometimes speak of music as a language. But such usages should be regarded only as metaphorical extensions of the meaning of the term "language"; and normal usage should limit the term to the narrower sense defined above.

What is involved in learning a language?

Although speculation on the historical origin and growth patterns of languages is inconclusive, a great deal can be observed about the development of speech habits in children. According to one authority,* for example, the earliest stage in learning language is that of response to the spoken sounds of one's elders, often with some feeble attempts at imitation. This stage is followed, usually between the second and tenth month of the infant's life, by a period of experimentation with sounds. In this second period the efforts toward imitation fall off, and the child, instead, tries out his own private language. The third stage begins with a renewed interest in imitation and a sturdier effort to capture and repeat the sounds with objects and situations. The fourth stage is that of *naming*, in which not only objects but also certain feelings and desires are given conventional linguistic forms. At this point language becomes, for the first time, a consciously communicative tool, to be improved and perfected gradually over many years of learning. In the naming stage, names of objects (nouns) normally come first. Then these may be converted into one-word sentences (e.g., "Milk!" meaning "I want some milk!"). Later, the child learns to form simple sentences with subject and predicate (in those languages which have subjects and predicates). Gradually the sentences become longer and more complicated, always following imitation of the spoken language, and often with correction from others (e.g., "Don't say 'bringed'; say 'brought' ").

Each of the above stages involves time and learning effort on the part of the child. There are trials and errors all along the way—for example, the child's *phonetic range* is at first very limited, so that even when he begins to attach linguistic symbols to objects, he frequently finds it necessary to alter or substitute sounds. Difficulties with sounds are especially noticeable where there is a combination of a front and a back consonant, such as

* M. M. Lewis, *Infant Speech*, especially Ch. 4.

pl, sp, sw, etc., or where a difficult tongue position such as *th* is involved. A child is apt to say "keem" for "cream," or "feet" for "sweet." In fact, I recall the case of a rather precocious young girl whose grammar was better than her phonetics. She corrected her older sister's grammatical error by saying "Hitter, don't hay 'heen' hay 'haw'" (i.e., "Sister, don't say 'seen' say 'saw'"). In general, the child substitutes easier sounds for the more difficult ones, until often these substitutions become so ingrained that good pronunciation later on is impaired.

More embarrassing and amusing difficulties may be caused by the early limitation in *vocabulary*. Since words are learned slowly, a few at a time, the first ones mastered must do duty for those not yet learned. As a result, the child with his limited vocabulary will extend the meanings of his words over a wider range of objects than a more developed and discriminating use would permit. For example, small children may quite unintentionally discomfit their mothers by addressing strange men as "daddy" simply because this word was the first one associated with the type of object we call man. Or a child learns that a certain four-footed animal is a cow. When he sees a horse it is promptly called "cow," this being the one word learned in his vocabulary up to this point which most nearly fits the object observed. Had the child learned "horse" first, he would no doubt have used this word for a cow.

As children become aware of grammatical patterns, they tend to fit the words they use into these patterns, even beyond the limits of accepted usage. For example, English verbs, like most verb systems in European languages, have a few less regular, or "irregular," patterns, while the majority of verbs follow the more regular patterns. A child tends to convert irregular verbs to regular patterns, as saying "swimmed" for "swam" or "standed" for "stood." Even pronouns may come in for the same treatment (e.g., "she's" for "her"). In learning a language, one must remember several patterns, some rarer and some more frequent.

Learning to write a language constitutes a correlated but in itself quite different process. Here a new set of graphic symbols must be associated with the spoken symbols, and secondly, with the referents for which these stand. This task may well seem tedious and overwhelming when looked at as a whole. However, the discovery of the power of graphic symbols can prove exciting to the child. Many children have gone on to experiment with new or secret symbol systems (codes) of their own.

Psychologists as well as linguists have paid much attention to the process of language learning, not only because of their interest in the learning process generally, but because knowledge of language is the basic clue to all other knowledge and to whatever one may mean by "intelligence." It is known that certain linguistic defects (e.g., aphasia, or loss of ability to speak) are not necessarily indications of lack of intelligence, but are usually traceable to brain injuries.

Why should we study grammar?

The term "grammar" refers primarily to the word and sentence patterns used in a language, and to the ways or situations in which they are used. As we have been emphasizing, every language has some patterns for word formation and word usage. We can, of course, learn a language simply by imitating the habits of others, without paying special attention to the grammatical patterns. However, without some direct attention to these, we would need to spend years listening to native speakers and imitating them; we would never be too sure of ourselves in certain cases of alternative linguistic possibilities; and most important, we would never get a clear idea of the structure of the language. Knowledge of grammar is thus not only a shortcut to the learning of a language, including our own; but it is also a means to the end of clarifying our thought, since it acquaints us with the linguistic structures underlying that thought.

If we are sometimes annoyed by the exceptions to grammatical rules, we should remember that these rules simply summarize the regularities created by the speech habits of a people; and, like human habits generally, these habits tend to change. The remnants of older uniformities cling on in a waning condition, while newer fashions of language usage take over. For example, in English the young child, as noted, has a tendency to regularize speech forms and to say such things as "he swimmed" instead of "he swam"; yet the forms "swim-swam-swum" or "bring-brought-

brought" simply reflect other, often older, regular patterns. The newer or larger regularities become dominant in the sense that they are the ones which will be applied to newly coined terms, whereas the older or smaller regularities merely cling on as vestiges of a past tradition.

We can test a form to see if it is living or vital by coining a new word and discovering which verbalizing or nominalizing suffixes we naturally use. For example, Old English had two ways of changing adjectives into nouns. Sometimes the ending added to the adjective was -th and sometimes it was -nes. Today the -th ending merely clings on in such forms as "truth" from "true," "depth" from "deep," "warmth" from "warm," etc. But we quickly discover that the -nes (now -ness) ending is the living one. Let us test these two endings on some unusual or modern adjective. "Chintz" is the name of a cheap cotton material originally from India. We have recently formed the adjective "chintzy" meaning "cheap." Now let us convert this adjective into a noun naming this quality. Will it be "chintzith" or "chintziness?" Obviously, the latter. We still say "warmth," while its correlative opposite is "coolness," not "coolth." However, "coolth" was once (e.g., in the Elizabethan period) a more acceptable form than it is today. Though we indicated above that the more dominant and vital form is probably the later one to arise, this is not necessarily the case. Both -th and -nes are found in Old English, which is sufficiently antiquated so that neither form would be called recent. But for some reason the -ness form has preserved a stronger appeal, perhaps because it is easier to add as a separate syllable.

It may be well to warn the reader against the notion that grammar is all we need to know of a language. Grammar gives us only the structural skeleton. To put flesh and clothing on this skeleton requires a degree of mastery of at least four major linguistic arts: (1) understanding the spoken forms of a language; (2) reading the literature of the language and becoming sensitive to the word qualities; (3) speaking in customary and readily acceptable grammatical patterns; and (4) writing a literary style. Most of us progress only a small way along the path toward language mastery, even in our own tongue. What we do to foreign languages is too often a shame and a disgrace.

Yet the ability to know and use a number of languages is a tremendous asset and source of illumination, since each language, owing to its special structure, grants us a somewhat different perspective and understanding of the world in which we live.

What's in a word?

Language is made up of words. But to decide just what constitutes a word is an extremely difficult matter. This is due to the fact that languages vary considerably from the extreme of those with rather loose or freely separable (called "unbound") short units, to those with tightly connected (or "bound") units which cannot stand alone. Languages of the first type are called *analytic,* or sometimes *isolating.* Languages of the second type are *synthetic,* or even *polysynthetic* at the extreme. As an example of a polysynthetic word we might take the Algonquian name for a lake in Massachusetts near the town of Webster. It is

Chargoggagoggmanchauggagoggchaubunogungamaugg

which means approximately "You-fish-on-your-side-I-fish-on-my-side-nobody-fishes-in-the-middle."* This "word" appears to be a complete sentence, or even three sentences; however, it is composed of tightly bound elements, like prefixes and suffixes in English, so that it is difficult to separate it out into words which would have the same feeling of independence about them as English words. At the opposite extreme is a language like Chinese, in which the monosyllabic units can readily stand alone or be associated with other monosyllables in idea compounds. For example, the Chinese call an elevator a "rise-descend-machine" and a parliament is a "discuss-govern-country-assembly." The philosophical idea of the absolute is "exclude-opposite." † These English translations may seem to be very much like the Algonquian example. The difference is to be found in the fact that the Chinese elements, like "rise," "descend," etc., can stand alone or in other combinations without undergoing changes, whereas the Algonquian elements for the most part cannot. In a language like Chinese, where inflections and affixes (prefixes,

* See E. D. Myers, *The Foundations of English,* p. 11.
† *Encyclopaedia Britannica,* 11th ed., article "China: Language," Vol. 6, p. 222.

infixes, suffixes) are lacking, the important index of meaning is the word order. In this respect English, with its lack of inflected forms, is much like Chinese; and the difference between two English sentences often rests solely on word order. For example, it makes quite a difference to the meaning whether one says "Charles hit Jim" or "Jim hit Charles" and this difference is shown only by word order. Most European languages fall somewhere between Algonquian and Chinese, for European languages normally have quite a variety of possible affixes.

Leaving *word* in its ambivalent condition, let us turn to *sentence;* for the sentence, being the unit of thought, should be easier to handle. Sentences, like thoughts, may become very complicated and involved. However, if we proceed from the simple to the complex, we can conveniently start our study of any language by seeking out the simpler and more prevalent sentence forms. If we are careful not to carry the image too far, we can think of a sentence form as a sort of slot machine into which hundreds of different coins (the words) can be inserted. These coins mean little by themselves, but once they are fitted into their places, the machine will operate (that is, the words become meaningful). Now, these slots may be compared to the *functions* which the words perform in the sentence. The traditional "parts of speech" (i.e., nouns, pronouns, verbs, adjectives, adverbs, articles, prepositions, and conjunctions) are really nothing more nor less than such functions. The parts of speech of Indo-European languages (i.e., those just mentioned) do not necessarily fit other languages, which, in turn, would have their own systems and their own elementary linguistic functions. For this reason, the grammar that we learn for our traditional West European languages is hardly pertinent to some other language families. For each one, new function systems must be established.

But let us keep to the Indo-European languages, and especially to English. Even here we find that words by themselves do not always have single functions to fulfill. The same word may be used in several different parts of speech. For example, the English word *run* may be either noun or verb depending on its usage or function in the sentence. In the sentence "I run," it is a verb, but in the sentence "He made a run for it," this same word is a noun. How do we know which it is? By knowing first the *functions* which each word fulfills in the sentence. Nouns in English serve one of three primary functions: (1) subject of a verb, (2) object of a verb, or (3) object of a preposition. They may also be (4) complements, or (5) appositives, but these are derivatives of the three basic functions. Verbs, on the other hand, serve the purpose of stating the action or condition of the subject. In the sentence "He runs" the verb (runs) states the action of the subject (He). But in the sentence "He made a run for it," the noun (run) is object of the verb (made). Oftentimes in English the same word may be serving two or more functions at once; for example, "pronominal adjectives" (or "adjectival pronouns") are both pronouns and adjectives at the same time. That is, they serve the function of a pronoun, which is to refer back to some object namable by a noun; and they also serve the function of an adjective, which is to qualify or modify a noun. Thus, "my" in "my dog" refers back to me and also modifies "dog." The word "whose" is three things at once: pronoun, conjunction, and adjective. In the sentence, "See the man whose wife shot herself." the word "whose" (1) refers back to "man," (2) conjoins or relates a subsidiary clause, and (3) modifies "wife." Thus, we can see that we hamper our understanding of grammar if we think that each word fulfills only one function (i.e., always occurs as only one part of speech, or even occurs as only one part of speech at a time).

We should also note that in English there are some traditional affixes (usually suffixes) which have the special function of converting a word from one function (part of speech) to another. We have already seen that the endings *-th* and *-ness* are used to convert adjectives into nouns. From Latin sources we also have *-ity* and *-ion* to do the same job. If we were to catalogue all the suffixes in English which serve to change word functions, our list would extend over two pages at least. Some of these (e.g., *-ment, -ure, -er, -ism*) convert verbs into nouns. Some (e.g., *-al, -en, -ic,* etc.) convert nouns into adjectives. Some (e.g., *-ly*) convert adjectives into adverbs. These endings are traditionalized in certain part-of-speech positions; but there is nothing to prevent them from being changed even from these traditions.

The fact of language which we have just been stressing brings up an important warning about the relation between grammar and its underlying logic: namely, that the actual word forms do not always reveal the functions of words in sentences, whereas it is these sentence functions which are more important for an understanding of the underlying logic. There are many examples of this in all languages, but to take just one simple illustration from English, we observe that the suffix -*ly* occasionally indicates an adjectival form (e.g., prickly) although normally it is the sign of an adverb. When we approach a language from the point of view of the linguist who is principally interested in word formations, the logic of the grammar may escape us; and when we approach the same language from the point of view of the logician, the word forms may easily lead us astray. So the warning is simply that we must not expect greater correlation between word forms and word functions than actually exists, and that we must approach languages with both a linguistic and a logical interest.

What are the elementary sentence types in English?

If, as we have stated, the sentence, not the word, is the place to begin an analysis of language, we might well start by examining the elementary sentence forms of our own language. Although these forms or models may be quite different from those in other language groups, we find that they follow in general outline the same tradition as the other languages in our language family—the Indo-European—which includes not only English but also Sanskrit, Greek, Latin, Slavic, Germanic, Celtic, and others. It is especially important for students of philosophy to remember that English belongs to the same family of languages as Greek, for the ancient Greek philosophers first developed logic and many of the basic categories of our Western philosophies appear to have been influenced by the linguistic structure as worked out in Greek logic.

Grammarians and linguists have devised many ways of analyzing and categorizing sentence structures. We are probably familiar with the method of diagramming sentences, which was popular for many years. An example would look like this

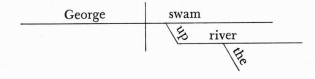

which divides our sentence, "George swam up the river," into two main parts: a subject (George) and a predicate (swam up the river). According to this diagramming, "swam" is an intransitive verb modified by a prepositional phrase used adverbially to tell where George swam.

More recently, especially since the advent of generative and transformational grammar, about which we shall say more later, the "tree" diagram has become more frequent. According to this method of diagramming, the above sentence would look like this

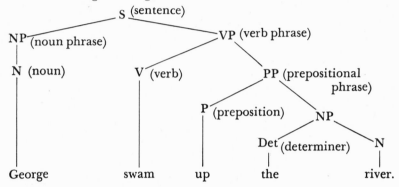

This latter type of diagram, as we can see, is much more explicit in showing the segments of the sentence and their relationships to the larger units.

Logicians have tended to look at sentence structures a bit differently from grammarians and linguists, since the logician's interest is more concerned with the types of relations implicit in sentence structure rather than in the parts and arrangement of the sentence as such. The following grouping of major sentence types, which shall be the basis of much that we do in this book, is based upon the logician's interest. We shall distinguish two main varieties of sentence, (1) the *doer-action* or simply *action* type, and (2) the *attributive* type.* Let us give some examples of each.

(1) *Doer-action or action sentences*
    (*a*) The horses walk.
    (*b*) The stablehand feeds the horses.

* The types of sentence here taken as basic are given by John Lyons in his *Introduction to Theoretical Linguistics* as examples of syntactic function of major parts of speech, pp. 319ff.

In the first example, the subject (horses) of the verb names the doers, and the verb (walk) names the action. In the second example, the subject (stablehand) is the doer, the verb (feeds) states the action, and the object (horses) is the recipient of the action. Thus, action sentences have two basic subpatterns: *(a)* doer-action *without object* (intransitive), and *(b)* doer-action *with object* (transitive). Notice a kind of symmetry in the second form, for there we have a simple order of noun-verb-noun (stablehand-feeds-horses). Here is the skeleton. The verbs state the actions and the nouns name the doers and objects. Even in complex sentences, if we can trim away the qualifiers (adjectives, articles, adverbs), we can observe the skeletal form. For example, we should be able to look at a sentence like

> The old lame horse, plowing through the mud, rubbed
> the barbed-wire fence and snagged his wispy tail.

and see its skeletal structure as follows:

Horse	rubbed	fence
and	snagged	tail.

In this case we have two simple doer-action statements with objects, connected by "and." The other words in the sentence are adjectives (old, lame, etc.) or adjectival phrases (plowing through the mud) which serve only to qualify one of the nouns. It is extremely important in helping us to understand linguistic structures that we are able to pick out the sentence skeletons in this way.

The simple transitive form may conceal a variety of relations between the doer (subject) and the apparent object of the action. For example, "He sails the boat" indicates a more direct action on the boat than "He sails the ocean" would indicate as action on the ocean, though "boat" and "ocean" have equally the position of direct object in the two sentences. The idea of the second sentence could be more accurately expressed as "He sails over the ocean," thus making clear the difference in relationship between the subject and object in the two sentences. However, the human tendency is to omit words like "over" if the idea seems clear enough without them. It is from cases such as this that the generative grammarian finds ammunition for his contention that ordinary surface sentence structures may not by themselves adequately reveal the conceptual meanings expressed in our sentences, even though these meanings are well understood in ordinary usage.

(2) *Attributive sentences*
    (*a*) Henry is tall.
    (*b*) George is the president.
    (*c*) John is a Boy Scout.
    (*d*) Cats are animals.

Here we have four sentences, all of which are alike in attributing some condition to the subject. In the first, we have a subject (Henry) *qualified by a predicate adjective* (tall), expressing the fact that the quality indicated by the predicate adjective is being attributed to the subject. In the second, third, and fourth, the subject has some condition attributed to it, *indicated by a predicate noun*. However, there are noteworthy logical differences in the relations between the subject and predicate nouns in these last three cases, which are not shown by any grammatical difference. In the second sentence the subject is *equated with* the predicate noun (i.e., George = the president). Here the relation is between individuals. In the third sentence the subject is an individual who is *a member of* a group named by the predicate noun (i.e., John is a member of the group called Boy Scouts). Here the relation is between an individual and a group. And in the fourth sentence the subject is a class of objects which is *included in* a larger class of objects (i.e., the class of cats is included in the class of animals). Here the relation is between groups.

There are a number of ways in which English sentences may combine action and attributive features in the same sentence. One way is through the use of objective complements in what we may call *complementative sentences*. For example, in the sentence "George painted the desk brown" an ordinary action sentence with direct object (George painted the desk) is supplemented or completed with another word (brown), which in this case is an adjective. Or the same formula may occur with a noun, as in the sentence "They elected Sam president" where "president," a noun, functions as the "objective complement." In other examples, the direct object may be omitted and an adjective used directly after an ordinary verb of action, as in "Jim is running *wild*."

A second variety which combines action and attributive features is the *transitional sentence*. Unlike the complementatives which refer to single actions (e.g., They elected Sam president) or continuing action (e.g., Jim is running wild) transitional sentences stress change from one condition to another. Such sentences as "The sky *reddens*," "Henry is *getting wet*," or "Joe *becomes* an officer" illustrate transitional sentences. In the first example (The sky reddens) the verb itself indicates change of condition. In the second example (Henry is getting wet), we have a verb of change (is getting) plus predicate adjective (wet). And in the third example (Joe becomes an officer), the verb of change (becomes) is followed by a predicate noun (officer). Some transitionals are even more specific in expressing the idea that the change is in its beginning phase (inceptive) or in its ending phase (terminative). While some languages have special verbal forms for such ideas, English resorts to combinations of verbs such as "Jack is starting to climb the mountain" (inceptive), or "Jack is finishing climbing the mountain" (terminative).

So we see that we can combine verbs into clusters by using infinitives or gerunds for the main verbal idea (e.g., Jack *starts to climb*). The verb which is inflected in these cases (e.g., *starts*) can be considered a helper or auxiliary verb. We should take note of one especially important group of auxiliary verbs, called *modal auxiliaries*, which are used to show the background conditions of the statement. These background conditions (modalities) often reflect the subjective attitude of the speaker. For example, the modal auxiliary *must* (e.g., I must go) indicates a sense of necessity; *ought* or *should* (e.g., You ought to come, He should be here) indicate a sense of obligation or probability; *may* (e.g., I may be there) indicates possibility or permission; etc. Modal forms have an interesting logic of their own, leading us from necessity through possibility (including probability and improbability) to impossibility. This problem has a long history in Western philosophy from Aristotle through Kant to present-day efforts to develop modal systems of logic. Questions of cause, chance, contingency, and probability are introduced by modal considerations. For our purposes here, however, it is only necessary that we should be aware of the existence of modal auxiliary verbs and recognize them in sentences.

By now it should be clear that the types of English sentences are numerous indeed. Fortunately, we can end our discussion here. Not being grammarians, we need not explore all the possible types but only the major and elementary ones.

From the foregoing examples, we see that our basic sentence forms are constructed around nouns and verbs. Ours is what is sometimes called a "noun and verb" language. This does not mean that the other word functions (parts of speech) are not also important. We have seen that adjectives are useful to modify nouns, both as direct modifiers (e.g., *wispy* tail) and as predicate adjectives (e.g., the tail is *wispy*). Articles (*the, a, an*) also serve an adjectival function, since they ascribe definiteness or indefiniteness to a noun. Adverbs modify verbs, adjectives, or other adverbs (e.g., That book is *highly* considered). Lastly, the prepositions and conjunctions are extremely important, and these we have been slighting so far. The preposition relates a noun or pronoun to the rest of a sentence by showing some relational concept (*in, on, under, after, near,* etc.). Conjunctions relate parallel structures, such as sentences or clauses, to each other (e.g., *and, when, since, because, whereas,* etc.). Both prepositions and conjunctions are basically *relaters*.

Let us look again at our basic word functions or parts of speech. We find that there are really *four* primary ones:

- Nouns or noun substitutes (pronouns, nominal phrases, etc.), which are used to name objects, events, situations.
- Verbs, which are used to assert actions or conditions that pertain to the subject.
- Adjectives, articles, and adverbs, which qualify or modify the named objects, events, actions, or conditions.
- Prepositions and conjunctions, which relate either nouns or sentences to each other.

Our whole analysis of philosophical thinking in this book will be based to a considerable degree on the foregoing fourfold classification, for it turns out very remarkably that around these concepts many of the most profound problems of Western philosophy have gravitated. As a quick preview, we might point out here that Chapter V, though concerned with all forms of abstracting will again mention these four categories, and that Chapters VI,

VII, and VIII will deal with qualifiers, relaters, and action forms respectively. At the end of Chapter VIII, with the advantage of a more thorough logical analysis, we shall again review the basic sentence types.

How are language and thought related?

Whenever thought goes beyond the stage of feelings, premonitions, and mere hunches, it depends upon an awareness and analysis of relationships. We may call this level of thought "conceptual," if we like, for the term "concept" is often used to suggest clear, well-analyzed notions. We express conceptual thought best through the use of a developed symbol system, such as we find in language. In fact, we are so dependent upon language in making our conceptualizations that it is difficult to conceive of thought without language. Certainly the language we learn as a mother tongue gives us the patterns that we are accustomed to use whenever we express our thoughts; and these patterns undoubtedly tend to focus and channel the thoughts themselves along the lines that are already established in the language. But this is only half the story. There is a kind of experience which we all have at times, namely of finding ourselves with fairly clear ideas that we simply cannot express in language. We grope around looking for the "right way" to say it, and frequently end up coining some new expression, or giving some new twist of meaning to familiar words, or even distorting the ordinary sentence structure. So the relation between language and thought seems to be a two-way process. On the one hand, our native language presents us with already formulated ways of expressing our ideas. But on the other hand, it is often necessary for us to break old habits by finding new ways of adjusting our language to our thoughts. Even then, the general structure of the language is preserved. For example, a poet, like Dylan Thomas, may use some strange locutions, as when he says: "Altarwise by owl-light in the half-way house / the gentleman lay graveward with his furies."* But if he had arranged his sentence as follows, "Owl-light house gentleman furies lay altarwise the half-way the graveward his by in with," placing nouns, verbs,

---

* "Altarwise by Owl-light" can be found in *The Collected Poems of Dylan Thomas* (A New Directions Book) , p. 80.

modifiers, and relaters in that order, the English syntax would have been so distorted as to reduce the sense almost to zero.

So a language, over and beyond its phonetic component, presents us with two things: (1) a set of common words and phrases, and (2) a traditional sentence structure or syntax in which to arrange these words and phrases. The different languages of the world vary considerably both in regard to the ranges of meaning* of even nearly equivalent words and also with regard to their syntactical patterns. The fact that most of our Western European languages share a common ancestor and have, therefore, a rather similar syntactical structure, at least as compared with some non-Indo-European languages, has made it possible for those speaking these languages to develop a common logic based on this structure. To see more clearly why there is a close relation between language and logic, it will be helpful to look for a moment at the way in which Western logic has developed.

The study of logic originated as a means of analyzing arguments in order to detect fallacious inferences. In brief, logic may be said to be the analysis and testing of patterns of reasoning. Now, reasoning involves at least two things: (1) a sense of particular structures or patterns, and (2) the ability to draw out and state the implications inherent in the structure or pattern. There are thus two aspects to logic—the awareness of structures, and the drawing of inferences. Since most arguments we make are couched in ordinary language, it was only natural that logicians should make use of the structures and relationships embedded in the syntax of conventional language. This is not to say that logical inferences are limited to linguistic structures. Arithmetic and geometry, for example, involve inferential reasoning just as much as arguments in ordinary language. In fact, a statement about geometric figures would involve two sets of relationships: those of geometry and those of linguistic syntax. For example, the concept *rectangle* implies a geometric structure consisting of two sets of parallel lines and four interior right angles. But the proposition "Rectangles are four-sided figures" contains the class-relation structure of sentence type 2*d* above. A logical implication of the geometrical notion *rectangle* would be that the lines in each set of parallel lines have

* See Chapter IV for a discussion of "ranges of meaning" or "extension" of terms.

the same length, whereas a logical implication of the linguistic proposition that "Rectangles are four-sided figures" would be that "No rectangles are non-four-sided figures," since all rectangles are included in the class of four-sided figures.

Aristotle was the first major developer in Western thought of a logic based on the analysis of ordinary linguistic structures. His language was Greek, and we might expect this fact to cause some difficulty in applying his analysis to English sentences. Greek, however, is an Indo-European language, like our own, and its syntax is sufficiently similar not to cause us this sort of problem. What is of greater concern to the logician, since he is interested in the structure of inferences rather than the structure of language, is to set forth and make explicit the key relationships on which the inferences are based. When dealing with an argument in ordinary language, then, it is convenient to select some basic type of sentence structure to use throughout an argument. This of course necessitates converting all other sentence types into the one selected, however inconvenient this may be. But if the logician were forced to deal with several different types at once, he would have to discover and formulate transformation rules among his sentence types. It is simpler to reduce all sentences to one type at the outset.

Which sentence type did Aristotle select for his model? We find that he preferred the attributive over the action type of sentence. There are probably several reasons for this. Aristotle himself employed the attributive sentence both with predicate adjective (e.g., The garment is white) and also with predicate noun (e.g., Men are animals), but eventually the latter became the preferred form in Aristotelian logic. This sentence type has had a notable success, no doubt because it utilizes a fundamentally important relation, namely *classification*. In classifying, a smaller subclass is conceived as part of and therefore included in a larger class, as is implied in a statement like "Cats (subclass) are animals (larger class)."

We may well wonder what happens to the other basic sentence types mentioned above when we convert them into the attributive type with predicate noun. The predicate adjective type (e.g., Cats are furry) is not difficult to convert. It would simply be changed from predicate adjective to predicate noun (i.e., Cats are furry things). This is not too distant in meaning; and actually it is easier to translate the adjective (furry) into an adjective plus noun (furry things) than it would be to translate a noun into an adjective, as we should have to do if the predicate adjective type had been selected as the key, for in that case a sentence like "Cats are animals" would be changed into "Cats are animally," or something of the sort. This experiment indicates one reason, no doubt, why the form with the predicate noun is preferred. Also, we should observe that the form with the predicate noun has a certain symmetry of noun-relation-noun which makes it possible to study what happens with regard to implication when the two nouns are reversed. The predicate adjective form is not so readily manipulated, and is therefore less useful in studying the possible implications of propositions. For example, the sentence "Some cats are jumpers" implies "Some jumpers are cats." But it is not quite so convenient to reverse "Some cats are furry," since one would first have to change "furry" into a noun and say "Some furry things are cats."

But what of the attributive sentences with singular subjects (e.g., George is the president; John is a Boy Scout)? Traditional logic translated these into the class-inclusion form by considering the subject as if it were naming an entire class of one individual (e.g., the entire class of George). Modern revisions of traditional logic have found it expedient to regard these second and third types of attributive sentence as exemplifying different relations. Thus "George is the president" indicates a relation of *equivalence* assuming there is only one president; and "John is a Boy Scout" indicates a relation of *member of,* assuming there are many Boy Scouts. So we would no longer need to translate "George is the president" into "the whole class of George is included in the whole class of the president," a procedure which hardly does justice either to the spirit or the logic of our language.

Trouble again develops in translating action sentences into the class-inclusion form. For example, if we take a typical transitive doer-action sentence such as "The boys threw the mud," we should have to translate it into "The boys are in the class of mud-throwers," which is certainly something of a distortion. Yet in fairness we should recognize that the language admits of translation from action to class-inclusion attributives more readily than the reverse order. Thus, if we wished to change "Cats are animals" into a doer-action sentence type, we would have to say something like "Cats animalize."

The class-inclusion type of attributive sentence, then, serves reasonably well as the key form for logical analysis when the basic relation is that of classification. This, however, is not the only relation in experience, and it is certainly not the one stressed in some languages. For example, some American Indian languages prefer to stress events and their characterizations, thus throwing primary attention upon the ways things happen.* In this case, the doer-action sentence would seem to be the best key model for developing a logic. But even with our typical doer-action sentence, there is still a stress upon the individuals that act and are acted upon. If we shifted the stress to the verbal idea, and subordinated the doers and recipients of the action, then we should come closer to the action-centered concept. It is difficult to force our language into this mold, but as suggested by one linguist, we might use the gerund with possessive pronouns to approximate this shift. Thus, in Greenlandic Eskimo, the sentence "I hear him" would come out something like the English "Sounding-his-my," where the action is considered as a condition that belongs to me and emanates from him.†

It would be interesting to experiment with logical systems based on different sentence models. Thus, instead of having to transform a sentence like "The boys threw the mud" into the class-inclusion form ("The boys are in the class of mud-throwers") we might reverse the order and transform all class-inclusion sentences, such as "Cats are animals," into action type sentences, like "Cats animalize." Or we might go even further and stress events, as in Greenlandic Eskimo, arriving at a key sentence something like "Animalizing is taking place cattily." If we were to construct a logical system using these forms, however, we should note that the main difference would be in the key relationships. The notion of implication or inference based on these relationships would remain

---

* See B. L. Whorf, *Language, Thought, and Reality,* especially pp. 134-159, for a discussion of the verbalizing tendency in American Indian languages.

† See W. L. Graff, *Language and Languages,* pp. 327-328.

the same, since implication simply depends upon making explicit what is already implicit in the chosen relations.*

This line of thought raises the interesting question of the degree to which there is a common logic underlying human languages. In Chapter I, we mentioned the hypothesis of B. L. Whorf that linguistic structures predetermine thought patterns to such an extent as to create different linguistically oriented world views. In an extreme form this notion would imply that complete translation from one language to another—especially where the languages have rather different structures—would be impossible. In recent years, however, this hypothesis has been countered by another stemming largely from the notion of the generative grammarians, like Noam Chomsky, to the effect that there are some underlying "deep structure" universals in human thinking out of which the various surface structure grammars are generated. The term "generative grammar" is used for one in which major attention is paid to the analysis of rules that would "generate" a large number of particular sentences from the basic set of structures, yielding, in the words of John Lyons, "a decision-procedure for any combination of the elements of the language. . . ."† Further, a grammar "that claims to assign to each sentence that it generates both a deep-structure and a surface structure analysis and systematically to relate the two analyses is a transformational grammar (whether it uses the label or not)."‡

The presence of these deep structures can be shown either by noting the differences in relational meaning between similar structures or by noting similarities of meaning between different structures. Our example above of two similarly structured sentences, "He sails the boat" and "He sails the ocean," which nevertheless contain a different conception of sailing in each case, will illustrate the first point. Here, it is pointed out, we are not confused by the similarity of sentence type into supposing that the sailor manipulates the ocean just as he does his boat. Our sense of deep structure lets us make allowance for the differences in these two cases despite the structural similarity of the sentences.

As an example of the second kind of evidence for a deep struc-

* We shall examine the nature of inference in more detail in Chapter XIII.
† John Lyons, *Introduction to Theoretical Linguistics,* p. 156.
‡ *Ibid.,* p. 248.

ture, we may take any active sentence and its corresponding passive form, which are different syntactically, but which appear to give the same basic meaning. Thus, the sentences "George gave James the book" and "The book was given to James by George" seem to connote the same event. This event may be described equally well by using either of the above surface structure forms. However, it may be argued that the shift in surface structures from active to passive does change the emphasis from the giver of the book to the book itself. These subtle shifts of emphasis are overlooked by the transformational grammarians, although they can be considered as having a connotational difference of their own which raises questions about the significance of the supposed deep structure.

If, nevertheless, we do accept the deep structure theory, then the transformations necessitated by Aristotelian logic in changing action sentences into attributive sentences, and especially into the class-inclusion type, should be justifiable on the basis of some deep structure similarity. For example, the deep structure similarity between "The boys threw mud" and "The boys are mud-throwers" should be obvious. Aristotle himself apparently thought so.* And certainly for the sake of a uniform system of logic, these transformations are extremely helpful. But this convenience should not obscure the fact that there is an inevitable distortion of perspective whenever we make them. The new sentence forms do not mean quite the same as the old. So, it may very well be that the notion of a deep structure justification for Aristotelian transformations is a dangerous one, at least if we are seeking some kind of rigor in transformational rules.

Let me propose here a major thesis of the present book, namely that there are many more distinguishable relationships in experience than any one particular language incorporates into its syntax. Consequently, each language omits explicit formulation of a great many of these relationships. Yet many of them are expressible in secondary and roundabout ways. Spanish, for example, distinguishes directly through two different verbs *to be* between more permanent and more transient attributive situations. English

---

* See *De Interpretatione*, 20a 4-7: "Where 'is' does not suit as a verb and we use 'walks,' 'has health' and the like, then the same sort of scheme is produced as we get, when the verb 'is' is used." (Cooke translation in Loeb Classical Library)

does not have this feature, but this is not to say that the same idea cannot be expressed in English by introducing some adverbial additives (e.g., "persistently" or "temporarily"), if it really seems necessary to do so. The difference is that in Spanish, the verb *to be* must indicate this difference if it is to be used at all. Differences of this kind exist between most languages, some recognizing certain relationships, and others recognizing different ones. The logician, however, in his search for a simplified system, must make some accommodation with languages, and select only a few centrally important relationships, abandoning the richness of any ordinary language.

How can the logical analysis of grammar help us in thinking clearly?

As one benefit of the logical analysis of basic grammatical patterns, we discover important ways in which we can directly improve clarity in our thinking and writing. In a language like English, for example, we notice that each full sentence is about something (the subject); and that what is said about it (the predicate) is the information added by the particular sentence. Now, for a clear statement, *both subject and predicate should be clear*. But often we are so interested in one of these, usually the predicate, that we tend to leave the other ambiguous or unexpressed. *We* know what we are talking about so we naturally assume that the communicatee will also know. For example, in student themes sentences are frequently started with pronouns (it, he, they, etc.) as the subject terms, the writers presuming that everyone will know to what these pronouns refer. The result, of course, is that the reader often has only a very foggy notion of what is being discussed. Our first rule for clarity, then, is this:

(1) Think about the subject and be sure it is clearly understood and properly named. Especially, do not refer to the subject by a pronoun unless the antecedent is obvious.

Next, one must make certain that the predicate says what it is supposed to say. This is a difficult matter which involves above all else a careful selection of words. A person with a larger vocabulary at his disposal naturally fares better here than one who has a limited vocabulary. However, it is not just size of vocabulary that counts. One must have a sense of the flavor of words, so that one can select those which best express one's meaning. Unfortunately, it sometimes appears that a person is not sure just what he wishes to say until he is well launched upon a sentence. This seems to happen because the process of formulating sentences itself serves to clarify thoughts. Writing has a certain advantage over speaking, for one can phrase sentences more slowly and then go back and rephrase them, if necessary. But a speaker must extricate himself in the most graceful way he can from the middle of an awkward sentence. Some people who have difficulty in formulating good spoken sentences tend to stop in the middle and start afresh. This is not good practice. It is much better to go ahead and finish the sentence in the best way possible under the circumstances, and then clarify the matter with a new sentence if necessary. Otherwise one may develop the annoying habit of never finishing sentences! Occasionally one may get so hopelessly entangled that it is possible only to stop and recommence, being perfectly frank in indicating that this is the case. We should not be embarrassed to do this; for after all in matters of communication pride is secondary to clarity. So, our second rule should be this:

(2) Have a clear notion of what you are to say about a given subject, and then select the most accurate words at your disposal for saying it.

In discourse involving reasoning, one should try to work out in advance the best sequence in which to develop an argument. This means having some sense of the outline of a discourse. If one can learn to do this quickly and in advance of one's remarks, logic and the general thought qualities will improve. A clear mental picture, especially of major relationships involved in the elements of the discourse, is very important. Thus, we may state a third rule:

(3) Organize your thoughts to lead smoothly from some well-considered observations to the implied consequences of these observations.

Finally, for good measure, we might add:

(4) Be critical of your procedure and review it whenever possible.

SUGGESTED READINGS

Cassirer, Ernst, *An Essay on Man,* especially Ch. 8.

Chomsky, Noam, *Aspects of the Theory of Syntax,* especially Ch. 3.

Lewis, M. M., *Infant Speech,* especially Section I.

Lewis, M. M., *How Children Learn to Speak.*

Lyons, John, *Introduction to Theoretical Linguistics,* especially Ch. 4.

Myers, E. D., *The Foundations of English,* especially Chs. 1-2.

Piaget, J., *Language and Thought of the Child.*

Sapir, Edward, *Selected Writings of Edward Sapir,* especially pp. 7-60.

Whorf, Benjamin Lee, *Language, Thought, and Reality,* especially from p. 233 to the end.

CHAPTER III

Symbols

Why are symbols important?

HAVE YOU EVER tried to add, subtract, multiply, or divide using Roman instead of Arabic numerals? If you have not, try it. You will find that the simple processes of ordinary arithmetic seem like operations in higher mathematics. But the operations are the same. The only difference is in the nature and structure of the symbols used. The ease with which a thought process is carried on depends very greatly upon the nature of the symbol system.

In fact, without symbols thinking would limp along on one cylinder, if it could go at all. Symbols are the visible and audible counterparts of our acts of thinking and feeling. They serve to show the nature of our inner sensations and concepts, not only to others but even to ourselves. Have you ever had the experience of having a vague sense or idea about something, and then when it is put into words (i.e., linguistic symbols) it suddenly becomes clear? If so, you will appreciate the very great merit of symbolization.

Some students of human nature have gone so far as to assert that the discovery or invention of symbols is the greatest of all human discoveries, ranking on a par with or ahead of the domestication of fire and animals. Symbols give man a new dimension of reality not possessed by the other animals. Cassirer puts it as follows:

> Man has, as it were, discovered a new method of adapting himself to his environment. Between the receptor system and the effector system, which are to be found in all animal species, we find in man a third link which we may describe as the *symbolic system*. This new acquisition transforms the whole of human life. As compared with the other animals man lives not merely in a broader reality; he lives, so to speak, in a new dimension of reality.*

What are symbols?

Concern with theories of symbolism has a long history, and this whole area of study, often known as semantics, has in recent decades come to be one of man's major preoccupations, especially since the importance of symbol systems has dawned upon him with the full impact of its influences. But there is to date no uniform set of definitions or principles to which a majority of semanticists can agree. The field, in a sense, is still wide open.

There are so many kinds and uses of symbols that we find it difficult to give a satisfactory definition of symbol in general. For example, in the preceding chapter we discussed language. Now, language itself is an elaborate system of symbols. Words and sentences are very familiar examples. But there are other forms of symbols which are not normally included under language. Thus, the railroad semaphore or signal is a symbol serving to inform the engineer about the presence or absence of other trains. Or take note of the great variety of religious symbols, fraternity symbols, weather symbols, flags, blueprints, maps—all of which are symbols of one sort or another, although they are not linguistic symbols.

There are two other terms, *sign* and *signal,* which are often related to or contrasted with symbol. It will help us if we examine these terms first before we attempt even a tentative definition of symbol.

What is a sign? Let us think how we use this word in common

* E. Cassirer, *An Essay on Man,* p. 24. Cassirer may not be entirely correct in denying to other animals the power of symbolizing to some degree, but man alone has developed an elaborate system of symbols.

speech today. In one sense, a sign is a clue to the physical presence of something else, as when we call a cloud a sign of rain. The cloud, that is, points to the possible presence of rain. Similarly deer tracks are signs of deer, in the sense that they are clues pointing to previous presence of a deer in that locality. Now, of course, clouds could also be taken as symbols of rain, or deer tracks as symbols of deer. But this would mean something quite different; for it would mean that we are using the cloud or the tracks merely as substitutes to stand for or remind us of the referents (the rain or the deer, in these cases). Symbols, that is, are not taken as *clues* or *pointers* to the presence of something, they are simply *substitutes* used to *stand for* that something.

In a somewhat different sense, we may use the term "sign" for warnings, or directives for future action. Road signs, for example, inform and warn us of what to expect and what to do. Billboards, similarly, are signs in the sense that they label something or recommend a course of action (for example, to buy something in case we are interested in the product advertised). Of course, road signs and billboards normally contain symbols as part of the sign. Thus the curved arrow, indicating a turn in the road ahead, is just as much a symbol as would be the word "curve," since it stands for or suggests the idea of a curve. Here the symbol for a curve is used as part of a sign which warns one to expect a curve. In general, then, we find that signs are (1) clues or pointers, and (2) devices for labeling, suggesting courses of action, or warning.*

The term *signal* is used especially to designate the signs or symbols which have an immediate warning, action-directing, or commanding function, such as stop and go lights, railroad semaphores, police whistles, all of which have the special task of warning and commanding action. But as with signs in general, we notice that signals contain symbols, frequently linguistic symbols, as in the "Stop! Look! Listen!" which once graced many railroad crossings.

So far, we have glanced at the common meanings of *sign* and *signal*, but now what of *symbol?* It has already been intimated that the task of the symbol, as such, is not to point or warn or

---

* In addition to the foregoing uses, "sign" is sometimes used to stand for highly conventional substitute symbols (e.g., the dollar sign).

direct action but simply to *express or suggest an idea by standing for it*. Remember the way in which we related symbol to concept and referent in Chapter I. The symbol, as we saw then, is the appropriate external medium (sound, visual object, etc.) through which a concept or idea can be expressed and communicated. The idea, in turn, refers to something else which is its referent. Apparently this statement of the case should suffice for our customary meaning of *symbol*. But does it? While we should agree, no doubt, that symbols do stand for ideas, is this all that they do? What happens, for example, when they are used to arouse or express feelings? We know quite well that many of our common symbols, linguistic or other kinds, do produce emotional as well as ideational effects. Shall we say, then, that symbols *stand for* both ideas and feelings and let it go at that? This would be a simple solution, but it does not quite ring true. Feelings do not have referents in the same way that thoughts do. For example, my idea of a new sports car is quite clear as an idea with a referent (the sports car itself). But the referent is not a feeling, though it is very likely to produce some feelings along with it; especially if I have been wanting a new sports car. So the symbol "new sports car" certainly does not *stand for* my feeling in the same way it stands for the idea of the object itself; and we must conclude that symbols often have a dual function: (1) that of standing for an idea of a referent, and (2) that of expressing or arousing a feeling. Some symbols, especially such as religious or patriotic symbols, are strong emotion arousers; but we must not forget that they also stand for ideas. Even the names of feelings have these two functions. Thus the word "love" does not primarily have the function of expressing or arousing a feeling, though it may do this; it primarily designates or stands for the idea of a particular kind of feeling. But observe that we said symbols *may* have these two functions. It is quite possible for some symbols not to arouse feelings, at least to any marked extent; and symbols which suggest the same idea to two people may arouse feelings in one but not in the other. On the other hand, *mere feeling stimulators* with no ideational content, if that is possible, would not be symbols—they would simply be stimuli. *Mere feeling expressers* without ideational content would be only signs, or feeling clues.

Going back for a moment to signs and signals, we should recognize that they too, whether or not they include symbols, may express or even arouse feelings. A simple automatic expression of feeling, such as a cry of pain, would be a sign in the sense of being a clue to a feeling. But, of course, as with symbols, signs and signals may be neither expressions nor arousers of feelings (e.g., a casual observance of a cloud as a sign of rain need not evoke any particular emotion).

To summarize our discussions of signs, signals and symbols, let us note again that signs are primarily clues or pointers; that signals are signs which have the special function of warning or directing or commanding action; and that symbols stand for or suggest ideas of referents. Furthermore, all three (signs, signals, symbols) may express or arouse feelings.

What are the various kinds of symbols and symbol-referent relations?

Symbols can stand for a bewildering array of referents and can thus be classified according to the subject matter of these referents. For example, in the section labeled "Arbitrary Signs and Symbols" in an unabridged Merriam-Webster dictionary* we find a classification all the way from AERONAUTICS to WEATHER. But more interesting for our purposes are the basic varieties of symbols and the ways in which they can be connected with their referents; for these ways are to be found in all subject-matter areas.

First, we discover that man has appropriated natural objects for use as symbols. Seashells, for example, are often taken as symbols for water, and thence for rain, as by the desert Indians of North America. Whether seashells thus taken also involve magical or fetishistic characteristics need not detain us here. In any case, they illustrate the way in which a simple natural object can be taken to represent something other than itself. We may further notice that the relation between the natural object and that for which it stands is normally one that depends upon either *similarity* or *contiguity*. In the case of the seashell, contiguity or contact with ocean water affords the basis of the connection.

* Second edition, 1934.

Suppose a spider web is taken as a symbol for the universe by someone who imagines that the orderly geometry of the web is similar to the geometry of the universe. In this case the connection would be that of imagined similarity.

Most of the symbols used by man have been artificial or man-made devices, not natural objects. Man-made symbols can include carvings, drawings, writings, noises, and the like, as well as the more common vocal sounds. These artificial symbols, like the natural objects, can be related to their referents by contiguity or imitation. Thus, one can draw a picture of a seashell instead of using the actual shell; or, one could name a bird simply by imitating its call, as may possibly have been the case with the names for owl and chicken.

While vocal sounds are apparently the most natural symbolic formations of man, pictographic drawing is also very natural. Pictographic drawings very quickly become simplified and conventionalized, just as do imitative sounds. For example, ⵍⵀⵣ is an early Chinese symbol for mountain, and ⌒⌒ is a common Pueblo Indian cloud symbol, both of which are clearly altered into easily represented and regular forms.

This matter of imitative symbols raises an interesting issue. Would a casual photograph of a scene or person be properly called a symbol of that scene or person? The answer is No. A photograph may become a symbol in a different sense, as when a picture of one's home is used to symbolize one's nostalgia for home. But a picture, as picture, is not a symbol of the scene it pictures. The difference lies in the fact that a symbol has as its main purpose that of standing for something, whereas the purpose of a picture is to look like its object. For this reason, imitative symbols need not be faithful representations. Their purpose is fulfilled so long as they are conventionally recognized as symbolizing a certain kind of referent. Ease in forming them thus takes precedence over exact imitation. For example, the Chinese pictograph for mountain, illustrated above, becomes modified to ⵚⵀ , which is a simpler and more easily made version of the earlier form. And notice how the Pueblo cloud symbol has already been simplified and regularized from the highly irregular shapes of ordinary cumulus clouds.

So far we have mentioned two ways in which symbols may be

naturally connected to their referents: by *similarity* and by *contiguity.** There is possibly a third way, namely, that which occurs when a sensation in one of the senses suggests an associated response in another of the senses. For example, if a high shrill sound is used in a musical composition to suggest lightning (a visible, not auditory, phenomenon), it would be appropriate because of the association between the piercing quality of the sound and of the flash of light. Perhaps such associations are merely cases of similarity in which similar qualities (e.g., piercingness) are abstracted from two sensory media. But it is possible that sounds may suggest visual images and vice versa in accordance with some internal mechanism. This problem of sensory interconnections is one considered by psychologists under the label "synesthesia," but investigations so far have been sporadic and inconclusive.† However, for our purposes, we should record the possibility of synesthesia as a third type of natural connection between symbol and referent. So we now have three possible bases for natural connection: by *similarity*, by *contiguity*, and by *synesthesia*.

A naturally connected symbol need not always be very *appropriate* to its referent. Natural connection of itself does not assure a high degree of appropriateness; for there may be some tenuous or unobvious connections which are still natural in the sense of having imitation or contiguity. For example, a college football team may have taken as its symbolic mascot a wolf, which suggests strength and ferocity and thereby has a natural similarity at least to the ideal which is held for the team. Many equally appropriate animals might have been chosen, all imitating the same hoped-for trait; but an animal that also frequented the region in which the college is situated and so had contiguity would have greater appropriateness than one that did not; for this would add a second natural connection. Thus, in western United States, a mountain lion would be more appropriate

---

* David Hume, in the eighteenth century, had already formulated a philosophy of knowledge based especially upon the relations of similarity and contiguity.

† Linguists have experimented with natural synesthetic suggestion of different phonetic sounds. See especially the work of C. E. Osgood and such articles as Brown, Black, and Horowitz, "Phonetic Symbolism in Natural Languages," *Journal of Abnormal and Social Psychology*, Vol. 50, pp. 388-393.

than a tiger. Or supposing among the several local animals a rather timid little animal should be selected (e.g., a field mouse) then, although the connection is still a natural (contiguous) one, the appropriateness would be lessened since the imitative trait of ferocity would be lacking.

On the other hand, we must notice that many man-made symbols are not connected with their referents either by imitation or by contiguity or even by any noticeable synesthesia. As with the majority of the words in any of the natural languages, the original basis of association would seem to have been pure arbitrary invention. So in contrast to the few clearly onomatopoeic words (swish, boom, roar, etc.) which show an effort to imitate the sounds to which they refer, most words seem to have been *arbitrarily invented* in their origin. Especially is this true of relating words like *of* or *with*. But even names of objects and actions are not often explainable as imitations of sounds. For example, does "dog" sound like a dog, or "house" like a house? Perhaps some words can be traced back to imitation, and perhaps the Anglo-Saxon *dacga,* from which we get "dog," was an attempt to imitate a bark. But to find such origins for the majority of words will lead us to very far-fetched assumptions. It may be enticing to follow the lead of some of the psycholinguists who suggest that synesthesia is responsible for many primitive word associations; but at the present stage of our knowledge on this subject, we can only hesitate. Certainly we still will have a large number of words that have no accountable natural connection with their referents.

When we call symbols "arbitrarily invented" we do not mean arbitrarily chosen. Nearly all symbols are *arbitrarily chosen* in the sense that some other symbol, natural or nonnatural, could have been selected for the same meaning. But only symbols without any apparent natural connections with their referents are what we mean here by *arbitrarily invented* symbols.

Many of our symbols involve combinations of the naturally connected and arbitrarily invented kinds. For example, we might paint an area blue on a map to symbolize water. The blue color would be an imitative, hence naturally connected, symbol. But now suppose we refer to the water simply by the word "blue" where we plan later to paint the color. Then this word is an arbitrarily invented symbol for the color which would be naturally connected. Or we might symbolize water by the letters H_2O. H and O are naturally connected only with the words *hydrogen* and *oxygen* of which they are the initial letters. The words hydrogen and oxygen, however, are arbitrarily invented symbols. But the implied atomic arrangement, we assume, imitates the actual water molecule, thus suggesting a third factor—the arrangement—which would have a natural connection with water molecules. Thus the symbol H_2O incorporates both natural and arbitrary features.

So far we have noticed that symbols can be classified according to (1) the *context* in which they are used (e.g., aeronautics, highway signs, music, physics, weather), or (2) the *source of the symbolic material* (e.g., natural or man-made objects adopted as symbols as against devices designed primarily to be used as symbols), or (3) the *relationship between the symbol and its referent* (e.g., various natural relations, such as imitation and contiguity, as against having no apparent relation). There are a number of other interesting and important ways in which symbols may be classified. Let us examine some of these.

In the fourth place, we may consider the *conventionality* of a symbol. A newly coined symbol which has not yet gone into circulation would be unconventional or preconventional. Only after a reasonable period of repeated usage can we consider a symbol to be fully conventional. Anyone, of course, is free to coin new symbols, though he does this at the risk of not being understood. I might propose, for example, to let the letters *puxyr* stand for the way two people look to each other under water. However, such symbolic innovations would have little utility for purposes of communication, unless one explains them in symbols that are already familiar. Coined symbols are usually chosen because they have some linguistic connection with other already familiar symbols. New symbols, for example, are often abbreviations of the old (e.g., U.S.A. for the United States of America). Or new symbols may be composites of two or more familiar symbols. An example of such composites is found in some of the words of "Jabberwocky" taken from Lewis Carroll's *Through the Looking Glass:*

> 'Twas brillig, and the slithy toves
> Did gyre and gimble in the wabe;
> All mimsy were the borogoves,
> And the mome raths outgrabe.

These words almost seem to make sense because they combine or suggest other words (e.g., *slithy* suggests *slippery* and *writhing*). Others of these words need translation, and Lewis Carroll in Chapter 6 of *Through the Looking Glass* does indeed offer us some translations, although these are presented facetiously with the attitude that anyone ought to know what these words mean. The words used in "Jabberwocky" are not completely nonsensical like the vocables used to fill up sounds in a song (e.g., tra-la-la), which could hardly be called symbols at all. Instead, words like *slithy* and *gyre* are suggestive of other conventional words.

It is important to recognize that *naturally connected* symbols, as well as *arbitrarily invented* symbols, may become *conventional*. For example, as we noted above, imitations of sounds, like *swish, boom, cock-a-doodle-doo,* were natural imitative symbols to start with. But they have become conventional words in English and, as a result, have taken on the normal characteristics of English phonetic sounds, as witness the fact that no self-respecting rooster crows "cock-a-doodle-doo" in the way we customarily enunciate this sound. Another evidence of this is the fact that imitative symbols, such as the sound of the rooster, may be conventionalized in different ways, depending upon the phonetic habits of a language. Thus, in German the same sound is characteristically expressed as *kikiriki*.

In the fifth place, symbols may be distinguished as to whether they are *substitutes* for some other symbol or are *primary* symbols. We have indicated already that symbols are frequently shortened or abbreviated, especially in writing. These abbreviated forms (e.g., U.S.A.) are then substitute symbols for the original longer version. In mathematics and logic we find that single letters are very useful substitutes for more complicated expressions, especially when the same expression is repeated through several operations (e.g., Let $i = \sqrt{-1}$). Also, the x which stands for a quantity yet to be determined is a kind of anticipatory substitute symbol. Even in common language we find an excellent case of substitute symbols in the humble pronoun. Pronouns, if not abused, are great labor-saving devices. For example, compare the two following statements of the same idea:

(1) George and William took George's and William's pet pony to the pet pony's stall and in the stall George and William fed the pet pony hay and oats.

(2) George and William took *their* pet pony to *its* stall *where they* fed *it* hay and oats.

Here we see clearly the economy of the substitute symbol.

Sometimes substitute symbols are not shorter but merely different. In translating from one language to another, we may regard the words in our own language as the original symbols (for us), and those in the other language as the substitute symbols. Frequently, the correspondence in such cases is not perfect, as we shall see in more detail in Chapter IV, but roughly at least *chien,* or *perro,* or *Hund* may be be considered a substitute symbol for *dog.*

A sixth way of distinguishing symbols is between *opaque* and *transparent.* This distinction pertains especially to the ability of the communicatee to decode. A symbol that is difficult to decode is opaque, whereas one that is easy is transparent. A transparent symbol, that is, has a meaning so clear that scarcely any attention is wasted on the symbol itself. One's thought is immediately focused upon the referent. An opaque symbol, on the contrary, is figured out with difficulty, like a message in some private code.

Symbols can also be divided into those which are secret or esoteric and those which are not. A secret symbol is one, like special fraternity or sorority insignia and passwords, which is supposed to be the private mark of some special group. Also, the various systems of codes used by nations are both secret and substitute symbols, being devices to prevent an enemy from understanding one's message.

A somewhat more subtle distinction is that of the degree in which symbols rely upon other symbols to acquire their meaning. Some symbols, such as a single word (e.g., "dog"), reveal something, but not too much, when used by themselves. One may say to himself, "Yes, I know what a dog is, but what about it?" We need a whole statement or proposition to give a fuller meaning (e.g., "Your dog just got out of the car"). And in language there are many matrix or relater words, like "in," which tell us still less by themselves. If someone were to utter just the word "in," we would wonder, "What is in what?" These linguistic symbols clearly need others to fill out even a rudimentary situation. Such symbols are sometimes called "discursive" symbols because they need to be contained in a discourse or sequence of sentences to gain their specific meaning. On the other hand, there are some symbols which can give a great deal of information just within themselves. Certain religious symbols, for example, assuming one knows enough about the religion, contain many implications and levels of meaning even though they appear without other symbols. Such symbols as the Christian cross are not dependent upon other symbols, but rather upon the knowledge of the religious tradition, for their meaning. Moreover, if we take the notion of synesthetic connection seriously, there may be some naturally revelatory symbolic elements which, when combined together, give quite a sense of the meaning of the whole.*

A bit like the preceding distinction is that of the internality or externality of a symbol with its referent. Some symbols, like abbreviations, are simply fragments of the larger whole which they symbolize. Similarly, any suggestive fragment of sight or sound may bring about within the perceiver a larger and fuller range of impressions. Pictorial and musical elements are strongly imbued with this expansive property, so that, as symbols, they are able to enlarge one's sense of the whole meaning.† On the other hand, the typical arbitrarily invented symbols of ordinary language are quite outside of or external to their referents. There are many interesting questions about the nature of internal and expansive symbols, and the reasons why they tend to produce stronger emotive responses than do externally related symbols. But I shall leave these questions for the reader to contemplate.

---

* It may be interesting to compare what Susanne Langer calls "discursive" and "presentational" symbols in her discussion of symbols in *Philosophy in a New Key*, Ch. 4. She correlates presentational forms with the notion of *Gestalt*, which is closely related to the notion of synesthesia. It is useful to compare W. M. Urban's treatment of "insight symbols" in *Language and Reality*, Ch. 10.

† In this connection, see Gordon Epperson's *The Musical Symbol*, Chs. 11-12.

What are the principal uses of signs and symbols?

There can be little doubt that the primary use of signs and symbols is *communication*. The other basic use is simple *self-expression,* that is, a use of signs and symbols for one's own sake alone, as in the explosive use of interjections when something goes wrong or as in talking to oneself or even writing notes to oneself. Even these may be considered a kind of self-communication. So let us look for a moment at the human infant as it learns to express itself and to communicate with those around it, and then let us note into what these expressions and communications develop as the child grows up.

First, we observe that the oh's and ah's expressive of feelings are distinguishable into expressions of pleasure or displeasure, approval or disapproval, which soon become designed to communicate and even to solicit social agreement (e.g., "Ouch, that pin pricked me!" or "Gee, isn't that a beautiful sunset!"). Such forms of symbolic expression become enlarged into forms of discourse. This first or *expressive* type then becomes *affective* in its effort to affect others with our own feelings. Eventually it turns *appraisive* and *evaluative* as we attempt some reasoned justifications for these feelings. Thus, we may view this first type of symbolic usage as falling into a developing sequence—expressive, affective, appraisive, and evaluative—as the simple symbol becomes elaborated.

Secondly, one of the first purposes of communication, we may notice, is that of making demands upon those around us. The infant, who is so much a bundle of wants and needs, naturally learns this demand function of language very early. He shows his wants, strivings, or "conations" in his use of language. We may therefore call this type of usage in its early stages a *conative* use of language (e.g., "Da!" or something of the sort, meaning "I want that!"). As he matures, he learns to use more and more refined language so that the demands are couched as polite requests (or at least they should be). Occasionally a man wishes to accomplish some large goal, for which purpose he needs to persuade those around him that this goal is the thing that should be achieved. His discourse becomes persuasive or even *incitive* and *exhortative,* as in oratory. Such discourse presupposes, and often includes, affective and appraisive forms, for, normally, one is inclined to persuade others to do what one would like done.

There is thus a close connection between expressive-affective-appraisive discourse and conative-persuasive-incitive discourse: expressing one's likes and dislikes is usually a prelude to urging these upon others. Yet the focus is on *appraisal* in the first case and on *persuasion* in the second. It is possible, after all, to appraise without persuading and even, unfortunately, to persuade without appraising.

In the third place, from the moment the infant attempts to imitate the sounds of his elders in order to attach to them the appropriate objects, he is using language to *designate*. When the infant says "Da!" and points, he may not mean "I like that!" or "I want that!" but merely "See, there it is!" Language so used may be called "designative." Now, as one matures, his designations become more and more complex, referring to things absent or past as well as present. Such a use of language might more properly be termed "informative." *Informative* discourse, moreover, may be regarded as twofold: descriptive and narrative. When we look at all human discourse, we discover that by far the largest part of it purports to be informative. Try the following experiment. Listen to any conversation and notice how much of it is, or purports to be, informative. Gossip, for example, is typical of discourse that purports to inform. But gossip illustrates the fact that some apparently informative discourses are less reliable than others, and that it should be our responsibility always to check our sources. However, the question of reliability is not one with which we are concerned at present.

In the fourth place, one may distinguish a type of discourse which is to be found at a very early stage in the development of language uses. The child may say "Da?" instead of "Da!" meaning "What?" or "Why?" In other words, discourse may be *interrogative*. Interrogation reflects the inquisitive temper so characteristic of the human mind, the desire to seek confirmations and clarifications* of initial understandings. But interrogation is a request for

---

* On the notion that desire for confirmation precedes desire for clarification, see M. M. Lewis, *Infant Speech*, Ch. 14. The confirmations there noted are (1) confirming that linguistic intercourse with others is possible and (2) receiving permission to act. Then the child asks *for* something absent, and finally he asks *about* things.

an answer, and so is incomplete in itself. If we include not only the question but also the answer as part of this type of discourse, then we should call it "interrogative-explanatory." A full-fledged spirit of interrogation requires answers and explanations, and as this spirit develops it will naturally lead to investigation and inquiry. Certainly the philosophical dialogues written by Plato offer one important paradigm for interrogative-explanatory discourse.

At this point we may well wonder if what we have called informative discourse could not also serve as the conclusion of an interrogation. Do not questions call for information just as much as explanation? Or is there any real difference between information and explanation? Certainly we must not overstress this distinction, but let us look at it this way: information, we said, appears either as simple description or narration; very little attempt is made to get at the underlying reasons or causes for events or at the possible interrelationships of objects. But explanation aims at giving underlying reasons in terms of some theoretical pattern or structure of interrelations. So, even though the distinction between information and explanation is not sharp, it is meaningful and useful; and interrogation seems more often to be a request for explanation than for simple information.

There is evidence that a child's early questions are actually more requests for confirmation of his proper use of symbols than they are requests for what we might call real explanations. But even so, it seems highly probable that a childish "Why?" stems from a sense of inadequate knowledge and that he wants as much knowledge as he is capable of assimilating, even though from the adult point of view this may not be much. If the child asks questions at all, he is presumably trying to get the feel of the situation, to see how he fits into it. The desired answer is not just informative, but should have elements of explanation as well. This is shown in the very prevalence of "Why?" questions at an early stage. "Why?" is basically a question requiring explanation, whereas "What?" tends rather to solicit information. Although it is usually said by the authorities on this subject that the child's "Why?" does not solicit explanation, but merely confirmation (as if the question were "Is that really so-and-so?"), it is curious that the "Why?" question predominates among children, and that the child seems better satisfied with some attempt at explanation than he does at mere confirmation. For example, one of my sons as a young lad of four or five once said, "Why is that man walking down the street?" When the answer came back, "I don't know why," he replied, "Well, think up something!" In other words, the desire for explanation here was stronger than the desire for mere information (including an honest answer). Some hypothesis which would explain the man's walking down the street was being requested.

In general, now, and by way of recapitulation, we may note that a child's "Da" may mean

- "I like that" (*expressive* leading to *appraisive* discourse).
- "I want that" (*conative* becoming *persuasive* discourse).
- "There it is" (*designative* as a prelude to *informative* discourse).
- "Why?" or "What is that?" (*interrogative* as requesting primarily *explanatory* discourse).

We may summarize these four uses of symbols and the kinds of discourse to which they lead as follows:

- *Expressive-appraisive* discourse, which primarily expresses feelings and emotions.
- *Conative-persuasive-incitive* discourse, which primarily expresses wants, requests, demands, urgings, and the like.
- *Designative-informative* discourse, which moves from mere labeling and pointing to full-fledged description and narration.
- *Interrogative-explanatory* discourse, which seeks further information along with clarification and analysis.

In terms of meaning, which will be the topic of our next chapter, we may note here that expressive-appraisive discourse focuses on emotive meaning, conative-persuasive discourse on practical or active meaning, designative-informative discourse on descriptive and narrative, or "referential" meaning, and interrogative-explanatory discourse on clarificatory or analytic meaning.

As the human understanding develops and matures, it is but natural that the forms of discourse become intermingled. The longer discourses, with which we normally are concerned, may well include most of the above varieties within one speech or writing.

Still, it is possible to discern certain predominances of type in various typical statements. For example, political oratory contains many appraisive and persuasive sentences; description and narration are characteristically composed of informative sentences, whether about real or imaginary events; and philosophical and scientific essays are more apt to have explanatory sentences, in that their purpose is to seek out general principles.

Language is, of course, an extremely flexible tool, reflecting all the temperaments and purposes of human beings. Just as it would be unusual to encounter language used solely as expressive, or conative, or informative, or explanatory, likewise it is not possible to tie these modes of discourse to particular grammatical constructions, such as the indicative, or imperative, or interrogative verbal forms, convenient though it would be to do so. It may be, however, that certain grammatical forms will *tend to predominate* in one type of discourse as, for example, the indicative in informative discourse or the imperative in persuasive discourse.

It would also be a mistake to bind the types of discourse to any one of the commonly distinguished literary or rhetorical forms. Thus, although some writers have sought to maintain that *poetic* discourse is purely emotive or expressive of feeling, it should be readily observable that much of what we customarily term poetry has appraisive, informative, interrogative, and even explanatory passages. In fact, poetic discourse is often difficult to distinguish from prose. There is no one way to do this, though we might characterize poetry as that which *in addition to* telling a tale *(epic* poetry) or describing a scene *(descriptive* poetry) employs language to call forth overtones of feeling or meaning or to sharpen one's sensitivity to a situation. These additional tasks may be accomplished in many ways: by choice of words, by use of metaphor, by metrical or rhyming schemes, and so on. Of all the poetic forms, the *lyric* is that which comes closest to being purely expressive discourse. Yet even a love poem will glorify in simile or metaphor the enchantment cast by the beloved. Conversely, there are times when the most austere scientific discourse will wax poetical. Man's feelings remain ever close to the surface and have a way of asserting themselves even when he is seeking to be most matter-of-fact. So, poetry is not just emotive or expressive discourse but a kind which may involve all modes of discourse, yet in which the emphasis is upon the artistic forms of language that enhance and sharpen what one has to say.

Narrative prose and *drama* are literary forms which inform us of events, whether these events be fact or fiction. (Customarily the recounting of presumably factual events is called *history*.) Whether narration deals in fact or fiction, it is primarily informative discourse. *Exposition,* as a literary form, on the other hand, is principally explanatory, though, of course, informative and even appraisive modes of discourse are often included in exposition.

Various writers have classified types of discourse in other ways. Typical is the treatment of Frye and Levi* which distinguishes the following major varieties: *expressive, practical, ceremonial, poetic,* and *logical*. The *expressive,* for them, is much what we have meant here by this term. *Poetic* discourse, in their way of looking at it, appeals both to feelings and to the imagination, but without intending to provoke action or to inform. Discourse which intends to provoke action they call *practical;* and discourse which intends to inform is what they mean by *logical.* We stated above that poetry may involve all types of discourse—expressive, persuasive (or practical), informative, and explanatory. Frye and Levi do not disagree, for they admit that poetry may incite to action (i.e., be practical) or may inform (be informative). But they stress the view that these are not the primary functions of poetry. Its primary function, they insist, is to evoke feeling and imagination. Such a view sounds very plausible, but we should be wary of too great a restriction on the meaning of poetry for it has traditionally included narration and description. Indeed, poetic qualities often appear in prose writings, serving to enhance and sharpen the apprehension of what is being said therein.

Practical discourse, according to Frye and Levi, has as its purpose a stirring to action. However, the term "practical" is ambiguous, for we do not need to think of all practical discourse as necessarily incitive or inflammatory. The directions on a game, for example, are certainly unimpassioned examples of practical discourse. The full context in such cases would be conditional statements of the form: "If you wish to play this game, then you must do so-and-so." This conditional type of practical dis-

* See Frye and Levi, *Rational Belief,* pp. 9-20.

course is really a variety of explanatory discourse rather than the persuasive variety used by demagogues.

Ceremonial discourse, as this term is used by Frye and Levi, refers to traditionalized and often nonliteral verbal forms which oil the social machinery. Such polite forms of discourse as "How do you do?" "Goodbye," "Dear Sir" do not necessarily mean what they appear to say. "How do you do?" does not expect the answer "I do very well." "Goodbye" is a long way from its original "God be with you." And "Dear Sir" at the outset of a letter is hardly to be taken as an expression of endearment. These ceremonial forms can most appropriately be traced back to the conative forms of speech; but when man is sophisticated enough to realize that his desires may be best gained by politeness and respect toward others, then ceremonial forms become standardized. Linguistically these forms can be distinguished only by their being remnants of earlier forms of speech which no longer retain their original meanings as they are now used, or by being current forms of speech used without much thought to their meaning. Liturgical discourse, which graces the ceremonies of most religions, is often ceremonial discourse, for here too the old meaning may be lost and not replaced by any new meaning, except a general impression of the purpose of the words. In liturgy and perhaps in ceremonial discourse generally, there is an underlying hesitation to give up the old forms which assume a special association of sanctity. In general, ceremonial discourse is a variety of expressive and conative discourse.

In addition to the above types of discourse, some writers distinguish a *valuative* form or use.* Such a use occurs when one expresses not only approval or disapproval, but makes a statement about the goodness or badness of objects and events. The whole problem of asserting value is highly complicated and leads into one of the major fields of philosophy (axiology). Some people maintain that assertions of value are merely expressive or appraisive statements ("I like that" or "I don't like that"). Most philosophers, however, insist that there is more to the act of valuation than simply asserting liking or disliking. If this is so,

* See especially C. W. Morris, *Signs, Language, and Behavior,* Ch. 5, in which sixteen types of discourse are discussed, including "valuative" as a major *use,* as against "appraisive," which is here called a *mode.*

then valuative discourse cannot be reduced to a variant of expressive-appraisive discourse. Without pursuing the problem further here, we can only suggest that what is involved over and beyond mere liking or disliking is some sort of analytic or explanatory principle of evaluation. Thus if we accept this view, valuative discourse involves not only expressive-appraisive forms but also analytic-explanatory forms, at least implicitly.

J. L. Austin* has added a further insight into the varieties of linguistic symbolic usage by distinguishing a category of statement or utterance called *performatives*. A performative utterance is one that does not have the primary function of describing or narrating something, but rather of reporting that one is doing or performing an action or changing a condition. For example, the statement "The book is gray" is clearly descriptive of the book, but if I should say "I am giving you this book," then I am reporting what I am doing with regard to it. This performative statement does designate certain objects and actions (you, me, the book, giving), but it does not primarily describe or narrate anything. Furthermore, it does not primarily express a feeling or emotion, as would the statement "I was scared to death by that book," nor does it persuade or incite anyone to some kind of action or response, as would the question "Won't you please take this book?"

Austin lists a number of types of performative utterances, such as asking, ordering, warning, promising, announcing a verdict, pronouncing a sentence on someone, and so on. Such statements are all examples of focusing attention on what one is doing in making a particular utterance. Austin also notes that whereas descriptive and narrative utterances can normally be questioned with regard to their truth or falsity, it would be inappropriate to raise this issue in regard to performatives. If you indicate that you are giving me a book, I could ask "Is it true that you are giving me this book?" but what I would mean in this case is something like "Are you sincere or in earnest in wishing me to have the book?" For Austin it is more appropriate to say that performative utterances "misfire" if for some reason the act indicated does not or cannot take place (e.g., your attention is diverted and you forget to give me the book), or that these utterances are "abuses" if the one making the statement is insincere (e.g., you did not really intend to give me the book at

* See J. L. Austin, *How to Do Things with Words,* especially Lectures 1 and 2.

all). Misfirings and abuses are "infelicities" rather than judgments of falsity.

In a later section of *How to Do Things with Words*, Austin widens his concept with new terminology. The act of "saying something" in the full normal sense of this expression he calls a "locutionary act." But in addition to simple locutionary acts, he notes those actions and phrases that indicate what we are doing when we say something. This what-we-are-doing aspect he calls an "illocutionary act." As he puts it, it is "performance of an act *in* saying something as opposed to performance of an act *of* saying something" that makes the difference.* Thus, performative utterances, such as "I promise," "I decree," "I advise," are indications of illocutionary acts. Finally, Austin wishes to distinguish a third kind of aspect that utterances may have: their "perlocutionary force." The perlocutionary force consists in the "effects upon feelings, thoughts, or actions of the audience, or of the speaker, or of other persons,"† which may be produced when we say something. There are some verbs (e.g., persuade, get to, bring to) which suggest a perlocutionary force or resultant effect of our speech (e.g., He brought me to my senses).

Austin's program for examining linguistic usage in an effort to find clues to the distinctions we do or should make is helpful and suggestive, although it does not seem to have been as successful as he probably hoped it would. Not every time we use certain expressions do they necessarily indicate that we are endowing our language merely with a locutionary sense, or also with an illocutionary or possibly a perlocutionary sense. For example, we sometimes use the verb *to persuade* in the sense of *trying to persuade* ("I was persuading him to come" may mean "I was trying to get him to come") without implying that the persuasion had an effect. It is questionable, then, whether *persuade* must indicate a perlocutionary force. But this failure is due, no doubt, to slovenliness in the ordinary use of language, and not to the lack of validity of Austin's distinctions. In fact, Austin's whole approach can be used as an illustration of my major thesis that there are many more possible relations to be discovered in experience than any one language incorporates. Austin's refined methods of analyzing language have indeed

* *Ibid.*, p. 99.
† *Ibid.*, p. 101f.

brought to light some of these relations, especially through examination of verbs and prepositions and conjunctions, and we should be grateful for these insights, even if our language usage itself is not an airtight index.

We could continue enumerating varieties of discourse as distinguished by various writers on the subject from the time of Aristotle on down. But for our purposes we have mentioned enough, remembering always that classifications in an area of this kind are merely conveniences for helping us to observe some possible grounds for differentiation. Let us review the types stressed in the present discussion: (1) *expressive,* leading to *affective* and *appraisive* discourse; (2) *conative,* developing into *persuasive, exhortative,* and *incitive* discourse; (3) *designative,* becoming *informative* discourse; and (4) *interrogative,* being answered by *explanatory* discourse. One could go on to correlate or add the traditional literary types, such as lyric, narrative (historical or fictional), dramatic, and expository; or the rhetorical types, such as informative, convincing, persuasive, inspirational, entertaining, and eulogistic. Such an exercise could be interesting and instructive principally in showing the great variety of communicational goals which man sets before himself, and perhaps in giving us some valuable clues to human cultures.

We still need to enlarge our horizon and consider for a moment the fact that symbols and symbol systems are not limited to language or discourses in the usual sense. Nonlinguistic symbols such as (1) substitute symbols (e.g., some mathematical symbols), (2) clarificatory symbols (e.g., maps and charts), and (3) religious, fraternal and patriotic symbols (e.g., national flags) occur in many contexts, both within and outside of discourses. However, of even more interest is the possibility of considering works of art in their symbolic dimension. The power of synesthetic suggestion and of symbolic overtones pervades all the arts, even linguistic arts (literature), carrying the one who is affected by a work of art into new worlds of meaning and feeling.

In summary, this section has offered a bare introduction to the complex problem of varieties of symbolic uses, paying special attention to linguistic symbols in various types of discourse. Two basic uses seem to have emerged from our discussion: (1) that of expressing and arousing feelings, and (2) that of communicating and explaining concepts. But, we must not forget that a single symbol or symbol system may perform more than one function, so that it is not possible to correlate precisely *types* of symbols with their *uses*.

SUGGESTED READINGS

Austin, John L., *How to Do Things with Words.*
Cassirer, Ernst, *An Essay on Man,* especially Ch. 3.
Epperson, Gordon, *The Musical Symbol,* especially Chs. 9-12.
Fingesten, Peter, *The Eclipse of Symbolism.*
Koch, Rudolf, *The Book of Signs.*
Langer, Susanne, *Philosophy in a New Key,* especially Chs. 3-4.
Morris, C. W., *Signs, Language, and Behavior,* especially Ch. 5.
Urban, W. M., *Language and Reality,* especially Ch. 9.
Whitehead, Alfred N., *Symbolism: Its Meaning and Effect.*

CHAPTER IV

Meaning

What is meaning?

THERE ARE MANY distinguishable meanings of "meaning." In a pioneer work on this subject, Ogden and Richards list sixteen major varieties.* Fortunately for our purposes, we can do with fewer.

When we examine the verb "to mean," the first and most obvious distinction to hit us is that between a person's *intention* or *purpose* (what I mean to do) and a symbol's *reference* (what a word or symbol means). There is an early connection between these usages, for one variety of what I mean to do is what I mean to communicate; and the symbols I use when I communicate something should reveal the reference of my original intention. But for the sake of clarity, let us take these two uses of "meaning" as distinct. The first we shall call *intentional* or purposive meaning, and the second *referential* or symbolic meaning.

Now, it is the nature of a symbol, we remember, to stand for, refer to, or suggest something over and beyond itself. So symbols have references, or "referential

* Ogden and Richards, *The Meaning of Meaning*, pp. 186-187.

meaning."* Some words, however, do not have references. For example, if someone hurts himself and exclaims "Ow!" he is probably just expressing a feeling and not referring to anything. Language used in this way is a clue or natural sign of the feeling; it is not a symbol having a referent. Furthermore, language is sometimes used merely to arouse feelings in others, to stir up their emotions, without any clear or precise referential meaning. In the strict sense, these cases are more like stimuli than like symbols. Nevertheless, we should be careful not to exclude meaning from the emotive use of language; there are very few cases of language use which merely express or evoke feelings without concurrent ideas. Most emotively oriented language accomplishes its purpose by building conceptual images which in turn express or arouse feelings. Lyric poetry, for example, which might be considered the typically emotive use of language, accomplishes its purpose through the evocation of conceptual imagery.

When we examine the varieties of linguistic discourse, we find that for the most part there is some combination of conceptual and emotive factors at work, so that the meanings which we express and communicate contain some balance of these factors. Spoken language in particular is apt to betray our feelings through the accompanying aspects, such as tone of voice or facial expression. For example, the utterance "He's a pretty boy" could have quite opposite meanings depending upon sincerity or sarcasm in one's tone. Furthermore, in ordinary uses of language, as in conversation, we

---

* The expression "referential meaning" is often limited in current discussions to references made to objects and events that are actually or potentially present in the experience of the person using the symbols, especially when referred to or designated by a given speaker at a given time. This restriction, however, is unnecessarily narrow. One reason for it is undoubtedly the desire to distinguish between what is merely being thought about (the unapplied or primary conceptual meaning) and what is being asserted about the world (the applied conceptual meaning). While recognizing that how a proposition is used on a particular occasion does introduce some special meanings due to the nature and context of the particular occasion, we must remember that these special meanings simply supplement the primary conceptual meanings of the symbols used. For a general discussion of meaning, such as this one, it is useful to think of "referential meaning" in its widest sense as including anything that can be called to mind by the symbols used, even if the referent is imaginary, and not as limiting our referents either to perceivable objects and events or to special localized applications of conceptual meaning.

do not stop to discriminate the conceptual referential from the emotive components of meaning. The two taken together form in our awareness the larger meaning of our symbols. So, although strictly speaking we might maintain that the symbolic function is purely conceptual, and that the emotive function is a separate aspect which simply expresses or evokes feelings, it is more reasonable to grant to the symbolic function in its entirety both a conceptual referential and an emotive force. It was in this sense that we spoke in Chapter III of symbols having a dual function.

A third aspect of meaning, however, could well be added. This aspect derives from the fact that when we use language, it is most often involved in other activities of the communicator, the communicatee, or both. For example, the "conative-persuasive-incitive" use of symbols mentioned in Chapter III strongly implies that some kind of action should be forthcoming. Whether the communicator is cajoling, persuading, or commanding the communicatee to do something, the activity called for is an integral part of the total meaning.

This active dimension of meaning, let us note, may be thought of as involving not only the overt actions called for, but also what Austin called "perlocutionary force" and "illocutionary act" including his "performative utterances."* In these cases, it is the sense of asserted or promised activity that gives the meaning its active dimension, even if the activity is not overt at the moment beyond the utterance of the symbols themselves. For example, if I am greeting someone, or uttering words that are part of a ceremony, the primary focus of attention is on the actions taking place and the fact that my utterances play some meaningful role in these actions. If I am announcing what I intend to do, and vouching for my intention, as in promising to return a book or pay a bill, then my present language indicates some future action of mine.

When the importance of this kind of active meaning is stressed, it is but a short step to viewing all meaning as dependent upon the particular circumstances and linguistic usages of the moment. Meaning then becomes largely a function of use. But such a view unwarrantedly reduces meaning to only one of its aspects. There is no need for so extreme a restriction of meaning, since we can

* See Chapter III, p. 78.

more justifiably expand the concept of meaning to include all of its varieties, so long as we are clear about what they are and their interrelationships.

From one point of view, the central core of meaning is its conceptual referential dimension. Emotive and active meanings normally presuppose this. For example, if someone were to yell "Stop!" this utterance would lead to no appropriate response if the communicatee did not understand the conceptual meaning of the term "stop." Likewise, emotive meaning when it advances beyond the level of mere indicators of feeling, such as facial grimaces or spontaneous exclamations, and becomes verbalized into expressions such as "That hurts!" involves conceptual understanding of the terms used. We see, then, that conceptual referential meaning is the primary kind wherever there is an intent to communicate by means of conventional symbols, such as language.* For this reason we shall confine ourselves hereafter to an analysis of this sort of meaning.

Let us first summarize the types and aspects of meaning which we have distinguished so far. These are:

(1) What one has in mind to do or say (*Intentional meaning*).

(2) What the symbols one uses stand for, refer to, or call to mind (*Conceptual referential meaning*).

(3) The feelings or emotions that are expressed or aroused by our utterances (*Emotive meaning*).

(4) The actions that are called for or indicated as being involved in our utterances (*Active meaning*).

One further point may help us to understand the nature of meaning. If we ask ourselves what it is not to have meaning, we discover that meaning depends heavily upon our conceptual, emotive, and active associations. For example, the cross as symbol of Christ has meaning because of its associations, not only with the crucifixion itself, but with all the further implications of that event. These associations are both numerous and important, especially for the Christian. For followers of other religions, the associations are no doubt fewer or less important. The cross to them would have less meaning or a different meaning because of fewer or different as-

---

* For further elaboration of this point, see my *Meaning in Language,* pp. 16-25.

sociations. Moving in the direction of fewer associations, then, that thing would have least meaning which has no associations. Something unidentifiable which arouses no concepts, feelings, or actions would be a mere meaningless "it."

What are the major varieties of referential meaning?

We will distinguish the varieties of referential meaning with the aid of a familiar word—*term*. "Term" is often used as a synonym for "word" or "symbol," especially a linguistic symbol. And "term" is also used in Aristotelian logic for the unit or element related to some other element in a logical relation (e.g., subject term and predicate term in a proposition), however many words may be included in each term. In the present discussion, since we are dealing with the semantic relations between symbol, concept, and referent, it will be convenient to regard as a term either the symbol or the concept or *both taken together*. We may show this in a diagram in which the C (for concept) and the S (for symbol), taken from the diagram in Fig. 2 of Chapter I, now combine to become "term"; and the R (for referent) now becomes the range or *extension* of the referents, marked by *x*'s in our new diagram (Fig. 1).

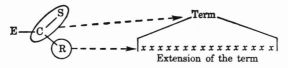

Fɪɢ. 1

Extensional and Intensional Meaning. The term "extension" is sometimes taken as a synonym for "denotation," and the contrasting term "intension" as a synonym for "connotation." However, usages of these words vary widely, so it will be necessary for us to select that meaning which is most useful for our present purposes. One usage takes the extension, or denotation, of a term to be the sum total of all particular cases or instances of objects, events, aspects, or situations to which the term normally refers (i.e., all customary referents). Thus the denotation of the term "cat" would be all animals customarily called cats. But another usage confines "denotation" to the present and observable examples (i.e., only the cats I am now seeing or can see). And still another refers to the simple primary or literal meaning of a term. "Extension" usually refers to all instances, actual or imaginary, to which a term refers (though sometimes extension is limited to the actual cases, excluding the imaginary ones, and at other times it is limited to subclasses instead of the particular individuals). But having noted these variations of usage, let us simplify the matter by considering "extension" and "denotation" to be synonymous, and by allowing them to stand for the whole set of particular individual referents, actual and imaginary, to which a term customarily refers. This set of particular referents can then be called the *extensional meaning* of a term.

We may think of a term on the analogy of a tent (see Fig. 1 above) which covers or *extends over* all the particulars to which the term normally refers. Conceiving the above diagram in this way helps us to see why the referents are called "the extension" of the term. It also indicates another important fact about extensions, namely, that they have limits (the sides of the tent); so we must think of the extension not only as including all a term's referents but also as indicating the limits beyond which the term no longer has reference. For example, the term "cat" extends over, or refers to, a very large number of particular animals which fall into many subclasses (Siamese, Persian, Burmese, Angora, alley). But there are limits to the extension of the term "cat." Quite apart from metaphorical extensions of meaning, which we shall examine later, we should be ill-advised indeed to include other animals, such as dogs, horses, cows, and camels, in the cat tent. A term, to be useful, must have more or less definable limits within which its referents are contained or "comprehended." For this reason the extension is sometimes called the "comprehension" of the term.

We have been speaking of extensions as including a multiplicity of particular individuals. But does every term refer to a plurality? Clearly not. Proper names and names of unique objects, like "universe," refer to single individuals only. Even group terms in certain circumstances, as when qualified by *this, that, the,* may designate single individuals (e.g., this man). Nevertheless, most names do refer to groups; so that the tent diagram, with a multiplicity of x's, will serve as the most usual case. Even if the term in question, like a proper name, does refer only to one individual, we can still regard it as a tent which covers only this one lone case. In fact, we may go further and imagine that there are no real perceivable *x*'s at all. The tent may be empty of perceivable referents and contain only imaginary ones. Thus, the terms "unicorn" and "centaur" would cover only imaginary referents.*

Turning now to "intension" or "connotation," we again find several traditional usages. The basic idea of intension† is that of the whole set of abstractable characteristics which the referents of a term must possess in order to be designated by that term. "Connotation" often means much the same thing, except that it may also include merely suggested or casually associated traits which are not part of the intension of the term; and sometimes its use is limited to these casual associations. For example, a slice of bread may connote butter; but butter is not part of the intension of the term "bread."

When we stop to think about it, we become aware of the fact that classes of objects (e.g., cats) or events (e.g., horse races) can be grouped together only by virtue of *similarities* which they all share. It is these similarities that the word "intension" indicates. For example, if an animal is properly called a kangaroo, it must have certain recognizable characteristics (jumps on its hind feet, carries its young in a pouch, etc.) which are traits of kangaroos, and which when taken together serve to distinguish this animal

* Occasionally writers on this subject wish us to distinguish terms with imaginary referents from those with a perceivable kind, by using different words for them. C. I. Lewis, for example, uses the word "comprehension" for all referents, both perceivable and nonperceivable, while reserving the words "extension" and "denotation" for the actual or existent things to which a term can be properly applied (see *An Analysis of Knowledge and Valuation*, Ch. 3). If we wish to make these distinctions, we could use "extension" for all referents, actual and possible, perceivable and imaginary; then "denotation" could refer to the perceivable referents only; and "designation," as it is often used, could refer to a given particular referent.

† We must be careful not to confuse "intension" with an *s* and "intention" with a *t*. Furthermore, the word "inten*t*ion" has two traditionally distinct meanings, for it not only refers to the intended purpose to do something (as we used it above), but can also be used to indicate that our terms imply or "intend" real objects or events as their referents. Thus, "intentional logic" refers to a logic in which the entities mentioned in propositions are assumed to have existence. All the meanings of "intention" and "intension" are derived from the Latin verb *intendere*, to stretch toward. "Inten*t*ion," in the first sense, refers to the stretching of a person toward what he wishes to do; and in the second sense, it refers to the stretching of the mind toward a real object of thought. "Inten*s*ion" refers to a stretching or straining toward the essential nature of a class.

from all other animals. It often requires two or more intensional aspects taken together to distinguish a class. For example, having two legs does not distinguish human beings from other animals, like birds, gorillas, kangaroos, etc., but having two legs *and* a double-curved spine would be distinctive of humans.

It may appear that the term "intensional" is but another way of saying "essential." This would be so if by "essential" we mean any aspect which is a necessary condition for membership in a given class. However, the notion of "essential" often adds the suggestion of a more basic reality, as if certain intensional traits were more fundamental to the nature of the type of thing included in a class than were other intensional traits. This meaning of essential is in part a result of the history of the term. To the meaning of essence we shall return in a later chapter. In the meantime we can indicate the intensional meaning of a term in our tent diagram by a set of lines from the particular *x*'s converging upon an area where we can imagine all common traits to be collected (Fig. 2).

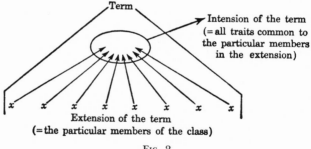

FIG. 2

If we wish, we may imagine that each tent has a gatekeeper, whose job it is to admit only the proper *x*'s into his tent. Each *x* presents its credentials to the gatekeeper, who then admits or rejects the *x*. The proper credentials would have to contain a list of the correct traits; that is, they would have to list the correct intension for whatever term it happened to be.

How does our imaginary gatekeeper arrive at a knowledge of the proper credentials? He could do this by examining the *x*'s already in the tent to see what traits they have in common. But what if there are no *x*'s in the tent? If the term is an arbitrarily invented symbol which has not yet become conventional, then the gatekeeper can establish his own choice of credentials. But if the term is already conventional, being new only to the gatekeeper, then he must learn its extensional meaning from people already familiar with it. Of course, we are the gatekeepers; and as children we began to attach names to classes of objects and events when we heard them named by our elders.

Once a thing is assigned a name, the child, as we saw in Chapter II, begins to extend this name to other similar things, often at first carrying the extension too far. Later he learns better where the limits of the extension normally lie, and which x's are admissible and which are not. Now, suppose a newly arrived x has most of the correct characteristics, but just one or two are lacking or are somewhat different. What is the gatekeeper to do? He may say "No!" quite emphatically and exclude this new arrival; or he may stretch a point and let it in anyway, thus widening the range of the tent's extension. The latter course is not at all unusual, and as a result, we find that the extensions of terms are often being stretched out. In fact, to carry our tent analogy a bit further, term-tents have quite elastic sides, which the gatekeeper may find it convenient not only to stretch out, but on occasion to pull in. So we must think of our tents as having flexible boundaries or *variable extensions.*

The intension is the set of common traits possessed by all the members of the extension. From each member (i.e., each x) we can abstract the traits which it has in common with the other members, and ignore for the moment the other traits. Thus, all cats have whiskers, and having whiskers is one of the traits which we can abstract from the other traits of a given cat as forming part of the intension of the term "cat." Having tails would not be part of the intension, since some cats (e.g., Manx cats) do not have tails; so this is a trait which we should have to ignore when looking for the intension of "cat." We see, then, that the traits in the intension are all of them abstractable from the more concrete objects (or events) which constitute the extension of the class in question. For a more detailed examination of the meaning of "abstract" and "concrete" we shall have to wait until we come to Chapter V.

We noted above that the extension may include only one individual, as when the term is a proper name. When this is the case, what is the intension? Obviously it cannot be the traits shared by a group of individuals if there is only one individual. What, for example, is the intension of Jack Jones? It has to be *all* the traits possessed by Jack Jones—his appearance, his modes of behavior, and so on. We can see, then, that there would be many more traits in the intension of the term "Jack Jones" than there would be in that of the term "man" or "boy," for the intensions of these terms would include only the traits possessed in common by all the Jack Joneses. So the fewer the variety and number of individual *x*'s which are grouped together in a class, the greater is the number of common traits and vice versa. Or as it is more often put, *the extension and the intension vary inversely.*

The inverse variation of extension and intension needs some further qualification. Adding more members to a class would not reduce the intensional similarities so long as these new members are in all major respects the same as those already included in the original extension. Thus, to add more folding chairs to others of the same type already in a room would not change the intension of the class of "folding chairs in the room." On the other hand, adding one different chair would reduce the intensional similarities, since the number of similar traits for the whole group would now be fewer. Therefore, the rule of inverse variation depends upon the degree of difference between members, rather than simply upon the total number of members in a class.

Specific and General Meaning. On the basis of the foregoing observations, we can easily distinguish what is meant by the more "general" and the more "specific" meanings of terms. Any term which covers a group of individuals is general when it refers to *all* the individuals that could be included within its tent. If it refers only to *some* of these individuals, but not to all of them, it is being used specifically. The *general meaning,* then, we can take to be one which refers equally well to a whole class. The *specific meaning,* in contrast, will be a reference to only a part of that class. Thus, the term "cat" in its general meaning refers equally well to *all* existing or possible cats. But a specific meaning of "cat" may limit the extension to some specific subgroup of cats, as "specifically" the cats now in the animal shelter.

The context in a discourse often indicates that a term is being used in a specific rather than a general way. A newspaper story may mention "the cats," and the reader understands that only the cats in a certain neighborhood are meant. The context of the story has implied this. But terms used by themselves, out of context, are as general as they can be in the sense that any individual that could be referred to by that term (anything that can be called a "cat") is a possible referent.

For many terms, when taken in their most general extensions, it is difficult to isolate the intensional properties—the similarities —that allow them to be grouped together. This is especially true where usage has enlarged the extension to include new referents that differ greatly from those in the original core meaning of a term. For example, the term *cap* has as its core meaning a soft article of clothing worn on the head. But this term can be extended to include tube or bottle tops, and even rock crusts on the earth's surface. In stretching the term to this extent, not only are some of the original intensional similarities lost (such as the association with the head) but others may be picked up (such as hardness of tube or bottle tops and rock crusts) which were not characteristic of the original set of referents. For this reason it has become popular in recent years to point out, following Wittgenstein, that many sets of individuals, even though named by a single term, have a "complicated network of similarities overlapping and criss-crossing," something like "family resemblances" where one trait links some individuals and another trait links others, rather than have a single dominant trait that clearly characterizes the whole set.* For ordinary usage, where context helps, such grouping of referents by family resemblances may be sufficient. But for precision in the usage of terms the gatekeeper who uses the term should pay careful attention to the similarities of his various candidates for admission.

Literal and Metaphorical Meaning. Precision in the use of terms is only one kind of goal. On the other side, it serves a useful purpose to stretch or even transfer the reference of a term to unusual situations, since in so doing, one achieves associations that not only tickle our fancy, but also help our understanding of the situation being described (as in calling a rock "cap"). When such transferrals

* See L. Wittgenstein, *Philosophical Investigations*, p. 31 and following. The quoted phrase, Anscombe translation, is found on page 32e.

of meaning are fresh and vigorous they are called *metaphorical* uses, in contrast to *literal* uses, which confine the application of a term to its normal or core extension. The tent analogy which we are using will help us to understand the difference between a term used literally and a term used metaphorically. A metaphor is simply a term or phrase used in an unusually extended sense. It refers to cases of referential meaning that fall well outside the normal limits of the term's customary tent. We may diagram this situation as in Fig. 3. The word "metaphor" means "carried beyond," in-

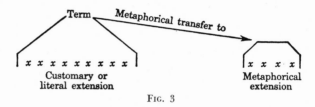

FIG. 3

dicating that the metaphorical or nonliteral reference of the term has been carried out beyond the limits of normal usage. "Literal" means "according to the letter," which is another way of saying "according to customary usage."

Now, let us examine two typical metaphors:

- The ship plows the sea.
- His marble brow.

In each case which is the word being used in a metaphorical meaning? In the first case the primary context appears to be that of ship in the sea. Thus the word which is nonliteral or out of usual context is "plows." In an abbreviated way, our attention is thus called to an analogy or similarity between the two situations: (1) a ship sailing through the sea, and (2) a plow making furrows in the ground. The characteristic of "moving laboriously through something" is all of the intension of "plow" which is needed here; and since the intension is so reduced, the extension of "plow" can be metaphorically transferred (Fig. 4).

Continuing our analysis of the nature of metaphor, note that the term used metaphorically (out of its normal context) highlights the primary context of the rest of the phrase or sentence. Thus, "plowing" highlights the motion of the ship, and not vice

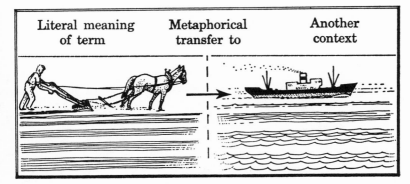

| Literal meaning of term | Metaphorical transfer to | Another context |

FIG. 4

versa. The literal referent of the metaphorical term in this way sheds the light of analogy upon the primary context to which it is transferred. This analogy is brought out indirectly, since it is only suggested by the associating of the two different situations or contexts. We can diagram the full situation, including both the normal or literal context of the term used metaphorically, and the primary context, or literal context of the nonmetaphorical terms, as in Fig. 5.

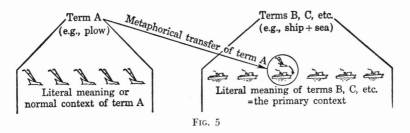

FIG. 5

It may help to clarify this situation if we experiment with a reversal of the two contexts. Suppose the literal context of Term A were made our primary context, and some key term in the present primary context were used metaphorically. We should then have a reversed metaphor (e.g., "The plow *sails* through the earth" instead of "The ship *plows* through the sea"; or "Browy marble" instead of "Marble brow"). The primary context now belongs to the normal meaning of Term A (e.g., plowing), and the term used metaphorically is taken from the other context of Terms B, C, etc. (e.g., sailing). In reversing metaphors, we often must change the part of speech of the key terms (e.g., Marble [adj.] + brow [noun] → Browy [adj.] + marble [noun]).

The principal force of a metaphor lies in its being more condensed than a simile (i.e., "The ship sails through the sea, as if it were a plow making furrows") and in being more vivid than a literal statement (i.e., "The ship pushes its prow through the sea, turning water back on either side"). Thus, a metaphor gives picturesqueness and economy to our descriptions.

In addition to the primary similarity stressed by the metaphor, there may be other more subtle suggestions of similarities. The idea of a plow furrowing a field contains an image of a certain way in which dirt is turned up or of a certain effort required to force the plow through the ground, etc. Some of these images may be carried over to the situation of the ship in the sea. Marble is not only white and cold but is solid and unmovable so far as its surface is concerned. These qualities are transferred in the metaphor to the brow.

But a metaphor must be taken sympathetically and seriously to have its proper cogency. It is easy to turn a metaphor into a ludicrous form of imagery if more than the intended similarities are carried over from the metaphorical image to the primary context. Cartoonists often make sport out of metaphors which are taken with too many suggested traits in the metaphorical image (Fig. 6).

Fig. 6. *Plowing back and forth hardly applies to boats.*

Our study of metaphor suggests the importance of context in determining meaning. How, for example, are we to know whether to take a term literally or metaphorically? The context will help. Thus, if someone says to us "See that man, he looks as if he had come right out of Dickens!" we should know better than to assume that "Dickens" is the name of a place or building out of which the man had just come. We should know this because we are fairly accustomed to the use of an author's name, not literally but as referring to his work; and we are also used to the meaning of "come out of" in this context, not as meaning that a person walks out of the books of an author but as meaning that he reminds us of the characters portrayed in those books.

With or without contextual help, is there a limit to the extending of metaphorical meaning? To find out, try the following experiment. Take any two normally unrelated terms of our language, make one an adjective and the other a noun, and then see if together they can make sense. For example, "grease" and "cloud" could be tested as "greasy cloud" or "cloudy grease." It is not difficult to find meaning here. But what of "wherefore" and "spirit" or "cow" and "of"? Can it mean anything to say "whereforey spirit" or "spiritual wherefore"? Or, "cowy of" or "ofy cow"? Certainly, to make any sense out of these expressions would require imagination.

How do referential meanings change?

It is a well-known fact of language that referential meanings are continually changing. Since the meaning of a term is simply what custom or convention dictates, this custom, like any other, may change. The tracing of the forms and meanings of a word back through its historical changes to its earliest known roots is known as etymology. The etymological careers of some words are quite varied and colorful. For example, the word "humor" is derived from the Latin word *humor* or *umor* meaning moisture or fluid. Its meanings have changed as follows:

(1) From moisture or fluid in general to the more specific fluids of the body—bile, phlegm, blood, and the like—which were once supposed to influence human temperaments.

(2) To these temperaments themselves.

(3) To that particular temperament which is capable of creating and appreciating the ludicrous.

(4) To the quality of any event which makes it seem ludicrous (e.g., "Did you find any humor in that situation?").

Note that Step 1 is a narrowing of the original extensional meaning; Step 2 is a transference to a related idea (namely, the temperaments believed associated with bodily fluids); Step 3 is another narrowing; and Step 4 is another transference. "Humor" may be used today in any of its four derived meanings but the first two sound decidedly archaic (e.g., "His bodily humors are out of balance").

When we examine many cases of shift in meaning, we find that there are just three possibilities: (1) the meaning (i.e., the extensional meaning) may *broaden;* (2) the meaning may *narrow;* or (3) the meaning may *be transferred.* These three types of change are illustrated diagrammatically in Fig. 7. It will be

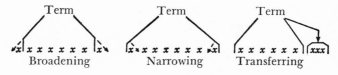

Broadening   Narrowing   Transferring

FIG. 7

helpful to refer to the first case as a "broadening" or "widening" of the meaning, not as an "extension" of meaning. "Extension" as we are using it refers to a given range of reference, and not to any change in regard to this range. So a given extension may be widened or narrowed or even transferred, but the term "extension" itself does not refer to any of these activities.

Can we assume that all transferred meanings are examples of metaphor? In the case of "humor," the two transferences (first from fluids to temperaments, and second from a sense of the comic to something which might cause a comic response) are both based on natural connections. But we can be more precise about these connections, if we like, by observing that they are connections by contiguity rather than similarity; and, according to the traditional terminology for figures of speech, we should reserve the term "metaphor" for connections by similarity, using "metonymy" for cause-effect, container-contained, or attributive relations; and "synecdoche" for part-whole, species-genus, or material-object relations. However, the terms "metonymy" and "synecdoche" are not often used any more, and the term "metaphor" is being broadened to take over all types of relation upon which transferences of meaning are based. So, broadly speaking, we can say that all transferences are, at least in their beginning stages before they become highly conventionalized, examples of metaphors.

What happens to a metaphor when it becomes conventional? First it becomes trite, and then it ceases to be a metaphor at all. For example, one Italian word for head (*testa*) and the French word (*tête*) come from a Latin word meaning earthen pot. This use was once clearly metaphorical, based on the similarity between a pot as a container and a head also as a kind of container. But in Italian and French this word has become the standard, literal word for head and the metaphorical character has been lost. It is interesting to observe how persistent this particular metaphor is, as illustrated by a modern Frenchwoman who would often refer to her head as a *vieille cafetière* ("old coffee pot"), thus reviving the lost metaphor, and by the German word for head (*Kopf*) which is a cognate of our English word "cup."

Sometimes metaphors which become trite, instead of being naturalized in their new domain, are simply dropped. In such cases the literal meaning of the term usually returns to its former habitat. But the human love of metaphor, with the sharp and pungent effect it produces, will certainly persist as a valuable asset to expression.

Vagueness and Ambiguity. Before leaving this topic, it will be useful to note one further distinction, that between *vagueness* and *ambiguity*. An *ambiguous term* is one which has *two or more rather distinct areas of reference*. These probably arose through metaphorical transfer in the first place; but mostly a term is considered ambiguous when the areas of meaning have become about coequal in frequency. For example, the term "law" is now ambiguous since it can refer either to the laws of physical nature or to the legal apparatus which man fashions for himself. Similarly, there must have been a time when the Italian and French word for head referred about equally to an earthen pot and a human or animal head. At such a period in its history this word would have been quite ambiguous.

A vague term, on the other hand, is one that has a large degree of *extensional variability.* Most terms have some amount of variability in their extensions due simply to the varying uses to which they are put, and which produce broadenings and narrowings of meaning. But certain terms have more than the customary amount of such variability and these are the terms which are vaguest. Thus, while ambiguity is a function of transference of meaning, vagueness is a function of broadening and narrowing. A diagram will help us to see this difference (Fig. 8).

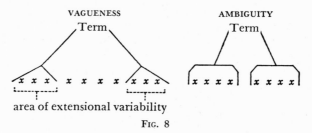

Fig. 8

How do languages classify experiences?

Different languages classify experiences in different ways. For example, in English the term "chair" refers both to armchairs and to armless chairs. In French, however, an armless chair is *chaise,* but an armchair is *fauteuil,* an unrelated word. The Eskimo have one word for snow on the ground (*aput*), another for falling snow (*qana*), and yet another for a snowdrift (*piqsirpoq*).*

Nature, we see again, is much more complex than any linguistic arrangement of it, so that every language, in its system of classifications, must limit or simplify natural complexities. At certain times and for certain purposes we may find one set of classifications more useful, while for other purposes a different set would be better. So

---

* See F. Boas, "Handbook of American Indian Languages," *Bulletin of the Bureau of American Ethnology,* No. 40, Pt. I, pp. 25-26.

we should never regard a classification as anything more than a convenient and approximate device for sorting experiences; and we must always be a little suspicious of the simple traditional classifications which languages make for us. Some of these schemes become quite absurd when extended too far, as for example, the distinction of masculine, feminine, and neuter in a language such as German.* Linguistic classifications, of course, may be based on reliable and accurate observations of natural similarities and differences, but often they seem to exaggerate distinctions which to later generations seem unimportant. Nevertheless, owing to the persistence of linguistic habits, these old distinctions continue in force. Improved techniques of observation and improved analyses of natural phenomena are constantly making the traditional arrangements and classifications of grammar somewhat obsolete. On the other hand, we should not discredit all of the old distinctions, for our ancestors had keener powers of observation about some things than we have.

These remarks on the variation in classifications among languages bring us to another matter that often perplexes us. This is the question of *translatability* from one language into another. Since one language carves experience in a somewhat different way from another language, many of the terms used in the one will not coincide precisely in their extensions to the nearest corresponding terms in the other. For the central focus of meaning (the core extension of a term), there will be, in all probability, an area of meaning which coincides closely between the two languages. Thus "boy" is a term which can readily find near equivalents in most languages. The difficulty arises toward the edges of the tent, since in some languages the concept "boy" would be stretched to include more cases than in other languages. For example, the term "boy" in one language may apply only to individuals under the age of puberty, whereas in another, the nearest corresponding term would include much older individuals. Each term also has connotational overtones dependent upon the culture in which it occurs, and these associations are quite changeable. Lastly, metaphorical extensions

---

* For a highly amusing satire on the uses of gender in German, read Mark Twain's essay entitled "The Awful German Language" which appears as Appendix D in *A Tramp Abroad*. Within this essay, it is "The Tale of the Fishwife and Its Sad Fate" which particularly pokes fun at the genders.

in one case may be more or less traditionalized along certain lines, while in another case these extensions do not occur. For all these reasons, translations are difficult, especially for the finer shadings of meaning such as are found in associational overtones or in metaphorical extensions. Despite all these difficulties, translations are constantly being made, and some are surprisingly close. But we should never forget that even the best translations are forced to leave out something of the original meaning and to introduce something else that was not intended.

How does the notion of extensional variability affect the analysis of class relations?

The class-inclusion sentence, which Aristotelian logic selected as its model type, has the primary form "All something (*x*'s) are included in something else (*y*'s)" (e.g., "All cats are animals," which is to say "The entire class of cats is included in the class of animals"). Other alternatives of this basic form were noted by Aristotle—first, when one takes a part of a class instead of an entire class (e.g., "Some cats" instead of "all cats"), and second, when one denies the relation instead of affirming it (e.g., "Cats are not dogs" instead of "Cats are animals"). This gave him four basic versions of the key sentence type:

(1) All *x*'s are included in *y*'s.

(2) No *x*'s are included in *y*'s.

(3) Some *x*'s are included in *y*'s.

(4) Some *x*'s are not included in *y*'s.

These relations are often diagrammed by circles (Fig. 9). Classical

Fig. 9

logic assigned the first four vowels of the alphabet to these four types: A to 1, E to 2, I to 3, and O to 4. If we imagine that our tents are circular tents, the circles would be the tents, or extensions of the terms, looked at from above, as in an aerial view. Of course, terms, unlike actual tents, can overlap each other.

But now, please notice that we have no indication here of the areas of variability around these extensions. If we add this factor by showing all circles as having two possible limits, a narrow and a wide one, we see at once that the relationships become much less certain. In fact, they can only be used successfully if we give some precise limits—narrow, medium, or broad—to our terms before we inquire into their relations to each other. Otherwise, we can readily see, what for one person would constitute a pair of mutually separate or exclusive terms would for another be overlapping terms. In classifying animals we usually have little difficulty—it would seem quite safe to say that cows are completely excluded from horses, or sheep from goats. But in the realm of human artifacts, the troubles mount. Are chairs completely exclusive of couches or is there an overlap here? Is an apartment building a house, or is it not? Is an apartment house a new and different term from either apartment or house? When these facts are taken into consideration, it means that class relationships in logic must cope with classes having variable extensions.

The danger lies in our assuming idealized precise classes where, in actual experience, they do not exist. For ease of analysis our logical relations have been simplified and the extensional variations eliminated. This situation poses no more of a problem to the logician than does the use of imaginary perfect points and lines to the geometer, or the use of a regularized and perfected integer system to the arithmetician, for, like mathematical concepts, logical concepts are idealizations which do not find precise application in experience. Experience contains only more or less rough approximations of our mathematical and logical refinements. For example, it is foolish to carry out some ratio to a fifth or sixth decimal when the data upon which this ratio rests can be no more accurate than would warrant a decimal of one, two, or possibly three digits. The mathematician can find the precise ratios or at least carry out his decimals for many, many digits in the case of irrational numbers, but such precision is of no great value when applied to experienceable situations where the lack of accuracy in measurement or enumeration is such that the decimals are meaningless. As an illustration, some universities and colleges assign different integers to letter grades, and then average grades out to five decimals. Yet the rough nature of the original letter grades makes such a refinement relatively meaningless. As with numbers, so with class logic, theoretical knowledge of perfect relations is very helpful, but *applications must always be made with a fair sense of the classificational accuracy appropriate to the experienceable content.* When we come to discuss the problem of definition, in Chapter XI, we shall again have occasion to take stock of this whole matter.

There is nothing fixed or universal about classifications. Different observers of the world see different bases for making their classifications; and these differences become somewhat stabilized in the various languages. Clearly, there is not going to be some one right classification, in contrast to which all others are wrong. But one may well wonder if some classifications are not superior to others, in that they separate objects or events by more important or more persistent traits which reflect the more basic natural distinctions. Aristotle, for example, regarded "rational" (i.e., capable of receiving and organizing knowledge) as a more important trait of human nature than "walking on two feet."* People may lose their feet or be born without them, but no human being, he thought, lacks the capacity to learn. We may not today regard the capacity to receive and organize knowledge as quite so distinctive of the human animal as Aristotle thought. Most animals learn up to a point, and not all human beings do a very good job of it. But we should certainly agree that receiving and organizing knowledge is a more important trait of human nature than walking on two feet, a trait which we share with the roadrunner and other birds, and which therefore needs the further qualification "featherless" to be limited to man. So, while classifications may not be uniquely based on "the one right trait," they can nevertheless be judged better or worse on the basis of the persistence of the trait selected, and how well it reveals the general character of that which it characterizes.

In conclusion, let us review the primary points we have discovered regarding conceptual referential meaning. Under this head, we have distinguished extensional and intensional meaning,

* *Topics,* Bk. V, Chs. 4-5.

specific and general meaning, literal and metaphorical meaning, and vague and ambiguous meanings. We have seen that referential meanings change by broadening, narrowing, or transferring their extensions; that extensions and intensions vary inversely; and that different languages classify experience in different ways. Finally, we have observed that classificational relationships can give us a very useful structural system for making logical inferences, but that the application of this structural system to the world of experience is only approximate, principally because of the variability of extensions.

SUGGESTED READINGS

Alexander, H. G., *Meaning in Language,* especially Ch. 1.
Alston, W. P., *Philosophy of Language,* especially Ch. 5.
Black, Max, *Language and Philosophy,* especially Ch. 2.
Cohen, M. R., *A Preface to Logic,* especially Ch. 3.
Lewis, C. I., *An Analysis of Knowlege and Valuation,* especially Chs. 3-4.
Wheelwright, Philip, *The Burning Fountain,* especially Ch. 6.
Wheelwright, Philip, *Metaphor and Reality,* especially Chs. 3-5.

PART TWO
Processes of Thinking

LET US TURN now to the more basic questions of what may be called the processes of thinking. The simplest and most elementary of these processes are here discussed under the headings of ABSTRACTING, IMAGINING, and GENERALIZING. Of the three processes, imagining —the altering of abstractions—is the crucial one for understanding the special nature of thought and its possible relations to reality. Abstracting, however, must be considered first, since it is the source of abstractions to alter; and generalizing is important because it sets ranges and limitations to terms.

Among our basic abstractions, three—qualities, relations, functions—are of sufficient importance to deserve special attention. Consequently, a chapter is devoted to each.

CHAPTER V

Abstracting

What is abstracting?

THE NOTION OF abstracting, unfortunately, covers a multitude of meanings. Some of these meanings can lead us into serious confusions concerning the nature of the abstractive process if we are not careful. "The abstract," for example, is sometimes thought to be that which is purely mental or even purely imaginary, as contrasted with "the concrete," which is then aligned with the perceivable or "physical" reality. But the basic meaning of the verb "to abstract" is to draw away mentally, and this suggests that there is something there to be drawn away and something from which to draw it away. The abstract, then, is not something that floats mysteriously into our thoughts we know not from whence. Rather it is something tied to experience.

We shall make better sense of the whole notion of abstracting if we follow the meaning of the term as used by A. N. Whitehead (1861-1947), which is well expressed as follows: "Each mode of abstracting is directing attention to something which is in nature; and thereby is isolating it for the purpose of contemplation."* In this sense, abstracting is not really removing anything at all. It is simply focusing our attention on some part or aspect of what we experience while neglecting to pay attention to other parts or aspects.

* See Whitehead's *Science and the Modern World*, p. 173.

To illustrate this notion of abstracting, let us try an experiment. First look at a table. Now center your attention upon some particular part or aspect of the table. Perhaps you are looking at one of the legs, or just the color, or the shape, or some decoration on the table. In any case, you are now abstracting a particular part or aspect of the table. But the table itself does not change or disappear. The part or aspect you are abstracting (focusing on) is still right there where it was—a part or aspect of the visible table.

But, you may say, the word "abstract" is derived from the Latin verb *abstrahere,* meaning "to draw away," and this implies the drawing away to a conceptual plane quite remote from the concrete level of experience. We need to go slowly here, for when we look at abstracting in this rather traditional way, it easily appears baffling and mysterious. Yet, what actually takes place is nothing mysterious, but something quite normal for all of us. It is a process of (1) *focusing attention upon some feature within experience;* (2) *holding this feature as the object of our immediate thought,* and (3) *possibly remembering it later.* Thus, the "drawing away" is already involved in the focusing. If I focus my attention upon the knob of a door, for example, I have in a sense drawn that knob away from the rest of the door—not physically, of course, as if I had actually removed the knob from the door, but only as an object of my attention when I consider it apart from its surroundings. When I do this, the knob becomes for me an abstraction. Thus, an abstraction is not some strange idea floating around in a realm of pure thought, but only the object of my limited attention.

There is a distinction to be made between *simple abstracting* and *imaginative altering of abstractions.* What we have described so far is only simple abstracting. But the human mind is also capable of imagining what objects or aspects might be like if they were different from the way they appear. We shall hold to the view that this process of transforming objects and imagining them in different ways is also a perfectly natural mental process, which is not just simple abstracting, but involves more mental activity than simple abstracting. It is quite possible that once we understand these two processes better we shall discover how most, if not all, of our ideas are formed by means of them. For the present, however, we must confine ourselves to the process of simple abstracting, and leave imagination to a later chapter.

Simple abstracting is not so simple that it stops when one has made a single abstraction. The process may continue. Suppose, for example, one starts with a desk. One might abstract (i.e., pay attention only to) one of the drawers, and then to the knob on the drawer, thus abstracting a part of a part. Or one could abstract first an aspect, such as the rectangular shape of the desk top, and then abstract an aspect of this aspect, such as the rectangular corner of the rectangle. Or abstracting first the color, one might then abstract its brightness. Thus, as long as one can find another part within a part or another aspect within an aspect, one can continue to abstract from abstractions. But as one continues in this way, less and less remains upon which to focus attention and more and more will fall into the leftover or residue area. Thus, we might abstract the square shape from a square tabletop, and then an angle from the square, and then the point at the corner of the angle; but what next? Here we seem to have reached the end of our abstractables. Of course, we could have abstracted any point from the lines in the angle, but once we have limited our attention to the one point at the corner, we have reached the limit of possibilities so far as abstractions from abstractions are concerned.

Now what of the leftover or *residue* area? Is it also an abstraction? Certainly the parts and aspects left behind when we made any of our abstractions could also have been abstracted in their turn. For example, if we abstract the color of the ceiling, then all the other parts or aspects of the ceiling are at this moment being eliminated from our attention. They are the residue of our abstraction. But we could just as well have selected any or all of them upon which to focus our attention, had we so desired. They are at least *potential abstractions,* capable of having become or of becoming abstractions.

These considerations point up one fact: when we abstract we are normally conscious of focusing attention upon the abstracted feature. At least we are conscious of this feature. But of the neglected or residue areas we are not particularly aware. Indeed, this factor of *awareness* constitutes the major difference between the abstraction and its residue. Yet just how much awareness is required? If one allows that there is abstracting when one is unaware of the fact that he is abstracting, is this really abstracting in the sense of a focusing attention upon? If so, then abstracting would be automatic, and it would turn out that all observing, insofar as it must limit the range of possible observation, is abstractive. So it is preferable to limit the meaning of abstracting to those cases in which we are definitely aware of the fact that we are making a selection from the total given range of experience; and then we shall need to admit that in every act of abstracting there is at least some slight awareness of the fact that there are residue or leftover abstractables. For example, if we are not only aware of the person we happen to be looking at or talking to in a group, but also of the fact that there are other persons upon whom we might have been focusing our attention, then we are aware both of the abstracted item (the person we are looking at) and also of the residue abstractables (the other persons). But we should not tell those other persons that they are "residue abstractables," for if we did, they would no longer be such.

We must, then, be slightly aware of the residue abstractables, but are we also aware of the act of abstracting itself? There is no reason why we could not be, for we can certainly be aware of our act of selecting one individual or feature as the object of our attention rather than another. The chances are, however, that this awareness of the act of selecting is even farther removed from our primary area of attention than are the residue factors, except in retrospect.

We have noticed three possible levels of awareness that are involved. First, there is the obvious awareness of the item being abstracted. Second, there is the less obvious awareness of the residue items. Third, there is the still less likely awareness of the fact that one is abstracting. For example, suppose you are about to spear a particular piece of meat on your plate. Having made your choice, you quickly lose sight of the other pieces. And in the process of eating one piece of meat, it is very unlikely that you stop to contemplate the fact that you were involved in a process of selecting (or abstracting). But normally we would have some secondary awareness, even if slight, of the residue factors and of the process itself. Indeed, without these awarenesses it would hardly be proper to consider the process as that of abstracting at all, for then we should be taking the entire given range of our awareness, even if quite limited, as the whole show, the whole concrete reality. Thus, if we become so wrapped up in one piece of meat that we are totally oblivious of all others and of our act of selecting it, then that piece of meat is at that moment our whole concrete reality. Unlikely as this may be, it illustrates the need for some awareness or consciousness of the act of selecting if abstracting is to be considered a process of thought.

What is the concrete?

The term "abstract" is often contrasted with the term "concrete." Let us see why this is. As already noted, when we abstract, we abstract from a given whole by focusing attention upon a part or aspect of that whole. The term "concrete," on the other hand, refers to the whole.* The concrete, then, is simply that from which nothing has been abstracted. Normally the objects of ordinary experience—tables, houses, trees, people—are thought of as concrete because we are not strongly aware of having abstracted them from anything more inclusive. It is with them that we customarily begin in making our abstractions. Nevertheless, when we stop to consider the matter, we realize that ordinary objects may be considered as parts of larger units. Thus, the table in a room is part of a larger context which involves all the furniture, and in fact all other features of the room. So when we look at anything in terms of greater inclusiveness, we find that what we took for concrete is already abstract. Is this true of the room itself? Is it not an abstractable part of the building? And the building—can it not be abstracted from other buildings in the city? If we follow this line of thought, we arrive at the conclusion that the only truly concrete reality is the entire total universe—nothing less. But the entire universe is beyond anyone's power to experience or conceive in all its detail. So, from our human point of view, the "entire universe" is a projection of many abstractions, projections which are imaginative activities, synthesized into what should be the most concrete of concepts.

Now let us return to the ordinary level of experience, the experience of ordinary-sized objects and events. These we may call

---

* "Concrete" is derived from the past participle of the Latin verb *concrescere,* meaning to grow together, to become congealed or hardened. Thus, the term implies that we are dealing with something that could be considered as separable into smaller elements. We also see why this term, by transference, is currently applied to a certain kind of building material; for this building material is a conglomerate of sand, rocks, cement, and water all "grown together."

our ordinary or everyday concretes (or *concreta*). They are the hunks of experience upon which our attention characteristically rests, and from which we can consciously make abstractions. They include OBJECTS, by which we mean any relatively stable individual things, such as tables, trees, persons, lakes, mountains; and they include EVENTS, by which we mean activities with reasonably clear-cut limits such as dances, games, races, lifetimes, and the like. SITUATIONS are more complicated sets of objects or events. If we think of situations as wholes, then objects and events are abstractions from them; but it is more normal for us to start our observations at the object-event level. What this indicates is the fact that "abstract" and "concrete" must be considered relative to each other; and that something which is concrete from one point of view may be abstract from another.

In general, then, "concrete" means taken all together, whereas "abstract" means taken piecemeal. But the concrete is also that which fills up a given range of attention. For example, if one starts with only the rectangular shape of the tabletop, and this shape is the sum total of his awareness, then for him at that moment this rectangle is concrete. Of course, one does not normally limit his range of attention in so drastic a manner; so it is more usual to regard the entire table as *the concrete whole,* and then the tabletop as an abstraction from the table, and the shape as an abstraction from the tabletop.

We use "abstract" as a verb much more often than we do "concrete." The dictionary allows "concrete" in a verbal usage, so that we could speak of "concreting" as well as "abstracting," if we wished. However, it is certainly not customary to speak in this way. The reason for this undoubtedly lies in the fact that the concrete level is the level of the given unit of experience with which we begin our analytic processes. We might expect, then, that when we have abstracted out various features from a given situation, we would turn around and put them back together, which would be to "concrete" them. The fact that we do not use "concrete" in this way suggests that we think of abstracting as a one-way process. Yet both directions are possible and certain great philosophers, for example Hegel, might well be termed "concretionistic" thinkers because of their strong urge toward wholeness and completeness in their developing world view. Others, in contrast, because of their desire for simple clarity remain abstractionistic.

What are the basic kinds of abstraction?

In general, we may distinguish two basic types of abstraction: (1) *parts,* or abstractions of features which could also be physically removed; and (2) *aspects,* or abstractions of features which could not be removed physically, even if we wished.* Parts include such things as tabletops, legs, drawers, and the like, whereas aspects are such things as color, shape, hardness. If someone asked you for a particular table leg you could saw it off and hand it to him; but if someone asked you for the color off a particular table what would you give him? You could, of course, remove color or shape by destroying the table, cutting it into pieces, painting it, etc. Paint, paint remover, hatchets, fire will enable you to change or destroy aspects, but they will not enable you to detach the aspect and give it away. Even scraped-off paint is not just color; it is colored material, and to this extent a *part* of the table. But in the act of abstracting we are only concerned with a mental and nonphysical action, that of focusing attention. When we abstract parts or aspects we need neither hatchet nor saw. It is only as a preliminary aid in distinguishing parts from aspects that we need to consider whether we *could also* use the hatchet or saw effectively. This distinction of parts as physically removable as against aspects which are not physically removable will do for now. In a moment we shall refine our meaning of "parts," especially when we are confronted with parts of aspects.

When we turn to aspects, we find that we can distinguish three primary sorts: (1) qualities, (2) relations, and (3) functions or activities. The qualities are simply those aspects which we take as units; the relations are those which are seen as connections between units; and the functions are those which involve action or change. These three types of aspect are so important in our understanding of the world that we shall devote a full chapter to each of them, and deal with them in detail there. For now, let

* Some people would limit the meaning of "abstract" to what we are calling aspects. However, there is nothing fundamentally different in the processes of abstracting parts or aspects that warrants such a limitation of meaning.

us raise another interesting question which is suggested by our distinction of parts and aspects; namely, what it would mean to abstract aspects from parts, or parts from aspects.

When we think about this question, we soon discover that there is no difficulty in abstracting aspects from parts, for any part (e.g., a table leg) will have some aspect or aspects (e.g., shape) that could be abstracted. But when we turn to the other part of the question and ask about abstracting parts from aspects, we run into trouble. The trouble arises from the way in which we have defined "part" and "aspect," for if a part is an element which could be physically removed, and an aspect is a feature which could not, then we see at once that it would be difficult to have a part (i.e., a physically removable element) in an aspect (i.e., something which is not physically removable). For example, the rectangular shape of the table-top is a typical aspect. But is not one side of the rectangle a part of it? We certainly do not find it inappropriate to refer to it in this way. And yet if we hold to our initial designation of a part as some element that is physically removable, we should not properly call a side of a rectangle a "part."

We can escape from this difficulty if we relax somewhat our specification that a part must be physically removable. Some aspects, particularly shapes or aspects having inner relations, do have what might be called segments or parts. It is quite traditional to designate these as parts, though they could not actually be removed in the way that a leg could be removed from a table. Certainly, when we think of a side of a rectangle as a part of that figure, we tend to think of it as something that could readily be regarded apart from the rectangle; but when we think of it as an aspect of the rectangle, we are more inclined to think of it as still located in the rectangle, even though we are focusing our primary attention upon it. So it turns out that a more refined meaning of "part" would be "a segment of a sort similar to that from which it is abstracted," whereas "aspect" would be "some feature of a different sort or on a different level." In this way we can justify speaking of parts of aspects. One large advantage of this way of speaking will be that it avoids using the rather ambiguous term "physical."

This solution of our difficulty will assist us when we start with events, rather than objects, as the raw concrete material from which we abstract. For example, if we take a particular football game as the concrete event and ask ourselves what are its *part* abstractions and its *aspect* abstractions, we could answer that any removable physical object (such as the ball, the players, the goal posts, the spectators) are part abstractions, whereas the aspect abstractions (such as duration, roughness, yardage) would not be removable. But now, suppose we ask whether one quarter of the game is a part or an aspect? Normally we would think of it as a part. However, it is really a part of the total elapsed time, which is an aspect. So the quarter turns out to be a part or segment of an aspect, like the side of the rectangle. Again, we can regard the term "part" justified here if we consider aspect (in this case duration) to be subdivisible into similar parts or segments.

Groups, as well as individuals, may have their parts and aspects. If, for example, one has a group of five apples, either one, two, three, or four apples would be part of the whole group; and the total weight or the quantity five would be aspects of the whole group. Stems and peelings, on the other hand, should be considered parts of individual apples; and the colors, hardnesses, and textures would be aspects of the individual apples. Clearly, the aspect of quantity or that of total weight could not apply to any individual in the group, but only to the group as a whole. So when groups are involved in events, as a football team in a football game, then the whole group is part of the event. Aspects of the group, such as total weight of a football team or teamwork of the team, would then be aspects of a part of the event.

Does the term "abstract" apply only to concepts?

There is a strong tradition which associates concepts with the abstract, and objects with the concrete. But, as we saw, this view of the matter is a rank oversimplification. If abstracting is basically a focusing-attention-upon, then not only is the concept, as limited by our narrow range of attention, an abstraction, but so also is the object upon which we are concentrating. For example, if we are paying attention only to a particular table leg and are thus abstracting that leg, we still have both the concept of the leg and the actually perceived leg in our awareness. Or if we concentrate upon just the color of the table, we still have both the mental concept of the color and the actually perceived color. So we discover that the abstracted referent (that upon which we are concentrating our attention) is at least a correlate of the abstracted concept.

Let us now turn back to our diagrams in Chapter I, which showed the relations between referent, concept, and symbol. We must resist the temptation to regard the referent as concrete, the concept as abstract, and the symbol as still more abstract, for such a notion simply does not do.* The referent, we recall, may be some perceivable object or event (e.g., horse, game) or even some concept which sorts out and brings together and possibly rearranges the elements of perceivable experience (e.g., unicorn, democracy). But the referent may also be taken either as a rather large chunk of experienced or imagined reality, or it may be narrowed down to some part or aspect thereof. So while in the former case the referent would be concrete, in the latter case it would clearly be abstract. In the second place, the concept, too, being a reflection of our range of attention, would likewise be capable of a broader or a narrower scope, and hence of being concrete or abstract. And finally the symbol, not as marks on a piece of paper, but as standing for something, could stand for an entire object, event, or situation, and so would be called a "concrete" symbol (e.g., a concrete noun), or could stand for a part or aspect only and thus be an "abstract" symbol (e.g., abstract noun). So it turns out that the referent, the concept, or the symbol may all three be either concrete or abstract —as reflecting the concreteness or abstractness of the concept, and not because one is abstracted from the other.

Then how did the notion arise that concepts are more abstract than referents? No doubt this idea stems from the fact, already noted above, that abstracting has been conceived primarily as a drawing-away, rather than as a focusing-attention-upon. But let us not be too hasty here. There may be another reason why abstractions have traditionally been associated with concepts in the mind, and this is because *the process of abstracting itself is a mental activity.* And as a mental activity, why should we imagine that it has any effect upon the objects of the real world, even though these objects may be considered by us either in larger and more concrete complexes, or in limited and more abstract portions

* This is one of the errors propounded by Korzybski and followed by many of his disciples (see *Science and Sanity,* Ch. 25) .

or aspects? Yet, before we speak of objects of the real world in this way, it is time we turn to some traditional philosophical doubts, and raise some fundamental issues about being and knowing.

We have probably been assuming that objects which we perceive exist exactly as we perceive them, whether we happen to be perceiving them or not. If so, this is a view which philosophers have called *common-sense realism*. In contrast to this view, however, there are a variety of idealisms which agree in regarding the world of "real" objects as in some way, wholly or partly mindlike. In British philosophy, for example, George Berkeley (1685-1753) argued the theory, sometimes called *subjective idealism*, according to which only perceiving minds and their perceptions exist. For Berkeley, knowable objects can only be objects of perception or arise from combinations of perceptions; and since perceptions are clearly within the perceiver, there is no use attempting to imagine some unperceivable and hence unknowable objects "out there." For Berkeley, indeed, it is a foolish extravagance to try to imagine the existence of that which by its very nature is beyond knowledge. We need not follow Berkeley to so extreme a view; but we must be prepared to face his embarrassing questions if we wish to reassert our common-sense realism. For example, we often speak familiarly of "physical objects," meaning the real external entities studied by the physicist. But what are physical objects (e.g., atoms) other than a number of observed phenomena which we try to explain in terms of some imagined model? The model is just the product of our own guesswork; and we cannot know for certain what it is that exists "out there." So if our realities are only objects of perception, we should do better to call them "phenomenal objects," not physical objects, and guard against attributing to phenomenal objects any *known* existence apart from perception. This position is sometimes called *phenomenalism*.

Berkeley's challenge to our naive beliefs about objects is a crucial and fascinating episode in the history of Western thought; and the efforts to answer this challenge could provide us with an extended journey into philosophical exploration. For now, however, we must be content only to mention this challenge, and to turn again to our discussion of the nature of abstracting, especially as it affects referents, concepts, and symbols. On this last subject, let us adopt the position outlined above that the qualifications "concrete" and "abstract" can apply equally well to referents, to concepts, and to symbols.

What errors are commonly made regarding abstractions?

If we follow out the implications of our analysis of abstracting, we find that several common notions regarding abstractions are mistaken. FIRST, it is sometimes thought that the abstract is "vague" and the concrete is not, the implication even being that all abstractions are vague. But following our analysis, abstractions, coming as the result of selecting and focusing attention, should be simpler and less vague than the concrete wholes from which they were abstracted. Vagueness, as we saw in Chapter IV, is due to the variable extension of a term, and does not vary with the concreteness or abstractness of the term. It may be that some terms for abstractions (e.g., justice) have acquired a considerable variation in meaning and are therefore difficult to locate precisely. Such terms are vague, not because they are abstractions, but because of their variable meaning. Especially is it the case that imaginatively altered abstractions are apt to suffer from variable meaning and therefore appear vague. On the other hand, many abstractions (e.g., rectangle) are quite precise and not in the least vague.

A SECOND confusion arises from identification of abstractions with generalizations. This confusion has a long and persistent history, no doubt because of the fact that we become aware of many abstractions when we contemplate generalizations, and all generalizations presuppose abstractions. Generalizing, however, is a process of grouping like units together into classes, whereas abstracting, on the contrary, is a process of selecting out by focusing upon. So these processes are, in one sense, just the reverse of each other. The reason that generalizations presuppose at least implicit abstractions is simply that the similarities presumed to exist among the members of a class are abstractable traits common to all the members. Generalizations, then, theoretically depend upon *abstractable similarities*. And these similarities would not be noticeable unless we had the whole class more or less in view or in mind before abstracting them.

But it is not necessary to start from a class in making abstractions. They can quite as well be formed from a single individual. For example, one can abstract a particular rectangle from a particular tabletop, and this does not make this particular rectangle in any sense general, even though as a shape it is capable of being applied to other objects (as when, for example, we might wish to make more tabletops of the same shape and size). Thus, we may conclude that although generalizing theoretically involves abstracting in order to find the similar or common elements, abstracting does not necessarily involve generalizing.*

The confusion of abstract and general is so widespread that some excellent thinkers fall into it. Thus, many persons who talk of levels of abstraction mean levels of generalization. That is, they refer to levels of greater inclusiveness of referents, not of greater selectivity of common characteristics. If we speak of levels of abstraction at all we should mean taking less and less from the given concrete situation from which we started, that is to say, abstracting from abstractions. "Levels of generalization," on the other hand, should refer to the conceiving of larger and larger or more inclusive groups of individuals.

In this same vein, we must not confuse *concrete* with *specific* or *particular*. If by "general" we mean a number of individuals taken together in a class, then a few individuals, by contrast, would be "specific" and a single individual would be "particular." On the other hand, if by "abstract" we mean an isolated aspect or part, then "concrete" means an entire unit taken together. Thus, the terms "particular" and "concrete" do not mean the same thing, though they are often used as if they did. In fact, we often have abstractions which are particular or specific, and general classes which are concrete, in the sense that they are composed of full-fledged concrete objects or events (see Chapter X).

A THIRD common fallacy regarding abstractions is the assumption

---

* In a study of the way in which concepts develop, the Russian psychologist Vygotsky noted that a primitive abstracting and a loose grouping or generalizing by family-type resemblances combine at an early stage. Then comes a greater use of abstracted traits in making analyses of concrete situations; but at this stage there is not yet enough awareness of the abstraction itself to permit its definition. Ability to define an abstraction by analyzing its own essential traits comes later; and lastly, with greater difficulty, one learns to apply the defined abstraction to new concrete situations seen as incorporating the particular abstraction. See L. S. Vygotsky, *Thought and Language*, Ch. 5.

that abstractions are necessarily unreal, in the sense that they are purely imaginary. If, as we have noted, abstractions are merely parts or aspects of experienced things and events upon which attention is focused, then it would follow that they are just as real (no more and no less) as the wholes from which they were abstracted. The leg of the desk or the color of the desk is surely just as real as the desk. The smile on the face of the Cheshire cat or the fatness of the present king of France is just as unreal (imaginary) as the Cheshire cat or the present king of France. This means that the test for reality must lie somewhere else than in degree of abstractness.

Why has this third confusion arisen? Is it that "concrete" as opposed to "abstract" somehow suggests reality? If so, this is based on an unusual meaning of "concrete"; for "concrete" merely means totality; and one can have a fictitious totality just as well as a non-fictitious totality. Or is it that "abstract," since it refers to isolating and concentrating upon, has come to suggest mentally withdrawn or aloof from reality? However, there is surely no reason why the act of concentrating upon some one feature of an object should make this feature unreal, even though the person who is doing the concentrating at the moment seems unaware of his surroundings.*

We must stress again that one can make abstractions from imaginary concepts (like unicorns, Cheshire cats, and present kings of France) just as readily as we can make abstractions from actually experienceable phenomena. Furthermore, we shall note later in dealing with imagination (Chapter IX) that many abstractions have been imaginatively altered after having been initially abstracted from some "real" experience. For example, if I abstract the precise shape of a poodle and then imagine this shape longer and squattier than it is, I have created a new shape which no longer fits the real (phenomenal) poodle. This new altered abstraction thus becomes imaginary or "unreal" insofar as it no longer refers to the given sense datum (i.e., the poodle as seen).

FINALLY, it is fallacious to imagine that aspect abstractions can exist by themselves as phenomena without the existence of the concrete object or event from which they were abstracted. To imagine that they can affords great entertainment for the fancy.

* The meaning of "abstract" as mentally withdrawn or aloof has become, it should be noted, one rather commonplace transferred meaning of the term. However, it is not the one discussed here, nor still the primary one.

For example, Alice in Wonderland sees the Cheshire cat fade away, all but its grin, and the grin (an aspect of the cat) is left. "Well, I've often seen a cat without a grin [thinks Alice], but a grin without a cat! It's the most curious thing I ever saw in all my life!" Indeed this would be curious in a world like ours where the grins are only as real as the grinners. After all, in our experience, abstracted aspects do presuppose the objects or events from which they are abstracted. The assumption that abstract aspects have a greater concreteness or substantiality than they do is sometimes called *hypostatizing*. It is closely akin to what Whitehead has called the *fallacy of misplaced concreteness.**

One caution needs to be injected here. The view that ideal forms and relations exist in some ultimate way as more basic and permanent realities of the universe than experienced phenomena is a view that has a very strong support in Western philosophy. In fact, this idea is central to the philosophy of Plato; and the Platonic tradition has always found adherents. It was, however, attacked by Plato's illustrious pupil, Aristotle, who preferred to regard forms and patterns as abstractions, though nonetheless genuine and real. The Platonists, on the other hand, would not regard forms and patterns as abstractions at all, but rather as the ultimately meaningful ingredients in experience which not only make experience intelligible, but also give it reality. For them, ideal forms and patterns are known not by the inspection of experienced objects and events, in order to determine and abstract the common and essential characteristics of these objects and events, as we have been asserting, but rather by an inner perceptivity of the mind, which can be trained to recognize the ideal forms directly. The reader must remember, then, that the present account has an Aristotelian, not a Platonic, orientation.

A famous criticism of "abstract ideas" which illustrates several of the foregoing difficulties stemming from the confusion over the meaning of the term abstraction is that of George Berkeley. Berkeley, whose subjective idealism was mentioned above, attacked the possibility of forming certain types of "abstract ideas" in order

---

* This is the "error of mistaking the abstract for the concrete" as, for example, assuming that the spatial points imagined by the laws of kinetics are concrete realities. See *Science and the Modern World*, pp. 74 ff., and *Process and Reality*, p. 11.

to undercut the notion that something independent of perception, and therefore for him unknowable, could be imagined. In particular, he attacked the possibility of imagining (1) generalizations, which he called "abstract general ideas," and (2) hypostatizations, or "qualities which it is impossible should exist separated" from some object in which they are perceived. But he was willing to admit the possibility of imagining simple abstractions, such as parts of a body, that could exist separately. It will be interesting to quote one of Berkeley's key statements on this point:

> Whether others have this wonderful faculty of abstracting their ideas, they best can tell; for myself, I find indeed I have a faculty of imagining, or representing to myself, the ideas of those particular things I have perceived, and of variously compounding and dividing them. I can imagine a man with two heads, or the upper parts of a man joined to the body of a horse. I can consider the hand, the eye, the nose, each by itself abstracted or separated from the rest of the body. But then whatever hand or eye I imagine, it must have some particular shape and color. Likewise the idea of a man that I frame to myself must be either of a white, or a black, or a tawny, a straight, or a crooked, a tall, or a low, or a middle-sized man. I cannot by any effort of thought conceive the abstract [general] idea above described. And it is equally impossible for me to form the abstract [general] idea of motion distinct from the body moving, and which is neither swift nor slow, curvilinear nor rectilinear; and the like may be said of all other abstract general ideas whatsoever. To be plain, I own myself able to abstract in one sense, as when I consider some particular parts or qualities separated from others, with which, though they are united in some object, yet it is possible they may really exist without them. But I deny that I can abstract from one another, or conceive separately, those qualities which it is impossible should exist so separated; or that I can frame a general notion, by abstracting from particulars in the manner aforesaid—which last are the two proper acceptations of "abstraction."*

We notice here that Berkeley disclaims an ability to abstract if "abstracting" is (1) imagining some quality (e.g., motion) or some object (e.g., a man) when it includes a wide variety of different examples, or (2) imagining *by itself* some quality which always occurs in experience combined with other qualities in an object; but he admits that he can abstract in the sense of considering

---

* George Berkeley, *A Treatise Concerning the Principles of Human Knowledge,* Intro. 10.

"some parts or qualities separated from others" when "they may really exist without them."* So, what he is objecting to is either conceiving a generalization (an "abstract general idea") as if it were a single simple thing, or a hypostatized quality as if it could exist by itself. He does not object to abstracting in the sense we are using it here, although he claims that the other two senses are the proper meanings ("acceptations") of the term, no doubt because of the frequency with which the term was used in these ways and was therefore confused with generalization and hypostatization.

Berkeley's major difficulties with abstracting could well be eliminated if he had adopted Whitehead's meaning of the term, as directing attention to and isolating a part or aspect for the purposes of contemplation, instead of taking abstracting in its more traditional sense of "holding a separate mental image." Berkeley's trouble with generalizations or "abstract general ideas" arose from his trying to visualize some variable quality or object as if it were unified and simple, and his trouble with imagining separate qualities which only occur in combination arose from his attempt to imagine them as if they did not occur in combination. But if abstracting is simply the focusing of our attention upon one factor at a time, then we could isolate the factor that distinguishes a quality in general (e.g., motion) from its lack (i.e., rest), or one kind of object (e.g., man) from some other kind of object (e.g., horse). We may understand this type of imagining better in the case of a simple geometric figure, like a rectangle, in which we isolate or focus our attention upon the four right angles at the corners and ignore the lengths of the lines between them. Similarly, we can focus on the traits characteristic of human beings which allow us to distinguish them from horses, or other things, and thereby imagine these traits as distinguishing features of human beings, even though they vary somewhat from individual to individual. In spite of Berkeley's disclaimer on his ability to imagine generalizations, we do make sense out of our linguistic terms for them (e.g., man, horse, city, etc.) and these terms do have referential meaning, as we saw in Chapter IV. Also, Berkeley's trouble with the imagining of hypostatized qualities would disappear if he were only required to isolate these qualities by focusing attention upon them

---

* Berkeley neglects to tell us which qualities he can imagine separated from others.

rather than by trying to think of them as somehow existing apart by themselves, like the grin on the Cheshire cat, when they really do not do so.

How are abstractions reflected in our language?

When we look at the structure of our language, we find various ways of dealing with the concrete and the abstract. (1) The realm of individual objects, normally taken as concrete, is symbolized by *primary* or nonderived nouns—man, dog, tree, etc. But we must not overlook the fact that some primary nouns (leg, top, side, etc.) may stand for parts, and parts, as we saw, are abstractions. (2) Types of doing or events, taken as concrete, are symbolized by *verbs,* at least with regard to what is going on. Of course, if one prefers to think of the whole complicated event with all its objects, parts, and aspects as the concrete unit, then the verb alone reflects only that aspect of the event which is abstractable as the functioning of these objects and parts. Let us consider a simple event: John shoots the deer. The idea of shooting is fairly concrete, and so one might take the verb to symbolize a concrete idea. But if one considers the whole situation, including the shooter (John) and what was shot (the deer), then the shooting by itself becomes only an abstractable aspect of the whole event. (3) Qualities, primarily symbolized by *adjectives,* will naturally be abstract aspects, since linguistically they qualify nouns, which is the same as saying that they are thought of as representing attributes of objects. Likewise, *adverbs,* in qualifying ways of doing or ways of qualifying, just symbolize an aspect recognizably abstract. (4) Finally, terms dealing with relations, namely *prepositions* and *conjunctions,* must symbolize abstractions also, since one cannot think of relations without a larger (more concrete) situation at least presupposed, for relations imply that there are things or events which are being related. Thus, of our four basic parts of speech (see Chapter II), only primary nouns (and pronouns when they replace these) and verbs taken as symbolizing an entire event will stand for normally concrete concepts. Other linguistic forms will suggest abstractions. But we must also remember that this verdict assumes the "normal" point of view. If someone starts from a customarily abstract element as his totality, then it would become for him concrete, and the linguistic symbol for it would likewise need to be regarded as concrete.

To summarize, (1) primary nouns normally indicate whole concrete *objects* or else abstractable *parts;* (2) adjectives and adverbs indicate abstractable *qualities* or *modes;* (3) prepositions and conjunctions indicate abstractable *relations;* and (4) verbs indicate either concrete *events* or abstractable *functions.* We must recall that this fourfold arrangement does not necessarily fit all languages equally well. Some, for example, center on the verbal idea and the concreteness of actions (see Chapter II). But for our purposes, it will be convenient to follow the grouping suggested by our own language, which gives the following basic varieties of abstractions:

(1) Parts
(2) Aspects
    (*a*) Qualities
    (*b*) Relations
    (*c*) Functions

The three aspects just named will be discussed in more detail in the next three chapters.

Let us turn our attention now to the matter of derived complex nouns, for they constitute the bulk of what are traditionally considered to be abstract nouns. In Chapter II we already noted that there were two common Old English endings used to change other parts of speech, usually adjectives, into nouns. These endings are *-ness* (good—goodness), and *-th* (true—truth). But there are many other endings, mostly from French, Latin, and Greek, which are used in English. Some common suffixes, in addition to the two already mentioned, are *-hood, -kind, -ion, -ce, -ity, -ment, -ism, -age, -er, -or, -ing.* On the whole, the endings *-kind, -ment, -age, -er,* and *-ing* suggest concepts somewhat more concrete than the others. The reason for this appears to be that they suggest either (1) *collective concepts* (like man*kind*) in which many individuals are considered together as a whole, losing their individuality in the notion of a mass, or (2) *concrete objects* or *events* named by one of the abstractable aspects of these objects or events (like think*er* or experi*ment*). These latter we shall call *concreted abstractions* to indicate that abstracted traits are now combined to name an ordinarily concrete object. Collective concepts and concreted abstractions would seem to fall somewhere between the concreteness of individualized objects named by primary nouns and the abstractness of nominalized qualities named by nouns ending in *-th, -ness, -hood, -ity, -ce, -ism,* etc.

We may well ask ourselves: Why bother to turn other parts of speech into nouns, since it involves all these cumbersome endings? There is a good reason for it. Sometimes we wish to call special attention to a quality or activity and point a finger at it. It is the job of the nouns in our sentences to indicate the objects of primary interest, that is, the things we are talking about. Thus the ability to nominalize other parts of speech gives us a verbal pointer of great value and adds vastly to the flexibility of our linguistic symbolism. Theoretically, any word whatsoever could be made over into a noun, if we wished. Note the following examples: (1) That is a very *true* (adjective) saying.—The *truth* (noun) of that saying is clear. (2) *Why* (adverb) did he come?—Can you give me the *why* (noun) of his coming? (3) The book is *upon* (preposition) the table. —Notice the *uponness* (noun) of the book with respect to the table. (4) He was admitted, *whereas* (conjunction) I had to wait.—The *whereas* (noun) of his being admitted was not clear to me.

We note that some words in the above examples are changed into nouns without the use of suffixes. In English one can form a noun frequently by using the word unchanged but placing a definite or indefinite article before it (e.g., the *whereas*). Many primary verbs are readily treated as nouns (becoming really derivative nouns) without changing the word at all (e.g., That was quite *a run* he made. Would you like to take *a walk?* etc.). English verbs also admit of two nominalized forms—the infinitive and the gerund. Thus we say, "*To run* (infinitive) a train requires skill"; or "*Running* (gerund) a train is not easy." The gerund may also function as a pure noun (not a verbal noun), as in the example "The *running* of the train is smooth," where the gerund itself does not take an object.

The ability to transfer words from one part of speech to another, or even to use a single word in two or more part-of-speech functions at the same time, is a great asset. It gives color to our range of expressions (e.g., "Amy *desked* her correspondence") and it also admits greater economy of phrasing (e.g., "There's George, *whose* car I borrowed," in which case "whose" is at the same time *three* parts of speech: adjective, pronoun, and conjunction). See p. 41.

Why is abstracting important?

The process of abstracting is the key to our thought processes. We discover how important it is when we recognize the role of abstracting in making an analysis. "Analyzing" literally means loosening up or unraveling. That is, it is the separate examination of all the components of an object, event, or situation, in order to find out how it is constructed and how its various elements function. Some objects, such as materials, machines, or organisms, can actually be taken apart, so that their components can be visually examined one at a time. But most of the things that we study cannot thus be broken up; and even machines and organisms do not tell us about the functionings of their various parts when we are looking at them in pieces. Certainly such a thing as a human society or government could not be studied except as a going, working, concrete set of events. And in such cases, analysis requires that we abstract the components by shifting our attention to them one at a time or in various combinations and noting their functional interrelationships. Then we can understand the whole as we synthesize it, or pull it back together again in our conceptual imagination. So, understanding, which depends on our ability to analyze and synthesize, must depend on our ability to abstract.

Practice in abstracting is therefore basic to our whole intellectual effort and to its success or failure. Since abstracting includes not only the ability to focus attention upon parts and aspects one at a time, but also the ability to hold each abstraction as an object of thought without allowing it to become entangled with other abstractions (at least until we are ready for this to happen), it follows that a large part of the difficulty which most of us have with deliberate and conscious abstracting is simply that of excluding those factors which we are ignoring and keeping them excluded until time to let them back in again in some orderly way. Were we more adept in doing this, much of the confusion arising from the intrusions of irrelevancies into our considerations could be eliminated.

SUGGESTED READINGS

For some philosophical approaches to "abstraction" see:

Locke, John, *An Essay Concerning Human Understanding*, Bk. II, Ch. 11.

Berkeley, George, *Of the Principles of Human Knowledge*, Intro.

Garnett, A. C., *The Perceptual Process*, especially Chs. 2-3.

Weinberg, J. R., *Abstraction, Relation, and Induction*, especially Pt. I.

Whitehead, A. N., *Science and the Modern World*, especially Ch. 5.

For psychological approaches to "abstraction" see:

Piaget, Jean, *Origins of Intelligence in Children*.

Pikas, Anatol, *Abstraction and Concept Formation*.

Vygotsky, L. S., *Thought and Language*, especially Chs. 5-6.

CHAPTER VI

Qualities

What are qualities?

ABSTRACTIONS, as we have defined them, are taken
from the areas of immediate experience, from the
realm of things as perceived. Now some of the aspects
which we abstract from the array of experienced objects appear to be quite simple and not subject to
being broken up into subordinate or smaller parts.
For example, the blue of a cloudless sky, when observed in some small region of the heavens, appears as
a simple unitary color. Even a shape like a rectangle
may be regarded as a single thing, that is, as a single
unitary aspect within the total field of our perceptions.
For convenience we shall call such unitary aspects
qualities. Although in normal usage the term "quality"
serves loosely as a synonym for "aspect" or "property"
in general, we are here giving it a somewhat restricted
meaning. We shall need, then, to think of qualities
not as *properties of,* nor as *complexities,* and certainly
not as marking something of *high degree* (as a "person
of quality"), but rather as *any simple unit of direct
perception.* A quality, in other words, will be for us
any aspect, abstracted from some larger segment of experience, which at the moment is being taken as simple
and unanalyzed.

Relations, on the other hand, which we shall examine in more detail in the next chapter, are *connections between related units,* and as such will necessitate, at least by implication, the presence of some items to be related. Thus a relation is more complex than a quality and presupposes qualities or parts which enter into the relation. It may happen that some trait or aspect, when first abstracted, stands out as a simple unit, as a quality; but after further attention to it, we discover that our supposed simple quality is composed of interrelated parts and aspects and thus becomes a complex set of interrelated qualities. A rectangle, for example, may be taken as a simple shape-unit, or it may be analyzed into its component elements of sides and angles related to each other in a certain way. When viewed in the latter manner, the rectangle is no longer a single, simple quality but is a complex of further abstractables which in turn are reducible to other qualities in relation to one another (i.e., lines and angles). Ultimately, in any abstracting process we should reach some simple primitive qualities which cannot be reduced further and without which there would be no units out of which to construct perceivable "objects."

A word of caution needs to be injected here. It is very tempting, when we analyze anything (break it up into its component elements) and finally arrive at some simplest element, to regard these as building blocks which have a kind of prior reality. So we may be tempted to regard our simple qualities as the very stuff of our experienced world. But any view which seeks to give to one kind of thing a privileged position, in regard either to reality or to ultimate importance, normally flounders when it comes to explaining the larger complexities. This tendency to reduce a view of reality down to some one kind of thing is often called *reductionism,* and we must be careful to avoid the trap which our reductionistic tendency sets for us. Even in regard to abstractions like rectangles, there is justification for taking them in two ways: either as large single units (or qualities), or as composed of other more elemental units related to each other.

Having distinguished qualities from *relations* on the ground that whereas qualities are single or all-of-a-piece, relations involve subordinate elements, there remains another variety of aspect-abstraction which we shall consider (Chapter VIII)—*func-*

tions. The term "function" will be used to designate the *active or changing aspects of experience.* Of course, qualities may change and relations may change, as when the colors shift during a sunset or one's distance from a certain town increases while traveling away from it; but we shall use the terms "quality" and "relation" to refer to the stable or instantaneous condition in which change is not our concern, and we shall reserve the term "function" for the changing aspects of any situation when change is our concern. A sunset may be a veritable kaleidoscope of shifting colors; but suppose we take a colored photograph of the sky; then we shall have caught the one set of qualities which the sky had at a particular moment. The photograph retains, or in a way makes permanent, the qualities and relations which existed at the time the picture was taken.

Our concept of qualities and relations is somewhat reminiscent of Plato's view of essences or forms. For example, Plato says of snow in the latter part of the *Phaedo* that snow, as snow, must remain forever unmelting; the essence of "snow" cannot melt. If it did, it would no longer have the quality of "snow." We may not wish to follow Plato through the argument which establishes permanent forms as the supreme realities, but we can agree that there is a kind of once-and-for-all-ness about a given quality, even in a world of change. We can even go so far as to assert that the very existence of a quality or relation at a given moment has a reality which can never be effaced from the total set of realities, and if there are influences or causal sequences at all, the influences of the momentary quality or relation will continue, without positing some Platonic realm of essences to allow for this permanence of a momentary condition.

What are the traditionally important varieties of quality?

The concept of quality has had a long and important history in philosophy. Indeed, the place assigned to quality in any philosophy is a good index of the basic orientation of that philosophy. It will be useful, therefore, for us to review a few of the major distinctions that have grown up around this notion.

Essential and Accidental Quality. In Plato's philosophy, we remember, the central importance assigned to permanent and unchanging forms is joined with the notion that each object of experience, or each kind of activity, copies or participates in some ultimate form of which it is only a partial and transitory example. The ultimate form is then the *essence** or real nature of the particular thing or activity.

Aristotle, we have noted, criticized this Platonic view for assigning primary reality to something so remote from everyday experience as these eternal forms. Instead, Aristotle preferred to locate ultimate reality in the world of experience here at hand. But he still retained the notion of essence as that which makes a thing what it is, and an *essential attribute* would thus be any quality which defines the primary nature of something or without which a thing could not be that thing. In contrast, qualities which can be altered without affecting a thing's real nature he termed *accidental*. For example, having a seat is an essential attribute of a chair; for without a seat an object could not function as a chair. But having the color brown (or gray or green or blue) is not essential to being a chair; and so for chairs color is an accidental quality. For some things (e.g., palomino horses) color might be essential.

Aristotle was much interested in biology, and he attempted to work out an extensive classification of organic life. But classifications soon bring us to the realization that traits which are essential to one class are not all essential to a larger and more inclusive class. While the color may be essential to being a palomino horse, it is certainly not essential to being a horse; and while having solid hooves may be essential to being a horse, it is not essential to being an animal. So Aristotle was made aware of the fact that an essence, in the sense of "what it is to be" something, must depend in part upon the limits of one's classification and the definition that goes with that classification. Nevertheless, he still regarded essential qualities as those which belong more directly and simply to the real nature of a thing, whereas accidental qualities are, as the term implies, more superficial.† The essence, that is, is closer to the inner nature or core reality of a thing and is not just a factor determined by an arbitrary classification.

* "Essence" is derived from the Latin verb *esse,* to be. The Greek word *ousia* used by Plato and Aristotle for "primary being" or "beingness" was translated into Latin as *essentia* (essence) .

† Especially in Book VII of the *Metaphysics,* Aristotle explores these concepts and their relationships.

But as noted in Chapter IV, with man-made objects (artifacts) it is more difficult to find the natural divisions between kinds; for human beings are quite inventive in creating hybrids, borderline cases, and new overlapping classes of objects. The arbitrariness of classifications in the realm of artifacts is well illustrated by the way in which different languages classify such things. As an example, consider again the English word *chair* for which having or not having arms is an accidental attribute. In French a *chaise* essentially does not have arms, whereas a *fauteuil* does. Thus, what is essential for a given class of objects in one language may not be essential in another. In fact, the more we examine classifications the more we discover the arbitrary element in them; and we are brought to the realization that essential attributes are nothing absolute in themselves, but are simply those qualities without which a thing would no longer *be classifiable* as that kind of thing.

It will help us to understand this classificational concept of essence if we refer back to our tent analogy (Chapter IV). Essential traits are those which constitute the minimum set of credentials necessary for admission to a given tent. For example, a chair must have a seat if it is to be admitted to the chair tent; but having or not having arms is nonessential, if it is the tent for the English word "chair." So intension, as we defined it, includes *all* traits common to a given class, and essence in the classificational sense, is simply that minimal part of an intension which is absolutely necessary for a given classification. There may then be some traits in the intension which are not part of the essence. For example, suppose that all the houses in town X have basements. Then having basements would be part of the intension (common aspects) of these houses. But for classifying any object as a house, or even as a house-in-town-X, it is not essential that it have a basement. Thus, having a basement is part of the intension but not of the essence in this case. And so we see that the intension of a term may include nonessential or accidental qualities.

Has the old meaning of "essence" as the "real nature" of something been entirely lost? Not quite; for we may regard some classifications as following more genuine natural lines of demarcation, and the essential qualities of these classifications would then be the more important ones for separating groups as thus classified. While geographical areas are not classes, we might think of an analogy here that will help. In the United States, some of the states have natural boundaries, such as rivers or mountain ranges, whereas most of the boundaries are merely lines laid out by the surveyor. So with classes: some appear to have divisions between them that represent a natural cleavage, whereas others are more a matter of an arbitrary drawing of lines. In the last analysis, whether an essence is to be regarded as something representing the "real nature" (a core reality) or whether it is only a matter of arbitrary line drawing will depend upon our philosophy of the objective and subjective components in what we call reality.

Primary and Secondary Qualities. Another distinction, not to be confused with the foregoing one, is that between primary and secondary qualities. Primary qualities are those which are believed to exist in objects, independent of any observer; whereas secondary qualities are those which are believed to exist only in the perceptions of the observer, perhaps as the result of external sources of sense stimuli. Here the question of objectivity and subjectivity is the central issue, but with regard to the qualities themselves, not with regard to classes.

The Greek philosopher Democritus (c. 460-370 B.C.) who, with Leucippus, is credited with giving the first developed statement of the theory of atoms, found it necessary to distinguish between qualities which he thought to be really in the atoms themselves and other qualities which would be merely the effects of atomic activity upon bodily sense organs. Of the first kind, later to be called *primary qualities,* Democritus probably distinguished shape, size, position, and arrangement.* All other qualities would be *secondary*—not qualities of the atoms themselves but only of sensation. The reason for this distinction arose from the fact that atomism was a highly reductionistic philosophy which took reality to be ultimately nothing more than physical particles ("atoms") moving in a void and colliding occasionally to form aggregates or bundles. Thus colors, sounds, smells, and the like would not be characteristics of atoms at all, but only by-products of stimulations caused by atoms.

* See Kirk and Raven, *The Presocratic Philosophers,* pp. 414-419.

The distinction between primary and secondary qualities was revived by Galileo, Descartes, Hobbes, and others in the sixteenth and seventeenth centuries. However, the principal formulator of the distinction, as we know it, was the English Philosopher John Locke (1632-1704). There was no fixed list of primary qualities upon which these philosophers agreed. Descartes (1596-1650) at one place named them as magnitude (or extension), figure (or shape), situation (or relation of bodies to one another), movement, substance, duration, and number.* Locke lists "solidity, extension, figure, and mobility" in one passage and "bulk, figure, number, situation and motion or rest" in another.† One thing that distinguishes these qualities from the secondary (such as color, sound, flavor, odor), Locke tells us, is the fact that the primary qualities remain present in an object no matter how much we break it up. For example, however much we cut up a piece of wood, Locke would say, we still have pieces with solidity, extension, figure, and mobility. Secondary qualities, on the other hand, were considered to be only our stimulated responses to the ways in which external objects affect us. They are not really in the objects at all, but only in our own nervous systems. Also, primary qualities may be detected by more than one sense, while secondary qualities cannot.

This idea of distinguishing primary from secondary qualities was accepted unchallenged until we come to Locke's follower, George Berkeley, whose views on abstracting we discussed in Chapter V. Adopting Locke's empiricism (the view that knowledge is traceable ultimately to sense impressions), Berkeley observed very simply that *all* qualities, as objects of perception, are just that and no more—something perceived. And if one inquires where objects of perception reside, one is forced to answer that they reside in perception. So, in effect, all qualities are alike in being aspects of the perceiver. What sense, then, is there in designating certain qualities as genuine qualities of external objects and other qualities as mere effects on nervous systems? Clearly, on Berkeley's grounds there is none. Certainly, the so-called primary qualities do not enter our perceptions endowed with certificates which would allow us to say of these particular im-

* *Meditations*, III, par. 19.
† *Essay Concerning Human Understanding*, II, Ch. 8, par. 9 and 23.

pressions that they are more objective than the others. So if we accept Berkeley's assumptions: (1) that it is foolish to assume a reality beyond the pale of the knowable, (2) that the knowable lies in the perceivable, and (3) that perceptions are a function of minds only, then we must dismiss the distinction between primary and secondary qualities as useless.*

David Hume (1711-1776), following the direction of Berkeley's thought, discovered that not only have we eliminated primary qualities, but also knowledge of substance and knowledge of self, if by "substance" we mean to imply some external reality independent of sense impressions, and if by "self" we mean some unified and enduring subject in which all our perceptions are held together. This skeptical conclusion of Hume's disturbed the philosopher Immanuel Kant (1724-1804) to such an extent that he worked out a radical new way of justifying permanent and universal forms under which perceptions must occur and judgments be made. Thus, in place of the old objective primary qualities, Kant gives us a basis for regarding certain forms of perception and modes of judgment as having a new kind of objectivity, the objectivity of a universal condition underlying all perceiving and thinking.

British philosophy, however, has tended to revert to a kind of pre-Berkeleyan realism, according to which objects do exist much

---

* See especially Berkeley, *Treatise Concerning the Principles of Human Knowledge*, 73: "It is worth while to reflect a little on the motives which induced men to suppose the existence of *material substance;* that so having observed the gradual ceasing and expiration of those motives or reasons, we may proportionably withdraw the assent that was grounded on them. *First,* therefore, it was thought that colour, figure, motion, and the rest of the sensible qualities or accidents, did really exist without the mind; and for this reason it seemed needful to suppose some unthinking *substratum* or substance wherein they did exist, since they could not be conceived to exist by themselves. Afterwards, *(secondly)* in process of time, men being convinced that colours, sounds, and the rest of the sensible secondary qualities had no existence without the mind, they stripped this *substratum* or material substance of those qualities, leaving only the *primary ones,* figure, motion, and such like, which they still conceived to exist without the mind, and consequently to stand in need of a material support. But it having been shown that none, even of these, can possibly exist otherwise than in a spirit or mind which perceives them, it follows that we have no longer any reason to suppose the being of *matter.* Nay that it is utterly impossible there should be any such thing, so long as that word is taken to denote an *unthinking substratum* of qualities or accidents, wherein they exist without the mind."

as we perceive them and quite independently of any perceiver. So the old distinction between primary and secondary qualities returns, happily wedded to the traditional view of the physical sciences and insisting on some knowable properties which are genuine characteristics of external physical objects.

There even has developed in recent times an additional notion of subjective qualities, called *tertiary* qualities, to accommodate the highly personal matter of tastes with respect to good and bad, beautiful and ugly. Tertiary qualities are simply feelings of preference which cause us to designate certain objects or events as good or beautiful, and other objects or events as bad or ugly. But again, for some good realistic British philosophers, tertiary qualities may seem too subjective. For example, the recent English philosopher G. E. Moore (1873-1958) developed a view that the value qualities (like good and beautiful) must be simple qualities. He would also have us sharpen our distinction between the *object sensed* and the *act of sensing* in order to realize that it is the latter, not the former, which is subjective, and that this subjective side needs the objective in order to be what it is.

There are many current philosophical views on these matters, especially with regard to the existence of value qualities. But before this question can be satisfactorily resolved, one must develop a clear meaning of what it is to be objective or subjective, and whether there may not be several varieties of objectivity or subjectivity which are easily confused. It may be that our difficulty also lies in what we take to be reliable tests for objectivity, for on the matter of tests there is also considerable room for difference of opinion. In the final analysis, whatever is selected as a test for objectivity must be selected on faith, for otherwise the test would have to be used to test itself, and this would prove nothing.

Kind and Degree. As a third and final distinction involving the notion of quality, let us explore what is meant by "difference of kind" as against "difference of degree." This is a distinction which for our contemporary stress on scientific and mathematical knowledge is probably more in need of our investigation than either of the two preceding distinctions.

When we speak of a certain *kind* of something (e.g., a kind of apple) we normally are thinking of a subclass within a larger class.

In fact, the word "kind," like its relative "kin," is a cousin of the Greek *genos* and Latin *genus,* meaning family group or class. But any class, we remember, is capable of being grouped together because of similarities. Thus if Golden Delicious is a kind of apple, it is because we have noted, or imagine, certain common qualities possessed by all Golden Delicious apples. Now the term "kind" may point to the class itself as a group of particular objects or events, or it may point toward the similar qualities. In other words, the term "kind" can be used to refer either to the extension or to the intension of a class. When it points in the direction of common qualities, or intension, the idea of quality comes to the fore. One curious usage of "kind" may help to demonstrate both its extensional and intensional meaning, for it may be used to refer to a *single entity* which does not fit into any group or class. Such a unique individual is said to be "of its own kind" or *sui generis.* The universe as a whole or God (in a monotheistic religion) is properly considered to be *sui generis.* In this case, "kind" does not refer to a class, unless it is thought of as a class whose extension includes only one member. The appropriate intensional meaning in this case would then include all the qualities of that unique individual.

The notion of *degree,* on the other hand, suggests that there is some stepwise or continuous variation from one end to the other of a scale. One of our most familiar examples of this situation is temperature, which we measure on thermometers marked off in degrees. This seems elementary enough; however, when we come to examine the possible range of this degree idea, we find quite a number of interesting possibilities. For example, even temperature may be thought of in two ways. We might go back to the days before thermometers and discover that differences in temperature were sometimes explained in terms of two different elements: the cold element and the hot element, which when mixed give us the cool or warm. If we think of the normal washbowl arrangement with hot and cold running water, and a mixture for warm water, we can easily understand the model for this notion. But then, with the advent of the thermometer, it seems much more reasonable to think of a continuously altering condition from cold to hot, which causes a corresponding variation in the volume of a gas or liquid, and which can thus be measured on some arbitrary scale. But even here, are we to think of two conditions, cold at one end of the scale, and hot at the other? Or shall we simplify our idea by thinking only of one condition, hot, which varies from its absence—called "cold"—to its increasing presence? And what about limits? We are told that there is a lowest limit to this scale, an *absolute zero,* beyond which there can be nothing colder. Is there also an upper limit, a hottest temperature? While we may not want to posit some absolute hot beyond which nothing could be hotter, it does stand to reason that in the universe there is some hottest temperature somewhere, and that the actual temperature scale does exist between the limits of absolute cold and maximum heat. The idea of a scale with two ends, like north and south pole, has given rise to the term *polarity* or *bipolarity* often used to express the general idea of two opposite qualities (hot-cold) with variations between the extremes.

The notion of polarity clearly involves a relationship between two qualities. It is thus somewhat more complex than the notion of a simple quality or kind, and we shall consider it therefore as one of the major types of relationships to be examined in Chapter VII. It also involves the notion of possible change or variation, and therefore could fall within the domain of Chapter VIII, which deals with change or "function." However, we need to consider this notion here as representing *degree* in contrast with the notion of *kind,* and from the light that it throws on the whole idea of quality, when qualities are regarded as related by polar contrast.

Actually, the polar relationship is highly ambiguous. Just in exploring the idea of hot and cold, we have encountered several alternative possible patterns for conceiving this relationship. One can, for example, imagine two absolute qualities, the hot and the cold, which as elements can be mixed to create the warm or cool. Or we can imagine two different qualities which vary inversely throughout a scale, so that the more there is of one quality, the less there is of the other. As another alternative, we can imagine one single quality, varying from more to less of itself, so that what is called the other quality is merely the absence or lack of the one positive quality. The first two of these notions are clearly *two-quality* ideas, whereas the last is only a *one-quality* notion, even though it does incorporate the idea of variation.

As another example of the one-quality idea, let us consider the qualities or kinds that do not seem to admit of degrees at all. Perfection, uniqueness, absoluteness, and the like, appear to be such notions. At least, we are often admonished against speaking of something as "more or less" perfect, or "more or less" unique. Not that there is anything grammatically wrong with these expressions: our language permits any adjective to have comparative and superlative forms (e.g., whiter, whitest, more unique, most unique), thus suggesting the possibility of degrees in all qualities. So the prohibition against introducing degrees into such a notion as "perfect" must be on logical grounds—that is, on the nature of the underlying pattern. Now, there is a way in which we can make good sense when we speak of something as "more or less perfect," and this is to think of perfection as the limit of a scale toward which, or away from which, a thing can move. Then, "more perfect" simply means "more nearly perfect"—nearer to perfection than the "less perfect"; and "more unique" means "more nearly unique"—nearer to uniqueness than the "less unique." Here we have in mind the model of a one-quality kind which constitutes the extreme limit of a scale along which one may approach this limit; but the quality itself admits of no degrees. Could we use this model for the one-quality temperature concept? We might, but we do not, for we do not normally limit the meaning of "cold" to absolute zero and call everything else "more or less" cold in the sense of being nearer to or farther from absolute zero. Rather, in the case of temperature, we now usually conceive of a scale which is two-directional with a zero somewhere in the middle in our own normal temperature range, as on a thermometer.

When we look at other examples of two-quality relations, we find not only the notion of two kinds being mixed (as hot and cold water in a washbowl) and the notion of two qualities (e.g., hot and cold) of the same category or kind (e.g., temperature) varying inversely throughout a scale (as on a thermometer), but we also find the notion of two different qualities that vary inversely in relation to each other. For example, the intensity of light varies inversely as the square of the distance that one is from the light source. Here the two qualities are (1) intensity of light and (2) distance from the light source. These are two quite distinct qualities which certainly could not be considered as one kind or category which varies along a scale from one limit to its opposite. In fact, we are rather extending the notion of polarity to include this type of two-quality relation under that heading. Yet, the two qualities here do vary inversely in a certain ratio, and are to that extent correlative qualities, the more of the one being correlated with a lesser amount of the other.

If we are to consider inverse variation under the general heading of polar relationships, we may also include direct proportional variation, in which case the more there is of one quality, the more there would be of the other. For example, if we think of horsepower of an automobile engine as correlated in this way with potential speed, then the more horsepower we have, the more potential speed. Or if we correlate size with value, as Americans have sometimes been accused of doing, then we would imagine that the bigger something is, the better it is.

There are other possible polar models which we might mention here. For example, we might have two absolute qualities which cannot vary in any way, and which cannot be approached or left. Admittedly such a concept would have little application to the world of experience which is filled with endless variations and deviations. But it is nonetheless an interesting theoretical possibility.

Or we may imagine a polar continuum in which there is a middle or neutral ground between two positive qualities. If, for example, we should take hot and cold as two positive qualities occurring only at the extremes, although they may have some degrees within themselves once we arrive there, then the middle ground between the hot and cold would be neutral, or neither hot nor cold. We may apply this model to our notion of good and evil to see if it fits. It would imply that within the area of good there may be more or less good, and within the area of evil there may be more or less evil, but between them, or independent of them, there is a neutral ground, say of behavior, which is neither good nor evil. Some people would no doubt prefer this model to the one that fancies good and evil to vary continuously with each other throughout the entire continuum. The task of the intelligent inquirer here is to become aware of as many of the patterns of polar relationships as possible, and then to decide which one best suits a given case.

Let us summarize the major varieties of one- and two-quality concepts which we have mentioned here, giving some diagrams to represent them. This list is not claimed to be exhaustive, for there are undoubtedly others that might be imagined.

(1) One or more absolute qualities, like the oddness or evenness of a numerical integer, that neither vary nor have any variable relations in regard to them.

(2) A single quality, like perfection, which is conceived as in itself unchanging, but with regard to which something may be nearer or further removed.

(3) Two absolute qualities which are thought not to vary in themselves, but which, like uniform hot and cold water in a wash-basin, can be mixed in different proportions.

(4) A single quality which, like heat when cold is considered to be only the absence of heat, can vary within itself.

(5) Two polar qualities within the same general category, like hot and cold within the category of temperature, which are thought to vary inversely.

(6) Two different qualities which, like intensity of light and distance from the light source, are conceived as varying inversely.

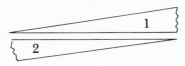

(7) Two different qualities which, like size and value, are thought to vary directly.*

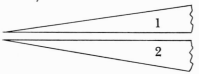

(8) Two qualities in the same category which, like hot and cold when measured on a thermometer in two directions from zero, are conceived as increasing in opposite directions from a midpoint.

(9) Two qualities in the same category which, like good and evil, can be conceived as having an intermediary neutral midground between them.

(10) Two qualities which, possibly like the events in a drama, increase in intensity to a midpoint or climax and then reduce in intensity.

In the foregoing list, we notice that from Example No. 4 through Example No. 9 the lower limits terminate in a point indicating a

* It is interesting to notice that whereas indirect variation may be thought of as two qualities in the same category, direct variation can only be conceived where the categories are different. The reason for this is that parallel increase through a single category, like temperature, would be possible only with one quality, or with two different names for the same quality (e.g., the more heat, the more hotness) , but inverse variation may be conceived as occurring either between two polar qualities within the same category (Example No. 5) , or between two related qualities in different categories (Example No. 6) . This consideration may suggest that it is better to regard Example No. 5 as affording simply two different quality terms for two possible directions of a single variable category (i.e., cold as negative heat and heat as negative cold) . And this in turn suggests that the single continuum of the temperature scale (Example No. 4) offers a better model for this type of relation.

definite end to the scale, but the upper limits are left indefinite, as indicated by the jagged lines. It would be possible to imagine the upper limits as also definite if there seemed some good reason to do so in the situation to which one wished to apply the model. In this case, the jagged line could be replaced by a straight line in the diagram, so that Example No. 4 would look like this

instead of like this

Examples 5 and 6 might have four alternative possibilities with regard to definiteness and indefiniteness. No. 5, for example, could be diagrammed as follows

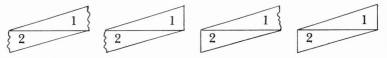

The point, again, is to find the most appropriate model to explain a given polar situation, or to help us understand how someone else is conceiving it.

As an example, we noted that Plato speculated that each kind of thing participates in an unchanging essence or ideal form. So, when he argued for the immortality of the soul in the *Phaedo,** he took the case of snow, which participates not only in snowness, but also in coldness, and fire, which participates in heat, to argue that the human soul, which has as its essence the life force, must forever participate in the life principle, and is therefore essentially opposed to death. The scheme represented in this argument is one in which opposite qualities have a reality of their own which is intermingled or mixed in the world as experienced. To the degree that the objects and events of experience bear in them the pure essential qualities, they are intelligible and eternal. The model suggested, then, comes nearest to our Example No. 3.

Let us turn our attention now to some common mistakes that are made with regard to difference of kind and degree. The first of these is the assumption that differences of degree are always quanti-

* See *Phaedo,* 103-106.

fiable, whether by counting discrete entities or steps or by measuring along a continuum with some selected unit of measure. But let us note that under the idea of degree we often include the notion of variable qualities which have not yet been measured and in fact may never be measurable. For example, before the invention of the thermometer, temperature was not measurable, and yet one could have experienced and thought of some days as *more* or *less* cold than others. Thus we see that capability of being measured is not necessary to the idea of *more* or *less* of a quality, and one often speaks of such unmeasured variations as having *differences of degree*. Our grammar seems to imply degree variation for all qualities that are named by adjectives (e.g., silly–sillier–silliest), whether or not there is a means of measurement available. Perhaps we assume that someday, when we have better scientific knowledge and equipment, all these qualities will become measurable. But this seems to be an expectation extremely unlikely to be fulfilled, for there are qualities (e.g., the value qualities good-better-best, ugly-uglier-ugliest) for which no yardstick is available or is ever likely to become available. At least, to date, any effort to invent a workable "valuometer" has proved inane. We might cite the case of Jeremy Bentham (1748-1832), who proposed that good and evil in human affairs could be measured in terms of pleasure and pain, assuming we can even measure pleasures and pains. John Stuart Mill (1806-1873), even though a follower of many of Bentham's ideas, saw the futility of this proposal and pointed out that there are different kinds or qualities of pleasure, as well as different degrees of pleasure. As he put it, "It is better to be a human being dissatisfied than a pig satisfied; better to be Socrates dissatisfied than a fool satisfied."* The difficulty with measuring value qualities is their subjective internal factor, for which there is no measurer. So we must beware of oversimplified schemes of measurement which omit the very thing we sought to measure.

There are two other dangers against which we must be on guard in thinking about differences of kind and differences of degree. The first of these is the danger of thinking that all differences of kind can ultimately turn out to be only differences of degree. Under the pressure of our urge toward knowledge which can be mathematicized it is a great temptation to look only for the measurable

* See Mill's *Utilitarianism*, Ch. II.

kind of data and then to shut our eyes to anything else. Ostrichlike, we may thus pretend to ourselves that quantities are everything. However, we must always remember that measurements are abstractions, which must therefore be measurements of *something,* and that this something is at least the *kind* of thing that is being measured. For example, when we measure temperature, temperature is that kind of thing that is being measured and it differs in kind from distance or a color scale, which are other kinds of things that could be measured. So, measurements by themselves may be interesting, but they do not mean much unless we know what kind of thing it is that we are measuring.

The second danger which lurks to entrap us lies in the opposite direction, namely, in thinking of kinds as always invariable. If we think of a quality or kind (e.g., black) as always that quality and as something that cannot admit of variation, then we are tempted to draw a sharp line around it and say to ourselves, "Well, it's either got to be this or its opposite: there is no in-between." However, as we should have seen by now, most qualities do admit of degrees, and their pure states serve only as imaginary limits of scales. In experience, a pure quality would be very rare, and most things would simply have more or less of a given quality. We might work hard to get a pure black paint, but it is doubtful that we could succeed. So we must guard against overextended uses of what is sometimes called either-or thinking, which may lead to such remarks as "Well, he's got to be either with us or against us," as if there were no in-between degrees. We are not here denying the utility of what is in logic called the principle of *excluded middle,* but we are saying that we must be very careful where and when we apply it. Under the idealized scheme in which our refined logical abstractions operate, the excluded middle is quite correct and useful. The naive application of this principle to subject matter for which it is unsuited is what we are objecting to here.

Can we formulate any rules for distinguishing our various patterns of degree-and-kind relations? Under which pattern, for example, can we best fit the notions of life and death, of movement and rest, of good and evil? Let us first ask ourselves if we need both qualities, or if one seems only to be the lack of the other. For example, the Neoplatonists used a one-quality pattern for good and evil, asserting that evil is merely the lack or deprivation of the good. But there are difficulties here which even the Neoplatonists could not avoid, notably the very real and positive nature of evil. If this pattern does not suit, then perhaps we should try in turn our two-quality patterns: the mixture of two elements or two qualities moving in opposite directions from a mid or neutral position, or two qualities varying inversely or directly, or even two invariable and unrelated qualities. Let us adopt tentatively the one that seems to fit best, but let us not close our thoughts to other possibilities, even some that we may not have considered here.

In what sense are qualities abstractions?

The empiricist, we have seen, begins with experience as the ultimate source of knowledge. Now, if experienced qualities are the units of that experience, out of which all is composed, then why are they not the basic units of our reality, and in a sense, that which is most concrete? Our answer to this question must turn back to what we said earlier about the relation of abstract and concrete. The concrete, we recall, is not something isolated and fragmentary (for that would be the abstract), but the largest graspings of experience of which we are capable. Qualities as simple unitary fragments would, from this point of view, be highly abstract. But even so, we may well ask ourselves what it is from which they are abstracted.

According to Aristotle, abstractions are to be made from some primary beings, or "substances," which as ultimate realities could only be subjects of our sentences and never predicates, that is, the things we think and talk about, not the things we attribute to them. If so, then these ultimate substances would be the concrete realities from which quality and other abstractions are made. But David Hume, as we saw above, noticed that when we commence with experience as the source of knowledge, we do not find any substances from which to make abstractions, for the substances would only be some kind of invisible or imaginary cement holding *clusters of aspects* together to create what we call "objects." Now, why assume such invisible creations of the imagination when we do not need them? Why not simply accept the idea that objects are nothing more than clusters of parts and aspects which usually stay together in experience? Thus, a table is not for Hume a substance possessing attributes (i.e., something having a certain shape, size, color, etc.) but a cluster of aspects which are customarily seen all together as forming a unit.

If we accept this *aspect-cluster* notion of objects, however, we can still take the separate aspects as legitimate abstractions from the whole cluster, in the sense that each aspect is capable of receiving our attention, and thus being abstracted, one at a time. So, as far as abstracting is concerned, it does not matter whether we adopt the view that there are ultimate substances or the view that there are only aspect-clusters. In either case, abstractions would occur as the separable parts and aspects of any given chunk of experience.

Hume's view leaves difficulties with regard to awareness of ultimate qualities as units of experience. William James, for example, regarded the level of percepts as a flux with no distinct boundaries, the boundaries being the result of conceptual activity. In a famous passage, he writes that if one can "lapse back into his immediate sensible life at this very moment, he will find it to be what someone has called a big blooming buzzing confusion, as free from contradiction in its 'much-at-onceness' as it is all alive and evidently there."* But this trick of "lapsing back" is not easy and contains no guarantee that it will show us the real character of preconceptualized qualities. Perceptual activity itself is a focusing on or unconscious abstracting of certain clusters of qualities out of larger areas. These clusters, when habitually associated in experience, present themselves as recognizable patterns to which our object names (hat, table, coat, etc.) refer. "Objects" in this sense are the normal concentrates of focal attention. But to abstract beyond these elementary groupings of qualities, we need to make a conscious effort toward locating and isolating the simpler and more unitary qualities (the red of a chair cushion, the tinges of color in the edge of a cloud, etc.). The painter, for example, sometimes resorts to eye-squinting in order to reach a conscious awareness of such simple qualities. It seems, then, that whether we start by assuming Aristotle's substances, or Hume's associated clusters of qualities, or James' big blooming buzzing confusion, we still need some abstractive effort or conscious focusing to arrive at what we here mean by "simple qualities."

* *Some Problems of Philosophy,* p. 50.

How does our language handle qualities?

There are, of course, many ways in which qualitative descriptions are capable of being expressed linguistically, but we are here concerned principally with grammatical habits of which we are all too often unaware. We have already discussed (Chapter V) the ways in which abstractions of all types are treated in our language, and so all we need now is to look at the treatment afforded qualities in particular. Quality abstractions are principally symbolized in language by *adjectives,* since an adjective is that part of speech which introduces a qualification of an object named by the noun which the adjective modifies. Thus, "blue goat" qualifies the named object (goat) by the quality (blue). There are in our language not only primary adjectives but also derived adjectives, and among these the verbal adjectives (present and past participles) are probably the most common. For example "stuffed" in "my stuffed hippopotamus" is a past participle of the verb "to stuff"; and "climbing" in "my climbing monkey" is a present participle of the verb "to climb." Nouns can be converted into adjectives by adding suffixes (*-al, -ful, -ish, -ic,* etc.) or by simply using the bare noun to function as an adjective. The *tar* baby, the *desk* stand, the *night* owl illustrate this latter practice. We may on occasion even wish to convert other parts of speech into adjectives, and if we are sufficiently inventive we should have no difficulty in doing so. For example, we might speak of "an *iffish* way one has of protecting his assumptions." Or we may say, "His path was extremely *to-y* and *fro-y.*" These are not customary English forms, but there should be little doubt as to what they mean.

Adverbs can also be classified as quality indicators. This is because adverbs primarily qualify verbs, which is to say that they have the primary function of qualifying an action or doing rather than an object. Thus the adverbs in "He left *slowly*" or "He left *rapidly*" show the manner or quality of his leaving. A great many of our adverbs are formed by adding the suffix *-ly* to the adjective. In this way the quality indicated by the adjective is made appropriate to characterize a verb, and we thus observe that the quality idea is still present. For example, the difference between *slow leaving* (adjective + verbal noun) and *slowly leave* (adverb + verb) is primarily due to the influence of the surrounding context and the way in which we wish to fit this idea into the sentence. Primary adverbs (*not, still, yet,* etc.) also indicate qualifications of the verbal idea. And of course, when we use adverbs to modify adjectives or other adverbs, they are still serving as special quality indicators.

Finally, the definite and indefinite *articles* (*the* and *a, an*) are in their way quality indicators. What, for example, is accomplished by inserting *the* before a noun, aside from merely showing that it is a noun? What is the difference between "cat" and "the cat"? The latter form of speech indicates that the speaker is referring to a definite or particular cat—presumably one that has been mentioned before. So the quality of *particularity* or *definiteness* is indicated by the definite article. Using the indefinite article ("a cat") shows the converse quality—that of no precise specification. Although these two qualities (*particularity* and *lack of particularity*) may seem to be not qualities of the objects themselves, but qualities of the way in which these objects are being regarded, they are nonetheless qualifiers. The expressions *the cat* or *a cat* show the quality of particularity or generality in reference to the notion of *cat*. But the expression *gray cat* indicates a quality of a particular cat. For this reason, adjectives like *gray* or *long* or *small* are sometimes called "descriptive" adjectives, whereas adjectives which indicate particularity or generality, like the articles and such words as *any, all, some, several,* are called "limiting" adjectives.

Qualities are symbolized in our language not only by adjectives, adverbs, and articles but also by nouns. We have already noted that many derived nouns (e.g., goodness) simply name a quality *as if it were an object*. It is, of course, not an object even in the sense of being an aspect-cluster. But it can be regarded as *objectlike* insofar as it is at the moment of abstraction being focused upon as the total area or *object* of our attention. It is at this point that we may be led into the error of hypostatization. For example, to speak of truth or blueness does not in effect do more than note that we are focusing our attention upon the quality *true* or the quality *blue*. It does not set up truth or blueness as separable concrete objects, even as aspect-clusters, nor allow us to imagine them as hypostatized entities. To avoid this fallacy, it will help if wherever possible we trace complex (derived) nouns back to the adjectives or other parts of speech from which they have come.

Let us add a word about the symbolization of qualities, based on a notation commonly used in symbolizing logical forms or statements. It is the purpose of logical symbols to give as general a form as possible, so that the bare structures of propositions and their elements can be clearly observed. In converting such a phrase as "gray cat" into a logically general form, we need a formula that will allow any similar phrase (dark house, grimy shirt, hot potato, etc.) to be symbolized by it. How can we do this? The conventional way is to use one letter of the alphabet, often a capital letter, to stand for the quality (more generally the "function"), and to use a small letter, usually x or y and often in parentheses, for the qualified object. Thus we would symbolize "gray cat," "dark house," "grimy shirt," or any such expression, by $F(x)$. Here the letter F stands for function or aspect, and the (x) stands for anything to which this function may be attributed. Since in the present treatment we are distinguishing between qualities, relations, and functions, it will be better for our purposes to use respectively $Q(x)$, $R(x)$, and $F(x)$, or xQ, xR, and xF, to stand for a *quality* of x, a *relation* of x, and a *function* of x. These uses will be further elaborated when we consider relations and functions in the two ensuing chapters.

SUGGESTED READINGS

On essence:
Aristotle, *Metaphysics,* Bk. VII (Zeta) , especially Chs. 2-6.
Lewis, C. I., *Mind and the World Order,* especially Ch. 5.
Blanshard, Brand, *Reason and Analysis,* especially Ch. 12.

On primary and secondary qualities:
Locke, John, *Essay Concerning Human Understanding,* Bk. II, Ch. 8.
Berkeley, George, *Of the Principles of Human Understanding,* Sections 1-33.
Hume, David, *Treatise of Human Nature,* Bk. I, Pt. IV, Section 4.

On polarities:
Plato, *Phaedo,* especially 103-106.
Aristotle, *De Interp.,* especially Ch. 7, and *Metaphysics,* Bk. XII (Lambda) , especially Chs. 1-5.
Bahm, A. J., *Polarity, Dialectic, and Organicity,* especially Pt. I.
Passmore, John, *Philosophical Reasoning,* especially Ch. 6.

CHAPTER VII

Relations

Relations: What and why?

ANALYSIS OF QUALITIES leads to an awareness of relations. Qualities, as defined here, are unified, all-at-a-glance impressions such as single colors or shapes. But when one begins to analyze—that is, to divide up into parts and aspects—one loses the unitariness of the quality and notes instead at least two or more elements with their interconnections. These interconnections are what we mean by "relations." For example, a solid green rectangular wall may at first glance appear to us as a single impression. But then one notices that it has (1) a color and (2) a shape. Each of these taken by itself is single—just one quality. But the shape may be separated or analyzed into subordinate aspects—sides, corners, etc. These inner aspects or parts of the shape are *related* to each other, and the ways in which they are related may be called "relations." On the other hand, the solid color (e.g., green) is not analyzable into subordinate parts or aspects. So it remains a quality. Of course, any color could be related to other colors in the spectrum or to the corresponding frequency of light **vibrations** which presumably is responsible for a given color, but these are relations which lead away from the color-as-seen. They are not, as with the rectangular shape, relations discoverable within the original impression. Thus, we note immediately that relations may be discovered either *within* a given quality (internal relations) or *outside* a given quality, between it and some other quality (external relations).

In general, whenever an association or connection can be distinguished as existing between two or more elements, we may refer to this connection as a "relation." For example, "book *on* table," "day *before* yesterday," "airplane *in* cloud," are relational phrases, the relations being indicated by the italicized prepositions.

There is also a special term for the parts, aspects, or elements which are connected by a relation. These are called "relata" (singular: relatum). Thus, in the examples above, book and table, day and yesterday, airplane and cloud are the relata.

Analysis into relations is the key to rational thinking. Every graph, chart, diagram, measuring device or measurement is a means to an understanding of the relations that exist in a given situation. It is only after a set of relations has been discovered and abstracted that we can have the kind of scientific knowledge which enables us to make successful predictions.

What are some of the major types of relations?

Among the thousands of relations that could be abstracted, certain ones stand out because of their importance as basic in our philosophical thinking. We shall here mention a number of these, indicating their general character and some of the interesting implications, especially where these have received notable consideration by famous philosophers. We shall also mention typical linguistic and logical modes of treating some of these relations.

Similarity and Difference. The relations *similar to* and *different from* are certainly as basic as any. Without similarity, for example, there could be no classes or classifications; there could be no generalization and no scientific knowledge. For example, a physician called upon to diagnose an illness must first decide what illness it is with which he is dealing. To do this, he must observe all discernible symptoms and seek to fit these into the pattern of some one of the recognized and known diseases. It is only by noticing the similarities and differences between various sets of symptoms that he can ever arrive at this knowledge, a knowledge which we hope is prerequisite to his making an appropriate prescription.

Language itself would be almost useless if all the grouping or class terms were eliminated and each particular object or event had to receive its own "proper" name. It is small wonder, then, that our traditional language-based logic should have taken the class relationship as its primary relational form.

While similarity and difference are closely related relations, they should be regarded as capable of being independently examined. Thus, one may inquire after the similarities between two situations without inquiring about the differences, or one may inquire after the differences without invoking the similarities. Thus it is necessary that questions which seek an elucidation of both relations should begin with the words "compare" (mention the similarities) and "contrast" (mention the differences). Of course, we normally assume that the greater the number of similarities between two situations the fewer the differences, and vice versa. If so, the relation of similarity and the relation of difference would themselves be related to each other by the relation of inverse variation. Since we are confronted here with a case of inverse variation, let us see what happens at the extremes. The term "identity" may be used for the extreme condition of similarity in which all difference has been excluded. But if this is done, then the characteristic of twoness, which implies some separateness or difference, must be eliminated. Hence, in this extreme sense no *two* things can be identical. Complete identity pertains only between a thing and itself. For example, two peas in a pod may look just alike in every respect, but to be *two* peas they must at least occupy different spaces and in this respect, not all difference has been eliminated. So two peas in a pod cannot be identical. (Of course, we often use the term "identical" more loosely than this, as when we speak of identical twins.) Complete and total difference is hard to conceive; for if we think of two things as different in all respects, there is at least one respect in which they are still alike: that is, that we are thinking of them both. Now if we eliminate this similarity, then we are no longer able to notice any difference, since we can no longer think about the two items.

To generalize, any relation will involve some degree of similarity and some degree of difference between its relata.

Opposites. When similarity and difference are taken together, we have the relation of *opposition,* which was discussed in connection with kind and degree (Chapter VI). When some quality (such as temperature) varies continuously from one extreme to another (i.e., hot to cold), we have an example of polar opposites or *polarity.* Here the opposition lies in the contrast of the two extreme conditions, but the pole or axis along which the variation occurs is regarded as a single kind of quality (e.g., temperature). So in a polar relationship there is both difference (the difference of the extremes, as hot *vs.* cold) and also similarity (the sameness of the underlying quality, such as temperature).

Polar opposition allows for continuous variation from one extreme to the other. Some opposites, however, do not vary in this way. Odd and even numbers, for example, offer a type of opposite without any variation from one to the other, at least in the realm of natural numbers. A natural number, other than zero, is either odd or it is even. There is no continuous variation from the one to the other, as there was with hot and cold. One number is not more or less odd than another. However, there is still something similar and something different in this case. The similarity lies in the fact that both opposites belong to the same class—the class of natural numbers in our example. The difference, of course, is that one kind (the odd) cannot be divided by two without a remainder, whereas the other (the even) can.

Philosophers have made use of the concept of opposition from the very earliest period of Greek thought. Anaximander (6th century B.C.) is reported to have conceived the universe as composed of a hot substance and a cold substance which contend with each other for dominance, and are periodically successful (hot in summer, cold in winter). The idea of opposites was investigated by Aristotle, who contrasted contrary opposites with contradictory opposites. Contrary opposites admit a third alternative or a middle ground between the extremes (e.g., the warm-cool range between the extremes of hot and cold). Contradictory opposites, on the other hand, do not admit an alternative, so that as with odd and even a middle is excluded.* The concern with opposites continues through a number of more sophisticated forms in Western philosophy, reaching a position of basic importance in German thought of the nineteenth century, especially in the dialectic of Hegel (1770-1831) where each of a considerable array of opposites constitutes an incomplete moment of thought and of reality, needing its opposite to become part of a more concrete and inclusive whole.

Part and Whole. It is very difficult to think at all without thinking in terms of part and whole. Very early we learn about parts and wholes, as when mother says to little Johnny: "What's the matter? Can't you finish all the food on your plate?" And Johnny replies: "I can't eat it all, just a part of it." Normally, the notion of part suggests something integrally or organically related to the whole, as a leg to a table or a nose to a face. Of course, the idea is extended beyond this organic type of a relation. Thus, the food on one's plate is not really integrally or organically related to the rest of the food (unless one is eating a chicken or a fish). So, looser aggregates are also thought of as having subportions. Thus, the idea of a class (e.g., all dogs), which as we noted emerges from a recognition of similarities, can be considered as divisible into parts (e.g., beagles, boxers, collies, etc.). But there is quite a difference between an *organic whole,* such as a whole chicken, and an *aggregate* or *class whole,* such as the whole class of dogs. The organic whole is not composed of a number of similar units (a chicken is not made of a lot of little chickens), whereas a class is composed in this way. So we must remember to distinguish between (1) the organic part-whole relation and (2) the aggregate or class part-whole relation, noting that this latter relation may also be thought of as the relation of species to genus or subclass to class-as-a-whole.†

Parts, we saw, constitute one basic variety of abstractables (Chap-

---

* See especially Aristotle's *Metaphysics,* Bk. X (Iota) , Ch. 7. Also *De Interp.,* Ch. 7 and *Topics,* Bk. V, Ch. 6. It is important to note that Aristotle's principle of excluded middle applies only to contradictory opposites and not to the contrary kind.

† A convenient way to test this distinction is to ask if the part is a *kind of* the whole (e.g., Is a cat a kind of animal?) . If the answer is Yes, then the relation is likely to be a class relation, not an organic, part-whole relation.

ter V). Any part of an object can be attended to or considered purely by itself. Now we are saying that the part-whole relation, just as a relation, can also be abstracted. How is this possible? It comes about in this way. First, we notice or abstract a part (e.g., a branch from a tree), then we notice that this part is related to the whole (e.g., the branch is really just a part of the tree). Now we are in a position to concentrate on this relationship and abstract it (e.g., we can abstract the *relation* of the branch to the tree as a whole, or the *relation* of the entire tree to one of its branches). In other words, this relationship of part-whole or whole-part is itself something upon which we can focus attention.

Our language provides us with no special technique for indicating part-whole relations. There are the words *part* and *portion* and the prefix *sub-* which we can use. The preposition *of* can indicate part as well as possession. *Part, portion,* and *of* are ambiguous in being able to refer to either the organic or the class part-whole relation. For example, we can speak of a dog as "one *of* the dogs" (membership in a class), and we can also speak of a branch as a "branch *of* a tree" (organic relation). The prefix *sub-,* on the other hand, normally indicates only a subclass or subtype (class relationship), thus being unambiguous when used to refer to a part-whole relation. Also, the figure of speech called *synecdoche* (Chapter IV), which uses a part to refer to a whole, or a whole to refer to a part, is unambiguous because it always indicates an organic part-whole relation.

Substance and Attribute. We have just observed that not only is a part abstractable from a whole, but that the relation of part-to-whole and whole-to-part may itself be abstracted. Similarly, not only can we abstract simple qualities from objects or events, but we can also abstract the relation of object-to-quality or quality-to-object. For example, a brand mark burnt into the hide of a steer becomes a quality of the steer. We can, of course, simply abstract the brand mark by focusing attention upon this mark and ignoring the steer. But we could also abstract the relation between the brand mark and the steer by focusing upon just this relationship. In general, the concept of an object (such as a steer) qualified in certain ways (as by a brand mark) presents the typical model of the substance-quality or substance-attribute relation.

Human beings probably arrived at the idea of substance-attribute relation from observing qualitative changes in things that otherwise remain much the same. For example, a man as he grows old becomes gray-haired. Yet we recognize him and regard him as the same person. Here we see one of his attributes (color of hair) changing, while his general configuration remains. We naturally come to think of the more transient quality (color of hair) as an attribute of some underlying substance (the real man), and we conclude that qualities (attributes) require substances in which they inhere. Our language has confirmed this notion through the attributive type of sentence (Chapter II) and the customary way of looking at the adjective-noun relationship. For example, when we assert "the cat is black" we are seeming to imply that one thing (the cat) as subject of the sentence is a substance that is qualified by a predicate attribute (black). Or if we say "black cat," the qualifying word (black) is taken as expressing some attribute of the underlying substance (cat).

Aristotle was the philosopher who was primarily responsible for taking the substance-attribute relation as a keystone to his thinking. But the implications which he drew led to certain difficulties, especially that of describing the substance. It turns out that whatever one says about a substance simply names one or more of its attributes, and the substance itself escapes description. For example, is the substance of a wooden chair the wood of which it is constructed? No, for the wood itself is describable and knowable only as a set of attributes such as its hardness or the patterns of the grain. But if we view the wood under a microscope, would this not give us a view of the substance? No more than before, for the cellular structure is still a set of attributes. But attributes of what? If all observable characteristics are to be taken as attributes, then clearly the "substance" is beyond observation.

As we have seen, it was Hume, with his rigorous effort to limit knowledge to that which is observable, who disposed of substance as some sort of necessary reality which underlies all attributes. The notion of quality or attribute can then no longer imply "quality of something" in the old sense; for the "something" becomes only an habitually associated cluster of qualities (Chapter VI). And yet, despite Hume, the need for conceiving of some kind of enduring reality in which qualities or attributes inhere and which keeps its underlying identity in spite of the changes of its qualities remains a dominant concept for us. Perhaps this concept illustrates one way in which a particular linguistic formula has perniciously dominated our thinking. But then again, it may be that the folk intuitions which discovered this way of thinking, primitive though they may be, were based upon an important insight.*

Possessor and Possessed. The notion of possession must be as old as human thinking, for many animals demonstrate a strong sense of possession, as when a dog growls at another dog attempting to steal a bone. Certainly, the concept of ownership with all its developments and limitations affords one fascinating key to the whole course of man's social and political history, including, as it does, the basis for ideas of defense and aggression.

The indicators of possession in languages are among the most universal forms, and we may presume, most primitive. In English, for example, the possessive may be indicated by the preposition *of* or by the genitive ending *-'s.* The possessive pronominal forms, *my, mine, his, her, hers,* etc., are also means of indicating ownership; and many common verbs, especially *to have,* can indicate possession.

Logically, it is interesting to note how the idea of property was carried over from the more usual kind of ownership to the possession of attributes by substances. Of course, this represents a rather large transfer of meaning, for there is quite a difference between my possessing a house and the house's possessing a roof or a coat of plaster. Thus, "I have a house" and "The house has a roof" hardly indicate a similar meaning of "have." And yet this mode of speaking is so common as to show a strong sense of analogy between these two situations. Somehow people must have felt that houses' having roofs is something like a person's possessing a house. Nevertheless, for the sake of clarity, we must not allow this common usage to blind us to the danger in this analogy, for, as we have just seen, the substance-attribute relation is a special one with its own distinctive problems.

---

* "All modern philosophy hinges around the difficulty of describing the world in terms of subject and predicate, substance and quality, particular and universal"—Whitehead, *Process and Reality,* p. 78.

Self and Other (or Subject and Object). The relation of oneself as *subject* to anything else as *object* is another basic relation which has played a major role in philosophical thought. In what sort of experience does one encounter this notion? It must emerge with the growing self-consciousness experienced by children, especially when they come to the ages of six or seven. Certainly, the moment a child becomes aware of himself as a special and unique existent, he is also forced to recognize that he is in some way distinct from his environment. On the one hand, there is oneself. On the other hand, there are all the other things and people around one. For most of us, once we are aware of this distinction and have adjusted our thoughts to the fact that we are separate selves set over against other persons and other things, the matter is dropped. We do develop some deep-seated attitudes toward our environment, which may be healthy or may be psychotic, but this is a matter for the psychologist to study.

Philosophers, however, have found much of interest in the insights suggested by the self-other or subject-object relation. In fact, the striking mark of Western philosophy since the time of Descartes has been the struggle to find some solution to the problem of the *self as knower* in his relation to the environment or universe as *object of knowledge.* Remember, for example, the argument of Berkeley, mentioned in Chapter VI, to the effect that all perception, and hence all knowledge, must originate within the self. The environment was for Berkeley an aspect of one's personal perceptions; and without Berkeley's recourse to a Divine Perceiver, one would be a prisoner within his own perceptions. This particular view (without Berkeley's recourse to God) is known as *solipsism* (alone with oneself); and for gregarious human beings, including human philosophers, it is distinctly unpleasant. All manner of reasonings have been adduced for justifying knowledge of the nonself or "other."

Especially important in this connection is the philosophy that developed in Germany after Kant, known traditionally as German Idealism. The emphasis in this philosophy, especially as given to it by Fichte (1762-1814), was to start from the realization that the self (Ego) is a more fundamental reality than the object or other, since the self as knower knows both the object and subject, whereas the object, as mere object, does not. But this position does not lead to solipsism, for the private or personal "self" needs a larger and more encompassing Self (a Transcendental Ego) as the larger source and field for its intellectual and striving activities. This whole philosophical avenue led in many directions—to Schopenhauer's Will as one kind of transcendental reality, and to Hegel's Dialectical Process as another kind in which the ultimate rational process of the universe is being fulfilled in human intelligence as we synthesize more and more concretely all polar opposites (including even the Mind-Nature or subject-object polarity).

The terms "self" and "other" are less ambiguous than "subject" and "object." To help us avoid misusing "subject" and "object" we might well spend a moment on their etymology. "Subject" is derived from a Latin word meaning "that which has been brought underneath" or "that which lies underneath" and was early used of conquered or subjugated individuals. Later it served as another word for substance, in the Aristotelian sense. In neither of these senses, however, does "subject" refer necessarily to oneself, for this meaning comes later.

"Object," likewise, started with a narrow meaning, namely, that which is opposed to one, especially an enemy or obstacle. Eventually it was broadened to include anything which is set apart or over against something else, as distinguishable from it. It is only rather recently that the term "object" has come to refer to that which is not oneself. We see this last meaning best, no doubt, in the forms "subjective" or "objective," which are now taken quite generally to mean that which has to do with the self and that which has to do with what is outside or other than the self. "Objective," however, has taken on another meaning based upon criteria set up independently of any personal or merely subjective ground.

For modern philosophy the subject-object relation is very much a live issue. There are still objective realists who regard things as capable of existing independent of being perceived or known. In this case one person's subjective self may be another's objective reality. Others, somewhat in the tradition of Berkeley, still emphasize the ultimate subjectivity of consciousness and all human reality. And still others recommend that we disregard the subject-object relation as being unproductive of human knowledge.

Probably some of our trouble stems from our linguistic forms. The actor in an action sentence, or the possessor of attributes in the attributive sentence, is called *subject,* whereas the recipient of an action after a transitive verb, or any noun after a preposition, is called an *object;* and these, we saw, are old meanings of these terms. The self-other distinction, on the other hand, is better illustrated by our pronouns, which we distinguish into first person (subjective), and second or third person (objective).

Cause and Effect. The relation of cause and effect centers upon the notion of a transference of force or influence from one object, event, or situation to another. For example, a tire blows out and the car goes into a ditch. Here we seem to observe a direct line of influence from the blowout to the swerve into the ditch. The blowout, we would say, was the cause of the car's going into the ditch.

But we can extend the cause-effect relation from such direct and immediate sequences of events to include preexisting conditions. For example, we might say that the cause of the accident was the slippery road. Here the preexisting condition of the road is blamed as cause, rather than some particular triggering event. Yet the slippery road by itself is not enough to produce an accident. It also takes a person driving a car in such a way as to skid. So we sometimes say that a slippery road is a *condition,* and the movement of the steering wheel that brought about the skid would be the *cause.* Similarly, a dry forest is a condition for a forest fire—in fact it is almost a necessary condition. But the burning match or wind-blown campfire or bolt of lightning would be the triggering cause. In general, we find that we need both the *necessary conditions* (e.g., a slippery road, dry forest) and the *triggering causes* (e.g., a turn of the steering wheel or a carelessly discarded cigarette) to account for the total cause of some effect. A *sufficient cause* would include the *necessary conditions* and the *triggering cause.*

We can even extend the notion of condition to include negative or preventive conditions. A wet forest might be said to be part of the cause of the nonoccurrence of a forest fire. In such cases, however, it would be better to speak of inhibiting factors rather than negative causes. Are inhibiting factors always preexisting conditions, or may they too trigger events? There is no reason why they cannot be the latter, as when one turns on a light regulated by two switches only to have someone else turn the other switch at the same moment. Then, the light does not go on because of the triggering inhibiting factor of the other person's turning the other switch.

How do we observe the cause-effect relation? When we observe two objects colliding we do not see any force conveyed from one to the other. So the feeling or sense of force can only be in ourselves or upon ourselves. For example, if I am driving a car when the tires blows out, I feel the pull on the steering wheel, so that in this case there is a direct feeling of force exerted upon me from the outside. Conversely, if I decide to move my desk to a different position, I can feel the force in the form of effort exerted by me to push the desk. Here I am aware of this feeling of effort followed by a moving of the desk. But when it comes to two observed objects, such as one billiard ball hitting another, then I can only imagine the presence of force. This I do probably by analogy with my own sensations of push and pull.

It was the philosopher Hume again who astutely pointed out that all we actually observe is mere sequence of similar occurrences from which we imagine the existence of a necessary or inevitable connection between causes and effects. We come to believe that our knowledge of causal connection is based on something more than observing similar sequences of events, and that this extra something is a force or power to produce the particular result that we observe; but when we attempt to track down our experience of this power it turns out to be nothing more than bare experience of repeated sequences. For example, when we observe that imbibing alcoholic beverages habitually leads to intoxication, we imagine a necessary connection between the alcohol and the state of drunkenness. But all we actually experience is the repeated sequence of a certain kind of drink followed by a certain kind of feeling. Even where I feel exertion, as in pushing my desk, I am only witnessing the sensation of exertion followed by the changing position of the desk. The fact that the latter continues only so long as the former continues and that they stop together does not add anything to the content of my awareness beyond a correlation of the two sensations. So, the causal relation, according to Hume, proves to be nothing more than an awareness that one event or object is "precedent and contiguous to another, where all the objects resembling the former are placed in like relations of precedency and contiguity to those objects that resemble the latter."* All we observe are the relations of sequence (precedency) and contiguity (proximity in time and space) and resemblance (similarity) of recurrences. From these experiences we come to imagine a necessary efficacy or force that connects cause to effect.

In spite of Hume, however, the conviction persists that there are genuine causal forces and connections. It does seem that explanations of phenomena in terms of such causal connections have practical value in our understandings of the world and the way we deal with it. This argument does not answer Hume's critique of the idea, for it cannot prove that we require more than his habitual associations of event sequences even to explain the whole of what constitutes scientific knowledge. But it does come closer to our ordinary understanding. Philosophers since Hume have given evidence of the strength of this conviction by attempting to give other justifications for a stronger idea of causality which would be based on more careful analyses.†

There is another difficulty with the cause-effect idea which ought to be mentioned. Among events there are only rather artificial and arbitrary points of division. If an automobile hits a light post and knocks it over, who is to say at what point in this sequence one event comes to an end and another commences? Perhaps we could regard it as one continuous event involving both movement of the car and subsequent movement of the light pole. However, there is a moment of contact, we must assume, when the car first touches the pole; and if we wish we can divide the two events at this point, arbitrary though it may be. The important thing is that we can separate events into classes or kinds, the same as we do objects; so that we can predict that one class of events (e.g., cars running into poles) will tend to produce or be followed by another class of events (e.g., poles being knocked over). Even Hume, in assuming contiguity of successive events, apparently accepted the notion of natural divisions between causes and effects. Whitehead, on the other hand, has done the most in seeking to develop a theory that would take into account both minimal events (actual occa-

---

* *A Treatise of Human Nature*, Bk. I, Pt. III, Section 14.
† Especially Immanuel Kant, *Critique of Pure Reason*, and A. N. Whitehead, *Process and Reality*.

sions) and larger more inclusive events which are "inter-related in some determinate fashion."*

What, then, when we think we observe a cause-effect relation, do we really notice? First, we notice a change in something (e.g., an unburning forest to a burning forest). Second, we look for some triggering event which will seem to explain this change (e.g., a match or spark in the forest). Sometimes we do not find the triggering event, in which case we have an effect (we think) but no known cause. Habits of associated sequences of events lead us to look for the cause in rather well-defined areas. However, when we are confronted by new phenomena, the search for causes may lead to wild-goose chases and ridiculous assumptions. The hunt for possible and likely causes is always with us, it constitutes the basic quest of what we call science.

The cause-effect relation, we may notice, has interesting linguistic and logical associations. In our language the sentence type called "action type" seems to imply a cause-effect relation in which the doer or agent is the cause and his action is the effect. Thus when we say, "I sing," or "the thunder pealed," there may be a suggestion that I am the cause of the singing, and the thunder is the cause of the pealing.

In logic the hypothetical if-then type of judgment, which is based on the relation of premise to inferred conclusion, or *ground* to *consequent,* as it is sometimes called, has a strong similarity to the notion of cause to effect. It was Kant who believed our very ability to make perceptions intelligible presupposes a kind of objective validity for our logical schemes, including this one, so that the necessity inherent in the logical relation must underlie ("a priori," as he says) our mode of seeing events arranged in cause-effect sequences. These necessary forms of thought must apply to experience, he insists, "but with a completely reversed mode of connection which never occurred to Hume—they do not derive from experience, but experience derives from them."†

In this chapter we have been discussing cause and effect *as a*

* *Process and Reality,* p. 113.

† *Prolegomena to Any Future Metaphysics,* Pt. II, Section 30. Revised translation by Lewis W. Beck, Library of Liberal Arts, No. 27. Or see Kant's *Critique of Pure Reason,* "The Analytic of Concepts," Ch. I. As against both Hume and Kant, Whitehead has asserted his belief in the possibility of perceiving what he calls "causal efficacy." See his *Symbolism,* p. 39, or *Process and Reality,* p. 256.

relation. But since it is a relation between events and implies changes, we shall need to consider cause and effect again under the heading of Function in Chapter VIII, for by *function* we shall mean abstractable aspects which involve change or action.

Spatial Relations. Spatial relations are relations in space—higher, lower, near, far, to the right, to the left, etc. The human mind has a tendency to symbolize all other relations in terms of spatial relations so far as possible. The spatial framework of human experience, it seems, affords the simplest and most direct set of relations that can be easily comprehended by way of visual imagery; and man's key to understanding seems to rely more on visual imagery than upon any other kind. We notice this fact readily when we consider the quantities of figures, graphs, diagrams, and the like, which we use in analyzing all types of problems. The simplest spatial notion is that of *distance* between two separate objects, such as distance or space between two trees. When we abstract the distance between two objects it is customary to conceive this as a line and to imagine lines wherever there are spatial relationships. In this way geometry develops from the study of the relationships between spatial abstractions, for geometry is nothing more nor less than the logic of spatial relationships. In our language, spatial relations are normally indicated by a variety of prepositions—on, under, near, around, etc.—and such prepositional phrases as "far from," "to the right of," "in the center of," "perpendicular to."

Temporal Relations. The relations in the realm of time are conceived largely by analogy with those of space. However, one's basic awareness of time grows out of a sense of passage of events, not out of an awareness of distance. Thus time is derived more from an inner feeling and a sense of sequence than from any external and all-together-given appearance of things. Kant sought to make the number system with its serial sequence the basic form of the time sense, just as geometry is the basic form of the space sense. This might be a satisfactory association if the number system were primarily ordinal (first, second, third, fourth, etc.), for in the ordinal series the suggestion of sequence is strong. But the simpler cardinal numbers may apply to whole groups as given-all-at-once;

so it would seem that the number system by itself is too broad to be associated only with the time sense.

Since time is characteristically conceived on the image of spatial diagrams, the flow of time is thought of as a continuum analogous to spatial dimensions. Events are then "located" in this continuum in relation to one another. When events are conceived as having durations of their own, more complex relations develop dealing with the various overlappings of events. In recent years the philosopher Bergson (1859-1941) has deplored this tendency to spatialize time, for he regarded the time sense as penetrating more deeply into the nature of reality than does the space sense.

In language, time is indicated not only by prepositions, prepositional phrases, and conjunctions—before, after, earlier than, later than, etc.—but more particularly by the tense structure of the verbs. Since we shall discuss the verb at some length in the next chapter, we shall leave the matter of verb structure until then.

Quantitative Relations. Quantities are primarily relations. We may have a rough all-at-a-glance impression of an amount—a qualitative impression of quantity. However, the moment we specify the *number* of a measurement or of a group, we are presupposing at least two things—the numerical quantifier and the thing or things quantified—which are related. This relational character is present both in the case of *measurement* and in the case of *enumeration*. Let us consider how this is so.

(1) Measurements are appropriate to situations which involve some gradual increase or decrease along a continuum, and where some unit of measure is available. For example, a simple distance can be measured by applying some unit of spatial measure—an inch, a foot, a yard, a meter, a mile—end to end throughout the distance, until one discovers how many of the units are contained in the length being measured. The resulting number is a relationship or *ratio* between two things—the *length being measured* and the *unit of measure*. This fact clearly shows the relational character of measurement.

Measurements also require that the quality being measured and the unit of measure be of the same kind (e.g., both lengths) or be correlated in some way. Thus a thermometer which has a spatial scale measures directly the amount of expansion or contraction of a liquid in a tube. Only indirectly and because of an assumed correlation can the thermometer measure temperature. Similarly, the hands on the clock indicate distance traversed by their tips, and this is a spatial measure. Only indirectly do they measure time; and then only if time is assumed to be a constant durational process, and the hands are assumed to be moving at a constant rate.

(2) Enumeration is simple counting of the individuals in a group where the individual units are readily distinguishable from one another. In this case there is no arbitrarily selected unit of measurement, so the relational aspect is not so apparent. However, if we consider the fact that in order to count the number of units (e.g., rugs in a house) one must first decide what is to be a proper member of the group to be counted (e.g., shall we include bath mats with the rugs?), we realize that there is still a decision to be made with regard to the units counted. Moreover, any class of discrete (individually separate) entities—rugs in a house, people in the world, etc.—has a total number which may be determined by enumerating the members of the class (provided that we are not imagining an infinite class). Now the number of these members stands in a relation (ratio) to any individual member, so that we find a relation in enumerating just as much as in measuring. For example, what do I mean by "three books"? I mean that the group or class of three books has a three-to-one relation (ratio) to any one of the books. It is for this reason that any rational number can be written as a ratio or fraction in order to show its relational character. Thus, 5 could be written 5/1, or 756 could be written 756/1, etc.

Quantitative relationships become more complicated when we consider their many inner relational possibilities. For example, if we divide a unit into four equal parts, each part is $\frac{1}{4}$ of the whole; if three of these fourths are now counted out, we will have $\frac{3}{4}$ of the original unit; etc. In this way, we see that we arrive at fractional relations by division, and the fractional units can be further related by addition, multiplication, subtraction, and division, and we soon encounter the complexities which beset simple arithmetic.

Mathematical and logical relations are sometimes considered a special kind of relation. However, what we have here said of quantity may well be generalized as a pattern for all such relations.

It is our thesis that arithmetical, geometrical, and classificational relationships can be abstracted from empirical sources; and then they can be imaginatively refined and explored to create the vast array of mathematical and logical systems already elaborated by human ingenuity (see Chapter IX). We must remember, however, that Platonists will object to this thesis on the ground that, according to them, the pure forms are not refined out of experience, but must in some sense come to our awareness first, before we can even recognize them in experience.

Biological and Social Relations. The relations of father to offspring, man to man, citizen to state, employer to employee, etc., constitute many complex sets of possible relationships based on genetic or social connections. The sense of belonging to a group as a member of it is no doubt a product of genetic and social relations much more strongly than it is of the property idea. So here again we find the group or class idea reinforced as a fundamental key to our analysis and understanding of our world.

The foregoing eleven varieties of relations are certainly not exhaustive, even of a list of the major relations discoverable in experience. For example, attitudes of human beings toward each other such as love, hate, sense of superiority or inferiority, and the like, constitute a whole set of possible *emotional relations* which might have been mentioned. In certain religious views man's relation to God is the central idea, so that we might have included *spiritual* or *theological relations.* But the reader is quite at liberty to formulate his own set of basic relations if he like. Suffice it to say that the ones we have discussed here in some detail have demonstrated their importance by the dominant roles they have played in philosophical thinking.

How are these relations expressed in language?

Many of the foregoing relations have interesting linguistic modes of expression. Not only do we have words for *similarity* ranging from "analogy" and "resemblance" to "identity," but the very existence of class names in a language, as we saw in Chapter IV, normally presupposes some degree of abstractable similarity.

Possession can be expressed in languages in many ways, from possessive adjectives and pronouns (e.g., my, mine) to verbs of be-longing (e.g., to have, to own, to acquire). Possession, as it turns out, may well be the primitive idea underlying such other relations as attribution and part-whole.

The notion of *attribution* in the substance-attribute relation is often assimilated to the relation of possession. Thus, an attribute, like the green color of the book cover, may be thought of as an aspect or quality possessed by the book, as shown by the fact that we often use the word "property" for "aspect." This way of con-ceiving attribution suggests that the possessed attribute needs a possessor, which may account for the notion that every attribute needs a "substance" as the possessor. This notion, we remember, appeared unfounded to Hume, who developed the aspect-cluster notion of an object to replace the old idea of the substance which was assumed to underlie attributes, though itself never visible.

The *part-whole* or *partitive* relation can be expressed in several ways. In expressing the *organic* part-whole relation, the idea of possession crops up again through the use of such possessives as *my* head, *his* leg, the leaf *of* the tree, etc. The *class* part-whole idea, on the other hand, is more often indicated by words like *some, all, several,* etc. Even these are sometimes assimilated to the notion of possession, as in the case of Chinese, where "some" (*yéu-də*) is literally "have-belonging."*

Causation is implicit in every functional doer-action type of sentence (see p. 165) in which there is the suggestion of an agent that causes the action, or is in some degree responsible for the ac-tion. Some languages have developed quite elaborate ways of in-dicating primary and secondary causal agents.

The *self-other* relation is normally shown by means of the pro-nominal system in a language. First, second, and third person pronouns are present in some form in most languages. And these indicate an awareness of the difference between oneself, the person or persons to whom one is talking, and other or "third person" individuals. Such a minimal set of linguistic distinctions does not, of course, imply any great level of sophistication in the direction of philosophical reflection concerning the self and the meaning of self-awareness.

Spatial and *temporal* relations can be indicated in language

* See Morris Swadesh, *Conversational Chinese for Beginners,* p. 139.

through the use of interrogative adverbs (e.g., where? how far? when?), or by means of prepositions (e.g., in, under, on, near, beside, before, after), or through conjunctions (e.g., where, when). Most verbal systems include some time indicators, such as one finds in temporal aspect distinctions (e.g., progressive, initiative, completive, reiterative), and in tense distinctions (e.g., past, present, future).

The idea of *quantity* is of course expressed in the number system of a language. Rough estimates of quantity are also shown through the use of certain adjectives (e.g., some, several, few, many).

I have omitted mention of the relation of *polarity* or polar opposites here, since it is not one that is strictly expressed through ordinary linguistic techniques. Of course, languages normally have techniques for negation, so that opposites can be indicated by denying a quality or condition (e.g., hot–not hot, mindful–unmindful, restful–restless, respective–irrespective, symmetrical–asymmetrical, and so on), but this is not the same as indicating a contrary polar opposite (e.g., hot–cold, wet–dry). To be sure, since the advent of dictionaries, lists of antonyms, or words with polar opposite meanings, are shown, but this is not the same as having indicators of this relation built into the language itself.

How can we further analyze and classify relations?

Relations, as already indicated, can be separated into *inner* and *outer*. When once an object or event is regarded as a unit apart from other objects or events, we may readily distinguish certain relationships as internal to the object (such as the angle between the back and the seat of a chair) and others as external (such as height of the chair compared to that of a bureau). The *position* of an object, for example, is due to its external relations in some frame of reference (such as the position of a chair in a room relative to a bureau).

Relations may also be classed according to the number of terms involved as relata. A relation of two terms is called *dyadic,* one of three terms is *triadic,* and so on. It is questionable whether there can be a relation with only one term (called *monadic*), though it is customary nowadays to extend the meaning of "relation" to include such an oddity. Reflexive relations especially may be considered monadic relations if we insist on the identity of a thing with itself (see the preceding discussion of identity and the following discussion of reflexive relations).

A more significant way of classifying relations, at least from the point of view of logical implications, is the following: (1) reflexive, irreflexive, or nonreflexive, where one relatum is involved though taken twice; (2) symmetrical, asymmetrical, or nonsymmetrical, where two relata are involved; and (3) transitive, intransitive, or nontransitive, where three or more relata are involved.

(1) If a relation always holds between a term and itself *(aRa)*, it is REFLEXIVE (e.g., the relation *identical with*). If it can never hold in this way, it is IRREFLEXIVE (e.g., *father of*). If it may sometimes hold and sometimes not, it is called NONREFLEXIVE (e.g., *mover of*).*

(2) Similarly, if a relation holds between two terms *(aRb)* and also necessarily between the same two terms reversed *(bRa)*, then it is called SYMMETRICAL (e.g., *equal to*). But any relation whose terms can never be reversed is ASYMMETRICAL (e.g., *father of*). If a relation may sometimes hold when reversed and sometimes not, it is NONSYMMETRICAL (e.g., *brother of*).

(3) Any relation which, if it holds between two terms *(aRb)* and also holds between the second term and a third term *(bRc)*, will always hold between the first and third terms *(aRc)* is said to

---

* The prefix *non-* may be misleading. It means simply that the classificational category is indeterminable, because it may sometimes be one way and sometimes the other. In fact, it would be clearer to speak of *plus, minus,* and *plus-or-minus* categories (e.g., "plus reflexivity," "minus reflexivity," or "plus-or-minus reflexivity"). We should also note that there are two distinguishable reasons why a relation can be considered to be nonreflexive, nonsymmetrical, or nontransitive (i.e., to have plus-or-minus reflexivity, plus-or-minus symmetry, or plus-or-minus transitivity). The first reason is that the situation itself may permit two conditions (e.g., living organisms may move themselves or may be moved by an external agent, so *mover of* is a nonreflexive relation). The second reason is that the term used to name the relation may be ambiguous (e.g., *brother of* is nonsymmetrical, since it is only symmetrical when both persons are male). However, one might argue that all the *non* (plus-or-minus) situations are due ultimately to ambiguity; for if languages were sufficiently explicit, the names of relations would refer to only one possibility. Thus, if a different term were used to specify *mover of* when referring to self-motivation as against external action on, then the term used for the relation would be clearly reflexive or irreflexive. And if our language had a different word for *brother of a brother* and *brother of a sister*, then this relation would be either symmetrical or asymmetrical.

be TRANSITIVE (e.g., *east of:* if *a* is east of *b* and *b* is east of *c*, then *a* must be east of *c*). If this condition is never true of a given relation, then that relation is INTRANSITIVE (e.g., *father of:* if *a* is father of *b*, and *b* is father of *c*, can *a* ever be father of *c?* No. He would be the grandfather). If a relation may sometimes hold in this way and sometimes not, it is called NONTRANSITIVE (e.g., *friend of:* if *a* is the friend of *b* and *b* is the friend of *c*, must *a* be the friend of *c* or can he never be a friend of *c*, or is it possible that he might or might not be the friend of *c?* Since the last case seems most appropriate, this relation is called nontransitive).

On the basis of the above classification, it will be seen that every relation can be analyzed with regard to its *reflexivity* (i.e., reflexive, irreflexive, or nonreflexive), its *symmetry* (i.e., symmetrical, asymmetrical, or nonsymmetrical), and its *transitivity* (i.e, transitive, intransitive, or nontransitive). To test a relation for reflexivity try it out with one relatum. To test it for symmetry try two relata. To test for transitivity try three relata. Thus, *father of,* when tested in this way, turns out to be irreflexive, asymmetrical, and intransitive; *equal to* is reflexive, symmetrical, and transitive; *higher than* is irreflexive, asymmetrical, and transitive; and *brother of* is irreflexive, nonsymmetrical, and transitive.

Knowledge of *reflexivity* is useful when we wish to study the ways in which something can be related to itself or can affect itself.

More useful, however, is a knowledge of *symmetry*. For example, it is necessary in traditional logical analysis to know whether a proposition (sentence) is capable of being converted (i.e., having the order of its subject and predicate terms reversed). If it is true that *all men are animals* would it follow that *all animals are men?* No, for the relation of including all of something in a larger class is not symmetrical. However, the proposition "Line *a* is perpendicular to line *b*" does imply "Line *b* is perpendicular to line *a*" because in this case the relation is symmetrical.

Knowledge of symmetry may also be applied to grammatical constructions, as in aiding us to distinguish between "coordinate" and "subordinate" elements in a sentence. Prepositions and conjunctions, as has been pointed out, are those parts of speech which are especially concerned with expressing relations. Prepositions relate single nouns or nominal phrases to other nouns or to the rest of the sentence (e.g., The seed is *in* the ground). Conjunctions, on the other hand, normally* relate sentences (called "clauses") to each other. Such conjunctions as *when, since, that, though, for, as,* and such conjunctive (i.e., relative) pronouns as *who, which, that,* introduce subordinate clauses (sentences) which are related in some way to the main clause. Now, from a logical point of view, "subordinate" clauses should be nonreversible with their main clauses, and the relation indicated by the subordinating conjunction should therefore be asymmetrical. Usually this is the case. For example, the sentence "We gave ground *when* the enemy attacked," contains two clauses: (1) We gave ground, and (2) the enemy attacked. If the relation expressed by *when* is genuinely asymmetrical, the sentence as given would not imply the reversed form: "The enemy attacked *when* we gave ground." And this indeed appears to be the case. Conversely, a typical coordinating conjunction (e.g., and) should be symmetrical. "Tom is fast *and* George is slow" should imply "George is slow *and* Tom is fast." However, traditionally subordinating conjunctions (e.g., as) are sometimes symmetrical, as in the sentence "The plane was preparing to land *as* it began to snow," where *as* means "during the same time that."

Subordination in its usual grammatical interpretation refers principally to inability to stand alone, rather than simply to a-symmetry. For example, the conjunctive pronoun *who* introduces a clause which cannot stand alone because the pronoun can only be used to refer back to an antecedent which has already been expressed in the main part of the sentence. We can test the symmetry of conjunctive pronouns only by replacing the pronoun with its antecedent when we reverse the order of our sentence (e.g., "The man is tall *who* came to see us" would be reversed as "The man came to see us *who* is tall," which requires moving the antecedent *man* into the other clause). Nevertheless, the grammatical condition of standing alone is not so easy to determine as the logical condition of symmetry; and our understanding of grammar might benefit from the application of the condition of symmetry to conjunctive relations. If we do this, we discover that coordinating con-

---

* Conjunctions *and, or, but* may be used in compound terms, however, as well as between clauses (e.g., Ike *and* Jake, Priscilla *or* Abigail, Not the horses *but* the mules, etc.). Such compound terms are sometimes assumed to be reduced clauses; but it is probably better to regard these conjunctions as simply relating terms rather than sentences.

junctions are sometimes asymmetrical, as when a time sequence is implied (e.g., "The house was finished *and* they moved in" could hardly imply "They moved in *and* the house was finished"). So we see that a logical analysis of grammatical relations can aid us in understanding the structure of our sentences and the basic character of the typically grammatical relationships.

Knowledge of transitivity is of great importance for any reasoning involving serial progressions. Transitive relations lead us on to the establishing of connections between *three or more* terms, so that a transitive relation may hold in an infinite series. For example, the number series itself can be examined in the light of the transitive relations *greater than* and *less than*. Yet the progressive relation *one more than* or *successor of*, which sets going the number sequence, is not itself a transitive relation (e.g., if b is one more than a, and c is one more than b, and d is one more than c, it does not hold that d is one more than a). It would perhaps be useful to consider PROGRESSIVITY or SERIALITY as another way of classifying relations, a progressive relation being one in which each new term is "one more something than" the preceding (e.g., one more foot long, one more number). Relations could then be judged as to whether they are progressive, unprogressive, or nonprogressive.

Returning to transitivity, we should observe that this is the essential relational trait of the traditional logical *syllogism* and of the *sorites,* or extended syllogism. Taking the class-inclusion relation of classical logic, for example, we can note the transitivity of this relation in the following:

> All students are clever *(aRb)*;
>
> All clever persons are thinkers *(bRc)*;
>
> Therefore, all students are thinkers *(aRc)*.

In this *syllogism* we observe that the a term (students) is tied to the c term (thinkers) by way of the b or middle term (clever persons). Here is the typical case of transitivity. The sorites is merely a syllogism which continues beyond three terms. For example:

> All students are clever *(aRb)*;
>
> All clever persons are thinkers *(bRc)*;
>
> All thinkers use logic *(cRd)*;
>
> All who use logic develop their structure sense *(dRe)*;

Therefore, all students develop their structure sense (*aRe*). Such series can continue as long as new terms can be found and the relation is transitive. We should also observe that other transitive relations besides that of class-inclusion are available for formulation of syllogistic reasoning. For example:

Mt. Everest is higher than Mt. McKinley (*aRb*);

Mt. McKinley is higher than Mt. Whitney (*bRc*);

Therefore, Mt. Everest is higher than Mt. Whitney (*aRc*).

Here the transitive relation *higher than* does just as well as the transitive relation *is included in*.

In summary, then, relations are abstractable connections. There are many varieties of basic and pervasive relations among which are:

(1) Similarity-difference
(2) Opposites
(3) Part-whole
(4) Substance-attribute
(5) Possessor-possessed
(6) Self-other
(7) Cause-effect
(8) Spatial
(9) Temporal
(10) Quantitative
(11) Biological, sociological, psychological

Relations can be classified with respect to whether they are:

(1) Internal or external
(2) Monadic, dyadic, triadic, etc.
(3) Reflexive, irreflexive, nonreflexive
(4) Symmetrical, asymmetrical, nonsymmetrical
(5) Transitive, intransitive, nontransitive
(6) Progressive, unprogressive, nonprogressive

SUGGESTED READINGS

Locke, *An Essay Concerning Human Understanding,* Bk. II, Chs. 25-28.
Hume, *A Treatise of Human Nature,* Bk. I, Pt. I, Section 5, and Pt. III, Sections 1-6 and 11-15.
Kant, *Prolegomena to Any Future Metaphysics,* Pt. II, Sections 28-38.
Blanshard, Brand, *Reason and Analysis,* especially Chs. X-XI.

CHAPTER VIII

Functions

What is involved in action and change?

SO FAR WE HAVE considered two types of abstraction: *quality* and *relation*. Neither quality nor relation, as here defined, implies anything dynamic or changing. But experience is not static and unchanging. The factor of movement, action, change, flux has long been recognized as of basic importance in any satisfactory interpretation of reality. As far back as Heraclitus (c. 535-475 B.C.) this factor of continuing change was singled out for special emphasis; for to Heraclitus was attributed the statement, "All things flow, nothing abides." In recent times the French philosopher Henri Bergson developed a philosophy around the notion of an ongoing creative process, basically temporal and changing in character. So, our discussion of key abstractions would be most one-sided and incomplete if we were to omit a consideration of the factor of change.

In the present chapter we are using the term *function* to stand for all types of activity, movement, and change. Functions (happenings, activities, changes, and the like) involve us in complex situations, with several elements implied, but the key meaning is always that of doing or performing or acting.

Let us look first at the simple notion of *action* or activity. By an "action" we normally mean any movement or process—kicking, running, throwing, augmenting, transferring, etc. The emphasis is upon a kind of movement or motion. However, it is difficult to conceive of action without also conceiving an *actor,* that is, something that does the acting. Where there is a kicking there must be a kicker; where there is a planetary movement there must be a planet. It was one of the cardinal points of Aristotle's philosophy that movements cannot occur without movers, that is, without something that moves. This point may appear trivial and commonplace, but it is not. Quite different consequences would follow from a philosophy constructed first around the idea of movement or change which then in some way entails more or less substantialized centers (something like lumps in a soup), and a philosophy like Aristotle's which starts with the substances (lumps) and then attributes motion to them. Perhaps it is just our Aristotelian tradition that leads us to take movement as an aspect of objects rather than the reverse. However, we should not reject it without good reason.

Another aspect of action is its association with the idea of *cause and effect* (Chapter VII). In the matter-oriented universe of early Greek philosophy it seemed natural to assume that unless things are being moved by some force or agent, they will be at rest. However, with the later development of the idea of *inertia,* motion becomes the standard condition, requiring exertion only to bring about a change in it, not to keep it going. Still, the altering or changing requires some external force or agent. But with the puzzles of modern astronomy and its supernovae, there is the possibility that some inner source of energy can cause explosions that fire up "matter" every so often to start off a new chain of events. Whatever our notions of the universe may be, some idea of a cause-effect sequence appears necessary. In fact, we are so habituated to thinking of any action as needing a cause that we have difficulty in separating out the notion of cause from the notion of action. But cause is so tricky a concept that we must beware of assuming it just because there is action present.

Another idea closely associated with that of action is *change.* The idea of change shifts the emphasis away from activities and movements toward an awareness of transition from one situation to another; and when we think of change we tend to stress the framework within which the action takes place. A good example is the clock with its hands moving around the face of the dial. These hands move or act as they *change* position from one place to another. So, in thinking of change, we become more aware of the positions or conditions between which the action takes place. Here we see more clearly that change is noticed relative to something unchanging; for the clock dial and the hands remain unchanging, while only their position changes.

Let us take another example: suppose we watch someone walking along the street. Now the person and the street remain recognizably the same; only the position of the person is changing. Of course, if we want to be pedantic, we may insist that the street too is moving, since it is on the surface of a moving planet; but we do not see the movement of the planet, and what we are saying here is that change *to be noticed* must be relative to something stable. The whole theory of relativity, in fact, was launched on its way because Einstein realized that we cannot measure velocities without simultaneities (or two events at the same instant), and we do not have simultaneities independent of the frame of reference of some particular observer. So, for measuring velocities we must accept, at least for the purposes of our measurements, some temporarily privileged frame of reference.

One way to bring home the importance of the unchanging in our awareness of change is to try to imagine a complete, total, and thoroughgoing change, one in which nothing remains. A complete change of everything would forfeit the continuing presence of the observer, and thus of any possible awareness of the change. But even imagining that everything changes except the observer— as if in a moving picture which, for the moment, is our whole absorbing reality, everything should shift abruptly to something unrelated to what has gone before—the effect would be that of two unconnected worlds between which we would be desperately looking for some connection. Senseless puzzlement would ensue.

Perhaps a more startling thought is the realization that if everything were changing proportionally—dimensions of the room we are in, all its furnishings, all the people, including ourselves— we could not possibly know it. In fact, this would not be change at all, unless it were observable from some vantage point from which it could be seen against an unchanging backdrop. So, again we are brought face to face with the importance of the relatively stable or unchanging wherever change is noticeable.

Heraclitus, whom we quoted above, is also reported to have said: "You cannot step into the same river twice." The idea he apparently suggested was that since some water had changed between steppings, it was no longer precisely the same river. The emphasis in this idea was on difference wrought by change, rather than upon the continuing sameness of the person stepping or of the river bank. Cratylus, a disciple of Heraclitus, according to Aristotle carried this trend of thought to its logical conclusion, remarking: "You cannot step into the same river once." His reasoning would assume that since all is changing, even the meaning of "same river" would have to change. Complete change, in other words, includes change of ideas and symbolic meanings. Words are, then, useless, and it is told that Cratylus ended by merely wagging his finger to show the uselessness of conversation if change is complete.*

So far we have been regarding change as primarily spatial—change in position. But there are other kinds of change to consider. Aristotle,† for example, distinguished four types: (1) change in *position,* (2) change in *size* or *quantity;* (3) change in *quality,* and (4) change in *existence* (coming into being and going out of being). Change in position we have already illustrated. Change in size suggests some continuously recognizable object either increasing or decreasing, as when a plant grows larger or dirt is removed from a hill. Change in quality suggests alteration of some aspect of a continuously recognizable object, as when a house is painted, or the peas on the stove get hot. Change in existence implies that what was previously nonexistent has come into being, or that what was existing has gone out of being, as when an animal is born or dies.

It is possible to consider Aristotle's four kinds of change as basically two types. Change in size is noticeable only as a change in place, since getting larger or smaller involves position. And change in existence might be considered simply as a change of *essential* quality as against *accidental* quality. At least, if we burn

---

* See Aristotle, *Metaphysics,* 1010a.
† See Aristotle, *Physics,* III, 1.

up a wooden table we would be changing its essential nature from table to ashes and smoke. And if life is considered essential to being an animal, then a dead animal is no longer essentially the same. Thus, Aristotle's four types of change appear to be two primary types: *change of position,* and *change of quality.*

There are other ways in which action or change may be analyzed. For example, when we think of change we may regard it as something continuous and gradual, varying from one condition to another, as when the sky gradually turns dark in the evening, or an object moves gradually from one place to another. Such *gradual variations* seem to be the most natural way of regarding change.

But now suppose the change is more abrupt. We may be watching a bird on the limb of a tree, and then suddenly the bird flies away. Or better, we see the bird, and then when we look back where it was it is no longer there. The bird has vanished. In a sense it has been negated. Thus the removal or *negation* of objects and aspects is a type of change, in fact a very simple type of change. If there is any place in experience from which the notion of zero or nothing can be derived, it must have been from just such experiences of disappearances; for "zero," when applied to experience, symbolizes the absence of some denumerable item, which, though expected, is not there.

Not only do things vanish; they also appear unexpectedly. As a counterpart to the experience of negation, there is the experience of sudden appearance or "creation." An empty tree limb may suddenly acquire a feathered visitor. From a sophisticated point of view, of course, this is an appearance, not a creation; for we reason that the bird must have flown in from somewhere. But to the untutored intellect, any unexplained appearance has the effect of an apparition, a novelty, even a *creation.*

Now, if we combine the disappearance of one object or aspect, and its replacement by another clearly different one, then we should call our experience that of a *substitution.* Thus, if we take one book from a certain place on the shelf, and then put another in its place, we have substituted the second for the first. Similarly, we can discern these two phases in any process of substitution: first there is the removal, and second the arrival of the replacement. And this is the case even if we substitute one color for another, as in painting a house with a different hue.

If we discount the factor of abruptness (and if we pay attention to the object or aspect that changes, rather than to the locus or frame of reference of its happening), disappearance, appearance, and substitution may all be viewed as examples of variation. Thus if we follow the bird as it comes to sit on the limb and then as it flies away later, we can see this whole action simply as a variation in the bird's position. Even the painting of a table with a new color could be regarded not simply as the substitution of the new color for the old, but rather as a gradual variation from one color to the other. Thus, in all the foregoing varieties of change, the issue is that of the scope of our attention. When things disappear *beyond our ken,* they are in effect negated, perhaps, at least for us, out of existence completely. When they appear *out of nowhere,* as it were, they are created. When something else comes to take the place of the old, there is a substitution. But when we follow through the phases of the change, it is a variation. Is it not in these terms, and with these metaphors, that we wonder about death? Does our individual consciousness simply go out of existence, or is it removed from the familiar to an unfamiliar realm? Whatever we may conclude, our speculations, we note, are always based on the familiar modes of experience.

What is meant by function?

We have been discussing the nature of action and change. But the term "function" was selected as the title for this chapter, since it has some modern connotations that will help us to see the general importance and place of change in contemporary science and philosophy. Let us begin by noting the several definitions of "function" in any large standard dictionary. We find that there are apparently three outstandingly different meanings:

(1) A type of activity or event in general (e.g., a social function).

(2) An activity associated with an object, either as something it does, or as something done to it (e.g., the function of a postman is to collect and deliver mail; the function of a chair is to be sat on).

(3) An activity or change associated with another activity or

change, usually in some definite ratio (e.g., the speed of a planet is a function of its distance from the sun).

In each of these three meanings the stress is upon an activity, either as a *type* of activity, or as an activity *associated with* some object, or as an activity *associated with* another activity. Let us examine each of these meanings in more detail.

First, as a general type of activity, function seems to refer to the full concrete event including all its parts and aspects. "Social function," "church function," and "athletic function" all suggest complete affairs, including place, time, people involved, subordinate actions which take place within the main event, and so on. What do we mean when we say, for example: "That was quite a function!"? Is this not simply an equivalent for: "That was quite an event!"? In effect, then, "function" in this first sense is hardly to be regarded as an abstraction, at least from the normal object-event level of concreteness. The word "function," however, is a derived noun (from the Latin verb *fungor*), and should normally indicate an abstraction. But abstracted concepts represented by derived nouns often come to refer to full concrete situations which include or are marked by the abstract aspect named. Thus, many if not most of our terms for events (game, dance, race, etc.) really indicate only one abstractable aspect of the total situation (e.g., "game" implies the playful, sporty, or competitive aspect of the total event). In common usage these terms refer to the full concrete happening; and "function" in our first sense may be regarded as indicating something as concrete as a normal object or event. If we like, we can call function in this sense an *event function*.

In the second sense (e.g., the function of a postman, or of a chair, etc.), the term is clearly an abstraction. The central idea here is that of doing or acting in a certain prescribed way, and this is an abstractable aspect of that which so acts. Thus the function of a postman is the prescribed task of delivering and collecting mail; and the prescribed function of a student is that of studying. These functions are the actions appropriate to the individuals or objects in question. Sometimes the function in this sense is not an action performed, but an action done to an object. Thus the function of a chair is to be sat upon, which is an action performed not by the chair, but upon the chair. We may extend the idea of performance, however, to include the notion of the chair performing the function of holding up the person who is sitting upon it. We see that this type of "performance" is really a passive sort of doing. However, we should include both active and passive varieties when considering "function" in this second sense. In either case, the function is one aspect of the object and may therefore be called a *qualifying function*.

Two derivative meanings of qualifying functions are worth noting. First, we may think of the function of an object as appropriate to it whether or not it is actively performing this function at a given time. The postman is still a postman even after he has finished delivering mail; and the chair still has the function of being sat on, although it may be vacant at any given time. So a thing's function may be considered to be a continuing characteristic or aspect of that thing, whether or not the activity indicated by the function is going on at the moment.

The second derivative meaning involves the idea of *purpose*. There is a close connection in our thinking between activity and purpose, as is demonstrated when we ask the question: "What is that for?" The answer expected is in terms of what a thing does— that is, its activity. What is a postman for? He is to deliver the mail. What is a chair for? It is to be sat upon. So we see that a thing's function is also its purpose (i.e., what it is for). For this reason, the term "function" is often used as a synonym for "purpose"; but we should remember that this is a usage derived from the correlation of purpose with the normal or expected performance of certain tasks or activities associated with particular objects, and is appropriate primarily in connection with human actions or man-made objects.

The third meaning of "function" is that of one activity or change associated with another activity or change, usually in some definite ratio. The stress here is upon the correlated character of the two (or more) activities involved. For example, normally when one turns the handle or knob of a water faucet, a stream of water comes from the faucet, and the more one turns the handle in the on direction, the more water flows out. We may consider this example a typical case of two variable activities—one the twisting of the handle, and the other the varying amount of water which pours forth—activities which are clearly correlative to each other. In many cases, such as this one, we can measure a quantity for each variable activity (amount of twist and amount of water) and then find out what the correlative ratio is. If the number of degrees in the angle of twist and the quantity of water follow a uniform or "constant" correlation, then we should be able to discover the rule or "law" which will tell us how much twist we need for various amounts of water. In this example we find the key to the importance of function in our third sense; for much of scientific and technological knowledge involves just such correlated measurable activities. Because of the key importance of correlational factors here, we can call functions of this type *correlated* or (simply) *related functions.*

Let us look at a more complex case of related functions. A good example is Kepler's second law of planetary motion, which we shall see is in its essential aspects analogous to the simpler case of the water faucet. Kepler's law involves also two changing variables: (*a*) the speed of a planet in its orbit around the sun and (*b*) its distance from the sun as it moves through an elliptical orbit. Kepler knew that the speed of a planet varied for different parts of the orbit; and being a great believer in natural ratios and harmonies in the universe, he looked long and arduously for the ratio that would fit these two variable activities. Finally he discovered one that seemed to work, though it was certainly far from the simple and obvious type of ratio that we might have expected; and it well demonstrates Kepler's imaginative powers that he was able to hit upon it at all. As we know, the ratio which he discovered to be the most successful of all those that he tried was this: the areas swept over by an imaginary line from any planet to the sun is always constant for any given period of time. Thus when a planet comes nearer to the sun, it moves proportionally faster, and when it is farther from the sun it moves proportionally slower, in exactly the right proportion so that the areas of the ellipse inscribed within the orbit, and subtended by the distance traveled by the planet—the sectors—are always equal for equal periods of time. So there again, even though the situation and the ratio are more complex than in the case of the water faucet, we have two changing variables related to each other by a constant ratio.

Correlation of functions seems to imply a causal connection between the two related changes. However, we must be careful of this implication. At least, it is quite possible to have two apparently unconnected changes which have some discernible constant ratio between them. For example, it was once observed that there was a close direct correlation between the price of corn on the Chicago corn exchange and the number of maternity cases in Chicago hospitals over a given period of time. Any attempt to infer causal connection here would certainly be dubious. Yet in most of the cases of such correlation there does seem to be as good evidence of causal factors as in most cases of assumed causality. Thus, the twist of the faucet handle would certainly be taken by most of us as part of the cause for the increasing stream of water; or the degree of pressure applied to an automobile brake would seem to be part of the cause for the slowing up of the vehicle.

This type of correlation is so frequent in our experience that we tend to think of one of the changing variables as *independent* (the cause) and the other as *dependent* (the effect). Thus, turning the water faucet is the controllable or independent variable, and the amount of water which results is the controlled or dependent variable. But in the case of Kepler's second law, how do we know which change to consider independent and which dependent? What meaning would there be in assigning independence and dependence here, unless we assumed that some agent was moving the planet? We cannot manipulate either the speed of a planet or its distance from the sun; and so it really does not matter in this case which variable one takes to be the independent one, and which the dependent one. We are probably inclined to take the variable easier to calculate as the independent variable, simply because we arrive at it first. But in this case, the idea of causal dependence has been overstepped, even though we are often, unfortunately, caught up in the causal association to such an extent that we tend to equate "function of" with "effect of."

The concept of "variables," both independent and dependent, has been much used in mathematics. How is it possible to transfer an idea which so obviously has to do with physical cause and effect to an area like mathematics in which one is concerned with imagined abstractions, where clearly the idea of physical cause and effect has been left behind? For example, the ratio known as the tangent in a right-angled triangle (i.e., for either one of the non-right angles, the ratio of the side opposite to the side adjacent to that angle) varies according to the number of degrees in the angle. So we have two interdependent variables: (1) the ratio of the side opposite to the side adjacent and (2) the number of degrees in the angle. Which of these should be considered the dependent variable and which the independent variable, or does it matter? It is a question principally of the one that is easier to imagine as manipulated first, in terms of which the other can be calculated. But actually it can be considered either way; and it would depend largely on the given information. If the number of degrees in the angle is given, then the tangent ratio would be the dependent variable; and if this ratio is given first, then the degrees in the angle would be dependent. Thus, the concepts of independent and dependent variable can be made to serve a useful purpose in mathematics, if we pry them loose from any connotation of the cause-effect relation and if we regard them as indicating merely a preferred order in the solution of a problem.

Owing to mathematical usage, there is one other transferred meaning of "function" which we need to take into account. "Function" suggests not only cause and effect, independence and dependence, but also the *set* or *table* of corresponding quantities (or quantitative values) which are implied by two interdependent variables, or the *graph* that might be constructed from these variables. The set of quantities and the graph represent, after all, the pattern of correlation which exists between the variables. This pattern indicates what the particular constant of variation is. Thus, in the case of the tangent of an angle, one can graph from a set on table of comparative values a diagram indicating the constant of variation in this case.* "Function" in our third sense is thus often broadened in meaning to include sets of quantitative values as tabulated or graphed, which represent possible changes, but are not in themselves changing. When we stress such sets of fixed relationships, we are moving in the direction

---

* For illustrations of the function of the tangent and its corresponding tabular and graphic forms, see any standard text in trigonometry.

of Platonism; for Plato's famous realm of Ideas is apparently something very close to and inclusive of what we mean by the fixed ratios or patterns that underlie related functions. Plato, it is true, assigned a more nearly ultimate reality to the Ideas than would be assigned to relational functions by the majority of contemporary scientists; since the scientist, as scientist need not be concerned with the metaphysical status of his functions at all. But insofar as science is a search for the laws and constants of nature, and insofar as these are akin to Plato's Ideas, one goal of science implies some belief in a modernized version of Platonism.

Before leaving related functions, we should observe that there are many ways in which two changes can be related. The simplest way is that of *direct* equal variation. In such a case, change of the variable x corresponds to a similar change in the variable y. The formula for this is simply $x = y$. But it is also possible that as one thing increases, the other decreases. In this case, the variation is called *inverse* instead of direct and the formula for an inverse equal variation is $x = 1/y$. Later we shall see that all such formulations as these are examples of the *propositional forms* or propositional functions of modern logic.

We have now distinguished action, change, and three meanings of function. They all center on the same idea, namely that of a happening or a doing, but with differences of emphasis. Thus (1) *action* centers on the simple movement itself, without concern for doers, causes, goals, objects, and the like (e.g., kicking); (2) *change* centers on the transitional aspect, the shift from one condition to another, usually associated with some changing object and some frame of reference (e.g., heating the peas changes them from cold to hot); (3) *event function* centers upon a complex event with many minor activities involved (e.g., a social function); (4) *qualifying function* centers upon a function as the appropriate activity associated with some object (e.g., studying is the function of a student); and (5) *related function* centers upon two or more changes related to each other (e.g., amount of water related to the turning of a water faucet).

For convenience, let us extend the meaning of the term "function" to include all five of the above cases. Thus, simple action will be the minimal case of an event function, and a full event will be considered an event-unit in which many simple actions are included. Change, likewise, is simply the before-and-after aspect of any function and is implicit in all functionings. So although qualifying and related functions are the more typical cases referred to by the term "function," action and change can be included at least as aspects of these. The full event-function is the most concrete of all five notions here considered; for the full event contains qualifying and related functions, which in turn contain actions and changes as subordinate parts or aspects. In other words, from full concrete events we can abstract qualifying and related functions; and from these we can abstract actions and changes.

How are concepts of function expressed linguistically?

The burden of expressing functions falls on the *verb;* and even verbs of relative inactivity—sit, lie, stand, etc.—are suitable for answering the question, "What are you *doing?*" So verbs basically express the idea of something *going on,* something *taking place,* something *acting.* Even the outstanding exception, the verb "to be," especially in its present participial form (being), connotes a going on in the sense of enduring, which is not far distant from the notion of doing something. However, it is customary to distinguish between *verbs of action* (meaning those that indicate the more active type of behavior) and *verbs of condition* (meaning those that indicate a more stable and enduring type of doing). And it is convenient also to distinguish a third type of verb, *verbs of transition*—verbs (e.g., becoming) which indicate change from one state to another.

In most languages verbs are very complex units. They not only express types of activity, condition, or transition but also perform many additional tasks, usually indicated by changes in the verb forms themselves showing tense, number, aspect, mood, etc.

Many of the characteristics of the verb in a sentence depend upon the basic sentence type. We recall (Chapter II) that we had two primary sentence forms: the *action* and the *attributive.* Under the action type, there were two principal subtypes: the *intransitive* and the *transitive.* An intransitive use of a verb simply names the subject together with the verb, without giving any object of the action (e.g., The man bites). A transitive use of a verb also names an object as receiver of the action (e.g., The man bites the dog). This use is called "transitive" (i.e., carrying across) because the *action* is carried across from the subject to the object. We must not confuse "transitive" in this sense with the transitive relations discussed in the preceding chapter, where the *relation* is what is carried across from two cases to a third.

Action sentences may also be distinguished with regard to order, as to whether they are *active* or *passive*.* If the subject is the actor or doer (e.g., The boy kills the rabbit), then the sentence and verb are said to be *active*. If the recipient of the action is named as subject (e.g., The rabbit is killed by the boy), then the sentence and verb are said to be *passive*. Intransitive sentences may be either active or passive: The man bites/The man is bitten. Transitive sentences, however, are normally considered active (The man bites the dog), whereas the corresponding passive form would be considered intransitive (The dog is bitten by the man), with the prepositional phrase (by the man) treated as an adverbial modifier of the verb. However, from a logical point of view, it is much more convenient to regard the preposition (by) as an adverb attached to the verb, and the object of the preposition (the man) as an object of the whole verbal element. If we do this, we can convert the active transitive form (The man *bites* the dog) into a corresponding passive transitive form (The dog *is bitten by* the man). In this way, the subject of the transitive form has an equal position in the sentence with the object, and the two are readily "converted," to use an operation from logic, by reversing position, and changing the verbal unit from active to passive. We now have the following possibilities:

(1) INTRANSITIVE ACTIVE:	*The boy*	*kills.*		
	SUBJECT	VERB		
(2) INTRANSITIVE PASSIVE:	*The rabbit*	*is killed.*		
	SUBJECT	VERB		
(3) TRANSITIVE ACTIVE:	*The boy*	*kills*	*the rabbit.*	
	SUBJECT	VERB	OBJECT	
(4) TRANSITIVE PASSIVE:	*The rabbit*	*is killed by*	*the boy.*	
	SUBJECT	VERB	AGENT	

* In traditional grammatical terminology, active and passive are called *voices,* presumably indicating that they sound different. It makes clearer sense, however, to call them *orders,* since they indicate the order of doer and done-to.

In action sentences, we normally think of the verb as indicating an activity. The form suggests this, and we tend to assimilate even verbs of condition to the pattern of more active verbal ideas (e.g., The boy sits in the chair). This assimilation is shown by the fact that such verbs as "sitting" or "sleeping" may answer the question "What is he *doing*?" So we may note that there are active and passive forms for verbs of condition, just as there are for more active verbs. E.g.: INTRANSITIVE ACTIVE: The boy sits; INTRANSITIVE PASSIVE: The chair is sat in; TRANSITIVE ACTIVE: The boy sits in the chair; TRANSITIVE PASSIVE: The chair is sat in by the boy. However, it makes little sense to apply the distinction of active and passive order to attributive sentences. Thus a sentence like "The boy is fat" is properly speaking neither active nor passive; it is simply attributive.

In addition to the (1) *intransitive-transitive* and (2) *active-passive* distinctions which involve verbal forms, there are several other characteristics of the event being described that also involve alterations of verbal forms in most languages. Verbal alterations may indicate (3) *tense* (past-present-future); (4) *temporal aspect* (continuing, momentary, repeated, customary, beginning, ending, etc., as characteristics of events); (5) *mood* (indicative, imperative, interrogative, dubitative, necessitative, optative, conditional, etc., as attitudes of the speaker in making a statement); and (6) *predication* (affirmative, negative). As an example of these various functions, consider the statement: "He will be coming after dinner." The verb "will be coming" is (1) intransitive, (2) active, (3) future tense, (4) continuing or progressive temporal aspect, (5) indicative mood, and (6) affirmative predication. Or take the example: "He may not have come yesterday." Here the verb is (1) intransitive, (2) active, (3) perfect tense, (4) momentary temporal aspect, (5) dubitative mood, and (6) negative predication.

How do verbs handle cause and effect, which as we have seen is a very important relation where functions are involved? In the first place, the subject of the doer-action or action   type of sentence is at least a very important part of the cause of the event named by the verb. In a situation such as that represented by the sentence "The boy kills the rabbit," we should readily admit that "the boy" is a large part of the cause of the event. However, causation, we know, involves more than just the triggering action; it may involve other agents and necessary conditions. For a more complicated situation in which causal factors are expressed, consider the following statement: "Dad had the hired man mow the lawn for him for two dollars with the new mower in order to improve the appearance of the yard." Here *Dad* is the instigator of the action or motivating force; *hired man* is the agent; *mowing* is the action; *lawn* is the direct object or recipient of the action; *him* (i.e. Dad) is the indirect object or that for whom the action takes place; *two dollars* serves as one inducement for the action; *mower* names the instrument; and the phrase *to improve the appearance of the yard* indicates Dad's purpose or goal. Thus we have mentioned in this illustration: (1) the primary actor or cause, (2) the secondary actor or agent, (3) the action itself, (4) the direct object, (5) the indirect object, (6) the inducement, (7) the instrument, and (8) the goal or purpose. Two verbs (*had* and *mow*) and one verbal noun (*to improve*) carry the burden of functional indicators in the sentence. However, all of the factors listed enter into a rather complex report on the whole causal situation. Not many causal situations, we can rejoice, are so completely expressed.

We have concentrated our attention on verbs since verbs are the principal indicators of the notion of function in language. However, there are other ways in which we can express this notion linguistically. For example, verbal nouns, like the gerund (e.g., the running) or the infinitive (e.g., to run) combine the verb and noun functions in our language. We can also use primary nouns which designate types of events (e.g., dance, game, hike) to indicate functions. Adverbs, as verbal qualifiers, express qualities of functions, or if we like, "functions" of functions (e.g., He ran *rapidly*). Likewise, any phrase or clause used adverbially can indicate a quality or function of a function.

Since we have distinguished between qualities and functions on the basis that qualities are considered static or unchanging whereas functions indicate change or action, it may be instructive to ask where to draw the line between the action type of verb (e.g., run), the static or "stative" kind of verb (e.g., sit), and the purely attributive qualifier type of predicate (e.g., is tall). We noticed that "sitting" and "sleeping" may still be considered somewhat active. At least they answer the question "What were you doing?" "Being tall" would not answer that question. So, this fact suggests that even stative verbs are still considered functions. But in English we can use the progressive form of the verb (e.g., he is smiling) as a kind of intermediary. The predicate "is happy" serves as a good example of an attributive qualifier, but the progressive statement "He is smiling" can imply either a statement of an activity, like "He smiles," or a statement of attribution, like "He is happy." However, the fact that this form is ambiguous in this way does not mean that there is no line of demarcation between the more static *quality* concept and the more active *function* concept. What it indicates is that in our thinking about the world we can see the same situation either in a static or dynamic light.

As with qualities, we noticed that *relations* are also ordinarily taken to be static rather than dynamic. Yet we do have dynamic relations, and from the point of view of language, the active transitive verb is a good example. In a transitive sentence (e.g., I drove the car) the action (drove) relates the subject (I) to the object (car). Active transitive verbs are, therefore, subject to the same analyses that we applied to relations in Chapter VII, including tests for reflexivity, symmetry, and relational transitivity. For example, the form "I kick myself" is reflexive; the form "I shake hands with William" is symmetrical if William is entering into the spirit of handshaking; and causatives such as "Samson pulled down the pillars, and the pillars pulled down the temple, so Samson pulled down the temple" would illustrate relational transitivity of an active transitive verb.

Do sentence structures reflect basic thought patterns?

Having reviewed some philosophical problems connected with qualities, relations, and functions, as well as some of our linguistic ways of formulating these abstractions, let us raise again the question of the relation between the linguistic structures and natural patterns of thinking. Linguists have been interested in these structures as reflected in actual languages. Logicians have been more interested in purely theoretical structures of thought, hopefully independent of any particular language. Our thesis, suggested already in Chapter II, is that many more possible relationships can be discriminated in experience than are noticed or formulated in any given language, or for that matter in any given system of logic. Languages and logical systems, however, do incorporate and expand certain ones of these relations—perhaps, indeed, those that are most important to us. It will help us to understand the problem better if we examine in an elementary way some of the characteristic techniques used by logicians and linguists for analyzing the structures with which they deal. We are now in a better position to do this than was the case in Chapter II.

The logician, in his analysis, has made good use of the mathematician's notion of *propositional form* or *propositional function*.* Let us imagine for a moment that a typical algebraic formula like $x + y = z$ might be used to represent any linguistic sentence. We would be looking for a formula of wide generality. The trouble here is that the algebraic statement is normally associated with only one kind of sentence—namely that in which quantitative relations appear. We therefore need a more general sort of formula, one at least that could express all the structures of our own language. For example, the form "Tom runs" is like the form "George runs" or "Henry runs." Now, if we substitute a generalizing symbol x for all the possible individuals who run (i.e., x runs), we would have a propositional form with one variable, namely, the subject term. But we could also vary the predicate term (e.g., George flies, George wrestles, George kicks, etc.). Then the functions of George could be generalized as "George F's," where F stands for any action that can be predicated of George. Finally, both subject and predicate terms can be generalized in the form "xF's" or more characteristically "$F(x)$," meaning "any x has an activity F associated with it."

The form $F(x)$ or xF indicates only one subject and one activity or condition (e.g., Rover barks). But supposing we wish to indicate a transitive activity having an object as well as a subject. This

---

* The use of the word "function" here arises from the fact that variables are involved, and variables, as the name indicates, stand for items that can be changed or substituted. However, in the mathematical use of the term "function," the meaning has shifted away from the variables themselves to the stable relationships or conditions into which the variables are fitted. Since this latter meaning is better satisfied by the term "form," we shall speak of "propositional forms" rather than "functions." An excellent discussion of the meanings of "function" is to be found in a rather rare book, Archibald Bowman's *A Sacramental Universe,* Ch. I.

notion could be symbolized by two variables, one for the subject and one for the object (e.g., x kisses y). Or generalizing the activity, we have xFy where F stands for any activity that can take place between any x and any y.

Now notice the similarity between the intransitive propositional form xF and that which we gave in Chapter VI for a qualitative abstraction xQ. Observe also that the transitive form xFy resembles the relational form xRy given in Chapter VII. The difference indicated by our symbols Q, R, and F is simply a matter of stability or change, since the Q's and R's indicate stable (unchanging) qualities and relations, whereas the F's indicate action or change. We could ignore this difference, if we wished, so that the form xF might be used for any intransitive sentence, and xFy for any transitive one. In such a case we would be considering xQ (e.g., John is tall) and xF (e.g., John runs) as analogous intransitive forms, and xRy (e.g., The book is on the table) and xFy (e.g., Sam catches fish) as analogous transitive types. If our goal is the logician's desire to find the fewest and most comprehensive propositional forms, then it would be reasonable to eliminate xQ and xRy; but so long as we are regarding the distinction between quality, relation, and function as a basic one—and it seems to be so for grammar—it will help us if we retain the xQ and the xRy.

Now we discover a considerable advantage in what we have done; for the propositional form xRy as we used it in Chapter VII can stand for *any relation* between two terms. That is, we can use xRy to symbolize such varieties of sentences as "x is *under* y," "x is *east of* y," "x is *father of* y," etc. If we consider R as standing for the *relation* between x and y, we cannot regard y as a predicate attribute of x; and for logical analysis, we do *not* wish to regard the relations as qualitative attributes of the subject term—although traditional grammatical analysis does precisely this. From the point of view of traditional grammar the expression "under y" in "x is under y" would be regarded as a prepositional phrase used adjectivally to modify the subject. Also, "east of" would be considered an adjective (east) modified by a prepositional phrase (of y), all modifying the subject. And "father of y" would be a predicate noun (father) modified by a prepositional phrase (of y), all serving as an attribute of the subject.

But for the simpler logical analysis here suggested, the x and the

y should be regarded as coequal terms with some relation predicated between them, so that "x is under y" can be replaced by xRy, where R stands for "is under." We can either assume that the R includes the idea of predication (is), or we can limit the R to the relation (under), and devise some further symbol (e.g., $\vdash$) to stand for the act of predicating. Usually the first procedure is followed. The advantage in this form of analysis is considerable, for it allows both greater ease in symbolizing and greater facility in showing inferences. For example, "x is east of y" ($\overrightarrow{xRy}$) implies "y is west of x" ($\overleftarrow{yRx}$), and "x is father of y" implies "y is child of x," for we see that these are relations with readily recognizable opposites, as indicated by reversing the arrows.

Using these propositional forms, with Q and R representing the relatively unchanging or stable qualities and relations, and F representing happenings or events, we now have the following elementary sentential types:

	ATTRIBUTIVE SENTENCES	ACTION SENTENCES
INTRANSITIVE	(1) $\quad xQ$ or $Q(x)$ e.g., The book is green.	(2) $\quad xF$ or $F(x)$ e.g., John runs.
DIRECT TRANSITIVE "Active"	(3) $\quad \overrightarrow{xRy}$ e.g., The book is on the table.	(4) $\quad \overrightarrow{xFy}$ e.g., John hits the ball.
REVERSED TRANSITIVE "Passive"	(5) $\quad \overleftarrow{yRx}$ e.g., The table is under the book.	(6) $\quad \overleftarrow{yFx}$ e.g., The ball is hit by John.

Compounds of the above forms are not difficult to symbolize. For example, a complementative sentence, like "John painted his desk green," would involve both a *direct transitive action* sentence, "John painted his desk," and an *attributive* complement, "green," thus combining (4) and (1). This could be symbolized by adding a Q to form (4), giving $xFyQ$. Or a sentence involving an action and a relation, like "John walks in the street," can be regarded as combining (2) and (3), giving $xFRy$. The system could be easily developed in this direction, showing the relative positions of the unit elements (x, y, etc.), qualities, relations, and functions. But it will be more instructive to apply it to our three basic types of function—event functions, qualifying functions, and related functions.

In the case of *event functions,* the sentence subject may be itself the named function (e.g., The dance was great sport), which could be indicated by replacing the more customary x with a small f, giving (fQ) where the f stands for the named event and the Q stands for the qualifier.

With regard to *qualifying functions,* the simplest type is already given by xF, where x designates the doer (e.g., John) and F designates the qualifying function (e.g., runs). But if the qualifying function is indicated by a noun standing for a professional or customary activity, as in "John is a postman," then the primary propositional form more appropriately becomes xRy to show that we now have the member-of-a-class relation (i.e., John is a member of the class of postmen), although the functional nature of being a postman suggests that we could substitute f for y, thus xRf.

Similarly, the relating of functions, or *related functions* (e.g., the bigger, the better) could be symbolized by f_1Rf_2 where f_1 stands for the first function (getting bigger), R stands for the relation between the functions, and f_2 stands for the second function (getting better). If the functioning objects are also included (e.g., This elevator goes up as that one comes down), we could write $xF\ R\ yF$, where x stands for the first object (this elevator), the associated F for the function of the first object (going up), R for the relation between the functions (as), y for the second object (that elevator), and the second F for the function of the second object (coming down). This, we notice, is the formula for the relation of the amount of water coming from a faucet to the degree of twist given the knob, which might be written, $wF\ R\ tF$, or "the function of the volume of water is related to the function of the degree of twist." If we assume, for the sake of illustration, that for every $30°$ of twist, the amount of water is doubled, then we could specify the relation as follows: $wF/1 = 30°/tF$, where each unit of water stands in a ratio to the degree of twist as 1 to $30°$. A similar formula could be written for Kepler's second law, and for all like related functions.

There are, of course, other ways of symbolizing and diagramming sentence structures. Two of them were illustrated in Chapter II (see pp. 42-43). The system proposed here, however, resembles more the techniques of the propositional calculus in modern logic, except that we have given greater attention to grammatical considerations, such as verb forms. The propositional calculus, on the other hand, can introduce symbols for "quantification" to indicate the class part-whole distinctions of traditional Western logic. These symbols include primarily the forms *(x)* meaning "for any *x*" and *(∃x)* meaning "there is at least one *x*, but not all *x*'s, such that etc." The first is the universal or whole-class quantifier, and the second is the particular or part-class quantifier. For example, the universal proposition "All cats are animals" could be symbolized as *(x) xRy*, or more specifically *(x) x<y*, which would be read "For any *x* (in this case *cat*), an *x* is a *y* (in this case *animal*)"; and the particular proposition, "Some cats are long-haired," could be symbolized as *(∃x) x<y*, which would be read "There is at least one *x* (i.e., *cat*), such that it is also *y (long-haired)*." In the notation of symbolic logic, it is customary to simplify the number of basic relations used by taking the universal class-inclusion relation as a case of the implication (if . . . then) relation, often symbolized by ⊃ and the particular class-inclusion relation as a case of conjunction (both . . . and), symbolized by a dot ·. When this is done, the symbolism is more specific with regard to classes and attributes. For example, the universal proposition above (All cats are animals) would appear as *(x)(Cx⊃Ax)*, meaning "For any *x*, if *x* is *C* (a cat), then *x* is *A* (an animal)," and the particular proposition above (Some cats are long-haired) would appear as *(∃x)(Cx · Lx)*, meaning "There is at least one *x*, such that *x* is both *C* (a cat) and also *L* (long-haired)."

Unfortunately this latter mode of symbolizing propositions raised an unnecessary question regarding the existence of members of the subject term. It was thought that particular propositions (e.g., Some cats are animals) implied such existence, whereas universal propositions (e.g., All cats are animals) did not. This view arose apparently because of the assumption that the universal categorical proposition (e.g., All cats are animals) is transformable into a corresponding hypothetical form (i.e., If something is a cat, then it is an animal), which leaves the existence of members in the subject term open to question. But the particular categorical proposition (e.g., Some cats are animals) was not considered to be translatable into a corresponding hypothetical form, although linguistically there is no reason against this (e.g., If some things are cats, then they are animals). So, it was assumed that the particular proposition retains an implied existence regarding at least one member of the subject term which the universal proposition does not. This assumption is underlined by the translation of the form "Some x's are . . ." into "There exists at least one x, such that it is. . . ." There is no need, however, for thus confusing an implication concerning existence with the distinction between particular and universal subject terms. These two factors could better have been treated separately in our current logical notation.

More interesting from our point of view is the fact that traditional logical analysis of propositional form has centered its attention upon the class part-whole relations, whereas grammarians have paid more attention to the singular-plural distinction, where quantification is concerned. The reason for this difference lies in the fact that the grammarian is interested principally in those relational differences that are indicated by linguistic elements, such as are shown by singular and plural forms of the noun. The logician, on the other hand, from Aristotle on, has paid more attention to classes and class relationships, whether or not these are exhibited by linguistic elements. Clearly, however, in accordance with our thesis that experience is capable of revealing many more relationships than those recorded in any one language or logical system, we should not discount the singular-plural distinction in favor of the class part-whole relation, nor vice versa.

Different languages have developed in such ways as to express different relationships. But this does not mean that languages which have no built-in means of expressing certain relationships cannot express them at all. There are two factors at work here: (1) an apparent selectivity in a language regarding the relationships which will be most dominantly or necessarily expressed and (2) the possibility of expressing other relationships in a less direct fashion. For example, whereas in English we *must* express the singular-plural distinction when we use ordinary nouns and verbs, we *can,* but need not, express the class part-whole relation by using certain modifiers (e.g., all, some, several, any, etc.). In this way, by enforcing the expression of some relations but not others, a language assigns greater or lesser prominence to the various relations.

It appears safe to say that most if not all languages express in some way the key relations mentioned in Chapter VII. But there may be wide variation in the priorities assigned to the relations. For example, if as noted in Chapter VII, the relationship of possession was taken as the key to attribution, then there would be a tendency to regard an attribute as a kind of possession or property of something, thus giving possession a dominant position. Or if possession is regarded as the key to the organic part-whole relation, as was also noted, then an organic part is conceived as belonging to or possessed by the whole. It would be natural in this case to extend the notion of possession to the class part-whole relation and regard a subclass or species as in some way the possession of the larger class or genus. There may be a good reason why the notion of possession was a dominant one for our ancestors, but it is entirely possible to reverse the priorities and regard possession as subordinate to attribution or subportion. These examples should suffice to indicate what a difference relational priority makes in our conceptual orientations.

If we are correct in the assumption that linguistic differences in the expression of relations and functions lie in the two factors of selection and priority, rather than in the relations themselves, we can account for both the view of Benjamin Lee Whorf that languages do embody and perpetuate differing world views and also the view of Noam Chomsky and the universalists in grammar that there are some fundamental deep structure uniformities in all languages. While the priorities vary (Whorf) the relations remain (Chomsky). These views only appear to conflict when either one is carried to such an extreme that the other hypothesis is necessarily excluded.

One advantage of the sentential symbolism proposed in this chapter is its ability to indicate both the structural similarities and the differences in priority or dominance as between languages. For example, the functional relation in the ordinary English version of the sentence "I hear him" would be indicated as xFy, whereas the Greenlandic Eskimo version, "Sounding-his-my," as formulated by Willem Graff,* would be shown as $F\ Ry\ Rx$ where F stands for the sounding activity or function, the Ry for the possessive relation relative to him, and the Rx for the possessive relation relative to me. Conversion formulas could then be worked out for these two languages showing the redistribution of emphasis in the syntactical differences. In this example, we might have $F_1\ Ry\ Rx$ becoming $Rx\ F_2\ Ry$, and then $x\ F_2\ y$, as the possessive relation disappears in the English version. The F_1 indicates the sound-emitting notion implied in the Greenlandic version, whereas the F_2 indicates the sound-receiving notion implied in the English. It is not my purpose here to develop further examples of this sort, but merely to offer some evidence for the major thesis here proposed, namely that linguistic differences in relational expression are a matter of selection and priority.

SUGGESTED READINGS

Aristotle, *Physics,* Bk. III, Chs. 1-3 (on motion and change) .

Bergson, Henri, *Creative Evolution,* especially Ch. 1 (on creativity and fixity in life) .

Whitehead, A. N., *Science and the Modern World,* especially Ch. 7 (on abstraction and events) .

Sartre, Jean-Paul, *Being and Nothingness,* especially Ch. 1, Section 2 (on negations.)

Bowman, A. A., *A Sacramental Universe,* Pt. I, Ch. I (on meanings of the term "function") .

---

* See Chapter II, p. 52.

CHAPTER IX

Imagining

What do we mean by imagination?

THROUGH THE PAST THREE chapters we have examined three principal varieties of abstractable aspects: qualities, relations, and functions. In doing this, we took occasion to review a number of crucial philosophical problems that have arisen in connection with these abstractions and their sundry types. But, although we have many times made use of imagination in dealing with some of the characteristics of these types, we have so far neglected an investigation of the ways in which the imagination allows us to move beyond the limits of direct experience. And yet through the use of imagination we can rearrange and alter our simple abstractions so as to create a fantastic variety of possible concepts. These concepts in the form of hypotheses about the world guide our understanding of it and in the form of moral ideals guide our notions of good and evil. The distinctively human world that we inhabit is in a profound sense the work of the imagination. So, to this phase of thinking, we must turn our attention.

The term "imagination," like most of the terms with which we have been dealing, has had considerable variability of meaning. At bottom it derives from the word "image," which suggests some sort of copy, as in a mirror. Imagination, in its simplest sense, would be merely a mental mirroring, taking ideas to be mirrorlike copies of sense perceptions. But even in this simple sense, imagination is not the same as mere perception. Imagination suggests that mental images are present through recollection rather than as direct perceptions. Thus, memories of one's childhood home would be more apt to come under the heading "imagination" than would the mental pictures formed from the immediate perception of the table in front of one.

The term "imagination," however, soon takes on other connotations. For example, it comes to mean the holding in mind and conceiving of abstractions, especially aspect abstractions. Thus my concept or mental picture of the blue sky or of the shape of a particular house may be thought to be somehow more imaginative than a picture of the entire visible sky or the entire visible house. Still, imagination in this sense is closely tied to direct perceptual experience. Even imaginings of abstractions arise from what has been perceived and are not yet the products of mental creation or fantasy.

It is what is sometimes called "creative imagination," rather than simple mental picturing, which has come to be associated with the highly extolled imaginative power, deemed especially important in human activities. Creative imagination is a reworking, remodeling, reshaping of abstractions, a kind of mental playing around with the parts and aspects that have been abstracted from experience. For example, to abstract the shape of a house and then to recall it in the form of a mental picture may involve a limited type of imagining (imagining in the first sense). But to conceive the shape of the house as altered, as longer or higher than it is, would be to change imaginatively what had been taken from experience. This would be *a going beyond experience*. The power of altering abstractions so that they are no longer as experienced is what we mean by "creative imagination."

Why is it that the imaginative altering of abstractions, or creative imagination, is so important to man? For one thing, without it he could form no new philosophical or scientific hypotheses, in which case philosophy and science would be impossible. And for the fine arts especially, the power of the creative imagination is all-important. These are matters which we shall demonstrate in more detail later.

There is one important point which needs clarification before we proceed. This is the question of *intention* or conscious purpose. Sometimes we associate imagination, even the creative type, with daydreaming or idle fantasy. The suggestion here is that imagining operates aimlessly and without a controlling purpose. No doubt this is often the case. But we must stress, on the other hand, that use of the imaginative power of thought may be accompanied by a highly controlled and very purposeful direction. Some persons may be tempted to associate the idle variety with the arts and the purposeful kind with the sciences. This, however, would be unfair, for scientific achievements occasionally result from what at the moment seem to be quite idle and daydreamish thoughts, and artistic achievements are more often than not the product of well-directed efforts. The important point here is not that of science versus art, but of the type and degree of intention and control which the mind exercises over its imaginings. Creative imagination needs freedom, but it also needs direction.

In what ways can abstractions be altered?

Creative imagination, we have said, is the mental manipulating or altering of abstractions. How does this alteration come about? The answer to this question was suggested in Chapter VIII where we were concerned with the forms of change. There we considered changes, actions, and functions as abstractions, thus implying that they constitute features or aspects which can be singled out from ordinary experience. Now, however, we wish to know how abstractions can be imaginatively altered over and beyond experience. A relatively simple answer to this question suggests itself; namely, that *changes, actions, and functions, having been abstracted from experience, can now become the models for purely imaginative alterations of abstractions.* As a simple illustration we may take the following case. We observe a rubber band stretched (or anything stretchable being stretched), and then having abstracted the notion of stretchableness, we can imaginatively apply it to any abstraction which has length, such as the top of a desk even though the desk top itself does not stretch. If we review all the ways in which ideas can be imaginatively altered, we shall find, I believe, that they are traceable back to experienceable changes. At least, let us accept this view as an hypothesis which will be worth exploring.

Change, we observed, is noticeable as negation, creation, substitution, or variation. Let us consider *negation* first, to see how it may be used in imaginative alteration. Awareness of negation arises when some accustomed object, part, or aspect is missing (e.g., My hat is not on the hook in the closet where I keep it). But imaginative negation occurs when we simply remove an object, part, or aspect in thought only (e.g., I imagine my hat not to be on its hook). Even ordinary noticing of the absence of something requires some sophistication, for it presupposes enough familiarity with a situation to have built up an expectation. Children learn early to ask for absent objects, but only after they have had experience with that object as present in the given circumstance. Imaginative negation must go considerably further. It must result from first abstracting some object, part, or aspect, and then consciously imagining it away, that is, as not there.

In the history of philosophy, imaginative negation has played a role of great importance. For example, it took considerable courage on the part of the early Greek philosophers to conceive of the universe as operating without the innumerable personified spirits which were supposed to inhabit streams, forests, mountains, winds, and the like. This depersonification of nature may seem commonplace to us today, since we would now consider the personified spirits of mythology as the products of fanciful imagination. But when an idea has become so long established in popular thought as this one was by the time of Thales (c. 585 B.C.), it takes a strong act of conscious negation to banish it. But probably the most developed philosophical effort toward negation is that to be found in Hindu thought, where one of the dominant ideas has been that of ridding oneself of the ordinary notions of experienced things, and even of personal feelings, in order to become better united with the ultimate reality. This ultimate reality is conceived traditionally in Hindu thought as transcending all differences.*

* See P. T. Raju, "The Principle of Four-Cornered Negation in Indian Philosophy," *Review of Metaphysics,* VII, No. 4 (June 1954) , pp. 694-713.

Language assists us in making negations, for negating elements are very common and readily available in most languages. For example, English has a number of negative prefixes, such as *un-*, *in-*, *(im-, ir-)*, *a-*, *(an-)*,* and the suffix *-less* (e.g., unblue, inefficient, irreflexive, asymmetrical, anemic, boundless). Such terms usually refer by abstractive negation to absence of an expected quality or condition. But·they may help to suggest imaginative negation, as when we try to imagine what something now seen as finite would be like if it were *in*finite or bound*less*. This concept of the infinite or boundless occurred early in Greek philosophy, when Thales' successor Anaximander imagined that the fundamental stuff of reality is the boundless. Though we are not quite certain what he had in mind, it is probable that he thought of "boundless" as referring not so much to the absence of external limits of the universe as to the inexhaustible nature of the basic material. The concept of the boundless or infinite has had an interesting history. We shall consider later how it might have arisen in the imagination.

The opposite idea from negation is that of *creation*. Where negation implies an abrupt disappearance, creation implies an abrupt appearance. We offered (Chapter VIII) the example of the sudden appearance of a bird on a previously empty branch as the type of experience from which the idea of creation could arise. From this type of experience the idea of creation could be extended imaginatively in many directions. For example, people have long wondered about the origin of the universe. They have answered this question by positing a sudden creation out of nothing, as suggested in the Book of Genesis. They have also conceived creation in a more modest or partial way, as in the case of the Greek philosophers, where some kind of eternally existing matter takes on new configurations or new directions of movement. The ideas of Empedocles (c. 495-435 B.C.) offer one illustration of this view. For him the material of the universe (earth, water, air, fire) alternates between a movement toward harmonious creation in which the force of affection or love dominates, and an opposite movement toward separation when anger and strife dominate. Since these two movements alternate endlessly, "creation" in this scheme would only mean the changing from one cycle to the other, or the particular creation of some kind or species during the period

* Note that not all *in-* or *an-* prefixes indicate negation.

dominated by love. Greek speculation was full of ideas concerning special modes of creation or particular creations, but the Greeks apparently never conceived of the possibility of a total creation out of nothing such as we encounter in the Old Testament.

Turning next to *imaginative substitution,* we find not only useful concepts but also a fertile source for the creation of all sorts of monstrosities. Imaginative substitution occurs whenever we think of some part of a given observable object or situation as negated or removed and then replaced by another element. If, for example, one should contemplate tearing down a building and replacing it with another, one is imaginatively substituting the new building for the old one. This sort of imagining is most useful. But the creatures of many mythologies involve imaginatively substituted composites formed from animal heads and human bodies. The harpy is a vulture with a human female head. The Minotaur is a human male with a bull's head. The Chimera is a flame-vomiting creature with a she-goat's body, a lion's head, and a serpent's tail. One author* has expanded on these combinations in a very entertaining publication having fifteen pages divided horizontally, with pictures of animals drawn across the split in such a way that the outer limits of the top part coincide with the limits of the bottom part. Thus in fifteen pages there are 15^2 or 225 possible combinations of animal drawings, some of which, needless to say, are very odd indeed.

Not only can objects and parts be interchanged and substituted imaginatively, but so can aspects. For example, in the case of Salvador Dali's famous painting of watches drooping over the edge of a table (The Persistence of Memory, 1931), one can notice that the quality of limpness replaces the expected quality of rigidity normal to watches. This substitution gives a startling effect. Substitution of both part and quality is a frequent type of imaginative alteration in surrealistic art, and Dali's work offers many notable examples.

Relations and functions too may be imaginatively substituted, as when a longer (or relationally different) nose is substituted for a shorter one in a cartoon, or when a movement is speeded up in a film, giving a different rate of action. But changes of relation or

* James Riddell, *Animal Lore and Disorder* (Harper and Brothers, no date) and *Hit or Myth* (Atrium Press) .

function, whether noticed or imagined, suggest variation more than substitution. Substitution, as we have been considering it, implies taking away one part or aspect and replacing it by another. This process itself may be either slow or rapid, gradual or abrupt. When a substitution is finished, however, this particular bit of change comes to an end. Some clocks, for example, show only the numbers representing hours and minutes. At each minute a new number pops abruptly into view. Here is a type of timepiece in which the changes are substitutional. Continuous gradual change, on the other hand, such as one finds in the ordinary clock where the hands move around a dial, we have been calling "variation." Variation and substitution are thus distinguishable only with regard to rapidity of the change, and this may seem a minor difference. Yet the orientation is quite different, especially the psychological effect, so that imaginatively the idea of steady change or variation gives rise to certain possibilities which abrupt substitution does not.

Let us consider, then, *imaginative variation*. Variation, like negation, creation, and substitution, may involve objects, parts of objects, qualities, relations, or functions. We find examples of abstractable variation all about us. A candle burns, and is reduced in size; a rosebud grows; the sky changes color during a sunset; a building is moved to a new site; a car accelerates. Imaginative variation follows the same possibilities; for all the examples just mentioned—and many more—could be imagined instead of being actually perceived. We could imagine the candle burning down, the rosebud growing, the sky changing color, etc.; and the imaginary possibilities may be carried in each case far beyond the perceived situations, or may be transferred from one kind of situation to another. Thus we can imagine a bean plant growing until it reaches the sky, or a modern skyscraper sprouting wings and flying away, or people traveling to other planets. These imaginings go beyond any present experiences; but they are possible as extensions and recombinations of experienced abstractions.

Changes, including variations, may be changes of quality, relation, or function. As an example of imaginative change of quality, let us think of the painter who runs through in his mind all the possible colors he may use for coloring a particular shape. He need not be bound by the way things look; and indeed he may select a blue color for a face rather than the more realistic flesh color, not necessarily because the blue is symbolic, but only because it balances better with other colors. Shapes, too, can be imaginatively varied before choosing a particular one. Thus, in twentieth-century painting especially, we find remarkable examples of variation of qualities.

It is in the area of changing relations that the greatest possibilities for imaginative extension seem to occur. We might test out these possibilities in terms of any of the major relations discussed in Chapter VII. Let us look, for example, at spatial and quantitative relations. Not only is there the beanstalk that grows to the sky, but there are Alice's unnatural ups and downs as she eats the cakes in Wonderland. Such imaginative changes in size are much less painful than those ascribed to Procrustes, who, according to legend, made all visitors fit his bed, either by stretching them out or by lopping them off. One can invert trees and even mountains, not to mention the more useful imaginative task of mentally redistributing the furniture in a room.

Turning to quantitative relations, we recall (Chapter VII) that there are two kinds: measurement and enumeration. Measurement is applicable to a continuum, whereas enumeration is suitable to discrete units. In either case, increase or decrease can be imagined; and it is the notion of quantity plus imaginative increase and decrease which gives us arithmetic. Thus the number system is, to start with, simply an imagined endlessly increasing addition of units. And what can be added can be imaginatively taken away. Eventually we must imagine taking away more than we had, thus leading us to the notion of minus or negative numbers. Having established imaginatively these extensions of observables, we are able to utilize these concepts for all types of further imaginary situations, such as an unending progression of days or an unending diminution of distance. With both spatial and quantitative relations the imagination is given a relational basis for projecting its notions out and beyond any given experience. Mathematics, indeed, is basically the imaginative playing around with spatial (geometry) and quantitative (arithmetic) relations in order to discover the necessary implications of such imaginative manipulation. The reader may find it profitable and enlightening to play around with the other key relations discussed in Chapter VII to see what fanciful alterations they may yield.

Not only are changes of qualities and changes of relations possible, but changes of functions are also possible. If, for example, one considers "function" in our second sense (i.e., a characteristic task of anything), it is easy to imagine a change of function. If the postman were to become a policeman, or an automobile were to be jacked up to run a pump, we would have examples of changes of function in this sense. Changes of function in the third sense (i.e., two or more related changes) are also conceivable. Thus we might imagine the acceleration or deceleration of a planet in its movement around the sun, with corresponding changes in position, as far greater than they actually are. Or we could imagine a change in Kepler's law of planetary motion itself, as for example, if the relationship between speed of a planet and distance from the sun were not that of constant areas swept by an imaginary line from planet to sun, but were instead speed dependent upon square of the distance from the sun. Remember that Kepler had to try out many such possible relationships *imaginatively* before he hit upon the best one. It is at this point in his work that the scientist must depend heavily upon his imaginative powers.

What are the levels of imagination?

We have seen how negation, creation, substitution, and variation can form the model for imaginative alteration of abstractions. Now let us look at the imaginative activity from the point of view of kinds or levels of imagination, starting with the very simplest and most obvious sort and proceeding toward the very limits of imaginative possibility.

Imagination, as we are using this term here, should be taken in a very broad sense, namely that of having some awareness, whether mentally pictured or not, of something or some condition that is not immediately present to direct perception. In this sense, even if we are looking at a scene and shut our eyes for a moment, then any awareness we may have of the scene while our eyes are shut would be a kind of imagination. This would be the simplest kind of recollective imagination, and would constitute our lowest or *first* level.

The *second* kind of imagination occurs when the object or scene remembered is no longer perceptually retrievable, often when the recollection has become dim with age. One's childhood bed will serve as an example for most of us, assuming of course that this venerable object has not been stored away in the attic where we can revisit it, refresh our memory of it, and correct any aberrations of recollection. Without the object, our forgetfulness will require more imaginative power to fill in the forgotten detail, perhaps correctly, perhaps not.

The *third* variety of imagination is a bit different. It involves the filling in and completing in our perception, thought, and understanding of what we are actually perceiving. We have all had the experience of filling in the wrong details and discovering later that we were mistaken about the object we thought we were perceiving. For example, as noted in Chapter I, we may mistake a cat for a dog or a raccoon for a rabbit when seen in the dark or at a distance. Likewise, we often fill in wrongly the unheard part of another person's spoken words, so that we construe his remarks to mean something quite different from what they actually meant. Such experiences may represent but the top of the iceberg when it comes to the vast amount that we are continuously filling into our experiences by way of imagination. No doubt these imaginary completions are suggested by previous experiences which help us to recognize whatever it is we think we are perceiving. We rarely take the time to examine the objects of perception with care; things are happening too fast for that. So we depend to a great extent upon what we may here call "completive" imagination.

A *fourth* type of imagining is closely related to the preceding, but clearly involves a greater imaginative effort. This type occurs when we fill in the details of some object or event that we ourselves have never witnessed, but which is being described or narrated to us by someone else. We naturally do the best we can in terms of our own experiences and our own previous imaginings. Knowledge of historical "facts" is largely of this kind, since we must there rely upon the testimony of others who either witnessed the events themselves, or whose testimony is in turn dependent upon the testimony of others who did. Often such testimony is based on imagined presuppositions and not upon observation at all. From considerations of this sort, we must realize that the so-called "facts of history" are highly imaginative, or at least seen through the perspective of various observers.

As a *fifth* example of imagination, let us turn to a kind that may be termed "reduplicative" imagining. Most generalizing is of this type, since it involves imagining more of the same kind of anything as those we have ourselves witnessed. For example, we have all experienced a number of dogs and cats. But what about all dogs or all cats? The ones we have witnessed are only a very small portion of the total class, especially if we include past and future examples. So what do we do? We reach out in our thoughts by imagining more and more like the ones we already know. Now clearly a generalization of this sort—and this is the case with most generalizations—is the product of reduplicative imagining. Only those few and limited generalizations which are entirely perceivable (e.g., all the chairs in this room) would not involve imagination in our sense.

Moving on to a *sixth* and more creative kind of imagining, we have those concepts that are produced by recombining experienceable elements or parts of observable objects. Many of the creatures of mythology, as noted, like the centaur (man and horse) or the Minotaur (man's body with bull's head), are imaginative combinations of experienceable elements. No doubt these creatures were imagined because of the greater power or terrifying character which they were assumed to possess. But whatever the reason, they represent a characteristic type of human imagining, and one that is still fertile in current science fiction. Since most of these imaginary creatures are composed of perceivable elements, they can be readily depicted and portrayed in drawings or statuary. So once having been imaginatively created and depicted, the pictures at least become perceivable.

In *seventh* place, let us note the kind of imagining which would take some experienceable object and extend it or reduce it in size. A giant, for example, is a normal human form enlarged—perhaps to as much as a mile in height. Or a world of miniature humans and miniature geography, as in Swift's land of Lilliput, would exemplify imaginative reduction in size. Here, as with the sixth type, we are still in the realm of picturable objects, even though their proportions to other things are different.

Let us in the *eighth* type move beyond the realm of the picturable.* Suppose we think of an infinitely tall giant, or an infinitely extended table top. We do this simply by conceiving of something without limits. But everything we experience and can picture is finite. We may imagine that a finite length can be infinitely divided into lesser and lesser portions, but such a thought carries us far beyond what we can actually see or portray directly in pictures. Are the infinitely great and the infinitely small (infinitesimal) based on any experience at all? There are at least two possibilities which show that they are. One is to examine the word *infinite* with the eye of the etymologist, and note that the negating prefix *in-* is used. *In*finite thus means "not finite," an idea that could be derived by first abstracting a limited or finite continuum (such as the edge of a tabletop), then abstracting from this limited continuum the bare notion of limits, and finally negating or discarding these limits. When the limits are negated, the concept of an infinite continuum results. The other approach is to commence with the abstracted idea of number (either the number of a group or of units in a continuum) and then imaginatively conceive the continuing addition of further numbers. Since there is no inherent limit to the imaginative act of adding, this process can be conceived as continuing without termination. Any progression or regression in which there is no inherent limit will lend itself to this type of imagining. Of course, indicating in this way that the concept of infinity is derivable from abstraction plus imagination does not aid us to conceive an infinity as actually existing. Here the paradox comes from our effort to think of a quality which goes beyond experience as if it were experienceable, and this we cannot do. Or as an alternative, it invites us to imagine a kind of existence that falls outside the experienceable, and this kind of existence has a vague meaning based on our effort to make it analogous to what we do experience.

The infinitesimal, like the infinite, is an instructive case of a nonpicturable imaginary concept. It was once conceived to be the result of a quantitative reduction of a continuum until all length was eliminated and only a lengthless point remained. Such a point

---

* One traditional use of the term limits "imagination" to the picturable kind, preferring some other term such as "conceptualization" for the nonpicturable. The justification for this practice would be that the term "image" suggests something picturable. However, there seems to be a continuity of imaginative activity in moving from the picturable to the nonpicturable which justifies the present usage.

would not have magnitude, however. It would only have position in a frame of reference, as with points in a Cartesian system of co-ordinates. But points without size are useless if we wish to think of them as constituting lines, for no matter how many such points are added together nothing having magnitude, like a line, is produced. As Zeno the Eleatic (c. 480-440 B.C.) clearly observed, one does not get something from nothing or magnitude from that which has no magnitude. So the infinitesimal cannot be conceived as having no magnitude. The mathematician is therefore compelled to regard the infinitesimal as a variable quantity which may become indefinitely small (smaller and smaller endlessly), but without ever reaching zero. Such a concept is bound to be both useful and troublesome.

The infinite and the infinitesimal are examples of imaginative extrapolation. We also have many examples of imaginative refinement, like the notion of a perfect circle, or any other perfect geometric figure. As Plato argued,* we never experience perfection in this world, and yet we have little difficulty understanding what a perfect circle would be. But we do not need to posit Plato's myth of reincarnation and recollection to explain the notion of such perfection. Objects in nature—the sun or a full moon—can suggest a circle which we could then imaginatively refine until our notion reaches the limit which the geometer wishes us to conceive as his perfect ideal form. Is this perfect limit something innate, something already within us, toward which our imagination must move? We need not even go so far as this, except to allow that once a line or direction of imagining has been suggested, we naturally (i.e., innately) carry it as far as we can.

With regard to nonpicturable imaginary extrapolations and refinements, one more point needs to be made. There is a strong tendency in human thought to objectify and hypostatize our abstractions.† This tendency is no less prevalent for our perfected imaginings. Thus, to carry the abstractions of power and goodness to a maximum limit and then to attribute these imaginatively perfected qualities to a perfect concrete being—a God, for example—falls quite naturally within the tendency of human thought.

I have reserved until last a very special sort of imagining—the

* See *Phaedo*, 65, for a statement about nonperceptible absolutes.
† See Chapter V, p. 121.

effort to conceive contradictory traits as if they could belong to a single object or event at the same time. The classic example is the famous (or infamous) round square. To imagine some single object which is both perfectly square and also perfectly circular at the same time is manifestly self-defeating and impossible. It is easy enough for us to propound paradoxical situations, like the round square, the finite infinite, or the encounter between the irresistible force and the immovable body. Where powers of imagination boggle is in the attempt to imagine these paradoxical traits together in one object or event. In all these cases, the imagination is successful up to a point—the point of imagining the two paradoxical traits. But only in an irrational feeling or a suprarational mystic ecstasy could one feel that he had achieved success in combining them. Actually there is nothing mysterious about imaginatively attempting the impossible. We only make trouble for ourselves when we assert rational success for these attempts.

We can simplify our classification of the varieties of imagination as follows: the first two kinds mentioned above could be called (A) "recollective" imagination, the third and fourth varieties would be termed (B) "completive" or "concretive" imagination in the sense of filling out the details of an object or situation in one's imagination, the fifth variety we can designate as (C) "additive" imagination in the sense that generalizing adds new imaginary examples to an already conceived class, and the sixth, seventh, and eighth types are all cases of (D) "reconstructive" imagination in the sense that parts and aspects are imaginatively moved around or altered in regard to position, size, quality, and the like, whether the result is picturable or not. The final case—that of paradoxical traits, like the round square, taken together—represents an effort toward completive or concretive imagination, but one that does not quite succeed for the reasons already noted.

How is imagination used in logic and mathematics?

The logician who constructs a logic dealing with precise classes instead of classes with variable extensions, the geometer who reasons out the relationships between "perfect" figures, and the arithmetician who concerns himself with pure numbers are all operating with imaginatively refined concepts. When these concepts are related back to the world of sense experience, they are applicable only to the degree to which they approach the experienceable world. For example, if one were asked to enumerate the items on an ordinary cluttered desk, he would have difficulty knowing what to consider as a "single" item. Would the sheaf of papers in a folder be one item or many? Depending on how the numbering is applied, different answers would be obtained. So one must refine and simplify one's initial abstractions in order to make them coincide with notions of logic and mathematics.

In another and even more important way, imagination plays a role in logic and mathematics. One can imaginatively alter some primary assumption of a logical or mathematical system and then discover the consequences of the new assumption. Thus, in non-Euclidean geometry, one can imagine a system in which parallel lines do meet if infinitely extended. This proposition produces new consequences for the system of which it is a postulate. Or in logic if, instead of the postulate of separate classes, one should assume that each kind stands in a relation of synthesis with its opposite kind, one would be conceiving the dialectical logic of Hegel instead of the independent class logic of Aristotle. The imaginative alteration of basic assumptions is vital to the construction of alternative logical or mathematical systems.

Empiricists claim that experience is the ultimate source of knowledge. Against this view the concepts of mathematics, such as the infinite and infinitesimal, pose one of the chief obstacles, for these concepts seem to have little to do with anything experienceable. Yet when we examine the way in which the imaginative power of thought can alter abstractions through all sorts of refinements and extrapolations, even the most inexperienceable of mathematical concepts can be given a reasonable derivation from simple primary abstractions. One more example may help us to see how this is so. The square root of -1 (or the square root of any negative number) has the honor of being specially designated as an "imaginary" number. Actually it is no more imaginary than many other concepts involving numbers. But be that as it may, let us see if we can trace its derivation to some primary abstractions. First, ordinary numbers are directly abstractable as quantities of different groups of objects. Then these numbers are imaginatively arranged in a series which can be indefinitely extended. Now, certain experiences with numbers introduce the notion of negative numbers, as when one's bank account goes in the red, or when we establish a scale, like that of the thermometer, which can increase in two directions from a central point. Having thus included negative numbers in our number system, there is no reason why we should not imaginatively try out all the arithmetical operations (including the taking of square roots) over our whole set of numbers. Presto—we have the case of the square roots of minus quantities confronting us, even though we also have a stipulation in our arithmetical system that any square must be positive (because any number multiplied with itself, whether a positive or a negative number, should give us a positive number). But why let this stipulation stop us? We can experiment imaginatively with square roots of minus quantities, can we not? When we do so, we find that there are some interesting and useful results; so we simply add a new category of numbers (imaginary numbers) to our other varieties. The point here, however, is not the utility of these numbers, but the fact that they are derived through imaginative operations upon primary abstractions.

What is the role of imagination?

In Science. Scientific thought could never have begun but for the mind's ability to alter abstractions imaginatively. Once natural human curiosity and the desire to explain are at work, the job of the scientist is fundamentally that of formulating plausible hypotheses or theories which will "explain" (i.e., give general reasons) why things are as they are or behave as they do. And remember that the testing of hypotheses would be impossible if there were not first some hypotheses to test.

We shall examine the manners of formulating hypotheses in more detail in Chapter XIII. Let us here simply note the role imagination plays in the typical inductive generalization (e.g., all crows are black) or extrapolation (e.g., there will be approximately one million college graduates in the United States in 1990). In both generalizing and extrapolating we are led to imagine a condition that lies beyond our range of direct experience.

More interesting from the point of view of imagination are those hypotheses which involve rather highly developed conceptual models (like the notion of the solar system or the atom). As scientific knowledge progresses, it is often necessary to modify or even revamp the hypothetical models which have come down to us. The need for such modification or revamping is normally indicated by the discovery of new empirical evidence not accounted for by the old model, or by the discovery of some logical contradiction or inconsistency as we explore the implications of a model or compare it with some other accepted model. When the need for modification becomes apparent, it is customary for the scientific imagination to borrow from some other area of experience where a model is already given, or to alter the structure of the older model. Sometimes both of these procedures happen together, as we shall see in the following illustration.

The concept of the *atom* affords an excellent example of the manner in which scientific imagination operates. The ancient Greek thinkers Leucippus and Democritus (fifth century B.C.) were apparently the first to hit on the idea of the atom, which they did as the result of the same logic that led Zeno to reject infinitesimals without magnitude, for they realized that if matter were really divisible at any point, there could be no smallest unit of matter. To avoid this difficulty, they suggested that there must be very small units having some magnitude, but themselves incapable of being divided further. They named these smallest units of matter *atoms*, meaning "indivisibles." These atoms were undoubtedly conceived on the model of little hard particles like grains of sand.

From the time of Democritus until about the nineteenth century the theory of atomism remained essentially unchanged. Thus even at the time of Dalton (1766-1844) and after, atoms were regarded as simply hard, impenetrable solids. Apparently they were also thought of as having various shapes, since Ostwald as late as 1904 refers to "those pernicious hypotheses" which place "hooks and points upon atoms." More important, however, the atoms of each chemical element were thought to possess a characteristic weight. It was also thought, although agreement here was not universal, that the atom was an inelastic body. The ground for this hypothesis was logical simplicity. For the atom to be an elastic body would imply movement among its parts, and the atom, by definition, is without parts.

THE VORTEX ATOM. The main difficulty with this atomic theory was encountered with regard to elasticity. If atoms are inelastic, then in the collision between atoms kinetic energy will be lost—a result thought to be contrary to experience. To meet this situation, William Thomson (the future Lord Kelvin) in 1867 proposed the vortex atom. Following the lead of Helmholtz, he imagined a homogeneous, incompressible, frictionless fluid within which vortices exist. The fluid has the property of inertia, but only the vortices, or rings, have the character of matter. This atom was more nearly ideal than any of the previous kinds suggested, but it was not clear how inertia could pertain to what is only a mode of motion of a substance, and not a substance itself.

The discovery of radioactivity and of X rays toward the end of the nineteenth century led J. J. Thomson to the discovery of the electron in 1897. With this discovery, the concept of the atom as an ultimate, indivisible particle of matter became untenable. The old difficulties with the atomic theory were thereby liquidated in favor of a new set of difficulties.

THE SPHERICAL ATOM. Around the year 1900, Lord Kelvin suggested a new notion of the atom designed to account for the new facts. This was the first model which included an internal structure. It was conceived as consisting in a uniform sphere of positive electrification permeated here and there by free electrons, "like raisins in a pudding." Kelvin remarked that "If the electrons, or atoms of electricity, succeeded in getting out of the atoms of matter, they would proceed with velocities which might exceed the velocity of light," and the body would be radioactive. J. J. Thomson analyzed this model, and as a result, it is often known as "the Thomson atom."

THE SHELL ATOM. A few years later, Lord Kelvin proposed a different model. This atom would consist of alternating shells of positive and negative electricity. The electrons were thought of as embedded in the positive shells, and, if unstable, could be ejected with varying speeds. The atom was now regarded as a sphere of positive electrification with electrons moving about on inner concentric shells. "Thomson [then] showed that a ring of rotating electrons will be stable till the number exceeds a definite limit. Two rings will then be formed, and so on."*

* See W. C. Dampier, *A History of Science*, p. 405.

THE NUCLEUS ATOM. The shell atom did not explain the amount of scattering of alpha particles passing through thin sheets of matter, such as gold. To meet this objection, Rutherford in 1911, following a suggestion of Nagaoka, modified it by turning it inside out. The positive charge was now conceived as concentrated at the center, "like a fly in a cathedral," as he put it, the electrons being distributed about this nucleus in such manner as to make the atom electrically neutral. The greater part of the mass of the atom was now held to be concentrated at the center and the atom itself conceived as mostly empty space. Thus a particle could now be thought to pass through an atom without hitting anything, yet to be deflected from its course by the attraction of the heavy mass at the center, much as a comet passes through the solar system and is deflected from its course by the gravitational attraction of the sun. Rutherford's atom was essentially a solar system in miniature.

Rutherford's atom could explain the scattering, but it was recognized that the atom must also explain the facts of spectroscopy, and this it could not do. If the electrons in Rutherford's atom moved about the nucleus with a given frequency, they should emit radiation of that frequency and thereby lose energy. Hence the atom should emit radiation at a continuously decreasing frequency. But the spectral lines of atoms are sharp. The shift from one frequency to another is abrupt, not gradual.

THE BOHR ATOM. To explain the evidence of spectroscopy, Niels Bohr in 1913 applied the principle of quantum theory to the atom. He allowed the electron to move only in certain orbits. The electron could move in a given orbit without radiating or absorbing energy. But radiation would occur when the electron moved from an outer to an inner orbit. Thus the atom was still thought of as a miniature planetary system. Later, the orbits were even plotted as elliptical, with nucleus and electrons moving about a common center of mass. Nevertheless, the laws which hold for this system are not those which hold for the planetary system as such.

THE WAVE ATOM. A later phase in the development of atomic theory is represented by the notion of the wave atom. In 1924 De Broglie studied the relation between energy of a unit particle and that of a wave. Now by relativity theory, motion increases mass but slows down frequency. Hence the two energies cannot be equated directly. But they can be equated if a particle, such as an electron, is regarded as always being enveloped in a group of waves. Later Schrödinger proposed dropping the particle from the picture as being unnecessary, leaving merely the wave group. This atom was to be visualized as no longer a planetary system with revolving electrons, but rather as a wave group or undulation.

However, difficulties inherent in this model have led most contemporary physicists to reject it as a picturable reality. Schrödinger's famous wave equations, which seemed to describe the electron as a three-dimensional wave surrounding the atomic nucleus are now interpreted in terms of probability waves. That is, the waves must be imagined as yielding the *probability* of the electron being at a particular location, but not as describing the mechanical structure of the atom.

At present there seems to be no generally accepted mechanical model for the atom. The behavior and nature of subatomic particles are believed to be such that the atom cannot be represented in visual images. Scientists talk of atomic "states" which describe the interior structures of atoms. But these states are highly mathematical abstractions, and the values of the observables with which they are supposed to correlate (e.g., position and momentum of electrons) are held to depend in a special way on the act of observation itself. Thus, contemporary "models" of the atom are more in the nature of charts representing the relationships between the various possible states of the atom. They are not to be thought of as pictures of what one might "see" if one could enlarge an atom sufficiently. The very notion of such imaginative picturings is now held to be meaningless in the realm of atomic theory. If we wish to speak of a model at all, we would have to say that the only adequate atomic model is composed entirely of abstract mathematical relations.

The foregoing account of the development of the concept of the atom illustrates how imagination can construct scientific hypotheses about entities which are beyond the reach of direct experience. It also illustrates how the concepts used in constructing these hypotheses are the product of either logical necessity or new empirical data. Lastly, it shows us the manner in which hypothetical models may be borrowed from many sources—grains of sand, the solar system, waves, and the like—or may be the product of imaginative rearrangements of existing models, as in the case of Rutherford's inversion of the Thomson model, which is both a rearrangement and a borrowing of the solar system model. In this way scientific imagination proceeds in its search for likely hypotheses. As students of science, our first requirement is to grasp clearly and accurately the hypothetical models or abstractions currently preferred. Then we can begin to look for ways of improving the models.

In the Arts. If by "arts" we mean the fine arts (literature, music, dance, drama, painting, sculpture, drawing, architecture, and the like), we should in all probability regard these as the very homeland of creative imagination; and it is certainly true that without creative imagination it would be as impossible to have art as it would to have science. How, then, does the creative imagination function in the arts?

First, the artist has a certain idea or feeling which through his art he seeks to portray. This idea or feeling is itself abstracted from experience and refined imaginatively. It is commonly compressed, as in the drama, where the events portrayed on the stage are pushed together in time. It may have certain features or qualities strengthened or enlarged to heighten certain effects, as in the paintings of El Greco, where human figures are elongated. Very often there is considerable rearrangement of parts or actions. A story writer may take a suggestion from a real episode; but then he transposes it and twists and adds or subtracts parts of the episode in order to create a well-rounded and interesting plot which will serve to bring out the character traits needed to heighten the drama of the situation. In all these rearrangements of subject matter, the artist must use his imagination.

Secondly, there is the question of medium. Each art is distinguished by the special medium or artist's material. The oil painter uses canvas and paint, the musician uses systems of sounds, the writer uses linguistic symbols, the dancer uses his own body, and so on for other arts. Each art has a chosen medium in which to express ideas and feelings. Now these media have their own abstractable aspects which can be imaginatively altered in many ways. For example, sound has pitch, intensity, duration, timbre (quality of sound—brassy, reedy, etc.), all of which can be altered by the composer within limited ranges. The literary artist's words have qualities of sound (euphony, rhyme, alliteration, etc.) as well as meaning, suggestion of symbolic overtone, and emotional coloration.

Having selected or discovered a suitable subject matter or theme, the artist is faced with the selection of appropriate media and with the many possible variable qualities that exist within each medium. The total work of art is the product of many acts of imaginative selection. Sometimes, for some of us, these acts seem to come spontaneously. For others, it is a tedious process of trial and error, testing, rejecting, and reworking. In either case, creative imagination is at work.

Additional mention should be made of the directive function of imagination at work in artistic creation. There are at least two directions in which this function can move. First, all the acts of selection mentioned above have as their goal what may be called "enhanced seeing." One does not select and concentrate his qualities and forms in a haphazard manner without some kind of directive guidance, but rather with an imagined goal or end product in view that will highlight and strengthen just those aspects that are important in producing new or unusual perspectives in whatever subject matter one has chosen. This *concentrative* act of artistic imagination operates not only at the level of perception, or literal "seeing," but also at the emotive level, especially in musical arts, and at the conceptual level, especially in the literary arts.

A second way in which imagination is of extreme importance in the arts is to be found in the domain of symbolism. The various elements in a work of art can suggest *extended symbolic meanings,* not just by using the traditional or conventional kind of symbol, but by creating new and metaphorical extensions in terms of the basic generic or natural symbols of human feeling and understanding. Thus, the elements of rhythm and tonal quality may suggest far-reaching characteristics of nature to be interwoven with other symbolic overtones. The imaginative use of symbolic extension in the creation and appreciation of art is that which above all else endows a work with meaning and significance.

Both of the above modes of imagining—the concentrative and symbolic extension—are as important for the receiver or appreciator of a work of art as for the artist himself. Without them the artistic enterprise would be dull and lifeless. They constitute the very heart of what we mean by creative imagination in the arts.

Yet creative imagination is not by itself sufficient to produce a successful work of art. It also takes what may be called *taste*. Artistic taste is a mysterious gift, but central to it is facility in selecting the most appropriate media and forms to represent or express a given theme. The great artists have all had the gift of taste. Great scientists, too, have a gift somewhat akin to artistic taste. In their case it is more a sense of the appropriateness of an imaginative model to serve as a successful hypothesis or theory for a given problem. A fertile imagination by itself will afford its possessor the possibility of conceiving a wider variety of alternative models, but scientific "taste" is also needed in helping one to select models which are most likely to prove fruitful.

In Philosophy. The philosopher must use his imagination in a number of ways. In fact, at every stage of the game some imaginative activity is involved. Let us review briefly some of these activities.

There is, of course, no well-defined philosophical method. Nevertheless, there are some characteristic stages or phases in philosophical thinking which seem to have a certain order to them. First, the philosopher, as the expert in ideas and beliefs, must have some ideas to examine. These may come to him as the result of his own observations and musings on the nature of things, or they may come from conversations and readings. Most of our ideas come as a combination of these sources. But however they come, they usually arrive in a vague and confused condition. Our first job, then, is to *examine* and *clarify* them. This means that we must take the bits of evidence from personal observations and from the reports of others and seek to make them more precise by delimiting them and filling in the detail. As we saw, filling in the detail of an idea requires an act of the imagination, for we must imagine the details that we do not perceive. And furthermore, in selecting the detail, we have a considerable latitude, depending upon the scope of our imagination. The wider our imagination, the more possibilities we have for selecting appropriate detail.

In the second place, our ideas as to the nature of things lead to beliefs that things are this way rather than that. These beliefs often come to us as part of our education. They have been worked out by our ancestors. But it behooves the philosopher to reexamine beliefs for himself, and not to accept them too readily. This is the stage of *critical examination* which is so important to a well-developed philosophical activity. Most often our critical activity takes the shape of looking for the assumptions upon which our casual beliefs depend. When we find these assumptions, they in turn must be clarified and evaluated. The clarification and testing of assumptions leads squarely to logic and a developed logical imagination.

We may assign to the *logical exploration* of assumptions a third place in our philosophical quest. The procedure here is not simple. It is not just a matter of selecting some clarified primitive assumptions, and then following through with simple deductions, for our logic will itself depend upon the set of relationships which we regard as fundamental. What normally happens is that some key image or key metaphor is taken as the best explanation of the character of things in the world that we are seeking to elucidate, to put in perspective.

For example, we may decide that the concept or key image of hard little particles of matter offers us the most fertile clue to the nature of reality, and so we make the assumption that the universe is at bottom composed of such particles, that they are the fundamental reality. Matter becomes our root image for developing a view which we would call "materialism." Or on the other hand, we may prefer to start with ideas themselves as representing that which comes closest to revealing the nature of ultimate reality. When idea and mind are taken as the key metaphor our philosophy is usually known as "idea-l-ism" (the -l- is for euphony). Or, as another alternative, we may assume that both matter and mind are equally important as key concepts, and then we have a mind-matter "dualism," in the style of Descartes.

There are of course a great many possible key concepts that we might select; but whatever one it is, we must then explore it in terms of its logical implications. This is done imaginatively by taking what we conceive to be the primary nature of our key concept and applying it in turn to the various aspects of the world. The logical process here is generous rather than rigorous. We might say to ourselves, for example, "if all is matter, then our thoughts too must be material, perhaps as a kind of material extrusion or secretion of the brain." But such is not the only conclusion we might reach. We may prefer to take thought as more like the whirr of a motor, a mere adjunct of matter in motion. It is not a kind of matter, then, but an aspect of matter in motion.

This kind of reasoning, let us observe, is not one that follows the more precise paths of mathematical and logical deduction where numerical, geometric, or classificational relationships are clearly laid down in advance, and the consequences that are drawn follow by logical necessity. That kind of deductive process is too restrictive for the philosopher's typical quest. His logical explorations require a wider latitude of imagination, an imagination which continues to reach out for more meaningful key concepts and better syntheses. We shall return in Chapter XIV to this question of key concepts and philosophical exploration.

In addition to making logical explorations of basic assumptions, the philosopher will normally seek *justifications*. To justify a theory requires at least two things: experiential evidence and logical consistency with other notions already accepted. Experiential evidence is sometimes given a wider, sometimes a narrower, meaning. In the narrow sense, it may be limited to the carefully controlled experience of the typical scientific procedure, where quantifiable situations are preferred. At the other extreme, experience and experiential evidence may include inner feelings and dreams which seem not to have come from any external sensory source. It may even include those experiences of the few who claim to have had unusual moments of mystic ecstasy. Logical consistency, too, may have various meanings. At one extreme, it may be limited to propositions that can be shown to be derivable by formal deductive procedures. Or, it may be broadened to include any proposition that does not obviously contradict the primary assumptions of a growing philosophical system. The point to note here is that philosophical use of imagination is involved both in the selection of the kind of evidence we wish to include in our justifications and also in the selection of the kind of logical implications we wish to use.

Finally, the outcome of this whole procedure is the development of a *system*. The urge toward greater and greater interrelating of

our various philosophical perspectives into a well-knit and systematic set of propositions is very strong. But, as there is a danger
of extending one's zeal for system beyond its appropriate limits,
it takes a well-tutored imagination to understand the possibilities
and limitations of systematization. The imaginative work involved
in philosophical system building can hardly be overestimated.

With philosophy, as with science and art, there is also a matter
of "taste." As in the other cases, the key to taste is the sense of
appropriateness. For the philosopher this means selecting and
weaving together those ideas which in the long run will make
most sense out of human experience and out of the kinds of reality
that man senses in his world. But also, as with science and art, it is
possible to have philosophical imagination without taste. A taste-
less philosophy would be one in which no rule of proportion relates
the imaginative extravagances of the philosopher. Taste, we might
say, is the twin genius of imagination.

What truth-status shall we assign to imaginary ideas?

Surely enough has been said to demonstrate the error of regarding all the products of creative imagination as mere idle fantasies.
Some imaginary ideas may be useless; but when we consider the
way in which scientific imagination has been fruitful in advancing
knowledge, we must recognize the tremendous value of ideas which
may have seemed to be pure fantasy at the time they were invented.

There are many cases in which a very simple altered abstraction
can be shown to have a superior truth claim to a directly perceived
abstraction. For example, there is the often cited case of the stick
in the glass of water. It appears bent at the waterline; and if we
abstract directly the shape of the stick, we abstract the bent shape.
However, when further investigation of the stick (lifting it out of
the water or running our finger along it) reveals that it is not bent,
we conclude that an imaginatively straightened stick would have
been truer than the bent stick that we perceived. Other examples
of direct abstraction are learned to be illusory (e.g., the sun is not
really the size it appears to us), so that we come to believe that our
imaginatively altered abstractions are truer than those we directly
observe. We do this when our imaginative ideas fit better into the

entire system of beliefs about reality than do the ideas based upon direct perception.

Even the artist, whom we may regard as characteristically exploiting his imaginative freedom to the full, is very often concerned with an effort to discover a forceful and effective mode of presenting not only particular qualities, but also generic traits truly embodied in the particular. Some arts, notably music, seem less concerned with the revelation of particular truths than with the creation of interesting formal patterns and their effective results. Nevertheless, the organization of affective qualities itself may be taken as a kind of musical truth, a truth not so readily expressible in any other medium.

Certainly the philosopher, who is the traditional seeker after truth, should not have his imaginative activity shortchanged by the judgment that philosophical speculation belongs only to the ivory tower or the cloister. Although the types of verification and confirmation which are available to the scientist are not ordinarily available to the philosopher, we should not let this fact detract from the positive contribution of philosophy. It is important to our understanding of the smallest detail that we also spend some time grappling with philosophical problems—problems of the widest scope—including the very problem of truth itself. In fact, since truth is one of the problems with which the philosophical imagination must come to grips, it is unfair to ask of a particular philosophical theory whether or not it is true. If a theory of truth is interwoven with the other strands on the philosophical loom, the whole fabric is not subject to some further external criterion for establishing its truth status. The value of philosophical speculation is broader than truth value alone.

We may conclude that creative imagination is necessary to knowledge; but if it is to bear its fullest rewards, there is also need both for control by good structure sense (logic) and by a sense of appropriateness (taste), whether we are dealing with it in the realm of science, art, or philosophy. This is not to deny the possibility of that sort of imagination which may be termed "idle" or even "wild," nor even to disavow a justifiable exhilaration in the power of such human fantasy. But it does claim that if we wish to do more than revel in a particular human ability, we need the additional guard of the aforementioned controls.

SUGGESTED READINGS

Locke, John, *Essay Concerning Human Understanding,* Bk. II, Ch. 17 (on the infinite).

Hume, David, *Treatise of Human Nature,* Bk. I, Pt. II, Sections 1-2.

Tyndall, John "Essay on the Scientific Use of the Imagination" in *Fragments of Science,* Vol. II.

Whitehead, A. N., *The Concept of Nature,* especially Ch. 4 (on extensive abstraction).

Cohen, M. R., *A Preface to Logic,* Ch. 5 (on the logic of fictions).

Alexander, H. B., "The Great Art Which Is Philosophy" in *Contemporary American Philosophy* (Adams and Montague, eds.), Vol. I, pp. 89-110.

Brown, Harcourt (ed.), *Science and the Creative Spirit.*

Ghiselin, Brewster (ed.), *The Creative Process,* especially the introduction and articles by Poincaré, Einstein, Sessions, Moore, and Coleridge.

Koestler, Arthur, *The Act of Creation,* especially Pts. II and III.

CHAPTER X

Generalizing

What is generalizing?

GENERALIZING (CHAPTER V) is the *process of grouping together to form a class, or of adding more members to a class.* Every *class,* whether of relatively concrete objects or events or of abstract parts, qualities, relations, or functions, is already a generalization, a product of an act of generalizing. It may help us to remember this if we look for a moment at the derivation of the word "generalize." The root of this word is *genus* which signified in Latin a tribe or race or eventually any group that could be thought of as having kinship, that is a *kind* (see Chapter VI). From this meaning, the word was broadened to refer to a bunch or class of any kind of thing grouped together because of similarity of the members (for example, the class of candy bars).

(1) We may suppose that the initial experience with some object registers very little with us except an impression of color, shape, smell, taste, and the like. But this object is given a name (e.g., "candy bar"); and the next time we meet a similar object we remember the name and associate it with the similar object. A third and a fourth example are added to our ex-

perience. Are these still candy bars? With the aid of confirmation by those already familiar with the grouping habits of our particular language, we gradually come to recognize the customary limits of the "candy bar" tent, after first tending to overgeneralize (Chapter II). Thus, by adding instance after instance of similar things (candy bars), an *extension* for this term (Chapter IV) is built up in our imagination. Now this first building up of a class extension is the primary meaning of "generalize," which we can illustrate in our tent diagram by Fig. 1. Let us call this a *simple generalization*.

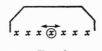

FIG. 1

(2) However, as we learned in Chapter IV, extensional meanings may change. They can be stretched out further or narrowed or transferred to a new area. When we stretch an already existing extension, we may think of this as a new act of generalizing. For example, when new objects are invented or become recognized, the tendency on the part of the users of a language is to extend old terms to cover these new cases. Thus the term "boat" once referred to small open craft moved by oars; but in the course of time this term has been extended to include tremendous ships, ocean liners, battleships, aircraft carriers, and so on. This second stage of generalizing can be illustrated by Fig. 2 and we shall call this an *extended generalization*.

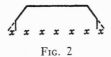

FIG. 2

(3) A third meaning of "generalize" occurs when one class is included in a larger, or "more general" class, for which there is a different and more general term. For example, all trees, and many other growing things as well, are included in the term "plants." So we can speak of generalizing "trees" into "plants." In this case, the term with the smaller extension ("tree") is in-

cluded within another term with a larger extension ("plant"). This type of relation is the basis of the class-inclusion sentence (All trees are plants), where the smaller class is related to the larger class as species to genus. "Species" in this sense merely mean a subclass of a larger or more general class. This third variety of generalizing is illustrated in Fig. 3 and can be termed an *inclusive generalization*.

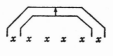

FIG. 3

(4) We sometimes use the term generalization to apply to the notion of a collectivity. In the concept of a collectivity, the distinct separateness of the individuals tends to be blurred, so that one thinks of a group as a mass or throng. For example, the term "mankind" often suggests this type of image with regard to human beings, since the separateness of individual persons is lost to view, and the notion of a mass of people stands out instead. This fourth type of generalization may be called a *collective generalization*. The only way we could show this type of concept in our diagrams would be by moving the *x*'s so close together that they would touch one another.

(5) A single object or event may be thought of as a generalization if it is considered as exemplifying an entire class. One would have to consider the individual to be a sort of prototype or model for the whole class, that is, a *typical particular*. Thus a very ordinary chair, but a typical chair, might be called a generalized chair. In this case, however, the group idea is no longer explicitly present, and the meaning of "general" is in effect transferred to its opposite, namely, to a particular. For this reason it seems better to avoid using the notion of generalization to apply to typical individuals.

(6) The five types of generalization which have been listed above refer to the generalizing of *terms*. However, a *proposition* may be called "general" or "a generalization" if the subject term refers to an entire class. For example, an attributive proposition with a predicate noun (e.g., All cats are animals) would simply express the class-inclusion relation implied in Fig. 3, where the smaller tent

is the lesser class (cats) and the larger tent (animals) is the one that includes it. But attributive propositions, we remember, may also have predicate adjectives (e.g., All cats are furry) in which case the predicate term expresses some aspect of the entire subject class. General propositions can also be action type sentences (e.g., All members of this class have learned to swim). These are all generalizations because the subject term is general. Fig. 3, however, only seems to fit the first of these three examples (i.e., All cats are animals) where we have a clear class-inclusion relation. However, as noted in Chapter II, it has been customary to translate attributive type sentences with predicate adjective and action type sentences into class-inclusion sentences. If we do this, then Fig. 3 can be made to fit them all.

What is the relation between abstracting and generalizing?

We observed in Chapter V that abstracting is not the same as generalizing. In abstracting one *selects* parts or aspects upon which to focus attention. In generalizing, on the other hand, one forms an initial class of similar items, or one extends such a class to *include* more.

But how are these two processes related? Must we, for example, abstract first before we can generalize, or generalize first before we abstract? Does the order in which abstracting and generalizing arise in our experience agree with or differ from the order required by some logical kind of priority? First, we need to observe that generalizations are *classes* of objects or events, taken together because of some similarity or similarities that they have in common. So, the abstracting of the similar traits, which determine the generalization, would seem to be prior (at least logically prior) to the knowledge that there is a "class" (e.g., if we see some apples, we must notice their similarities before we can be sure that they are all "apples"). However, the awareness of the similar traits would depend upon the prior presence in experience of the individuals from which we are going to abstract the similarities (i.e., the "apples" must be experienced first for us to observe their similarities). It seems, then, that we must first have an awareness of something that may turn out to be a general class; and this awareness may be considered as a kind of primitive or embryonic generalizing. But the step of abstracting is necessary before we can be sure that it is a class. Also, repeated examples of the same thing help us to see the similarities which we are going to abstract from them. Both processes (abstracting and generalizing) are equally important for learning and for understanding. Let us conclude, then, that whereas the selective act of abstracting is logically prior to and simpler than the inclusive act of generalizing, in actual practice the two usually go together.

As we explore further the relationships between abstractions and generalizations, a number of interesting questions come to mind. For example, are all generalizations concrete, or are there also generalizations of abstractions? We should remember from our discussion of abstract and concrete in Chapter V that even the objects of ordinary experience, which we are accustomed to consider concrete, can be regarded as themselves abstractions from larger wholes. And if we pursue this thought to its conclusion we wind up with the entire universe as the only concrete; and the universe is no generalization at all, but a particular individual, large though it be. However, if we start with our everyday concretes, the houses, trees, and thunderstorms of ordinary experience, we do of course find that these are all capable of being symbolized by general terms, a capacity which brings us to think of them as generalizations. Since such generalizations are groupings of the normal particulars of experience, let us not begin with them, but inquire about the possibility of generalizing the abstractions which we make from them.

Part abstractions cause little trouble; they are constantly generalized. The top of the table may be generalized into a class of tabletops, and the branches of trees may be generalized into a class of tree branches. But what of aspects? Can color or shape or size be generalized? Why not? We often speak of colors and shapes and sizes in the plural, thus indicating that we are conceiving a generalization of abstract colors or abstract shapes or abstract sizes. For example, all the rectangles that are abstractable from an assortment of tabletops can be generalized into a class of rectangles, and then we can enlarge this class to include all conceivable rectangles from square to long and narrow, and from small to large. So we see that general classes should not be limited to our everyday concretes; they may also include *generalizations of abstractions.*

Let us now look at Fig. 4 where we have diagrammed the relationship between the abstracting and the generalizing processes by two intersecting lines. The vertical line represents variation from

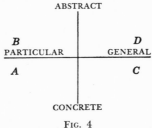

Fig. 4

the most concrete at the bottom to the most abstract at the top and the horizontal line represents greater inclusiveness of individuals from the single or particular individual at the left to the most general group or class at the right. In the mid-area of this diagram, just below the horizontal line, we can plot our everyday concretes (e.g., tables). Then just above the midline we would have our first-level abstractions (e.g., tabletops). Further up would be the aspect abstractions (e.g., rectangular shapes), and so on. So, starting at the left just below our midline, we can imagine a single table; and somewhere in the middle moving to the right would be small groups of tables (e.g., all dining tables); and finally at the extreme right would be all possible tables. We can now note four possibilities, marked by the capital letters: A for an everyday concrete particular, B for a particular abstraction, C for everyday concrete generalizations, and D for generalizations of abstractions.

On a line above our table line, and just above the midline, we could have another horizontal line representing first-level abstractions (e.g., tabletops), with a single tabletop at left, and all possible tabletops at the extreme right. Above that there might be another horizontal line for tabletop shapes, from one particular shape to all possible shapes. Suppose, now, we select just the rectangular tabletops, and from these generalize all rectangular shapes. We could move up to a higher level of abstraction reflecting merely the right-angledness of all rectangles, and then propose a new horizontal line at that level for all right-anglednesses. But the question arises, is there a possible plurality or class of right-angled-ness? Is not right-angledness only a single aspect, wherever it appears? It would seem so, for the notion of a variety of right-anglednesses makes little sense. There is only one possible aspect designated by the term "right-angledness." And with other abstractions, it is similar. We always wind up at the top of our diagram with some single aspect which it makes no sense to generalize. Thus we find that generalizations occur only in the mid-portion of our diagram. The entire universe at the bottom was a particular individual, and the ultimate abstractions at the top are always particular individuals. We have attempted to show this condition in Fig. 5 by superimposing a trapezoid on Fig. 4, a trapezoid which

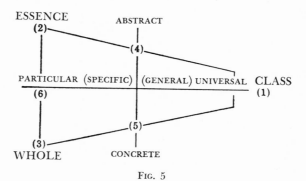

FIG. 5

roughly outlines the possibilities within which our concepts can be found with respect both to their concrete-to-abstract and particular-to-general ranges.

Fig. 5 can further illustrate two ways in which classes can be formed. The first and most obvious way is simply by moving straight across the diagram from left to right—that is, by including more and more of a similar type of particular to form a class. This route is represented by our first three diagrams. But there is also the possibility of using a single abstraction to generate a class. For example, instead of looking at a whole class of particulars (e.g., all the cats in a cat show) and then abstracting their similarities, we might start with one abstractable trait (e.g., furriness) and then go on to generate the class of all furry things.

Unfortunately, our language has no suffix for conveying the idea of these embodied or concreted abstractions. We might speak of this class as "the furries"; or we might adopt such a suffix as *-thum,* as was once suggested,* and speak of "the furry- thums." But most often we indicate these concreted classes generated from some abstraction by means of adjectives or participles used as nouns, with the implied modified noun left unexpressed. For example, we might say "Susan was among the unexpected," where the participle (unexpected)refers to unexpected people, or something of the sort. If we had the suffix suggested above, we could express ourselves by saying "Susan was among the unexpectedthums," but without such a form our language offers us no better way than the use of the participle for expressing the notion of a class generated by an abstraction. At least, among ourselves, we can make use of the *-thum* suffix to test whether or not a particular adjective or participle is being used to express a concreted abstraction. Thus if we are given the sentence "Susan was among the unexpected," and it makes sense to us to say "Susan was among the unexpected-thums," then we know that the word in question ("unexpected" in this case) is a concreted abstraction.

The labels in Figs. 4 and 5 will help us understand the character of a concreted abstraction: a single abstract trait in B, abstracted from some concrete particular in A, can serve to generate a class in C. If we like, we can imagine a line from the trait in B slanting downward to the class in C as representing the process of concreting an abstraction. Thus by abstracting the round shape of a wheel and concreting this abstraction, we can generate the class of all round things (or roundthums). Moreover, the diagrams help us to see the major difference between *generalized abstractions* (e.g., circles), on the one hand, which would be represented in quadrant D, horizontally across from the single abstract circle; and *generalized concreted abstractions,* on the other hand, which would be represented in quadrant C.

The diagrams which we are using here raise certain questions which are not easy to answer, but do bring out some interesting and illuminating considerations. For example, we have been assuming that the general class horizontally across from a particular individual has the same degree of concreteness or abstractness as the particular. But we know that any class as a whole has more as-

* California Associates, *Knowledge and Society,* page 34.

pects in it than would any of its particular members. Would not the class, then, properly be more concrete than the particular? And furthermore, is not the member of a class an abstraction from that class? For if we start with any class of particulars, there is no reason why we could not center attention upon (i.e., abstract) just one of these particulars. There are answers to these questions which will, I believe, allow us to regard these horizontal lines as representing the same degree of concreteness throughout. Let us take the question of the number of traits first. Suppose we have an alley full of cats, and all of these cats represent a plurality of rather similar individuals, so that the number of aspects per individual would not vary greatly. Then the concreteness of the class as a plurality of individuals can be judged in terms of the average number of aspects per member, rather than in terms of the total number of aspects for all the members. This answer suggests one for the other question as well, for when we are concerned with an aggregate of individuals, we are not concerned with a class-as-a-whole. To be sure, the class-as-a-whole might be taken as something more concrete than any of its members; but a class-as-a-whole, when taken as a whole, would itself be an individual and would not properly speaking be represented on the right side of our diagram at all, but on the left side where individuals belong. These points serve simply to illustrate the fact that on the right side of the diagram we are representing a class only as a plurality of particular individuals, and not as a more concrete unit. There is nothing mysterious about the ability to consider a class either as a plurality or as an individual unit. We are constantly faced with this alternative, as is indicated by the fact that we often have a tendency to use a plural verb with such a term as "class."

What is the relation between imagining and generalizing?

In Chapter IX, generalizing was mentioned as a simple kind of extrapolative imagining whenever it moves beyond the confines of a limited class of objects, events, or aspects that are all perceivable at a given time. Thus, the generalization "all the chairs in this room" would most likely include only objects that could be seen at a given time and would not involve imagination. But the generalization "all chairs" would be much vaster, and would include not only all presently existing "chairs" wherever they are, but also past and future "chairs." To attempt to give content to such a generalization would certainly involve an imaginative effort.

For the most part, however, we content ourselves with a simple recollective imagining of a few cases of whatever we are naming, whether "chairs" or "fights" or "red colors" or "religions" or something else, which we take to be typical of the whole class, and we let it go at that. But if we are asked to give a "definition" of the class we have in mind, then we are forced to think about the entire possible class and its proper boundaries, so that we will not include more or less cases than we should in our descriptive formula which serves as definition. To do this is a very valuable exercise in preventing us from forming a hasty generalization based on the few examples that come readily to mind. It also forces us to use our extrapolative imagination to think of the possible cases that we have not personally experienced.

When a generalization becomes fairly clear in its outlines, whether or not we have taken the trouble to formulate a definition, then we can use this knowledge as a guide or rule for deciding which items to allow into our generalization tent and which to exclude. We must remember, however, as noted in Chapter IV, that the extensions of our common terms (e.g., "chair") may vary considerably from language to language. This indicates that the boundaries we set are often the result of human custom or convention. Where nature does seem to "divide at the joints" as in the plant and animal world, there can be more precise formulations for delimiting a term's range. Even here, nevertheless, it is frequently difficult to find satisfactory boundary criteria, as for example in trying to separate human beings into "races." Abstract spatial forms, such as we have in geometry, fare somewhat better, because of their simplicity. A plane rectilineal figure having three angles and three sides readily identifies a plane triangle.

We can also observe that repeated events which set up a recognizable and perhaps measurable pattern of recurrence, as in the case of the rate of acceleration of a falling object, will give rise to some rule or "law" for this type of event which is an extrapolatable generalization and allows us to make predictions. This, of course, was what Galileo did in formulating his famous rule, $s = \frac{1}{2}gt^2$, in which s stands for distance, g for the rate of acceleration, and t for the time interval. A formula of this sort is simply a generalization of a type of event. It is imaginative in the sense that we imagine it to apply to any event of the kind designated, whether or not the event has been observed or yet taken place.

In noting how generalizations regularly involve imagination, we have also noted that they can serve as rules for categorizing and predicting features of our world. But we must never forget the difference between those categorizations or classifications that depend largely on human convenience and convention and those that rest on some observable regularity or uniformity of nature. These latter serve as the basis for our scientific projections and predictions, if we adopt the faith of the scientist, which is precisely a faith in the uniformity of nature.

What are the dangers in generalizing?

There are a number of hazards in generalizing—we have already encountered many of them in one form or another—which it will be helpful for us to enumerate and review. Let us go back to the processes represented by our first three figures and see what specific hazards each one may bring about.

Generalizing, according to Fig. 1, is simply the original creation of a class in our thoughts. The most common hazard here is that of overgeneralizing, giving the extensional meaning of a term a range too broad to correspond to the conventional limits of the term. As we noted in Chapter II, this tendency is especially marked among the young when first learning the proper extension of terms. We can, of course, run afoul of the opposite tendency—that of giving the extensional meaning too narrow a range—but those who do this are more apt to be the careful discriminating users of a language who wish to retain unusual precision in their meanings. Neither of these tendencies would constitute a hazard except when communicating with others who may have different limits for the same terms.

When the generalizing process is that illustrated in Fig. 2, the danger stems from the fact that adding new and considerably different members to a class will change the intensional meaning of the term. We recall that as the extension is increased to include new members of a different character, the intension (or common abstractable parts and aspects) is correspondingly decreased. Now if within the intension there is a well-recognized set of essential traits and if we alter this intension by adding to the extension, these essential traits will be changed. For example, if we have a fairly common and well-recognized meaning for the term "book," but we extend the class to include looseleaf notebooks, we have thereby reduced the intension of the term and possibly removed some of the traits normally considered essential. Again, as in Fig. 1, the principal danger is to communication and common understanding. We can ward off this danger by calling the attention of others to our new extensional meaning. But we should also remember that any time we change the extension of a term, we may cross over and obliterate what to many appear to be natural lines of cleavage between classes.* Perhaps these lines were simply artificial ones which had become encrusted by tradition and needed to be obliterated; on the other hand, they may have recorded some genuine natural boundaries that should be preserved. At least, when we break down traditional extensions, we must be prepared to defend our new groupings.

Fig. 3 represents a kind of generalizing of a more complex sort. Here two terms are involved, one for the smaller tent, and another for the larger tent. The dangers here are (1) that the two terms may represent some relation other than the class-inclusion relation and (2) that the term representing the larger tent will not be sufficiently broad to include all the members of the smaller tent. Let us consider each of these possibilities in turn.

(1) Two terms sometimes look as if they should be related to each other by a class-inclusion or species-genus relation; but on closer inspection, the relation turns out to be a different one (e.g., cause to effect or concrete† to abstract). We must remember that the larger and more inclusive class should have the same degree of concreteness as the smaller and less inclusive class. For example,

---

* See Chapter IV, pp. 98-100 and Chapter VI, p. 133 f.

† Special care is needed in keeping "specific" distinct from "concrete," since these two terms are often confused. "Specific" refers to the less general subclass or smaller set of referents relative to a more general class (e.g., cats to animals) ; while "concrete" refers to a less abstract or more fully qualified concept (e.g., tree to tree shape) . Frequently that which is specific is also concrete, but there are also specific abstractions and concrete generalizations (see Fig. 4 and p. 119).

if we generalize tabletops into the class of shapes, we commit the error of moving toward the more abstract instead of toward the more general. Tabletops are not a *kind of* shape; they *have* shapes, which is a different relationship. Or suppose we try to generalize furnace into heat. Again the relation is wrong, for furnaces *give* heat or are a *cause of* heat, but are not a *kind of* heat. We can correct this error by making "heat" into a concreted abstraction, "heater," since furnaces are a kind of heater. Other relations may cause us trouble in this way. Thus, we might want to say that logic is a kind of rationalism. But attention to the meanings of these terms soon reveals that "logic" refers to inferential reasoning based on the analysis of regularities and structures, whereas "rationalism" refers to a belief or set of beliefs which take the rational process as the ultimate basis for the establishment of knowledge. Now both of these terms have to do with reasoning, but they are not related to each other as species to genus; so it would be wrong to say that logic is a kind of rationalism.

A famous case of the fallacy of mistakenly assuming a class-inclusion relation is illustrated in the following syllogistic argument: white is a color; snow is white; therefore, snow is a color. The fallacy is not in the form of the syllogism, which is correct, but in moving from abstract qualities (white, color) to a concrete embodiment (snow), as if they were on the same level of concreteness. The syllogism would have been correct if the class-inclusion relation in the minor premise and in the conclusion had been replaced by the relation of possession of an attribute as follows: white is a color; snow has whiteness; therefore, snow has a color.

In eliminating relations other than the class-inclusion relation, we may find it helpful to use the "kind of" test (Chapter VII). If it seems correct to say A is a *kind of* B, we can presume that our relationship is an authentic class-inclusion relation. Even here we must be careful to take "kind of" in its strict sense as referring to a larger class, for sometimes we use "kind of" more loosely. We might say, for example, "Apples are a kind of pear," meaning only that there is some family resemblance between them, and not that apples are a subclass of pears. When using "kind of" as a test for class-inclusion, this usage would have to be avoided.

(2) Suppose now, as represented by Fig. 3, two terms do have the same level of concreteness or abstractness, and they do seem cor-

rectly related in terms of species to genus. It still may be the case that the larger class is not sufficiently large to include all members of the smaller class. We remember that because of the factor of variable extension (Chapter IV) it is easy for some terms to be included in a larger class most of the time, but to be enlarged at other times beyond the scope of the larger term. For example, it would seem safe enough to say that automobiles form a subclass of vehicles, but someone might wish to extend the term "automobiles" to include the old, junked cars in the wrecking lot, and restrict the term "vehicles" to means of transportation that are still functioning. In this case, the "automobile" tent, by being stretched, would exceed the "vehicle" tent in one area.

It is worth noting that when we state the inclusion of a small class within a larger class we have a generalized proposition of the form "All x's are y's." Now if we commit the error of trying to force the smaller subject class into a predicate class which is not sufficiently large, we commit the fallacy of *hasty generalization*. Hasty generalizations vary from those which are obviously hasty (e.g., All Russians are Communists) to those which are only hasty if not carefully specified with regard to the limitations of the terms as they are being used (e.g., All automobiles are vehicles). Most generalizations fall somewhat in between, so that they seem reasonable at first glance, but on second thought we realize that there are too many exceptions (e.g., All shoes are made of leather). Even some of those propositions that would seem least hasty (e.g, All crows are black) may need some qualification. For example, in the case of "All crows are black," do we mean all observed crows, or all possible crows, including future ones? In the future, crows might change color, and still we should wish to call them "crows," because of their other characteristics. And if today we find an albino crow, do we wish to rule him arbitrarily out of the "crow" tent? A safer generalization, because it belongs to the basic definition of the term, would be "All crows are birds." But even this case precludes the possibility of using "crow" in an extended or metaphorical sense, where "crow" might refer to nonbirds.

Very frequently we cannot find a convenient term to use for the genus which safely includes all the members of the smaller class, especially if the term used for the smaller class is ambiguous (i.e., stands for more than one kind of extension). For example, since words ending in *-ion* may refer either to an activity or to the condition resulting from the activity, it would be necessary, when naming a genus for terms ending in *-ion*, to mention both activity and condition. In this book we have tried to eliminate this ambiguity by using the gerund (e.g., abstracting) for the activity, and the word ending in *-ion* (e.g., abstraction) only for the resultant condition. Unfortunately, this is not general practice, and so the genus for a word like "abstraction" would need to mention both activity and condition.

We should further notice that generalizing in the third sense (Fig. 3) is the basis for making *classifications*. Attention to making an appropriate and useful classification is a very important preliminary step in any science or area of knowledge, and even has a special name—taxonomy—to represent this kind of activity. Ideally a classification should consist of an inclusive genus term with a number of subclasses or species terms covering the area within the genus. The subclasses may in turn have lower level subclasses. The subclasses at each level should be exclusive (i.e., not overlapping) and exhaustive (i.e., together they cover the field). Furthermore, the members in each class should be parallel at the same level of concreteness or abstractness, so that, for example, something as abstract as "structural design" would not be classified under a genus term as concrete as "building materials."

These ideals, however, are difficult to achieve. For one thing, the objects and events that we wish to classify do not break up into neat parallel subclasses with clear-cut junctures or breaking points between them. For example, if we decide to make our classificational division between plants and animals on the traits of moving as against stationary, then the coral and sea anemone would be plants. But they have other characteristics that are more animal-like. And when we turn to the complexities of man-made objects, like furniture, the problem is aggravated by human inventiveness plus the fact that ordinarily we do not need extreme precision. Where we draw the line between desk and table, for example, is not clear, and in some cases it probably will not make much difference which term we use. It is interesting that more ideal classifications can be achieved among abstractions, such as triangles, than among more concrete objects and events. But even triangles cause problems. If we divide them into equilateral, isosceles, and all others (scalene), this third category does not seem quite comparable to the other two. And then there is the important cross-cutting category of right-angled triangles which may be either isosceles or scalene. How we classify depends on the dividing traits that we take to be important, and this is largely a matter of purpose and preference.

The reasons for the difficulty in achieving an ideal classification in most cases are notably (1) the factor of variable extensions, which makes it practically impossible to eliminate overlapping and thus arrive at exclusiveness; (2) the multiplicity of subclasses when dealing with smaller species, which makes it difficult for a classification to be exhaustive; and (3) the tendency to be careless about parallelism of terms, allowing some to represent more concrete and others less concrete concepts. But if we (1) define our terms in order to eliminate as much of the variable extension as we can and (2) select a genus that is not too broad in comparison with the subclasses involved and (3) apply the "kind of" test to make sure that we have proper class relations, then we should be able to improve our ability to classify.

What are universals?

One concept which has traditionally been the center of much controversy is the notion of *universal*. Since the term "universal" is often taken as a close synonym to "general," it will be appropriate to turn our attention to some of the major meanings of this term. The diagram in Fig. 5 will assist us, for each number in that diagram suggests a different possible meaning of universal, some of which have been historically important.

Starting with the position marked (1), we have the *class* concept of universal. In this case, the term would refer to any complete group as an entire class of individual members (e.g., all elephants). The noun "universal" would thus be synonymous with "genus," and the adjective "universal" would coincide very nearly with "general," although the expressions "general," "in general," and "generally" are often taken a bit more loosely to mean "for the most part." "Universal," on the other hand, whether noun or adjective, preserves the strict sense and rarely if ever means "for the most part."

The term "particular" is the traditional opposite of "universal," whereas the term "specific" is normally opposed to "general." Again, the term "specific" is not so extreme as the term "particular," for "specific" only implies a reference to a "species" or smaller group as contrasted to a "genus" or larger group; but "particular" indicates only a single individual.* So, on the horizontal line in Fig. 5, we should place PARTICULAR at the extreme left, then SPECIFIC a little to the right, while UNIVERSAL would be located at the extreme right, with GENERAL a little to its left.

This first meaning of universal, meaning an entire class, is traceable primarily to Aristotelian logic; and for convenience we may call this the *Aristotelian* universal. Aristotle himself, however, uses the term "universal" (*katholou*) both in an *extensional* and in an *intensional* sense. Sometimes he speaks of a universal as "that which is of such a nature as to be predicated of many subjects,"† and gives "man" as an example (Socrates is a man, Plato is a man, Democritus is a man, etc.), where "man" is being taken in an extensional sense. But he also speaks of universal as what many things have in common,‡ thus giving it the intensional meaning of referring simply to the abstractable parts and aspects of a class. So in calling position (1) the Aristotelian universal, we must remember that this is only partly accurate.

Now let us look at position (2). Here "universal" would be purely intensional and might even be limited to the essential traits or *essence* of a class. Moreover, it should be considered singular, rather than plural as in position (1), for the entire set of intensional or essential traits can be taken as a unity. It will be convenient to designate this second meaning of universal as *Platonic,* since Plato's Ideas are often called universals in the sense that they are archetypes or master forms from which the particulars of experience derive their character and even their reality. However, we should be clear that Plato's universal archetypes are not to be regarded as abstractions from experienceable classes, as would be the case even

---

* In Aristotelian logic, "particular" also has the technical meaning of a subportion of a class—all the way from at least one member to nearly all. However, this meaning must be carefully distinguished from the one mentioned in the text, which limits "particular" to a single individual.

† *De Interp.*, Ch. 7.

‡ *Metaphysics* VII (Zeta), Ch. 13.

with Aristotle's intensional universals, for in Platonism universals are prior realities. More accurately, to start with position (1), the total plural class of particular objects or events as the primary universal, and then to derive the intensional universal at position (2), is to follow an Aristotelian order. But to start with the archetypal universal at position (2), and derive the particulars at position (1), is to follow a Platonic order. So, as representing different starting points, we can call position (1) Aristotelian, and position (2) Platonic.

Dropping down to position (3), we have "universal" meaning the entire totality of all that is, the entire *concrete universe* itself. From this point of view, everything within the universe, part or aspect, would be an abstraction from this single totality. To emphasize in this way the importance of the ultimate concrete universal is suggestive of the philosophy of Hegel, who developed the view that any idea of a more inclusive and therefore more concrete type comes closer to reality than does any abstract idea. By a system of synthetically combining opposites (e.g., logic and nature, the subjective and objective), Hegel believed we could reach more and more concrete universals, finally bringing us to the most fully concrete concept of all, which he called the Absolute Idea. Thus Hegel's effort to move our ideas toward an understanding of the ultimate concrete universal, position (3), makes it appropriate to call this, for convenience, the *Hegelian* universal.

Fig. 5 also shows three intermediate positions. What do they represent? Position (4) lies somewhere between the class universal indicated by position (1) and the essential or archetypal universal indicated by position (2). Position (4) represents a *collective* universal like the collective generalization mentioned above. This idea, we saw, can be illustrated by considering the usual meaning of "mankind" as between "human beings," on the one hand, and "humanness," on the other. "Mankind" suggests the collective idea, which is characterized by the notion of a mass or throng, where sharp demarcations between individuals are rather obliterated in one's idea. "Human beings," representing position (1), suggests instead the idea of an aggregate of separate individuals. "Humanness," representing position (2), suggests the intensional or essential universal. The word "humanity" seems to vacillate in meaning between something fairly close to "mankind" at times and something closer to "humanness" at other times. But probably "humanity" most often coincides in meaning with "mankind" (i.e., the mass of humanity), thus being principally a collective concept.

Position (5), by contrast with position (4), would represent a collective concept that is tending toward the concrete, since it falls somewhere between the notion of a class of separate individuals at position (1) and the concrete universal at position (3). In ordinary usage this meaning would probably not be distinguishable from that of position (4), but it is quite possible that such a term as "mankind" at times means something fuller than just an indistinct mass of human beings. If the concept indicated by "mankind" should refer not only to the bare mass of human beings but also to the many relations that exist among them and around them, relating them to their environment, then this concept would be more concrete than either the abstract collective (the bare mass of human beings) or the simple class plurality (the class of human beings). It will be useful, therefore, to distinguish a *concrete collective* at position (5) from the *abstract collective* at position (4).

Finally, position (6) represents a single or particular individual, which, like the fifth type of generalization mentioned above, is simply a typical example. If, for example, someone were to refer to a particular instance of a falling body as a "universal," it would only be because this single event exemplifies the universal rule for falling bodies. However, there is no more excuse for calling a *typical particular* a "universal" than for calling it a "generalization"; and we shall do well to stay away from both of these usages.

Let us now summarize our six meanings of universal:

(1) A whole class of individuals, which we have called the *Aristotelian* universal.

(2) An essence or archetype, which we have called the *Platonic* universal.

(3) The concrete totality, which we have called the *Hegelian* universal.

(4) An *abstract collective* universal.

(5) A *concrete collective* universal.

(6) A *typical particular* universal.

What existential status should be assigned to universals?

Since the center of the controversy about universals has been their existential status, we may profitably digress for a bit to sketch out something of the history of this aspect of the problem.

Plato's essential or archetypal universals had an existential priority in Platonism, just as, much later, Hegel's concrete universals had an existential priority in Hegelianism. The existential priority in Platonism lies in the notion that the archetypal essences are considered eternal and unchanging, whereas the particular objects and qualities of experience are transient and evanescent. Thus particulars from the Platonic point of view are only poor imitations of the eternal primary realities.

Aristotle, we remember, was dissatisfied with this arrangement and wished to assign a more definite reality to the particular objects of sense experience. So he characteristically stressed the reality of individual substances as the primary beings. These individuals, however, are not universals, although they may be collected into universal classes and they may possess universal attributes. For Aristotle, moreover, knowledge is a matter of universals, for any knowledge about particulars is always in terms of their class participations and their universal attributes.* When it came to the traditional Greek types of matter (earth, water, air, fire), Aristotle also wished to include them as one sort of primary being,† even though they only become fully actual when given some sort of form; and of course in Aristotle's view the form itself, as that which really determines what a thing is, assumes a very large share for the reality of anything. At times he seems to ascribe to form almost as much importance as did Plato. Nevertheless, Aristotle consistently adhered to his basic insight, which was to regard the particular as not only the most immediate, but also the primary reality, and its class membership or its attributes are then simply the means by which we come to know it.

The Aristotelian view of the status of universals produced some interesting consequences in the medieval controversy between "Realists" and "Nominalists." The Realists in the medieval sense of this term carried the Platonic emphasis upon ultimate reality

---

* See *Metaphysics* III (Beta) , 1003a 15.
† See *Metaphysics* V (Delta) , Ch. 8, and VIII (Eta) , Ch. 1.

of essences to an extreme, while the Nominalists took Aristotle's emphasis on particulars to an opposite extreme. In the extreme Nominalism, particulars alone have reality, and all universals—or even the apparent similarities by means of which we form classes—are fictions of imagination. Such an extreme view raised more questions than it could settle; and a more moderate disciple of Aristotle, St. Thomas Aquinas, adhered to the view that universals do exist in three senses at least: inherently in particulars, as abstractable essences in the human intellect, and ultimately in the mind of God.

The controversy, however, continued; and the British empiricists at a later date again returned to a skepticism in regard to the possibility of knowing abstractable similarities and essences. Berkeley, we remember, wrote: "It is . . . impossible for me to form the abstract idea of motion distinct from the body moving, and which is neither swift nor slow, curvilinear nor rectilinear; and the like may be said of all other abstract general ideas whatsoever."[*] In other words, the abstractable idea of motion which would be universally present in all motions, Berkeley claimed he could not conceive. Hume agreed with Berkeley, but admitted that similarities, or "resemblances," as he called them, are detectable, and that mainly "by custom we are able to give meaning to general ideas."[†] The objections raised by Berkeley and Hume were not directed against particular abstractions, but against *general* abstractions, that is, abstractions when they are applied equally to an entire class.[‡] In this case, the inability to form a precise mental image of a given abstract aspect, as it would exist in all the various particulars of a class, was for Berkeley sufficient to destroy credence in such notions. It would be impossible, he would say for example, to form a mental image of a rectangle, without its being some particular rectangle. Hume was more circumspect than Berkeley and claimed that we can attach meaning to abstract general ideas, even though our mental images may not be so vivid and precise as we might wish them.

Hume's position is certainly a sounder one than Berkeley's, for

* *Principles of Human Knowledge,* Introd. 10. See p. 122.
† *Treatise of Human Nature,* Bk. I, Pt. I, Section 7.
‡ When Berkeley speaks of "general abstractions," he apparently means what we have called above "general concreted abstractions" and not "generalized abstractions."

we not only make constant use of concrete generalizations, which must be based on abstractable similarities (e.g., cats) but we also make meaningful generalizations of abstractions themselves (e.g., rectangles). The test will come at the next higher level of abstraction (i.e., rectangularity). Can we give some meaning to such a notion, which in this case is the common abstractable property of all rectangles? It would seem so, if we do not require the precision of the empiricists' simple, clear mental image. Actually, we need only admit that we are not forced to think of rectangularity as the quality of having four *particular lengths* of line joined by right angles, but only as the *particular quality* of having four lines joined by right angles. It is not too difficult to imagine these lines, joined in the prescribed manner, without specifying what length they should have, and then to call this condition the particular abstract quality of rectangularity which is to be found in all rectangles. The same could be done with motion or any other abstraction from which a more concrete class is generated.

Such a view as the one just expressed may satisfy the meaning of universality in the case of simple abstractions, like rectangles, but what about ordinary concrete concepts, like dog or cat, table or chair? Here is where Wittgenstein's notion of "family resemblances" may seem more appropriate (see p. 91). Using the term "game" as an example, Wittgenstein questioned whether there is any conceivable common aspect for all types of games: card games, athletic contests, children's games, etc. Each kind of game, he thought, may have something in common with another type, but without there being any one aspect applicable to all games. Card games and athletic contests, for example, are both contests. Athletic games and some children's games, like ring-around-the-rosy, involve exercise. But sometimes we use the term "game" to refer to children's play which simply imitates adult activities and which involves little if any element of contest. What, then, is the common aspect of all "games"? We may have the notion that there must be at least one common trait simply because the same term is used for all of them. Wittgenstein warns us against this assumption on the ground that language usage is loose and there is often no discoverable common element for every class term. It will do no harm to concede that there are terms, like "game," which cover subclasses that have little in common with other subclasses. But we should also notice that dictionaries are filled with terms for class universals for which it has not been difficult for the dictionary editors to find common aspects. In this connection, we should remember that the referential range of terms can be widened, narrowed, or transferred, so that it is not uncommon for dictionary words to have several alternative ranges of meaning due to these shifts. And there are often discoverable threads of meaning which explain the shifts, as in the case of metaphor (see pp. 91-95). For this reason, we must beware of exaggerating Wittgenstein's strictures against the possibility of common aspects for class universals.

Sometimes a distinction is made between ordinary class universal terms, which are usually nouns or verbs, like "tree" or "run," and words or word elements which have the function of showing relationships, like "in" or "if," or the inflectional suffixes and other affixes in most European languages. It is claimed that whereas the ordinary nouns and verbs may have identifiable common aspects, this is certainly not the case with the relaters. The difficulty here is largely the result of the lack of enough different words or word elements to show all the relational complexities that are distinguishable in the world. For example, the preposition "by" may indicate several rather different types of situation, such as (1) near or alongside (The house was by the river), or (2) agent (The ball was hit by George), or (3) time when (He came by day), or (4) added or subtracted amounts (His salary was increased by fifty dollars per month), etc. It would indeed be difficult to find a common identifiable thread of common meaning for all these usages. But this does not mean that there are no common meanings within each usage; and one might even wish to claim that all usages of "by" imply a sense of two more or less parallel objects or events being related to each other in some fashion, although such a generous meaning would not be limited to "by" but might include other relaters, like "with." In any case, it is safe to conclude that there may be more reason for applying Wittgenstein's admonition against common traits in the case of relater words and elements than in the case of ordinary class universals, like nouns and verbs.

Finally, we need to note the difficulties surrounding complex universals, such as "religion," "government," "democracy," and the like. Each universal concept in these cases covers a variety of different objects and actions which are related to one another in a tightly knit and interdependent fashion. For this reason, it is hard to select some one or two dominating traits which will clearly supply the common element of meaning for all usages of the term. The term "religion," for example, normally implies at least a set of beliefs with a high degree of commitment to them, some traditional legends, some ritual practices, and some commandments for human behavior. But all of these traits are closely interdependent. The beliefs are associated with the legends, the legends with the rituals and with the commandments. Moreover, it would be difficult to say which is the dominant trait or the more essential one, for they are all connected even though, for different religions or different individuals, one or another of these traits may seem to be the crucial one. In cases of this sort, therefore, we must expect to find a number of equally strong and interdependent traits.

It is interesting to note that Hume went beyond mere resemblance in the case of certain concepts by introducing the notion of *analogy*. As examples of analogically unified concepts, he mentions (1) the notion of large numbers built up through the use of decimals, (2) being aided in recalling a verse once memorized by having the initial word given, and (3) concepts suggested by such terms as "government," "church," "negotiation," and "conquest."* The first of these is a notion universalized on the basis of imaginative extrapolation, the second is only a memory clue, but the third represents good examples of our complex universals described above.

The problem of universals and their relation to particulars has certainly not been settled in any conclusive way. The difficulties heretofore encountered will continue to recur with each new generation of thinkers. Here we can simply point to the basic nature of the problem and cite, as we have, a few of the best known positions relative to it.

What are some of the cautions that should be taken with regard to universals?

If we take "universal" as meaning applicable to a whole (e.g., a whole class), then we must realize that there are many kinds of wholes with regard to which we can use the term "universal."

---

* See Hume's *Treatise of Human Nature,* Bk. I, Pt. I, Section 7.

Failure to distinguish which particular whole is meant often leads to serious confusions.

Possibly the most common error is that which confuses a *universal belief about nature* with a *universal aspect of nature*. If everybody in a given group (e.g., all the people now on earth) holds a certain belief, then we might call this a *universal belief*. And if some aspect (e.g., having some degree of temperature) actually exists throughout nature, then we might call this a *universal aspect* of nature. There is no reason for confusion here, except that we tend to use universality of belief as evidence for objectivity in nature. We might, for example, judge that having some degree of temperature is an objective trait of nature simply because everybody believes this to be so. But universality of a belief is not very good evidence for objective reality, as has often been demonstrated in the past. The confusion between objective and subjective universality most often surrounds the expression "universal truth." For the term "truth" itself suffers from the subjective-objective ambiguity. If, as we are taking it, truth is most properly thought of as a quality of beliefs (when they are reliable or correspond with the facts), then a "universal truth" should mean a universal belief and not a universal aspect of nature.

A second source of confusion arises when we associate the term "universal" too closely with the universe and take it to mean only that which is applicable to the whole universe. If "universal" means applicable to any whole, then we must admit the possibility of rather limited wholes. Thus, furriness is a universal trait of cats and is in this sense a universal, even though the universe itself is certainly not furry. Every class, no matter how small, can have its own universals. For example, if all the members of the Class of '70 in XYZ College buy class pins, then the purchasing of class pins is a universal with regard to this class.

Obviously, then, there are degrees of universality. An aspect that exists very widely (e.g., the existence of living organisms) is clearly more universal than a more limited trait (e.g., being furry). Furthermore, both spatial and temporal limits must be considered. If the existence of living organisms is limited to this planet, then it is a spatially restricted trait, so far as the entire universe is concerned. On the other hand, if the existence of living organisms is spread throughout the universe now existing, then clearly it is a more universal trait, but still not so universal, we may assume, as the existence of temperature. The time dimension also can be brought into the picture. For example, if there was a time when no living organisms existed, but when there was temperature, then the existence of living organisms is a trait less universal, temporally as well as spatially, than the existence of temperature. So the term "universal" operates within limits of which we should always be aware.

There is a tendency to reserve the term "universal" for the larger and more extensive universals. An interesting example of this is found in the physical sciences, where the term "constant" is often used to mean a limited universal, and the term "universal" is suggestive of the larger ones. Consider a famous example of this. Galileo formulated a law for falling bodies, $s = \frac{1}{2}gt^2$, in which the g stands for the *constant* rate of acceleration of a falling body. Now, this rate varies with distance from the center of the earth and with air resistance encountered by the falling body; so it is only a limited universal applicable under specified conditions. Then Newton formulated a more general law, $F = G(M_1M_2/d^2)$, which indicates the mutual attraction of any two masses and in which the G is called the "universal of gravitation." Newton's G is clearly more universal than Galileo's g, but it too has its limitations, for it could only operate where we assume mass to exist. So both the "constant" and the "universal" are relatively limited universals.

A third common confusion is associated with the expression "absolute universal." Literally, the term "absolute" means set free or released from any dependency upon something else. From this root meaning, the term has been extended to apply to anything conceived as complete, perfect, unchanging, or at an extreme limit beyond which it could not go (e.g., the "absolute zero" of the temperature scale). It is natural, then, to associate "absolute" in one of its senses with something completely universal. But in all fairness to these terms, we should recognize the possibility of limited absolutes as well as limited universals. If "absolute" means complete or at an extreme limit, then we can imagine all sorts of limited absolutes (e.g., complete rest, complete dark, etc.). In fact, wherever anything is completely determined, we are apt to say, "That's absolutely it!" Thus even limited universals can have their absolutes. For example, if we observe that all the chairs in this room have backs, we could say that this characteristic is an absolute universal with regard to these chairs. So neither "absolute" nor "universal" need refer to the widest and most complete extension only.

What we have been saying about universal aspects will of course apply equally to that kind of subjective universal which we distinguished a while back, namely, *universal beliefs*. We could say with probable accuracy that the belief that the earth is a flat disk was once universally held, which means only that within certain restrictions of time and place, this belief was universal. But after a glance at the way in which beliefs have changed down through human history, it will seem likely that many, perhaps all, beliefs have changed, at least in some respects. This thought then leads to the conclusion that in all probability there are no beliefs which will remain universal throughout time *exactly* as they are now. But there still may be beliefs that will remain for a long time without much change. After all, we can only guess about beliefs; we cannot prove or disprove the possibility of their being universal beliefs, especially in the sense that certain beliefs may recur over and over again throughout the entire class of believers, past, present, and future.

In conclusion, the important thing to remember is that most universals are applicable to wholes within prescribed limits, and we must be careful to prescribe these limits.

SUGGESTED READINGS

Plato, *Phaedo*, 100ff.

Aristotle, *Metaphysics,* Bk. I (Alpha), Ch. 9, and Bk. VII (Zeta), especially Ch. 13.

Thomas Aquinas, *On Being and Essence,* Ch. 3.

Locke, John, *Essay Concerning Human Understanding,* Bk. III, Ch. 3.

Hegel, G. W. F., *Encyclopedia of Philosophy,* Sections 109-139 (the Concept).

Blanshard, Brand, *Reason and Analysis,* Ch. 9.

Aaron, R. I., *The Theory of Universals.*

PART THREE
The Nature of Rational Inquiry

WE ARE NOW READY to apply our discoveries concerning
the world of symbols and the processes of thinking. Rational knowledge is our goal. But what is it, and how
do we attain it?

In this domain the philosopher and the scientist move
together. The scientist chooses his special domain within the scope of all possible knowledge, and works away
with special tools and techniques. The philosopher is
both more general and more critical. He is general in
encompassing the whole domain of knowledge, and he
is critical in his effort to assess just what constitutes
knowledge. He willingly leaves to the scientist the task
of exploring particular domains with particular tools.
But he reserves the business of estimating and evaluating all kinds of knowledge, whether scientific and rational or not. His goal in its most comprehensive scope
is that of constructing a system of beliefs that will hang
together, give us a perspective on ourselves and our
world, and lead to useful orientations in the conduct
of our lives. He may stop short of this goal, and rest
content with a simple critique and estimate of knowledge, but those who pass for "philosophers" in the
great tradition of our cultural history have been the
ones who worked far along the road to systematization.

In Part Three, we shall examine what may generally
be called "the nature of rational inquiry" as it affects
both science and philosophy.

CHAPTER XI

Defining

Why and when are definitions important?

WHEREVER CLARITY OF THOUGHT is desired, definitions are important. This is especially the case in philosophy, where one is concerned with a reexamination of basic concepts, with their implications, and with the systems of ideas that may emerge from such a study. Defining is important in the philosophical enterprise; for a definition is much more than a mere restatement of an equivalent meaning in other terms. Nearly every term we use has had a long history of usages and has a number of current usages, all of which give it a character of its own and special perspectives from which to view the referents to which it directs our attention. These perspectives may change, sometimes drastically, our manner of understanding a given concept and bring about nuances and distinctions which are extremely illuminating for the overall philosophical meanings that we seek.

The most illustrious prototype of the philosophical inquirer is Socrates, fearlessly pushing the argument wherever it leads as he pursues with a tireless zeal the nature of the virtues. This Socratic quest, immortalized for us by Plato, may be regarded as a search for definitions, definitions which will reveal the essential nature of his quarry. That the quarry should prove elusive must not blind us to the notable increase in understanding that is accomplished simply by the chase itself. As a fine example of the Socratic method, let us examine a typical Socratic dialogue, the *Euthyphro*.* Here we find Socrates inquiring of Euthyphro, a man portrayed as notable for his religious zeal, about the nature of holiness or piety. As often happens, Euthyphro's first attempt at a definition is a miserable failure; for he gives not a general rule, but merely a particular instance. "Well, I say holiness is to do just what I am doing now —to prosecute the wrongdoer in a case of murder or sacrilege, or any similar offender . . ." (Euthyphro was on his way to court to prosecute his father for allowing a slave to die.) Socrates presses him again, and Euthyphro does better: "I say, then, that what the Gods love is holy, and what they do not love is unholy." But do not the Gods often disagree among themselves? "Yes, but not in this case." So far, so good; but Socrates wants to know if holiness is "loved by the Gods because it is holy, or is holy because it is loved?" Unfortunately, Euthyphro asserts the former alternative and so, being loved by the Gods cannot be the sufficient reason for an action's being holy. He must try again; and he says: "The kind of righteousness that I call pious and holy is the kind that has to do with the care of the Gods. The rest has to do with the care of Man." "Righteousness" is here the genus, and the differentiating characteristic is "that has to do with the care of the Gods." It sounds as if Euthyphro had at last hit the bull's-eye. But Socrates is not satisfied; for when one cares for something (like horses or dogs) it is to benefit them. But the Gods do not need benefiting. So Euthyphro suggests that perhaps these benefits are not for the Gods themselves, but are simply acceptable to them, and we are back where we started, saying that holiness is that which is acceptable to or loved by the Gods. Socrates and Euthyphro must stop. Perhaps another time the discussion can be resumed with better success.

The Socratic search for definition is the expression of a philosophical faith—the faith that there are essences not only of objects but of aspects, like virtues; and that these essences can be at least

* F. M. Stawell translation (Dent & Co., 1906).

partially glimpsed through the diligent inquiry to which Socrates characteristically subjects key ideas. To be sure, a perfect understanding may not lie within the capacity of earth-bound men; but by a superior intelligence the perfect forms can be clearly and directly intuited in all their essential glory. Such, at least, is Plato's faith, already implicit in the method of Socrates.

But if earth-bound men must give up hope of ultimate success, why try at all? The only logical answer is that the greater understanding afforded even by a partial glimpse is sufficient to justify the whole undertaking, and that an excursion into meanings and natures by way of a search for definitions is a vastly rewarding affair. Let the Socratic hope, then, be our guide; and let us not regard the quick proclamation of a definition as the end of the matter, as if we only awaited the solemn *ipse dixit* of some high authority. Rather, let us continue to seek to improve our definitions and thereby our understandings; for ultimately clarity of thought must depend upon the clarity with which we know both our key notions and the relationships between them.

What is a definition?

The anatomy of a definition has long been a subject of interest to philosophers, first carefully studied by Aristotle in his *Topics,* and a full discussion of this anatomy becomes quite involved. However, the basic nature of a definition can be very simply stated: *a definition is a statement which seeks to give the referential meaning of one term in other terms.* For example, the dictionary informs us that "deep" means "extending or lying comparatively far below the surface." Here we have a term to be defined (deep) restated in other terms (lying or extending comparatively far below the surface). The term to be defined is called the *definiendum,* and the defining statement is called the *definiens.* A definition is a kind of *equation* in which the same extension is referred to in two ways (see Fig. 1).*

Most often a definition is sought in order to *disclose* or *clarify*

---

* Remember we are taking extension to include all possible referents, whether perceivable or not (Chapter IV). If we limit the extension to perceivable referents only, then we can have intensions without extensions, and there can be purely intensional definitions. But since we have taken extension in its widest sense, every intension has a corresponding extension.

Definiendum

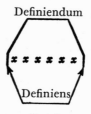

Definiens

FIG. 1

meaning of an unfamiliar term. Normally it is with this clarificatory end in view that we consult a dictionary. However, there is
another equally important purpose for defining—that of *fixing
more precisely* the boundaries of the extension. Terms, we remember, are like tents with loose sides that may be pulled out or
in by users of the term. So, for more precise understanding of
our meanings, it becomes necessary to peg down these tent sides—
that is, to fix the limits of the terms we use. We may wish to peg
them down at a narrow or at a wide extension or somewhere in
between; the important thing here is to know as exactly as possible
what limits we are placing on a term's extension (see **Fig. 2**).

Definiendum

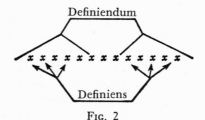

Definiens

FIG. 2

In order to accomplish a precise delimitation of the extension,
one needs terms in the definiens that are already precise. But it
often happens that these more precise terms are the more technical
terms in the various areas of knowledge. As a result, definitions
which have as their primary goal the function of pinning down
the extension may not be particularly helpful in clarifying the
primary meaning (for example, "Circle = a closed plane curve
such that all its points are equidistant from a point within called
the *center*"). On the other hand, definitions which disclose meanings of unfamiliar terms by using terms that are familiar may

not be very precise definitions, since the more familiar terms are apt to be somewhat wavery in their own extensions (for example, "Folk = a group of kindred people forming a tribe or nation"). Nevertheless, the ideal, as Descartes reiterates, is to have terms that are both *clear* and *distinct*.

Primarily, then, a definition involves two parts, the *definiendum* and the *definiens,* related ideally by the relation of *equivalence*. Is this equivalence primarily an extensional one or an intensional one? We should expect it to be both. The key to this equivalence, however, is the extension, that is the referents themselves, with whatever degree of concreteness they may possess. If the intension is carefully limited to the entire set of common abstractable properties possessed by all the members of the extension, then extensional equivalence should give rise to intensional equivalence as well. If, however, the intensional properties named in the definiens, as is usually the case, do not include the entire set of common abstractable properties, but only a few of them, then the same extension may be defined by different intensional properties. For example, *man* may have the intensional properties, "thinking abstractly and using symbols to stand for abstractions," or he may have the properties "walking erect on two feet, having an opposable thumb and a double curved spine." Obviously these two sets of intensional or essential traits are in no way equivalent to each other, although they do refer to the same extension (human beings). So partial intensions need not themselves be equivalent for an equivalent extension.

Also, terms used in the definiens will have their own special connotational overtones that may give different emphases to the various ways in which a term can be defined. Moreover, there may be special connotations of the definiendum which are not caught by the definition. For example, we noted that "deep" may be defined as "extending or lying comparatively far below the surface"; yet there is nothing in all these defining terms which suggests the heavy, profound, or serious quality often meant by "deep." Even close synonyms usually have connotational differences. For example, the dictionary indicates that "foam" and "froth" are synonyms; yet one must forget the special connotational features of each in order to regard them as precise equivalents. "Foamy" certainly is not quite the same in meaning as "frothy." So, if we ask the crucial question about defining—namely, how far is it legitimate to substitute some symbols for others for the purpose of giving equivalent meanings—our answer will be that so long as we are concerned only with indicating the referential range of a term, our definitions can be considered sufficient and useful, but if we are concerned about differences in connotational overtones and stresses in the meanings of the words we use, then we should not expect any definition to be quite adequate.

What effect will different types of terms have upon defining?

"Term," as we are using this word, includes both the symbol and the concept for which it stands, and there are a number of distinguishable types of symbols and terms for which differences in defining may well be appropriate. What would they be?

(1) Symbols, we remember (Chapter III), can be distinguished on the basis of *conventionality*. There are those which are newly invented, as against those which have a reasonably long tradition of usage. The great majority of our symbols, especially our linguistic symbols, are well-seasoned; but occasionally we are required to invent a new symbol, especially for a newly discovered object or for a new idea. When one is called upon to define a new symbol, the definition must be what is called *prescriptive* or *stipulative;* whereas the usual definitions of the old symbols are called, by contrast, *descriptive, lexical,* or *conventional* (since they describe the established vocabulary meanings). However, even definitions of well-established symbols, within their traditional areas of meaning, for some special purpose may need to receive greater refinement of extension than is normal. If so, such a definition would be prescriptive or stipulative to the extent that it specially determines limits of the extensional meaning for the particular use of the term that one has in mind. In such cases, a definition would be partly descriptive, since the traditional meaning is being described, and partly prescriptive, since there is an additional refinement of this meaning.

(2) Sometimes traditional symbols are used with *new meanings*. If so, the new meanings will need to be stipulatively or prescrip-

tively defined, if one does not wish to rely merely upon the context to indicate the sense of the term.

Terms which are carried over to refer to new extensions, when used *metaphorically* (Chapter IV), need not be defined, however. The force of a metaphor rests upon the strength and freshness of the new perspective that is thrown upon a situation by the importance of a meaning traditionally associated with another context. The context alone should suffice to call forth the desired image, and the need for defining would constitute a detrimental distraction. Old terms used in new senses need defining when they are being arbitrarily assigned to their new meanings, and not when they are being metaphorically transferred.

Since the extensional meanings of terms are continually being changed, either by a broadening, a narrowing, or a transferring of them, it is important that conventional lexical definitions be dated and that dictionaries be brought up to date. For this reason certain definitions are marked *obs.* (obsolete) or *arch.* (archaic), and the *Oxford English Dictionary* actually includes dates of first and last usages. The usage of terms also varies with different geographical areas and with different technical uses. The dictionary recognizes these differences by marking certain meanings as *colloq.* (colloquial) for common or *dial.* (dialetic) for regional usage, and by inserting the name of the field or profession in the case of technical meanings.

(3) Terms may refer to a *particular* or *general* extension. The best example of terms with particular extensions are proper names; and these do not need defining. This is so because the idea of defining implies the delimitation of a class of particulars, and a single particular is not a class that needs delimiting. One does not speak of *defining* John Smith, though one may *describe* John Smith. General terms, on the other hand, can be defined, for they have an extension over many individuals. The definition of a general term is in fact a description of all members of a class, but it is a description with a special purpose, namely, to give just those traits which will mark out or delimit that class from other classes. In a sense, one might speak of defining John Smith, but this would be the same as describing him, since his definition would include all his traits. Proper names are not the only particular terms. For

example, class terms can be made particular when they are preceded by *the* or *this* (e.g., this book). But such a particular term would be defined in terms of the class of which it is a member, and not in terms of the one particular to which reference is being made.

(4) Terms may be *concrete, collective, abstract,* or *imaginatively altered abstractions.* Which one it is will determine where one looks for examples of the items to be defined. Visible concrete objects (e.g., monkeys) can best be defined by examining their common characteristics. Collectives (e.g., mankind) are taken as whole groups characterized by the common traits of the individuals in the group. Abstractions (e.g., squares) will need to be defined by looking rather at the set or class of similar abstractions—all squares. Ultimate abstractions—squareness or rectangularity—are definable as simply naming the common essence of a class of abstractions. And imaginatively altered abstractions—centaurs—would depend upon the basis of their imaginative creation for their definition. These differences are very important in formulating our own definitions; and so they will enter into our considerations in Chapter XII, where we shall be directly concerned with constructing definitions.

What are the principal ways of defining?

To summarize our discussion of variations in definition, let us note again that people generally define a term for one of two reasons: either (1) to establish a new meaning for a term which they are inventing or for one which they are using in a new and special way; or (2) to clarify and delimit more precisely what others usually mean by a traditional term in one of its traditional senses. Definitions resulting from the first motive are called *stipulative* or *prescriptive.* Those resulting from the second motive are called *conventional, lexical,* or *descriptive.* Further, metaphorical transferences are normally not defined until they become established in their new habitat and are no longer metaphorical. Finally, particular terms are not to be defined except as being examples of a general class or as incorporating the essential abstractions of a possible class.

(1) If one is interested only in clarifying a term, and not in delimiting its extension, then one may simply point to a particular

and presumably typical example. Such pointing, if dignified by being called a definition at all, is said to be an *ostensive definition*. However, from the mere designation of one example, we cannot know the range or limits of the extension of a term; and so ostensive definition cannot delimit. Nevertheless, dictionaries often use a kind of ostensive definition when they include a picture of an example of the definiendum. Such picturings are of course limited to visible objects and are never more than supplementary to the full definition.

(2) One might attempt to define a class by naming over all the various subclasses; but this would be in most cases very tedious and unsatisfactory. For example, to define "tree" as elm, birch, pine, oak, alder, linden, fir, palm, etc., etc. would certainly be tiresome and difficult if one were to attempt to name all the sub-varieties. However, *enumerating subclasses* may be a very helpful aid in defining; and in fact, dictionaries often include some examples of subclasses to supplement a full definition.

(3) Perhaps the quickest and neatest manner of giving a meaning to a term is to find another familiar term with as nearly equivalent a meaning as possible—*defining by synonym*. For example, one might define "sleeping" as slumbering. However, as has already been pointed out, synonyms lack connotational equivalence even though they may have rough extensional equivalence. And in perhaps most cases, the extensional equivalence is not very precise (see Fig. 3). Dictionaries may use synonyms as adjuncts in

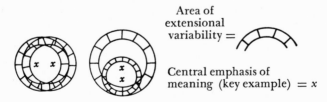

FIG. 3. *Possible ways in which the extension of synonyms may be related. Imagine we are looking down on the circular tents.*

defining, but the better dictionaries take pains to point out the major connotational differences under the heading *Syn.* for "synonym."

(4) The fourth way of defining is the classical form called *defi-*

nition by genus and differentia. Here at least we come to a case in which a serious attempt is made to delimit the extension and give some precision to the range of meaning. The genus names the larger class in which the definiendum is to be included as a species or subclass. The differentia names the set of intensional aspects or traits which, as nearly as possible, delimits or differentiates the subclass to be defined from all the other subclasses in the genus. The differentia, in other words, should give an essential or partial intension of the definiendum. A clear example of a definition by genus and differentia is the following:

A circle	is	*a closed plane figure*	*whose points are equi-distant from the center*
(definiendum)		(genus)	(differentia)

Here the differentia typically appears as a relative clause modifying the genus. But in other cases (e.g., A horse is a large, solid-hoofed, herbivorous, short-eared, four-footed mammal) the differentia may appear as a set of adjectives modifying the genus. If there is both an adjective or adjectives modifying the genus and also a relative clause, the adjective may be taken either as restricting the genus (and therefore constituting part of it, as in the case of "closed plane figure" above), or it may be taken as part of the differentia, if one prefers, thus leaving the genus much larger (e.g., *figure* alone would be a larger genus than *closed plane figure,* for it would include not only open figures, but three-dimensional ones as well). In any case, the distinctive character of a definition by genus and differentia is that it first places the term to be defined in a larger class (or tent) and then eliminates the unwanted subclasses of this larger class by giving the essential intensional properties which presumably are possessed only by the class being defined (see Fig. 4).

While definition by genus and differentia remains a very efficient way of handling logical definitions, it should be observed that it is primarily designed for defining nouns. Nouns, we recall, name objects, events, situations, qualities, etc. But is it not possible to find a more efficient way of handling the definitions of the other parts of speech? Of course, we can convert any part of speech into a noun,

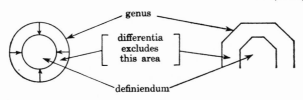

FIG. 4

and allow it to function in a sentence as a noun. For example, if we wish to define an adjective (e.g., soft), we may start out "Soft is that condition which . . ." thus including the condition "soft" under the general heading "condition." Here "soft" has become a noun and the term "condition" serves as genus for it. Or if we wish to define a verb (e.g., "to lift"), we can formulate the definition as follows: "Lifting is the action of moving something in an upward direction." Here "lifting" is a verbal noun, and "action" serves as its genus. Since prepositions and conjunctions indicate relations, we could use the word "relation" as genus in these cases (e.g., "In" is the relation of one thing to another when the second encloses or includes the first). But these formulations seem somewhat forced into a mold primarily designed for nouns.

(5) We therefore use what may be called a *contextual* definition in cases where the genus and differentia formulation seems awkward. After all, we are basically interested in the statement of some equivalence, and if we can find two roughly equivalent formulations of a sentence in which the word to be defined is replaced by another word or words in the same syntactical position, we should be satisfied. So instead of starting "Soft is that condition which," we say merely "*x* is soft when it is pliant, gentle, or gives way to the touch." This gives us a contextual definition of soft. Or let us define "to lift" in this way: "*x* lifts *y* when *x* moves *y* to a higher position." Likewise, "*x* is in *y* when *x* is entirely enclosed by *y*" defines "in."

Conjunctions pose more of a problem when defined contextually, because they normally link or conjoin clauses (i.e., full sentences). But let us see what we can do with the word *since* when used as a conjunction. This word is ambiguous, having both a temporal and a causative meaning; and a contextual definition which takes account of this ambiguity would be: "Event *x* occurred since event *y* occurred, whenever either *x* occurs after *y*, or *x* occurs because of *y*."*

Note that in contextual definitions *we have dispensed with the genus,* and all we have left in effect is the differentia. Actually it was the differentia all along that was the key to a definition by genus and differentia. The genus served principally to mark off and focus our attention upon a large general area within which our meaning was to be found. Naming the genus does have the advantage of a preliminary focusing of attention in the right direction. But when it comes to the task of delimitation itself, it is the differentia, as statement of the essential intension, which does the job. Actually it is always possible, and often quite useful, to convert a contextual definition into a genus and differentia form.

Much has been written in recent years, especially in regard to philosophy of science, about what are called *operational* definitions. However, this involves something other than a question of an alternative method of defining, for operationalism is a whole philosophical point of view based upon a rather restricted empiricism, which, in the interest of observational confirmation, attempts to keep imaginative inventions or "constructs" to a minimum, and to give a definition only in terms of the observable activities (or operations) of the definiendum. According to Hempel, a narrow empirical definition may be stated as follows: "Any term in the vocabulary of empirical science is definable by means of observation terms; i.e., it is possible to carry out a rational reconstruction of the language of science in such a way that all primitive terms are observation terms and all other terms are defined by means of them."† An operational definition further demands "that the concepts or terms used in the description of experience be framed in terms of operations which can be unequivocally performed."‡ But as Hempel points out, only terms for

---

* The ambiguity of *since* is somewhat lessened by our habit of using a compound tense (has occurred) more often in the temporal case (e.g., Since I came in, the book has fallen off the table) , and a simple past in the causative case (e.g., Since I jiggled the table, the book fell off). However, the situation referred to in each case is the best determinant of causal or temporal meaning.

† Carl G. Hempel, *Fundamentals of Concept Formation in Empirical Science,* p. 23.

‡ *Ibid.,* p. 41. Hempel is quoting a statement by P. W. Bridgman in an article "Operational Analysis," *Philosophy of Science,* V (1938) , p. 119.

which there could be manipulations, as in a laboratory, could be so defined, excluding "the most powerful theoretical constructs" of science, or else one must broaden the meaning of "operation" to include mental operations, as in mathematics, whereupon the key idea of empirical operation loses its force. Futhermore, according to Hempel, good scientific definitions require a whole system of interdependent concepts tied together by a general theory, and such definitions, being also hypotheses, must be regarded as never completely verifiable or falsifiable.* How, for example, should the scientist define the term "atom"? Obviously it will be more satisfactory if it is given in terms of the best current theory of the nature of an atom; and a theory of this sort cannot be limited to the merely observed effects, such as are noticeable in laboratory experiments. Basic scientific concepts, such as this one, will need some hypothetically imagined model or "construct" as part of the explanation, and therefore part of the definition. But also, as we noted in our review of the history of the concept of atom in Chapter IX, we may expect the present best definition to give way in the future to another.

In general, we must beware of the reductionistic tendency of empirical science to limit definable items to those which can be measured under well specified laboratory conditions. Many terms which are not only useful but essential to science would be eliminated. And many other terms such as "consciousness," "intuition," "will," "value," and the like, are placed under a cloud of suspicion, simply for lack of an ability to give them that degree of precision which the scientist seeks.† The antireductionistic point of view expressed here is that one cannot eliminate genuine realities simply because of our inability to define them precisely.

By way of summary, let us recall that definitions may be (1) ostensive, (2) by enumeration of subclasses, (3) by synonym, (4) by genus and differentia, or (5) contextual. But we need not consider operational definitions as constituting another variety of

---

* On the question of falsification of a theory leading only to a probable conclusion, see Paul Schmidt, "Truth in Physics," *American Journal of Physics*, Vol. 28, No. 1, pp. 24-32.

† There is a famous statement by Aristotle near the beginning of the *Nicomachean Ethics:* "It is the mark of an educated man to look for precision in each class of things just so far as the nature of the subject admits (1094b 23-25, Ross translation).

definition, for operationalism is simply a recommendation concerning the type of data from which to formulate the differentia of a genus and differentia definition, or the conditions of a contextual definition. It does not offer a new mode of defining.

What are the qualifications and tests of a good definition?

There are certain traditional qualifications for adequate definitions. These follow from the two basic purposes of descriptive definitions: (a) the clarificatory and (b) the precisional or delimitative. In fulfilling its task as clarifying a term, a good definition should have a definiens which (1) is as unambiguous as possible (that is, no term used in the definiens should have two or more alternative meanings which are equally plausible); (2) is noncircular (that is, terms used in the definiens should not be derivatives of the term which is the definiendum, as "love is a kind of loving," or should not give a term which is then defined in terms of the definiendum, as "sleep is slumber and slumber is sleep"); and (3) is at least partly positive (that is, the terms in the definiens should not be merely statements of what a thing is not). These goals are rarely capable of being completely achieved. As we have seen, most terms have some ambiguity about them, a condition as apt to pertain to those used in the definiens as to any others. As for noncircularity, this is a condition which can be maintained only within the immediate definition, for inasmuch as the number of synonymous symbols or symbolic expressions in a language is limited, if one pursues a definition far enough, he will inevitably return to some of the terms already used (see Successive Definition in Chapter XII p. 298 f.). The important thing, however, is that the terms in the definiens should be more familiar and not in need of further defining. Finally, the tabu against merely negative terms arises from the hopelessness of saying all the things or conditions that a thing is not. Yet in order to delimit properly, it is useful to differentiate by not only giving the positive essential intension of the definiendum, but also by indicating what type of borderline cases should be excluded.

The foregoing qualifications were directed primarily toward the goal of clear definitions. What is required for definitions which seek to delimit an extension as precisely as possible? We can require simply that the definiendum and the definiens should be extensionally equivalent and that the limits indicated by the definiens should be as precise as possible. But how are we to achieve this, or test to see that we have obtained this condition? One test which has been devised is to ask if the differentia states both the *necessary* and the *sufficient conditions* which anything must possess to belong properly to the definiendum in question.* Some conditions may be sufficient only, and others necessary only. For example, "If *x* is a boat, it has a keel" states a condition of boats which is too narrow for the whole class of boats (for there are flat boats which do not have keels). However, having a keel is a sufficient condition for being a boat, even though it is not a necessary condition. On the other hand, "If *x* is a boat, then it is designed to float," states a condition which is necessary but not sufficient, for there are other things, like buoys, which are designed to float but which are not boats (see Fig. 5). If we could find a

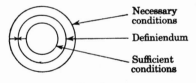

Necessary conditions

Definiendum

Sufficient conditions

Fig. 5

differentia which states both the sufficient and necessary conditions, our definition would be logically adequate. The formula for this is "if and only if" where "if" shows the sufficient conditions and "only if" shows the necessary conditions. In the case of rather variable concrete objects, like boats, it is not easy to find some simple set of sufficient and necessary conditions. A "boat," according to the dictionary, "is a small open vessel, or watercraft, usually moved by oars or paddles, but often by sails, or power mechanism." By way of test, let us propose that "*x* is a boat if and only if *x* is a small open vessel or watercraft, moved by oars,

---

* In Chapter VII we discussed necessary and sufficient conditions in connection with *causes and effects* (i.e., what is a necessary condition for some event to happen and what is a sufficient condition to cause it to happen) . Now we are concerned with necessary and sufficient conditions simply for *being* a certain kind of thing.

paddles, sails, or power mechanism." If we have really named both the necessary and sufficient conditions, we may consider our definition satisfactory.

As a test, then, we must try to find differentiating conditions which will be neither merely necessary nor merely sufficient, but which will be both together, thus converging upon and demarking the extension of the definiendum which we wish to show (see Fig. 5).

The ideal of logical perfection, as we should suppose, is much more nearly attainable for abstractions. For example, a given geometric form is a "circle if and only if it is a closed plane figure whose points are equidistant from a center." *If* anything has these conditions it must be a circle, so the conditions are sufficient. And *only if* a thing has these conditions can it be a circle, so the same conditions are necessary. Or we could say that "*x* is a husband if and only if *x* is male and is married." Here the conditions when taken together are both sufficient and necessary. Either one by itself would be necessary but not sufficient. But if there are no married men who are not husbands, then being a married man is also a sufficient condition for being a husband.

Lastly, in discovering the sufficient and necessary conditions for use as definiens, it is better to select centrally important ones than incidental or trivial ones. For example, we know something more important about human nature if we define *man* by using the conditions: thinking abstractly, using symbol systems, and developing a continuing social tradition, than we do if we use the conditions: having a double-curved spine and being a featherless biped.

In summary, then, a definition for clarity should be (1) unambiguous, (2) noncircular, and (3) partly positive. For precision it should (1) have equivalent definiens and definiendum, (2) be as precisely delimitative as possible, and (3) point to important rather than trivial traits.

Tests for the adequacy of definitions presuppose the ideal goals of clarity and precision. Such goals are useful in pointing us in the desired direction. However, it is always foolish to expect goals of this kind to be readily achieved. Definitions rarely give more than an approximation of a term's extension.

Furthermore, some ideas will be more difficult to translate into

other terms than will other ideas. So some terms are more definable than others. This is not to say that any symbol, if it is
capable of standing for a communicable notion, cannot be given
some definition. It is only to say that we must not expect more
than the degree of clarification and delimitative precision of
which a given idea is capable.

What cautions should be observed
with respect to definitions?

Definitions are very useful when we know what they can do
and what they cannot do. On the positive side, defining a term
directs our attention toward the presence of the intensional similarities (both parts and aspects) shared by the members of a
group. These similar factors are implicitly there whenever we
use group terms; and since nearly all the terms we use are group
terms, this means that we are constantly assuming the presence of
similar factors. But it may be that in many cases Wittgenstein was
right (Chapter IV), and that instead of some clear-cut similarities
or common factors running throughout a group, we have only a
set of "family resemblances" with different similarities joining
various members of the family. Even in this case, however, defining will *bring out the hidden ambiguities,* especially if we are
careful to define by first examining a good number of diverse
particular examples to which the term is customarily applied.

The process of defining also enables us to *decrease vagueness*
by narrowing the areas of extensional variability. When we do not
know where to draw the line around the extension of a term, we
expose the term to the danger of one kind of misinterpretation,
not only by others, but even by ourselves.

Finally, *newly invented terms or terms appropriated to new uses
need to be defined.* In this connection, defining is highly important in the sciences, where new discoveries are producing new
concepts and terms, for these concepts must at first be adopted
rather arbitrarily by those working in the field. A clearinghouse
of terminology and definition is always useful when this is the case.

To philosophers, from Socrates and Plato on, the definition has
served both as the pivotal point in clarifying a view and as the
principal tool in shaping the growing philosophical edifice. The

danger comes only when we begin to regard definitions as ultimate conclusions to which we are irrevocably committed, rather than as tools for better understanding.

On the side of caution, defining runs several risks. First, too often *we expect definitions to accomplish something different from what they are intended to do;* and so we are disillusioned by them. For example, since it is the primary purpose of a definition to delimit more precisely the extension of a term in a given use by stating only its minimum essential traits, we should not expect a definition to serve either as a *full description* or as an *explanation.* A definition is only a minimal description of a set of referents with the emphasis upon those traits which best serve the purpose of delimitation. A full description, especially of the referent of a term which is used in a particular context, would involve much more than this. A "rose," for example, is definable as "a shrub or vine having compound leaves and regular five-petaled, red, white, pink, or yellow (but never blue) flowers, with many stamens." The description of a particular rose could contain the mention of many more aspects, including associated feelings, if one wished. So the purposes of description are not best served by definitions.

An explanation normally involves an interest in causal relations, whereas a definition is concerned with similarities among the members of a class. For this reason a definition should not be expected to serve as an explanation, although causal relations may, on occasion, enter into the list of essential similarities mentioned in a definition. For example, the relation of a fossil to the living organism which caused it and of which it is the form may be taken as an important part of the explanation of the fossil. This relation could also be part of the definition of fossils. But as part of the definition, the emphasis is not upon the causal factor as explaining fossils, but rather upon this factor as something common to all fossils.

Second, *we must beware of expecting that there is going to be just one right definition.* There are many possible definitions for most terms, depending on the limits one wishes to assign to its extension and upon the various terms available to be used in the definiens. So, all that "right" could mean is "the best possible selection of defining terms for the particular extension or context we have in mind." The term "right" does not mean "the one and only."

Third, *we should not use the terms "true" or "false" of definitions.* If by "truth" we mean "reliability" (see Chapter XII), especially the reliability of an idea, then we see that the truth quality of an idea or a term is not directly relevant to the way it is defined, for the definition, as definition, is concerned with limits assigned to the extension of the term, and not with the descriptive reliability of the defining statement. For example, up-to-date knowledge will give us a definition of "atom" different from the older ones. The most recent definition, we hope, is truer. But all definitions of "atom," early and late, are equally correct as definitions for concepts held at a given time. Thus we are tempted to call any definition "false" if it disagrees with the prevalent conventional meaning of a term (e.g., defining "horse" as a extinct pachyderm). But since the meanings of terms can be stretched or transferred, it is more correct to call such definitions not "false" but "unconventional." Let us reserve for statements intended as descriptions and hypotheses the qualifications "true" and "false," and not attribute them to definitions as such.*

As a fourth caution, *we must beware of imposing our definitions upon others, or of allowing others to impose their definitions on us.* Definitions are not laws nor sacred edicts. They are trial statements in terms of which we can explore the further characteristics of the concept being defined. There is, in fact, a special danger when definitions are implicit or disguised. Suppose, for example, someone says something like: "Well, you've got to admit that that just isn't art!" while pointing to a painting. The speaker is enforcing an implied definition of art on the person he addresses. If, on being pressed for a definition, he retorts perchance, "Art is anything I like, and I don't like this," then at least he has given an initial definition of "art" even though it is

---

* Aristotle clearly indicates this distinction as follows: "If a thesis . . . asserts either the existence or nonexistence of a subject, it is a hypothesis; if it does not so assert, it is a definition. . . . [As, for example,] the arithmetician lays it down that to be a unit is to be quantitatively indivisible; but it is not a hypothesis, for to define what a unit is is not the same as to affirm its existence" (*Posterior Analytics* 17a 19-24. Mure translation) .

not going to be of much use to anyone else. To be useful for mutual understanding, we may note, a definition should be a cooperatively worked-out venture.

Finally, our fifth caution is *against the assumption that some terms simply cannot be defined.* Unless we are confronted with a language so poverty-stricken that no synonyms or synonymous expressions are available for most of its terms, then definitions are possible. But persons who stress the indefinability of certain ideas usually have one of two things in mind: (1) definitions, as noted above, fail to give complete understandings or (2) certain ideas and their symbols are so bound up with personal feelings and extra connotations that associating them with other terms seems to miss their main character. Now if we deny the possibility of definitions on the first ground, then we are expecting more than we should of a definition. And if we object on the second ground, then we are not denying the possibility of a definition, but rather its relevance to the important aspects of the idea. It may indeed be the case that defining is of no great service to highly intimate and individual experiences, any more than it is when applied to individual persons. But definitions are always possible and are useful to the extent that we are dealing with more or less general terms, whose members have features in common.

In summary, a definition is valuable and useful if we know what to expect of it. We should not expect it (1) to give a full description or an explanation, especially of particular referents, (2) to be the only correct definition, (3) to be true or false, (4) to be imposed upon us by some sacred authority, or (5) to be impossible wherever there are any terms whose referents have recognizable characteristics.

SUGGESTED READINGS

Plato, *Euthyphro* (to see how Socrates criticizes Euthyphro's definitions).

Mill, John Stuart, *A System of Logic,* Bk. I, Ch. 8.

Lewis, C. I., *An Analysis of Knowledge and Valuation,* Ch. 5.

Hempel, Carl G., "Fundamentals of Concept Formation in Empirical Science" in *International Encyclopedia for Unified Science,* Vol. II, No. 7, pp. 1-20.

Robinson, Richard, *Definition,* especially Chs. 3-4.

CHAPTER XII

Forming Definitions

Why and when do we need to formulate definitions of our own?

WHEN UNFAMILIAR WORDS bother us, our first recourse is most likely to be to the dictionary. However, when we are involved in a discussion—especially a philosophical discussion—the requirement that we define our terms often arises, not because we are unfamiliar with the term we are using, but because we need to clarify and shape its meaning to the purpose at hand. Of course, we may still want to go to the dictionary to find out whether or not our meaning agrees with the definitions given there. But this is not apt to be very helpful if we are more concerned with the clarification of our special meaning and its implications than we are with the conventional meanings of the term in question. So in philosophical discussion we need some handy method of procedure whereby we can begin to formulate our own definitions. In this chapter it will be our purpose to suggest such a procedure.

One caution needs to be mentioned at the outset. It may happen that persons who are unfamiliar with the purpose and nature of defining will express irritation and annoyance when definitions are called for. It is easy to gain the impression that the main goal of the discussion has been lost to view, and that we have become bogged down in "futile hairsplittings" or "mere semantics." On such occasions we must be patient and hold on to the idea that in the long run the futility of hairsplitting is apt to be much less than the futility of arguing over vague or ambiguous terms. Indeed, it is well to remember that arguments are often settled simply through the expedient of defining a few key terms.

To avoid a sense of futility, it is especially important that we do not fall into one of the common errors about definitions which were mentioned at the end of Chapter XI. Since definitions, as we saw, cannot reveal the full meaning of a term, we should not criticize them for a failure to do so; and if someone else criticizes our definitions on this ground, we should hasten to disabuse him regarding his misconception of the nature and function of defining. We should also be willing to consider any and all definitions that are seriously proposed by others; and then examine these definitions in order to discover (1) if they lead to any inconsistencies, and (2) how well they fit into our developing theory. Our attitude in a discussion should always be that of a cooperative exploration of meanings for the purpose of improving our understandings; and we should never permit discussion to degenerate either into a game of intellectual mastery or into expressions of emotional attachment or dislike for one meaning rather than another.

As a result of the process of defining, we often find that the word or expression we have selected may not be the one best suited for our purposes. Then we must hunt for a better word. It is at this point especially that some persons may object to our procedure as being "a mere matter of semantics." But such an objection usually reveals an impatience on the part of the objector, which stems from the fact that he is not aware of some important connotational overtones suggested by the terms in question. To him, then, it is only a trivial terminological quibble (or "a mere matter of semantics"), unless we can show him the importance of the connotational differences.

Defining terms is important not only for discussions but also for developing a position in a written essay. Here, though the writer is not challenged (being his own master), the reader should be kept in mind, and sufficient delimitations of meaning should be given to avoid puzzlements and confusions. This is especially necessary where more or less familiar terms have been given new extensions. In more formal treatises, the crucial definitions should be stated explicitly at the outset; but in more informal essays, definitions may better be worked in as needed and in fact may often simply be suggested by the context.

How shall we formulate definitions?

The type of term and the type of purpose will make some difference in regard to the best procedure for constructing our own definitions. If the term to be defined is new or is to be given a new extension, then the definition is prescriptive and we are at liberty to stipulate what meaning best suits our purposes. But if, as is more often the case, our purpose is simply to clarify meanings when some vagueness or ambiguity is detected in the ordinary use of language, then what we are seeking is a way of delimiting more precisely the extension or extensions of some traditional term. We then presume that we have some acquaintance with the "normal meaning" of the term in question and that we simply wish to find a procedure for clarifying and refining its meaning, either for ourselves or for someone else, or both.

Attention has already been called to the fact that terms may refer (1) to ordinary concrete objects or events (e.g., men), (2) to more collective referents (e.g., mankind), (3) to abstractions (e.g., triangle), and (4) to imaginatively altered and constructed concepts (e.g., infinity). Where we begin in formulating a definition will depend in part on which type of referent we have at hand. If the referents are a class of ordinary concrete objects, we could first examine the typical cases of such objects. The order, then, would proceed from the instances themselves to the intensional properties we are seeking, and by analogy with inductive inference, it will be convenient to call this *inductive** defining. How-

* A definition that starts with an examination of essential aspects and then proceeds to the particular examples or more concrete embodiments would then follow a *deductive* order of defining. The terms "inductive" and "deductive" are used here only by loose analogy with their stricter meanings, which we shall examine in Chapter XIII. Except for the convenience of the shorter terms, it would be more exact to call the two orders of defining (1) the "extensional-to-intensional" order and (2) the "intensional-to-extensional" order.

ever, when an imaginary concept is the referent, we clearly cannot begin with observable cases. Instead, the order would be that
of first examining the abstractions involved and then the ways in
which they have been altered.

Let us now look at the four categories of terms just mentioned, in order to discover what procedures may appropriately
be followed in formulating definitions in each case. The empirically oriented or inductive order will be most appropriate for
the first case and may indeed serve as a model for the others. At
least let us see how far we can carry such an approach, since this
would be in keeping with the general orientation of the point
of view developing in this book.

Defining Concrete Terms. Most appropriate to the defining
of ordinary concrete objects and events will be a procedure which
looks first at examples contained within the customary extension
of the term to be defined. From an examination of these examples, we should presumably be able to abstract their intensional parts and aspects and decide which among these are the
essential ones for the precise delimitation we are seeking. Remember that in the initial building of a class (see Chapter X, Fig. 1)
we start with some central core example or examples, about
which there would be no question as to their proper membership
in the class in question. Using this core example, or paradigm
case, as a basis of comparison, we can explore other examples of
similar objects or events in order to discover what limits to place
on the class that we are defining. Let us illustrate by taking
some very commonplace example like "rug." We should start by
thinking of a particular rug which would unquestionably be
called a rug. Our paradigm case here is certainly not going to be
wall-to-wall carpeting, but some ordinary smallish floor covering
made of woven cloth material. In other words, we start by thinking of some example or examples that fall well within the conventional meaning of the term being defined; and we assume, of
course, that our prior knowledge of the term's extension allows
us to do this.

Next we must examine the area of variability. To do this, we
should concentrate on the borderline cases, in order to decide
where to draw the membership line. In our example, shall we
push the term "rug" out to include wall-to-wall carpeting, or

not? It is at this point that we must become stipulative and decide for ourselves. Our decision will depend in part, no doubt, upon the use we intend to make of the term. Perhaps our feelings and prejudices may enter in to dictate to us which items to retain and which to exclude; but if we regard the procedure as exploratory and tentative, we need not and should not let our feelings cause us to have vigorous attachments for some special extensional limit. If we do discover some fairly obvious "natural" breaks or divisions between the extensions of one term and some others, then we may well take advantage of these breaks. But usually there are either gradual mergings or a number of equally available breaks, so that the ultimate decision will still be arbitrary.

We shall also need to decide on the type of definition we wish to formulate. As we saw in Chapter XI, the traditional genus-differentia definition and the contextual definition are the most satisfactory. In either case, we shall need a differentia which will state the necessary and sufficient conditions for membership. Especially when we are defining nouns, we find it helpful to use the genus-differentia formulation since the genus (or larger class; see Chapter X, Fig. 3) focuses attention on the general area within which the extension of the term being defined will fall. So, if a genus is to be used, it will be necessary to find an appropriate one, and name it, providing we observe the cautions mentioned in Chapter X.

Our last step is the crucial one. It is to determine the differentia (or necessary and sufficient conditions). For this, we must abstract from our chosen examples the parts, qualities, relations, and functions which are essential to these examples and serve to exclude unwanted cases. All the traits named in the differentia *when taken together* should accomplish this task. This part of our formulation will center on finding the set of credentials which any particular case must possess to be admitted into our tent. It is here that our examination of the borderline cases must be taken into account. For example, suppose we wish to define *horse*. We might start by including horses in the genus *animal,* and then differentiating them from other animals as being large, solid-hoofed, and herbivorous. Any one of these traits alone would be inadequate to differentiate horses; for elephants are certainly large, there is a special breed of hogs that is solid-hoofed, and many animals besides horses are herbivorous. But taken together these traits go far toward delimiting "horses" and establishing the necessary and sufficient conditions for horses. Yet, what about mules, donkeys, and zebras? Clearly they are still included. If we wish to narrow our tent so as to exclude mules, donkeys, and zebras, we shall have to add more traits to our differentia (e.g., short-eared and nonstriped). There may be other borderline cases to be considered (e.g., Shetland ponies), and it may be that further traits will need to be added, some affirmative (e.g., short-haired) and some negative (e.g., nonstriped), in order that our refinement of the concept *horse* may progress to a satisfactory point. How far we wish to go in the direction of making the concept precise and diminishing the area of variability will naturally depend upon the use to which we are going to put our definition. For ordinary purposes, roughly outlined areas of reference may suffice, but for careful reasoning, more precise definitions are necessary. Now let us summarize this procedure in a series of four steps.

STEP I. *Think of several core instances of the term to be defined.* These instances should be (1) varied and (2) particular. Do not concentrate on a number of very similar examples, but on some which are as different as possible, yet still fall within the tent. Also, do not think of concepts just a little less general than the term being defined, but rather seek out cases *as particular or specific as possible.* For example, if we are defining *chair* we might think of the old kitchen chair at home, of dad's overstuffed easy chair, of the old broken rocking chair in the attic, of a particular antique chair we remember, etc. These examples are both various and particular. We might have thought of rocking chairs, school chairs, kitchen chairs, easy chairs, etc. These would have been various, but not particular; we would be looking only at subclasses. However, there may well be some reasonable proportion between the generality of the definiendum and the specificity of the examples we are seeking; so that for more general terms less particular examples, such as subclasses, will be adequate. In fact, it may help us to name subclasses in any case; for they will direct attention to a wider variety of possibilities for inclusion or exclusion; but we should also try to think of some very particular examples, with all the parts and aspects such examples would have, lest we ignore some trait that will prove important for our later discriminations.

STEP II. *Think of some instances of items which should be excluded.* These items should include both those which are definitely outside the kind of thing being defined and also some borderline cases. For example, in the case of *chair,* we know we do not want to include desks or tables or beds or street lamps. But we must ask ourselves rather critically if we wish to include stools, settees, love seats, chaises longues, etc. These are borderline cases. Some we may wish to keep in our tent, others will no doubt be left out. Borderline cases are important; for it is through a consideration of them that we discover where to peg down the tent more definitely.

STEP III. *Select an appropriate genus.* Assuming we are following the method of genus and differentia, we shall need a genus. As discussed in Chapter X, the principal question to ask ourselves here is *what kind* of thing we are defining. The rules given for finding a proper genus should be applied, namely (1) be sure the smaller class is genuinely a subclass of the larger and (2) be sure the larger class is really larger. That is, check (1) the *kind of* relation and (2) the *inclusion* relation. Supposing we look for a proper genus for *chair.* We might say *chair* is a kind of furniture. But then we notice that something is wrong; for the term "furniture" like "mankind" is somewhat collective. We need to individualize it again by speaking of "pieces of furniture," or something of the sort. We might have selected a wider genus for *chair,* such as *artifact.* But since the usefulness of the genus depends partly upon restrictiveness of the range it gives, it is clearly preferable to select a small or proximate genus, so long as it safely includes all members of the subclass being defined.

STEP IV. *Formulate a differentia.* Now we must examine the particular cases which we wish to include in our tent, and abstract from them their essential and delimiting aspects. (Re-

member that "aspects" may be qualities, relations or functions.) These will be the aspects which when taken together
should pertain to all members within the group being defined
and will not pertain to outsiders. For example, in the case of
chair, if we decide to exclude stools and settees, chairs will
have the following properties: (1) seats, (2) backs (otherwise
they would include stools), (3) legs, pedestal, or some device
for holding the seat at a normal sitting distance above the
floor, and (4) the function of being designed to seat one person comfortably (otherwise we are including settees, benches,
couches, etc.). Each trait named should be checked to make
sure it pertains to all members of the group we are defining.
It will also be useful if each trait named serves to exclude
some borderline case which we wish to eliminate. However,
we must remember that language is loosely used in normal
speech. If we discover that we have excluded something we
wished inside, or included something we wanted outside, we
must not be surprised. For example, our definition of *chair*
above would seem to eliminate children's high chairs for
they are above the normal sitting height. Yet if we take out
the trait of "normal sitting height" we let in those high
counter stools with small backs which may be found in of-
fices, bars, etc. So if we wish to keep in the high chairs and
eliminate the bar stools, we shall have to search further for
differentiating criteria. Try it.

After completing the above four steps to our satisfaction, we
can go on to state our definition in a proper genus-differentia
formula. This formula is as follows: "An x is a (genus) which
(differentiating properties)." Thus, we might propose "A chair is
a (piece of furniture) which (has a seat, a back, some legs or
pedestal to raise the seat to a normal sitting distance from the
floor, and is designed to seat one person comfortably)." Such a
definition is of course but a minimal description. Additional information about the subvarieties of the class may be helpful, as
when the dictionary supplements its definition with some enu-
merative statements. And if we, like the dictionary, can also give
pictures or synonyms, better yet. But the crux of the whole matter
is the differentia.

Defining Collective Terms. Some concepts, as we have seen, are collective in the sense that they convey the image of a mass or throng rather than a set of individuals. Now, will the method of defining outlined above apply to collective concepts as well as to classes of individual concrete objects or events? If such a term as "furniture" or "mankind" is to be our definiendum, we may have more difficulty in thinking of the particular cases to include or exclude. But if we ask ourselves what are some "pieces of" or "bits of" or "cases of" the mass in question, then we should be able to locate the particular instances which we need.

For example, if we wish to define *furniture,* we can first think of typical pieces of furniture. Thus we arrive at the notion of a bed or a table or a chair, etc., and we have only to survey our experience with pieces of furniture to find what extension we may wish to give this term. After thinking of enough examples, we shall need to find a genus; and for collective terms we can often use *collection* as a suitable genus. Thus we might define *furniture* as the "collection of the larger man-made objects used in and around buildings." Or as another example of a collective noun, let us take *knowledge.* We should look first for cases of or bits of knowledge. We shall probably think of the various disciplines in the curriculum which claim to divide up the realm of knowledge and some characteristic pieces of information to be obtained from each. Then we shall notice that these disciplines tend to establish requirements before any particular bit of information can be called knowledge. But once it has passed the requirements, the bit of information takes its place in the total body of knowledge. So we may formulate our definition as follows: Knowledge is that collection (or body) of information assumed to be true in accordance with some criterion established for the discipline within which the particular bit of information falls. Of course we need not be satisfied with this definition; and indeed it should bring to mind any number of questions, such as the meaning of "true" or the nature of the criteria required or their underlying principles.

Defining Abstract Terms. We have seen that we can adapt our method of inductive defining to collective terms. Now we must see what happens in the case of simple abstractions, such as blue or square or true. The problem will be first to find particular concrete objects or events which embody the abstraction in question. For example, in the case of blue, we might start with the blue rug in the bedroom or Jane's blue sweater or the blue sky or any other example of something blue. Next we must look for the limits of the extension which should be assigned to the term "blue." We shall discover that things we ordinarily call blue vary considerably in hue, ranging from greenish to purplish, not to mention variations in brightness and saturation. With regard to hue, limits will need to be established on the color spectrum, beyond which it would no longer be suitable to call some color "blue." If we follow the usual convention, these limits would fall at about 467 and 482 millimicrons of wavelength. But their determination is partly a cultural and arbitrary matter. For example, the Navaho have one term covering some green and some blue and centering in the green-blue or turquoise area of the spectrum.

In the case of *square,* we can start again with some typical square objects—windowpanes, acoustic ceiling blocks, the village square, etc. What variability of extension do we find here? We notice that some squares are larger and others are smaller; but we can ignore size, since no matter how large or small a square may be, it is no less a square. Some square objects, like the village square, are less regular than others; but then we would be inclined to say that they are only approximate squares and not true squares. So we find no significant variable extension here. The reason for this is that when we are dealing with geometric figures, we normally think only in terms of the refined and perfected variety; and for these the variable extension is easily eliminated. As a result it is relatively easy to formulate precise intensional conditions for simple and regular geometric shapes. But refinement and regularity in geometry, as we saw, is the product of imagination. The notion of a perfect square is an imaginary concept, and the question of its definition can be deferred until we turn our attention to the defining of such concepts.

Let us look now at the concept *true.* Can it be defined inductively by starting from particular examples? First, we must ask ourselves in what situations or contexts would the term "true" be applied. Sometimes we speak of a measuring ruler as having a true edge, which suggests that its edge is not jagged or curved and is therefore trustworthy or reliable for drawing straight lines. Sometimes we speak of a pair of lovers as being true to each other, meaning that they do not consort amorously with other individuals. Again the term seems to point to trustworthiness. Sometimes an object or aspect is termed true (e.g., a true home) meaning that it fulfills all requirements for being that kind of thing. But most often the adjective "true" is used as an attribute of ideas or beliefs, which we call true when we think they agree with reality.

We have just noticed quite a wide range of things to which the term "true" is often applied. If we admit all of them, our definition of the term is going to be wider than if we limit it to some particular kind of situation. We may be tempted, for example, because of the frequency of usage, to limit "true" to ideas when involved in beliefs. We may even wish to be still more restrictive and limit its applicability to beliefs when they are expressed by propositions which either affirm or deny something (e.g., "It is raining"; "There is no God"). If we follow the lead of those who pin their faith on the scientific method, we may go still further and limit the proper application of the quality "true" (and "false") to affirmations or denials that can be scientifically or empirically verified or falsified.

Clearly, for a term like "true," some decision is going to be needed with regard to the range of applicability that we are to select. This consideration was not so important for "blue" or "square," largely because there has not been so much extensional variability in the application of those terms. But it is important in the case of "true"; for if the extension of "true" is to include straightedges and human trustworthiness, we should not want to incorporate in the definition some insistence on scientific verifiability.

"True" has not only a range of applicability, but also a range within its own abstract level, as had blue between green and purple. We can think of this as its *extension on the abstract level,* as against its *extension on the applied or concrete level.* The range here, as with so many aspects that have polar opposites, is between "true" and "false." If we refer back to our earlier discussion of such opposites, we shall remember that there are a number of patterns or models which may serve us (see Chapter VI). Shall we take true and false to be irrevocably separated and nonoverlapping? Or is one unchanging and the other variable, as we should conceive it if we take true as always perfect, and falsity as anything less? Or do truth and falsity vary inversely along a scale, so that what is half false is also half true? And in this case, does the scale have limits, or is it limitless? Here is another range of possibilities among which we shall need to decide. If we take a perfectionist or idealistic position, for example, and limit "true" to that which is completely and absolutely true, then we have placed this concept, along with geometrically refined squares, in the category of imaginary notions. If, on the other hand, we are willing to allow "true" to be a more-or-less quality, then we can find it in ordinary experiences wherever anything is shown to be more or less trustworthy or reliable. As a matter of fact, we may very well be able to find a simple definition of "true" without raising these questions, for if some synonyms can be found which also share the same conditions as "true," then we can use at least one synonym as the key term in our simple definition. In the case of "true," it is not difficult to find at least two synonyms, "reliable" and "trustworthy." But when we formulate this kind of simple definition ("true is the quality of being reliable or trustworthy"), we must realize that we have not yet tackled the questions about the limits of application and extension of this quality. We have merely postponed them.

In our foregoing discussion about defining abstract terms, we may have noticed that finding a suitable intension (or differentia) is on the whole easier than was the case with the more concrete terms. Thus, "blue" can be given an intension in terms of its position in the color spectrum; "square" is readily defined in terms of lines and angles (four equal lines connected by right angles); and even "true" can be given a simple definition by synonym. This should not surprise us; for abstractions are normally simpler and more precise than concrete concepts. Finding the intension of an abstract concept may be helped if we pay attention to some concrete embodiments or concreted abstractions. This will give us a better idea regarding the ways in which the abstraction in question is actually applied. For example, the term "democracy" can be applied to the simple town-meeting type of government, or to a form of government wherein representatives are elected to a governing body, or to a type of socialism in which the emphasis is upon human equality and managed economy promoted and maintained by a party oligarchy, as in the "peoples' democracies" of the communist world. We can, of course, decide in advance to define the term so as to exclude some of these varieties, especially if we have a strong feeling about what the term ought to mean. But let us not be too hasty. There may be a common thread of meaning running through all of these applications which will allow us greater insight into the reasons for such a diversity of usages. We are often aided in these cases by examining the history of the word in question to discover its earlier meanings. "Democracy," for example, is an ancient Greek word indicating the "power of the demes" or rural (as against urban) peoples. The rural people were considered untutored and "common," so the term came to mean "rule of the common people." Later this was interpreted as the power of the people as a whole, regardless of rank or wealth, and therefore of all considered equal. From this meaning came the stress on human equality, whether political or not. So, we see that the meaning has been transferred from (1) power or rule of the rural people to (2) rule of the common people to (3) rule of all people regardless of wealth or rank to (4) stress on human equality in all respects, not just political. It is in this last sense that socialist and communist oligarchies or dictatorships can appropriately be called "democracies," for they proclaim as their goal a condition of human equality. But with us, the term still is used largely in its third sense to mean the rule (via the ballot) of all persons of age regardless of rank or wealth. Terms like "democracy," as we shall see when we consider defining imaginary concepts, are readily idealized by the imagination. In these cases it becomes especially important to distinguish between what we mean by the term when applied to actual as against ideal situations.

Before we leave the defining of abstract concepts and turn to the imaginary variety, a word should be said about appropriate genera, in case we wish to formulate a genus-differentia type of definition. For abstractions which are parts (e.g., leg), the term "part" can be used as genus. For the majority of abstractions which are aspects, the term "aspect" itself will serve as a very broad genus. If a more proximate genus is desired, then "quality," "relation," or "function" may be used; and under these are many still more proximate (or specific) possibilities (e.g., *blue* is a quality, but more specifically it is a color; *square* is a set of relations, but more specifically it is a figure).

Defining Imaginary Terms. We have outlined a method for formulating inductive definitions of ordinary concrete terms, collective terms, and abstract terms. But will this method also serve for imaginary terms? When we turn our attention to concepts of this type, we are faced with the difficulty of not having any experienceable concrete examples from which to start. Here, it would seem, we cannot commence as before, with a number of observable instances.

Nevertheless, if our general thesis is correct, namely, that imaginary concepts are traceable back to ordinary abstractions which have been modified, we can at least start with those abstractions and then see what has been done to them. For example, unicorns are derivable from horses plus horns, and centaurs from horses plus human beings. Similarly, the creatures encountered today in science fiction, if we look with sufficient diligence, find derivations based on experienceable objects. Definitions in these cases would simply state what combinations or alterations have been made upon recognizable items of experience. For example, one could define a *unicorn* as an imaginary animal composed of a horse with a single horn, usually spiraled, coming from the center of the forehead.

However, there are other imaginary concepts that are not so clearly traceable back to experiences. What should we do, for example, with the notion of an *n*-dimensional universe? We could start with the idea of a single dimension which is abstractable in spatial terms from, say, one edge of a tabletop. Then we could imagine a two-dimensional plane surface, and then a three-dimensional solid. Now we have set up, at least in spatial experience, the beginning of a series (one-dimensional, two-dimensional, three-dimensional). Any series readily permits *extrapolation* as an imaginary procedure. So now we can continue in our thoughts to construct the concept of four dimensions, five dimensions, six dimensions, etc., on up to any number of dimensions—that is, *n* dimensions. Here we have gone beyond what is observable in experience, or even what is mentally picturable so long as we are thinking in terms of spatial dimensions. It is possible to generalize the notion of dimension to include not only spatial dimensions but also a time dimension or even anything measurable (e.g., a hot-cold dimension, a light-dark dimension, etc.). So if we wish to define a concept such as *n*-dimensionality, it will be necessary to trace the notion of dimension back to its sphere of meaning, giving it the extension which we desire, and to indicate what we mean by the *n* and how this notion of multiplicity can be correlated with the notion of dimension. In other words, *we must define each ingredient in the total concept, and then show how they are related.*

Thus our way of dealing with imaginary concepts is different from the inductive procedure outlined above. We do not start with some recognized examples taken from the core area of the term-tent in question; but instead we start with some familiar abstractions and then note how they are recombined or altered to form the new concept. The abstractions plus the particular operations involved in the recombinations, refinements, or extrapolations will give us the necessary criteria for our definitions. It may be helpful for the novice who is unacquainted with some special imaginary concept to trace its origin back to the level of experienceable abstractions, but this is not necessary for an adequate definition. Most of the notions of advanced mathematics and formal science, for example, can be directly defined in terms of other altered and refined concepts in current use. It is only for the beginner that the process of tracing back is of paramount importance, and normally those working at the frontiers of knowledge are not concerned with the beginner. If the beginner wishes to catch up as quickly as possible, he must use his imaginative powers in tracing out these concepts for himself. So the kind of definition needed for an imaginary concept will depend in part upon the sophistication of the audience in regard to prior knowledge of the meanings of the major abstractions used.

Perfect geometric shapes, as already observed in the case of *square,* are examples of imaginatively refined concepts, for which it is usually pointless to refer back to concrete experience. Unless we are rank beginners in the realm of geometry, it is a waste of time to inventory a large number of experienceable squares or circles in order to discover the criteria for squareness or circularity. Whether man first noticed rough shapes in nature and then refined them, or whether (to believe Plato) an incipient knowledge of these shapes was born in human intelligence, is an interesting question, but is not our main concern here. What is important is that in defining these concepts they must be clarified by reference to their key abstractions, and these in turn can be correlated with visible embodiments, if necessary.

Somewhat more perplexing are moral ideals where the visible embodiments are not so evident. Generally, an ideal is a desirable type of behavior or condition toward which we believe we should strive, but which does not yet exist, and in fact may never exist in experience. An ideal, then, is something imaginary; and we may well wonder where to look in experience to find the key abstractions which can be extrapolated to create the concept of an ideal. One answer is that we observe in the array of human actions and conditions some which are distasteful to us and seem less desirable as over against others which we regard as more desirable. Then by imaginatively extrapolating and integrating the more desirable types, we arrive at the notions of the various ideals. For example, we admire unselfishness as witnessed in human actions of dedication and sacrifice. From these observed examples, even though they may be rare, we can extrapolate to the notion of a more ideal selflessness in which dedicated and unselfish action is projected into a saintly perfection. The trait itself which we are extrapolating thus becomes the intensional character we need for a definition of unselfishness.

Moral qualities, we must note however, involve not only the observable acts and conditions just mentioned, but also the sense of their desirability or undesirability. No doubt the factor of desirability can itself be directly experienced as a feeling within oneself, and this would be enough for our own personal evaluations of human actions and conditions. But this is not enough if we wish to take into account the moral norms established by social custom. These norms may be the result of earlier feelings of desirability and undesirability which the society has erected into a moral code; but for each individual who becomes aware of them only as a code, they are presented as already established and as something simply to be learned. In this case there is another type of experience which can enter into the definition of an ideal, that is, experience with the moral code. For example, the act of removing some object from one place and putting it in another (such as taking money from a cash drawer and putting it into a purse) may or may not be classifiable as an act of theft. To decide whether a particular act is conventionally theft, two things need to be known: (1) the full circumstance of the act and (2) the social conventions according to which an act is considered theft. But this presupposes that the social code has already defined theft. If a new definition is desired, or if it is our own moral ideal that we wish to develop, then we must go further and ask about the origin and adequacy of the previous definition. When we embark upon this undertaking, we find it necessary to consider not only particular moral goods and evils but also the whole set of these qualities in order to integrate them in some harmonious fashion. The resulting image of an ideal society is called a "utopia," a word derived from the Greek for "nowhere" and first used by Sir Thomas More (1478-1535) as a recognition of the nonexistence of such imaginary ideals. We must remember, however, that imaginary ideals, like imaginary geometric figures, have great practical utility as guidelines to what is or could be experienceable.

These observations upon the defining of moral ideals lead to one highly important caution: there is a dangerous ambiguity present whenever we are dealing with terms which may include ideal meanings, since on the one hand we may take them as representing the actually experienceable conditions, or on the other they may stand only for the imaginary ideals. Where concepts of this kind are involved, we should constantly guard against the confusion that may result from a failure to recognize this type of ambiguity.

Among the value concepts which are often given both actual and ideal meanings, political forms are prominent. Democracy, for example, may be defined as "a form of government in which the supreme power is retained by the people and exercised through a system of elected representatives." Such a definition readily fits existing governments. But one might define democracy as "a form of government in which the sovereign powers are equally exercised by all the people," or as "a society in which all members have equal rights and exercise equal powers." We can readily see that these latter definitions could exist on earth only among a very small number of human beings, and even then with great difficulty. They represent ideal rather than practical or actual democracy. It is possible to define any form of government either as a practiced mode or as an imagined ideal, so that it is a favorite trick of the demagogue to confuse the public by assuming the ideal meaning when talking of his own program and the reverse when talking of his opponent's program. In the arena of political oratory, therefore, it is especially important to be on guard against confusing an imaginatively idealized condition with existing conditions which are always at the mercy of human weaknesses. The demand for a clear definition can be crucially vital in these cases.

To sum up our discussion of defining imaginary concepts, we should first remember that these concepts are usually interpretable as recombinations, refinements, and extrapolations of ordinary abstractions. To define them, we can best start by noting the ordinary abstractions and then name the ways in which these have been altered to form the imaginary concept, or if, as with simple concepts, this step is not necessary, we can analyze directly the essential traits of the concept. But we should not look for or expect to find visible embodiments, unless these are something we can create or approximate ourselves (e.g., pictures of unicorns).

How can definitions help us avoid ambiguities?

There are two primary obstacles to clarity: vagueness and ambiguity. Vagueness, we remember, is the result of too much extensional variability; and this in turn is usually due to lax usage. We have examined ways in which defining concrete terms, collective terms, abstract terms, and imaginary terms can eliminate some, if not all, of the extensional variability that surrounds most terms. More attention, however, is needed in regard to the matter of ambiguity.

Ambiguity occurs when a term has two or more rather widely separate extensional ranges (Chapter IV). Very often ambiguous terms started out as metaphorical transferences of meaning, and ended up becoming equally conventional in the old and new areas. To define ambiguous terms, the simplest thing, of course, is to give alternative definitions. The dictionary does just this, listing major and minor differences of meaning, with different numbers attached to each meaning. When making our own definitions, we may wish to do the same, though it is apt to be confusing in a discussion if we do not appropriate different definienda for our different meanings, or at least different qualifying words that can be easily remembered.

James MacKaye* has suggested a useful technique for weeding out misunderstandings due to ambiguity, especially when they lead to contradictory assertions. Consider, for example, the following pair of statements:

> Logic is a science.   Logic is not a science.

Both of these propositions, says MacKaye, may be true depending upon the way in which we define "logic" and "science." Assuming we know what logic is, let us look at the term "science." In its broadest sense, it should mean any kind of knowledge, and in this case logic would certainly be a science. But in more modern and narrower senses, "science" is limited to studies for which laboratory methods are useful, and in this case logic would not be a science. If we examine current dictionaries, we should find at least five rather different meanings of "science"; according to some of them logic would be considered a science, and according to others it would not. Taking stock of alternative meanings will usually put an end to the typically futile dispute over whether or not something is something else.

Certain ambiguities are fostered by the language itself, especially in the case of certain nominalizing suffixes. For example, *-ion* words can indicate either an activity or condition resulting from the activity. Thus the word "abstraction" may refer either to the process of abstracting or to the kind of concept that results from this process. To avoid ambiguity in the present book, where possible we have used the -ion ending for the condition resulting from a process, and the -ing ending for the process itself. Another suffix which is ambiguous in the same way is *-ment*. Usually words ending in -ment (e.g., embodiment, employment) refer principally

* See *Logic of Language,* Ch. 5.

to conditions, although the correlated activity is simultaneously suggested. More apt to cause trouble is *-ism,* used as a noun ending for Greek verbs terminating in -ize (e.g., baptism from baptize). Again the -ism suffix may stand for action or condition or both. But then this particular suffix was appropriated to designate a doctrine or theory, and it has been lavishly attached to a great many roots, Greek and otherwise (e.g., rationalism, dualism, Berkeleyism). So, -ism words may indicate (1) actions, (2) conditions, or (3) philosophical positions; and we must be on guard against this ambiguity. It is of interest in this case that "socialism" and "communism" make use of the -ism suffix, instead of the older *-cracy* (power) or *-archy* (rule) endings traditionally used for political types. The reason for this, no doubt, is that socialism and communism are nineteenth-century formulations which started as philosophical ideologies and have only gradually and imperfectly been actively put into practice. In this connection, it is well that we remember not to confuse the ideal with the actual, for ideal socialism or communism, like ideal democracy, is a concept quite different from anything we can observe in actual practice. It is also important for us to realize that socialism and communism have envisioned much more thoroughgoing reforms of human nature than is usually accomplished by a change in political form. For this reason, the political form, especially in the case of communism, has characteristically been dictatorial, excused on the ground of temporary expediency in bringing about the envisioned transformations in human attitudes and practices.

Cases of ambiguity are not limited, of course, to human affairs and sociopolitical forms. We have mentioned these at some length only because the dangers here are greater, where misunderstandings and intemperate attachments to certain meanings can cause so much human misery.

How far shall we go in defining a term?

One more point needs to be made. Since a single definition which aims at clarification of one term may introduce other vague or ambiguous terms, we may wonder if we should not go on and define these too. If the best terms we can find for the definiens are indeed vague or ambiguous, then certainly we shall do well to carry on the process of defining far enough to include definitions of these terms. This procedure may be called *the method of successive definition.* On most occasions it will very shortly reach a point of diminishing returns and we can drop the formulating of definitions to return to the main line of a discussion. But in a looser sense, we are always defining successively: each new answer that we give raises new questions, not only of definition, but of the larger meanings as well. For example, if we define *science* as any kind of knowledge, we have obviously made a start; but we have not gone far until we ask ourselves what knowledge is. Varieties and styles and criteria of knowledge may well emerge from our inquiry, and what we discover will be of great help in showing us what science is and what it is not. But then we shall no longer be forming definitions in a narrow sense; we shall be using our initial definitions, as they should be used, to reveal the larger problems of our subject matter. It is in this way of expanding our meanings and understandings that exploratory philosophical inquiry is properly based upon definitions.

SUGGESTED READINGS

MacKaye, James, *The Logic of Language,* especially Chs. 3 and 5.

Moore, G. E., *Principia Ethica,* especially Ch. 1 (concerning the "indefinable" nature of the concept "good").

Wheelwright, Philip, *A Critical Introduction to Ethics,* Chs. 1-2 (concerning definitions of ethical terms).

Werkmeister, W. K., *The Basis and Structure of Knowledge,* especially Ch. 4 (concerning meanings of "truth").

Austin, J. L., *Philosophical Papers,* No. 4 (more on "truth").

CHAPTER XIII
Inferring

What is an inference?

DEFINING, AS WE HAVE SEEN, has as its goal the clarifying and delimiting of the concepts which we must
use in discriminating better understandings. But defining by itself is only the opening step. The next step
on our journey requires us to make inferences;* for
the task of exploring ideas and discovering their consequences and their underlying assumptions depends
upon our ability to infer. Therefore, it is to this task
of inferring that we find a major portion of the philosophical enterprise devoted. Indeed, the processes of
inference are central not only to philosophy but to all
rational investigations, including the sciences.

Inferences occur whenever anyone draws out from a
situation or concept some further knowledge or meaning which was not directly given. Inferring, that is,
goes beyond immediate experience and thus involves
imagination. For example, you are out in the woods
and you happen to notice some marks in the ground.

---

* Let us avoid one common error. Do not say of concepts,
terms, judgments, or propositions that they "infer" something!
Only people infer. Concepts, terms, judgments, and propositions
may *imply*, but they do not *infer*.

Because of past experience, you infer that these marks are animal tracks. If your previous knowledge is sufficiently extensive, you may even be able to infer what animal made them (e.g., a deer) that the tracks were made within the last 48 hours by a buck weighing approximately 250 pounds, and much more. Such inferences would be made from some directly observed clues, but the observable marks are only clues. They need past observations and past knowledge to permit the inferred ideas to be built up with a reasonable chance for correctness.

Not all inferences need be made from direct personal observation. Someone might say to you, as you are preparing to leave a building, "Did you know it is raining?" Now, if you trust your informant, even though you yourself have not observed the rain, you would probably infer the advisability of fetching your raincoat or umbrella. Thus it is that the fabric of inferences which one normally makes involves a great variety of clues, only a few of which are likely to have been matters of direct observation.

The first characteristic of inference, then, is that it leads us beyond what is directly observable. But is this not also the chief characteristic of imagining? If so, how should we differentiate between inferring and imagining? Upon closer inspection, the difference turns out to be a matter of following out some suggested pattern or order in the case of inference, whereas imagination is more often regarded as something free and fanciful. We can, however, conveniently regard inference simply as that type of imagination which uses some pattern or order as a basis for inferring something beyond what is given or already known. Thus, in the case of the animal tracks, you infer a deer as the most probable cause because of the pattern of the previously observed correlations. A more fanciful type of imagining might lead to the suggestion that odd-shaped hail stones or men from Mars had caused the impressions in the ground.

If inferring, then, is imagining based upon patterns or orders, where do we find these patterns, and how do we make use of them? In answering this question, it will be convenient to follow the old distinction between inductive and deductive inferences, since the basic distinction here is concerned with the type of given material in which the patterns and orders are found. Let us take the case of induction first.

What is the nature of inductive inference?

Inductive inferences start with observed patterns of correlations which we abstract from experiences and on the basis of which we make guesses about extending these correlations beyond the given material. As an illustration, let us take again the example of the supposed deer tracks. Before we can hazard the guess that they were made by a deer, we must have had some previous experience, direct or indirect, which would connect this type of imprint with deer. Implicit in our thinking at this stage is the *inductive generalization,* all tracks of this type are made by deer. Our confidence in this generalization depends in part upon the frequency of our past experiences with deer tracks, and in part upon a lack of alternative explanations for the same phenomenon. Perhaps the tracks were made by elk or rabbits, rather than deer; but the adequacy of our generalization will depend upon the adequacy of our own familiarity with like situations. We can diagram the generalizing type of reasoning (Diagram I). We see that each additional case of A being correlated

CASE 1	CASE 2	CASE 3	CASE 4 ⟶ CASE *n*	
A (tracks)	A	A	A	A
↓	↓	↓	↓	↓
B (deer)	B	B	B	B

Diagram I. Inductive Generalization

with B suggests more strongly the generalization (*n*) that any case of A is correlated with B. It is on the basis of this implicit generalization that we complete our inference concerning the particular footprint which we are now observing, and assign to it the probability that it is a deer track.

There are other varieties of inductive inference. One of these which is closely related to generalizing is *reasoning by analogy.* It is closely related because generalizing moves ahead by way of similarities (analogies) between the cases.* In each similar case of repeated phenomena there may be a different number of

---

* Analogies usually imply similarities of structure in such a way that a missing factor (part, aspect, agent, etc.) of one occurrence of a phenomenon is assumed to be probably there because of its presence in one or more other occurrences of the same type of phenomenon.

aspects which are analogous. Thus, the deer tracks may be of the same size and shape as those last observed, in which case both the elements of size and shape are similar; or they may be of a different size, in which case only shape is similar. In generalizing, reasoning moves from few to more cases of a repeated correlation, ending in the guess that this correlation always prevails. In reasoning by analogy, on the other hand, one is concerned with at least two cases in which one infers a trait not yet revealed in the second case from its existence in a first case which is in most other respects similar.

For example, suppose you observe an animal about fifteen inches long, having fur, long whiskers, a twitchy tail, and a meow, and this animal is called a cat. Suppose then that you observe another animal about the same size with similar fur, whiskers, and twitchy tail; then you may infer by analogy that this animal too should be able to meow, even though it has as yet made no such sound. It also seems reasonable to suppose that the more numerous the observed traits which the two animals have in common, the more likelihood there is of other common traits being present. That is, on the basis of size, fur, and whiskers alone, you should be more cautious about predicting the meow than you would on the basis of size, fur, whiskers, and twitchy tail. Still, the meow may not be there; so the analogical inference, even from several common traits, is only an imaginative guess. Analogical inferences can be shown as in

	CASE 1	CASE 2	CASE 3	CASE 4	CASE 5
A (e.g., size)		Given A	Given A	Given A	Given A
B (e.g., fur)		B	B	B	infer B
C (e.g., whiskers)		C	C	infer C	C
D (e.g., twitchy tail)		D	infer D	D	D
E (e.g., meow)		infer E	and E	and E	and E

Diagram II. Analogical Inference

Diagram II. In Case 1 all five traits are observed to go together. In Cases 2, 3, 4, and 5, fewer and fewer traits are given and more and more need to be inferred. Thus in Case 5, only the size is given, so the fur, whiskers, twitchy tail, and meow all need inferring. As can be seen, such an inference would be more dubious, whereas in Case 2, where four traits are given and only one needs to be inferred, the inference would be much safer.

We can observe in Diagrams I and II how the order of generalizing and the order of analogizing are related. The order of generalizing is indicated horizontally as new cases with similar traits are added. The order of analogizing is indicated vertically as more common factors are given from which to predict additional ones. Of course, we can have generalizations with any number of similar traits in common. For example, that all cats are furry is a one-trait generalization; that all cats are furry and have whiskers is a two-trait generalization; etc. However, even to recognize what is meant by "cat" already involves several recognizable traits—the cat-identifying traits—so that at least implicitly there is analogical reasoning involved in a one-trait generalization. Some amount of analogy, as we have seen, must be present in all generalizations; and conversely, every noting of analogy involves at least two cases, which is a minimal generalization. The point to remember is that analogy increases by having more factors in common between two or more instances, and generalization increases by having more instances in which there are common (similar or analogical) factors. Thus, the two involve each other, but the emphasis changes from additional factors in the case of analogical reasoning to additional like instances in the case of generalizational reasoning. Reasoning by analogy often seems to bypass any generalization. At least we seem to ourselves to go directly from a trait associated with one case to the expectation of the same trait in another similar case without any awareness of an underlying generalization. Yet upon reflection we discover that analogies are only minimal generalizations.

In addition to inductive inference by generalization and analogy, we can infer inductively by *extrapolation* and *interpolation*. In these cases, the instances normally have some quantitative or measurable aspects which enable one to plot and graph a series (e.g., the population of the United States by decades, both past and future). The pattern of observed change is used to make predictions by extending the graph beyond the area of present observability. In this case we would be reasoning by extrapolation. Or we may find it necessary to plot intermediary positions on our graph, positions for which data were not originally given. For example, census figures are given only on the decades (1930, 1940, 1950, 1960, etc.) and if we wish to determine the probable population figure in any intermediary year from the position of a line on a graph as it would fall when the known positions are connected, we should have to find this figure by interpolation. Neither extrapolation nor interpolation can give assured knowledge, for we are always guessing in such cases. Thus the prediction of what the population was in the year 1955 is a guess just as much as the prediction of what it will be in the year 2000.

The chief difference between inductive inference by extrapolation and interpolation, on the one hand, and inductive inference by generalization and analogy, on the other, lies in the fact that our inductive basis in the extrapolative-interpolative type of reasoning shifts to the *changing factors,* whereas in generalization and analogy, it is centered on the unchanging factor or factors. For example, in our generalization about deer tracks, we were looking for more and more similar (i.e., unchanging) cases of a track with a certain shape. But in the case of plotting population figures, we are looking for the new or changed population figure at different time intervals. If we examine this matter a bit further, we find that extrapolations and interpolations are generalizations of a sort. Quantitative extrapolations and interpolations can be derived from algebraic equations, which are a form of generalization. For example, the simple formula $x = 2y$ is a generalization of the form "every time you add or subtract some quantity to or from any quantity assigned to y, you must add or subtract twice as much to or from the quantity assigned to x." However, the extrapolation or interpolation is not quite the same as the generalization, for the generalization refers to the *same* ratio which runs through all applications of the formula, whereas the extrapolations and interpolations refer to the *changing* quantities obtained.

In Chapter IX we considered imaginative variations such as expansions or reductions in size, which can be conceived in our thoughts even though never experienced. When these imaginative variations are controlled by some formula, so that the imagined increases or decreases can be plotted, they will be examples of imaginative extrapolation or interpolation. For example, if we imagine a line uniformly being reduced in length until there is nothing left except the imaginary point where the line ends, then we are in effect extrapolating toward a limit. Such imaginative extrapolatings or interpolatings constitute one very essential part of mathematical reasoning. They are similar to the extrapolative-interpolative inductions which enable us to make predictions about the experienced world, except that in themselves they have no concern beyond the realm of imaginary concepts. They explore the patterns which may at some time be usefully applied in the world by a science. They may even follow procedures somewhat similar to scientific induction, although the term "induction" is normally limited to inferences which lead to hypotheses about the experienceable universe.*

There is another type of statement, the *statistical,* which may be considered a further variety of inductive conclusion. A statistical statement is one in which some trait is ascribed to a percentage of a class of objects or events, rather than to the entire class. This type of statement has the peculiarity that it does not specify which individuals in the group have the trait. It names a portion, precise only with regard to its percentage, but indefinite with regard to the particular individuals. For example, the statement "Thirty-five percent of the trees in this forest are affected by a blight" has the characteristic of saying precisely what portion of the group of trees in question is affected, but not indicating with regard to any particular tree whether it has the blight. Presumably a statement of this kind was reached by examining the whole group of trees and noting how many of the total number have the characteristic named. The person making the original observation may well have known which individual trees were affected but he may not have been interested in this aspect when making his statistical

---

* In the case of "mathematical induction," there is an inference based on the assumption that what is true of a natural number and also of its successor is then true of all the natural numbers. Such an inference presupposes that we assume a uniformity of all numbers, even though the set is infinite. If we were simply extrapolating on the basis of a few observed cases to some characteristic of an entire class, then the procedure would be clearly inductive. But if, as appears to be the case, the inference depends upon our previous definition of all natural numbers then this type of inference follows deductively from the definition which includes the notion of "successor." Hence, so-called "mathematical induction" is not strictly induction.

judgment. In this case, we presume, it was not important to make a map and mark on it all the trees, showing by some special sign those with a blight. The interest was in the ratio or percentage only.

A statistical generalization* is normally based on a *sample*. It is, of course, possible to examine all the members of a limited class, and to note carefully exactly what percentage of the class has a certain characteristic (e.g., 35 out of 100 trees have a blight). The resulting statistical statement, like any completely known or "perfect" generalization, would be a description and would not involve any imaginative extending beyond experience. However, a genuine inductive inference leads beyond what has been observed. Thus, in the case of a statistical generalization which is the product of inductive inference, we start with a sample group (e.g., of trees in the forest) and note what percentage of this group has the trait in question (e.g., a blight). Then we extend this ratio to a larger group (e.g., the rest of the trees in the forest) and guess that the same or some other percentage prevails there. The question of how to select reliable samples is a difficult one. The art of the pollster, who must select his "random" samples with extreme care, basing them on various categories of individuals so that they are actually no longer random, illustrates the typical problem of statistical inductive inferences.

Inductive inference, as so far noted, may proceed by generalization and analogy, by extrapolation and interpolation, or by statistical estimates. In Chapter IX when we were discussing imagination, we mentioned generalization and extrapolation, and we could have mentioned analogy, interpolation, and statistical statements as examples of imaginative processes. But we also mentioned another very important process, namely, that of *constructing hypothetical models,* a process which has played a key role in scientific and philosophical thinking. Now, let us ask ourselves, shall we extend the meaning of the term "induction" to include this

---

* A statistical statement is a kind of generalization, for in effect it says "All of such and such a percentage of a group have or probably have a certain characteristic," (e.g., All of 35 percent of the trees have a blight) . This type of generalization refers only to a whole percentage (all 35 percent) without specifying which individuals belong in the percentage. Statistical generalizations are the only kind available in cases in which individuals are too numerous or too minute to examine separately.

process as well as the others? It will be a great convenience to do so, although we must remember that "induction" has traditionally been limited to generalization, analogy, and statistical statements and that we have already extended it slightly to include extrapolation and interpolation. But perhaps we can justify including the process of constructing hypothetical models on the ground that the *inductive process in general leads to formulation of hypotheses,* whatever the route taken to arrive there. Inasmuch as supposed generalizations, analogies, extrapolations, interpolations, statistical estimates, and explanatory models are all hypothetical, they may all be regarded as the legitimate products of inductive inference.

When we include the construction of models within the scope of induction, we move closer to free creative imagination, for the factor of following out given patterns is less here than it was in the other more traditional forms of induction. Patterns, however, are not eliminated: new empirical data, or logical inconsistency, may dictate a new model (Chapter IX). More generally, since the purpose of any hypothesis is to construct a likely concept of the state of affairs, which hopefully can be checked in some way, this governing purpose exercises a major control over any formulation of hypotheses. But such a purpose is usually absent from the freer fantasy of artistic imagination.

In summary, then, induction as we are treating it here may take the form of (1) generalizing, (2) reasoning by analogy, (3) extrapolating, (4) interpolating, (5) forming statistical estimates, or (6) constructing hypothetical models.

What is deductive inference?

Whereas inductive inference starts from direct experience, deductive inference starts from terms and propositions. The act of inferring in this case depends on that of analyzing clearly the meaning of the given term or proposition, and stating explicity what was previously only implicit or implied. In performing such inferences, certain rules of noncontradiction or consistency must be followed to assure us that the implications are properly derived.

How is it possible for terms and propositions to have implications? Let us recall that "term," as we are using this word, applies to both the concept and its symbols. Similarly, "proposition" may be considered to apply to both the judgment underlying a sentence and the sentence itself, which is the set of linguistic symbols expressing that judgment. Although only propositions, not single terms, make assertions that can be judged true or false, both terms and propositions can have implications. Let us consider how this may be.

First, how can a single term have implications which will allow for deductive inferences? Terms have been likened to tents, having a range of coverage, or *extension*. Within this extension there is normally a central core area consisting of cases which, as the users of a language would agree, without question belong in that tent. Now, as we have seen, this core area has certain common aspects which constitute the *intension* of the term. These are the aspects which we utilize in constructing a definition; and it is these aspects which are necessarily implied by the term, so long as the definition holds. For example, the term "elephant" implies a large animal, having a trunk, thick skin, ungulate feet, and so forth. Thus, the entire definition of elephant, including the genus (large animal) and all the common characteristics (trunk, thick skin, ungulate feet, etc.), is implicit in the term. We may call this the *definitional implication* of a term, and note that all terms, to the extent that they are definable, have such implications.

When definitional implications are put into words, they normally take the form: "If anything is an *x*, then it is a *y*, having the characteristics *a, b, c,* and so on" (e.g., "If anything is an elephant, it is a large animal, having a trunk, thick skin, ungulate feet, and so forth"). This statement includes a typical inferential indicator, *if . . . then*, which shows that an implication is present. Certain adverbs (*therefore, consequently, hence, so*) can also be used as inferential indicators when placed before an implied conclusion. Such inferential indicators are used both in inductive and deductive reasonings, although in most cases they are used to show deductive inference.

Now let us note that a genus-differentia definition (e.g., All elephants are large animals, having a trunk, thick skin, ungulate feet, etc.) does not itself include any of the inferential indicators. However, the definitional form stands behind and implies the inferential form. For example, defining "elephant" as "a large animal having a trunk, thick skin, ungulate feet, etc." implies that these characteristics belong to the class of elephants, and that therefore, if anything is an elephant, it will have these characteristics. Definitional implication, then, is simply the making explicit of any of the conditions of a term as defined.

In addition to the terms themselves, propositions (sentences) have implications. This is because of their implicit relations. To draw out the necessary consequences of these relations affords us another type of deductive inference, based on what we may call *propositional implication.* Characteristically, such implications start with one or more propositions, called *premises,* from which another, called the *conclusion,* is inferred. When *one* proposition implies another, it is traditionally called *immediate inference,* and when there is more than one premise it is called *mediate inference.* As one type of immediate inference, the assertion of any proposition implies the falsity of its contradictory or contrary. Thus, if we assume as premise that "Fido is a dog," we could immediately infer that "Fido is not a non-dog," i.e., he is not something other than a dog. It should be noticed, however, that we are assuming clear-cut classes and we must have a precisely defined predicate term before we can apply this kind of inference to a given situation. For example, if we assert that "The sky is sunny," we can of course infer that "The sky is not other than sunny." But does one cloud in the sky fall under the "sunny" category or under the "other than sunny" category? We should have to know where we are drawing the line between "sunny" and "other than sunny" before we could apply this kind of inference. Nevertheless, traditional Aristotelian logic recognizes double negation or "obversion," where one negation is placed on the propositional relater and one on the predicate term, as a legitimate form of immediate inference.

Another legitimate form of deductive inference from a single proposition is that in which the two terms of a symmetrical statement are reversed. For example, from the proposition "No monkeys are elephants" we can legitimately infer "No elephants are monkeys." The process of double negation, called *obversion,* and the process of reversing the terms in symmetrical statements, called *conversion,* are only two forms of immediate inference.

When one considers two or more propositions from which to draw deductive inferences, the possibilities increase. The *syllogism* is the classical case of two propositions which are taken together as *premises* and from which a third proposition is inferred. For example, the propositions "All American universities make a business of intercollegiate athletics" and "This university is an American university" when taken together will imply the proposition "This university makes a business of intercollegiate athletics." The syllogism constitutes only one of many possible forms into which deductive arguments may be cast. It is the business of formal logic to study these forms (see Chapter VII on transitivity).

With regard to deductive inferences, two points should be stressed. The first of these is that in the strictly deductive phase of reasoning, one is not concerned about the *factual truth* of one's premises, but only about the *formal truth* or *validity* of the inference. This is because the relation of our assertions to reality is not our concern here, but only the clarification and implications of whatever ideas we assume at the moment. Thus, if we assume that the moon is made of cheese and that cheese is edible, it follows deductively that the moon is edible, since the form of the reasoning is correct without regard to the truth or falsity of the content. In the whole process of reasoning, the ideal, of course, is to have both true premises and valid deductions; but the successful analysis of reasoning requires that we be able to separate the question of truth from the question of validity.

The second point concerns a difference between deductive and inductive inferences. It is customary to point out that whereas inductive inferences lead only to *probable* conclusions, deductive inferences lead to *necessary* conclusions. To understand why this is so, let us return to our definitions of induction and deduction. Induction, we said, starts with observed patterns of correlations abstracted from experience on the basis of which we make guesses about extending these correlations beyond the given experience. Even the simple inductive generalization (e.g., All crows are black) carries us beyond what can be observed or known with that type of certainty which is based upon direct experience. For this reason, an inductive inference hazards a guess that the patterns we observe are accurate and will continue. In other words we are betting on the uniformities of nature and their continuance. In the case of crows, we bet that they will keep on being black. But we are not sure; and so the conclusion is only a matter of probability. Furthermore, the complexities are such in the case of most inductive inferences that we cannot reduce them to a model that is simple enough to offer a calculable probability. All we can say is that most of our inductive reasonings have some unascertainable degree of probability.

Deductive reasonings, on the other hand, are necessary inferences. To infer deductively, we said, is to make explicit what was implicit in a term, proposition, or group of propositions. If what we infer deductively was genuinely implicit—if it was really there as part of the meaning of the terms or propositions—then bringing it out in the open and making it explicit is necessary only in the sense that what has been brought out was a necessary part of the original meaning. To say this is not to assert that any particular deductive inference is the only one that could be made, or even to assert that every person must make it. It only asserts that when a deductive conclusion has been legitimately drawn, all who analyze the terms or premises in the same way should see that it is contained in and follows from the original meaning.

If deductive reasoning is simply pulling out and making clear what was already contained in a term or proposition, has one really done anything? If, for example, we know that (1) Jack is taller than Henry and (2) Henry is taller than Patricia have we really added any new knowledge when we say, "Therefore Jack is taller than Patricia"? On this point, the arguments have gone in both directions. One can stress the fact that the deductive conclusion, no matter how obscured to start with, was already there in some sense. Then the act of bringing it out into the open does not add anything new. On the other hand, one may argue that the act of deduction at least puts the matter in a new way, enabling us to see the whole affair from a new point of view, and that this is an important kind of novelty which should not be overlooked. It is certainly the case that many deductive inferences are not at all transparent and that some may be downright surprising to those who make them. Also, it is difficult to explain in what sense a possible deductive inference is "there" if no one has yet made it.

The above question is closely related to the problem of *analytic* and *synthetic* propositions. An analytic proposition is a statement in which the predicate merely states (as in a definition) what is revealed in the subject term upon analysis of that term. In other words, the statement of a definitional implication of a term or a part thereof (e.g., An elephant is an animal) is an analytic proposition. The predicate is part of what is necessarily contained in an analysis of the subject. A synthetic proposition, on the other hand, is any statement which states something not contained in the analysis of the subject term (e.g., The elephant is in the zoo). Most propositions, it should be observed, will be synthetic. The German philosopher Immanuel Kant raised the very interesting question whether there can be synthetic propositions which are not derived from observation, but rather from the necessary structuring activity of the mind.* He maintained that such a statement as "7 plus 5 equals 12" is a synthetic proposition, even though it does not take any sense observations to establish it. The question hinges upon whether, in our opinion, a complete analysis of the subject (i.e., of the concepts of "7" and "plus" and "5") will necessarily produce the consequence "equals 12." If it does, Kant was wrong, and the proposition is analytic. But in defense of Kant, we may point out that the notion "12" does seem to add something not strictly contained in "7 plus 5," namely, the idea of a single group of 12 objects, and not two groups which are merely added together. Much of the question depends upon the fullness of meaning which one is willing to attribute to "7 plus 5." Kant, however, was convinced that every act of making a judgment prerequires some potential structuring of thought in accordance with which an act of synthesis, or putting together of ideas, must take place. In other words, he was much impressed with the role of what we have termed man's "structure sense" in making knowledge possible. The ultimate limits of direct experience or observation as against the inner working of the structure sense are difficult to determine, and the limits between the pure analytic judgment, the innerly structured synthetic judgment, and the experientially derived synthetic judgment are matters often debated by philosophers.

Formal reasoning may proceed backward towards underlying assumptions from which a given statement could have been deduced. For example, the statement "George is happy today" not only has consequences which may be deduced from it, but also has a large number of possible presuppositions, some of which we

* See Kant's *Prolegomena to Any Future Metaphysics*, Preamble, §2. See also what was said of Kant's position in Chapter VII.

might reconstruct, such as "Whenever it rains, George is happy; and it is raining today." This backward direction of reasoning is especially important in constructing the underlying assumptions of a theory and may frequently enter into the process whereby a new hypothetical model is formed. In philosophical reasoning, especially, the search for underlying assumptions is extremely prominent, for in philosophical reasoning one often starts from one's primary assumptions in order to discover what other assumptions underlie them. For example, the ancient Greek philosophers rather generally assumed that the material universe remains ultimately the same in total amount, although changes do occur. But such an assumption, we notice, presupposes that there must be some primeval matter or material elements which are capable of combining and recombining in various ways. Here, then, we are led from one basic assumption to another underlying assumption, which is the ground for the first assumption.

The inverted deduction that we are here discussing is distinguishable from induction by the fact that attention is concentrated upon the search for premises which would necessarily imply the conclusion, from which one is reasoning backward, whereas an inductive guess simply proposes a probable hypothesis. However, inverted deduction would lead to endless possible premises, unless some inductive guidance were also exercised.*

What cautions should we observe in connection with induction?

(1) *Hasty generalizations* (Chapter X) should be avoided, or at least their tentative character should be stressed. Any moving beyond experience involves a hazard, unless we are interested only in refined abstractions or formal properties, as in mathematical concepts (perfect squares, systems of integers, etc.) When our inductions are supposed to relate back to and "explain" empirical data, we must guard against assuming a greater truth for these inductions than is warranted.

---

* See Kant's footnote in his *Prolegomena,* Preamble, §5, in which he distinguishes between *progressive* and *regressive* orders of reasoning. His regressive order of reasoning, which aims at setting forth the conditions under which a given hypothesis is possible, would resemble to some extent what we here mean by "inverted deduction."

(2) The inductions given by people are frequently *irrelevant* as explanations for the case in question. Suppose, for example, that someone notes all the evidence in favor of biological evolution and then asserts that this evidence inductively leads to a denial of the Judeo-Christian religion. Here is a case in which the conclusion, apparently reached inductively, oversteps the limits of relevance that could legitimately be made. It may be that acceptance of evidence from historical geology contradicts the account of the earth's history as given in *Genesis* and interpreted by Archbishop Ussher.* But the appropriate induction here simply establishes a hypothesis about the earth's history based on geological data, which leads to the denial of the hypothesis of Archbishop Ussher. A further argument (viz., that the religion itself stands or falls on the Ussher chronology) would be necessary to infer a denial of the whole religion; and for most believers this chronology is not an essential or relevant part of Judeo-Christianity.

(3) When we are forced to make inductive inferences on the basis of *secondhand information*, it is necessary to evaluate the reliability of this information. This may be difficult. We must depend upon our own experience with authorities. Textbooks, for example, constitute one large class of authorities, a class which is all too likely to be accepted unquestioningly. Yet we must take them with the proverbial grain of salt, resolving neither to credit them wholly nor to discredit them wholly. A testing is needed to ascertain the reliability of any authority, and this testing in the end must come back to our own experiences and understandings. However, it is wise to assume that our understandings may not be adequate and that while some statement appears false to us, it may be that eventually we shall come to agree with it. In such cases, a wait-and-see attitude is the best one to adopt.

(4) Finally, in making an inductive leap, especially in the construction of imaginary models, one should keep an eye upon the nature of other hypotheses that have proved fruitful. While a wide-ranging imagination is of unquestionable value in bringing into consideration the possibilities that may pay off and may not occur to the unimaginative, it is still well to remember that induction is

---

* James Ussher, 1581-1656, reasoned that the creation of the world took place in 4004 B.C. His chronology formerly appeared in the margins of Bibles.

the product of *controlled* and *directed imagination.* The control here is largely that of experience with the variety of hypotheses which in the past have seemed most successful in any given area of knowledge.

What cautions should we observe in connection with deduction?

In deductive reasoning, the dangers are of a somewhat different order. Here the problem is that of accurately tracing out implied consequences of some given notions and premises. Persons who are inexperienced in these matters or who have never made the particular deductions in question may very easily get off the path. It is the business of formal logic and mathematics to clarify and map out these paths and to give us means to check them, so that deductive errors can be eliminated. One of the chief dangers of deduction is that of making large "intuitive" jumps in one's reasoning. Of course, if we are familiar with the path, we need not tarry over every step; but a path that is new, either because it has never yet been explored by anyone, or because we are learning it for the first time, should be followed with care and caution. It is due to this very situation, in fact, that a major difficulty arises in the teaching of mathematics and logic. The teacher is normally the one who is familiar with the path and readily jumps many "obvious" steps without realizing it. On the other hand, the student, for whom the path is new, has difficulty in following the teacher's "demonstration." The teacher, then, should tailor the minuteness of his delineation of a deductive path to the imaginative capacity of his audience. But the audience, too, has the responsibility of following with all possible attention and of halting the teacher whenever he proceeds at a gallop.

One other caution needs our attention here. It is a characteristic of a deductive process that it takes at the very least a term and its definition, or a premise and a conclusion, before there can be a deductive statement. A single term (e.g., wisdom) or a single statement (e.g., Wisdom is good) will not indicate any deductive reasoning. Nor will even a series of statements (as in description or narration) necessarily be an expression of such reasoning. Some inferential indicators (*if . . . then, and so, therefore*) should be present to show that a conclusion is being drawn. However, these guidemarks are sometimes omitted, and remarks often involve hidden deductions even though the remarks themselves contain no expressed premises and conclusion. In such cases, what is expressed does not reveal the deductive path, and the reader or listener would be at a loss to know it unless he could grab the author by the collar and say to him, "How did you arrive at the conclusion you have just expressed?" or unless he can reconstruct it for himself.

Where do induction and deduction fit into scientific inquiry?

Insofar as man is able to solve his problems, he needs to use the mental process which we have examined. There is a method, more or less clearly delineated, and sometimes loosely called *the scientific method,* which is widely considered the most successful general procedure for handling problems where empirical evidence is pertinent. The steps in this method may be listed as (1) observing, (2) formulating hypotheses, (3) making relevant deductions from the hypotheses, and (4) checking hypotheses. The order of the steps as given here is not meant to indicate a prescribed sequence that must be followed, for they may occur in various combinations and interminglings. Furthermore, although each step may sound simple, a careful examination will reveal a great complexity in each case. However, with the aid of our study of basic mental processes (symbolizing, abstracting, imagining, generalizing, and their application in defining and inferring) we should be in a position to give greater meaning to these traditional steps. Let us consider them one at a time.

Observing. Where do we begin when we "make observations"? The obvious answer would be that we use our eyes and ears and other external sense organs to collect impressions. Yet observation, as a stage in the method of scientific inquiry, implies a great deal more than mere awareness of sense data. The observer is, like the good reporter, one who pieces together his impressions to form some sort of connected mental picture of a set of interrelated events.

There are several prerequisites for observing in this sense. One is curiosity, or a motivation to investigate and look for explanations. Without such a desire, it is difficult to conceive how any serious observing could even start. But more important is the ability to imagine. Every set of observed events is filled in and rounded out by the use of imagination. Explanations, furthermore, depend upon imaginatively bringing to bear some appropriate classification or model into which the bare observations of the moment can be fitted. So, as background experience and understanding is increased, the quality of observing is improved. In sum, curiosity and imagination are the preconditions of observing; prior experience and understanding give adequacy.

Formulating Hypotheses. Observation may give us the basis for description, but it is inadequate for what we normally mean by "explanation." Explanation requires that we construct some hypothetical concepts or models, usually models of events involving cause-effect relations, in terms of which we can fit the particular impressions into a larger scheme. Suppose, for example, that we wish to know about the fossils we observe in the earth. We must obviously travel in our imagination beyond the given impressions of immediate experience. We must piece together the many bits of evidence gained from our observations and attempt to formulate a series of probable events which would tell the history of earth life and "explain" the bits of evidence.

In formulating hypotheses we see clearly the key importance of the processes of abstracting, imagining, and generalizing. To analyze, we must abstract. That is, we must separate out our conglomerate sense impressions into their component aspects and parts, and discover those relations and functions which give us our best understanding of both the structures and sequences of things. For example, the paleontologist, working only from excavated bones, must discover clues which will enable him to distinguish reptilian from mammalian forms, or one particular reptile from another. These clues become the important abstractions for him in his task. Other abstractable aspects, such as stratigraphy, will suggest hypotheses about sequence.

The attempt to formulate hypotheses is nothing recent in human history. The ancient Greeks in the sixth century B.C. were already imagining elaborate models of the universe. And even the most primitive peoples seek explanations that are the best they can construct. For example, eclipses, since they occur at infrequent intervals, have puzzled the human intellect from most primitive times. Many hypotheses, or guesses, have been suggested to explain them. According to Buriat mythology, when the moon is eclipsed it is being devoured by a monster.* According to Northwest Coast Indians, when the sun is eclipsed, it has dropped its torch. One of the ancient Greeks, Anaximander, suggested that there are holes in the sky behind which there is a fire that shines through, and these holes close periodically.

As knowledge of the nature of the solar system progresses, the guesses become more "reasonable." That is, the explanations are such that they accord with more aspects of the total hypothetical situation. Our present hypothesis, or inductive guess, is that occasionally the earth comes between the sun and the moon, casting a shadow on the moon, and at other times the moon comes between the earth and the sun, casting a shadow on the earth. These suppositions are readily correlated with easily constructed models of the solar system on the basis of which the patterns of the movements of the various objects involved can be plotted, so that prediction of eclipses becomes quite accurate. The success of these predictions appears to confirm the hypothesis.

But why, we may ask, should we select between several alternative hypotheses? We have intimated that we tend to prefer that one which accords best with most of our other guesses. Thus the notion that the sun and earth are globular objects, moving relative to each other, accords better with a number of experiences than the supposition, for example, that the sun and moon are brother and sister who commit incest during an eclipse (Eskimo).† But one must have as many correlatable guesses about the nature of things as possible, all of which accord with each other. Thus the increase of correlations in one area improves the chances in another area, and the person with the widest spread of knowledge is in the best position to "know." Even so, we must guard against the possibility that many correlated items may still turn

* See Leach and Fried (eds), *Dictionary of Folklore, Mythology, and Legend*, Article "Eclipses."
† *Ibid.*

out to be less acceptable eventually than a whole new set which will do the job better. For example, the Ptolemaic notion of the solar system, in which the earth was at the center and the planets moved around in circles with epicycles, explained the observable phenomena quite satisfactorily up to a point. Switching to the Copernican notion gave a tremendous jolt to man's basic notions of astronomy, simply because it involved so many correlated assumptions. Every so often the developing of new hypotheses leads to just such jolts, and we should be prepared for them by not becoming too firmly wedded to our prevalent concepts.

Making Relevant Deductions. The deductive process, which is that of discovering what is analytically implied in our assumptions, is of tremendous assistance in clarifying our inductive guesses. For example, to jump to the notion that the moon is devoured periodically by a monster might raise the question of its reappearance. The notion of devouring leads naturally to the idea of permanent disappearance. Yet the moon reappears after its supposed devoration. How is this possible? We shall be forced to return to our initial assumption and add to it a supplementary clause to the effect that the monster in this case does not digest the moon but regurgitates it as an indigestible morsel. If so, why does the silly monster try it again? So we must assume further that the monster has a particular fondness for the moon and simply cannot resist trying to eat it every so often. Here we see the role of deduction in the whole process. First we drew out the consequences of the hypothesis (e.g., that the monster must regurgitate the moon); then we discovered what other assumptions must be put with the first one to make it more acceptable. When this procedure leads to too many absurdities, we should be willing to abandon the first guess and try another.

The deductive tool par excellence is formal logic, including all formal logical and mathematical systems. Here we have entire patterns of deductions already worked out from certain premises. When we adopt any one set of these premises, the deductions follow readily for those who are acquainted with these systems. It is for this reason and for their relational clarity that science seeks premises statable in terms of some system of formal logic or mathematics (e.g., algebraic equations), for here the deductive ramifications are easily followed.

Checking Hypotheses. When is an explanatory guess or hypothesis confirmed? Is it when deductible predictions turn out to be experienceable? Such results might on first thought seem to be all that we need to "verify" a theory or hypothesis. But finding that what a theory predicts is actually the case only tends to confirm the theory; it does not prove it. For example, after what I assume to be enough observations of the effect of alcoholic beverages on people, I may predict that a particular given amount of alcohol will produce a drunken stupor. Now I see that Joe is drinking too much, and I warn him that if he keeps on he will succumb. But he disregards my warning, and my prediction is borne out. So I say to myself, "See, I was right; that proves it." But I should realize that poor Joe's fate is just one more bit of evidence for my generalization and that it only lends additional confirmation. The next fellow may drink just as much as Joe without succumbing. In other words, an hypothesis cannot be positively verified by observing predictable consequences unless one knows that there can absolutely be no other hypothesis which would account for the result, and that the results are always the same. But we rarely have such complete knowledge. Normally we should leave room for further qualifications of our hypothesis or for alternative hypotheses which will do a better job of accounting for the phenomena.

In evaluating hypotheses, there are several matters which should be taken into consideration. First, when observations are not made personally, but only reported by others, we must consider the *competence of the observer*. An untrained observer is less likely to give a trustworthy report than a trained observer. But this again is a matter of probabilities.

Second, some evidence may be more directly related to the hypothesis in question than other evidence; and some hypotheses may allow only for *indirect evidence*. For example, if one can measure a certain height directly, as the height of a room with a yardstick, this evidence is apt to be more reliable than the less direct measurement of the height of a mountain by surveyor's instruments, unless the indirect measurement has greater precision because of the

instruments used. Even so, it is necessary to assume that the indirect measurements are positively connected with the trait in
question. Measuring temperature by the expansion or contraction
of a liquid or gas depends upon our assuming a correlation between expansion and heat.

Third, we may find it convenient to distinguish *verification* from
confirmation on the ground that verification requires simple direct
evidence for a given hypothesis. Where verification is possible,
precise conditions of falsification should also be possible. Confirmation and disconfirmation, on the other hand, are the result
of more or less indirect evidence which simply adds to or subtracts
from the likelihood of a hypothesis. If we accept this distinction,
then we should prefer to deal with hypotheses for which conditions
of verifiability and falsifiability can readily be given. For example,
if an archaeologist hypothesizes that a certain area in a prehistoric
village was a burial ground, he should be able to say in advance of
any excavation what type of evidence would verify or falsify this
hypothesis. On the other hand, if no burial ground is discovered
near the site, the archaeologist might propose as explanation that
the ancient inhabitants thoroughly cremated their dead and then
scattered all the ashes leaving no traces whatsoever. Such a hypothesis would not be subject either to verifying or to falsifying evidence. If pictures of acts of cremation were found on pottery vessels
or other objects connected with the site, this would serve only as
indirect confirmatory evidence.

Many of the hypotheses of traditional philosophical interest are
such that conditions for verifying or falsifying them are not only
unavailable now, but by their very nature such conditions could
never become available. In fact, they may not ever receive much
confirmation or disconfirmation. For example: Is the universe
finite or infinite? Did the universe have a beginning in time, or
has it always existed? Is matter ultimately composed of units which
can have no further subdivisions, or will all units turn out to be
complex? These are some of the questions which Kant declared
out of bounds for either confirmation or disconfirmation.*

Nevertheless, scientists are normally not skeptics. They accept

* See Kant's famous "Antinomies of Pure Reason" in the *Critique of Pure
Reason*, Transcendental Dialectic, Bk. II, Ch. 2, or the *Prolegomena*, Pt. III,
Ch. 2.

their hypotheses with varying degrees of confidence, depending upon the evaluation of the evidence. Philosophers, too, even though more often concerned with insights and theories for which there is little if any possibility of establishing empirical tests, usually avoid skepticism, a view which is difficult to defend. A philosopher, furthermore, has the responsibility of examining the very assumptions underlying any theory of verification and knowledge, whether for himself or for the scientist, and of reaching some theory of "truth." So let us look briefly at some of the traditional views on this subject.

What is truth, and how do we test it?

From time to time in the course of this text we have mentioned some characteristics of the notion of truth. We have said, for example, that the adjective "true" is generally a synonym for "reliable" or "trustworthy." We have pointed out that in its most typical, but restricted, sense "true" pertains to beliefs or hypotheses about the way things are when these beliefs are thought to correspond to the realities. This view of truth, dating back at least to Aristotle, is sometimes called the *correspondence* notion of truth and suggests that the mind is a sort of mirror which more or less faithfully copies external realities.

The notion that a true belief is one that involves ideas which accurately correspond to the way things are seems so natural to us now that we may wonder why we need inquire further. The difficulty arises, however, when we try to explain erroneous beliefs or establish some check by which to determine just when a belief does accurately mirror reality. If, for example, our mental mirror continually distorts everything in exactly the same way, we could never know it. The trouble is that we cannot get outside our ideas to compare them with the external situations they are supposed to reflect. So we have no basis for comparison such as we have when we can see both an object and its mirrored image. We must therefore look for some indirect basis for checking on the accuracy or adequacy of our beliefs.

Among the commonplace habits which we find ourselves following is that of checking one sense impression against further sense impressions. If I am not sure what time it is by my watch,

I check it against another. If I discover something to be a mirage, it is because additional sense impressions in which I have greater confidence convince me that my first impression was only an optical illusion. I am normally inclined to accept the larger number of sense impressions or those that are verified by my companions or those that coordinate best with my preconceptions about the nature of things. Under ordinary circumstances a check by *comparison of sensory impressions* is enough. However, we must realize that this type of check is not infallible nor is it applicable to all beliefs. It may fail if all my sense impressions and those of my companions as well are in error. It may also fail if my preconceptions are erroneous but are so strong that they prevent me from making accurate and impartial observations. And as for application, we must recognize that further simple sensory impressions are of no service when we wish to check on the truth of imaginary concepts, such as those involved in hypothetical models (e.g., of the atom).

One recourse at this point is to adopt the view of the pragmatist, who says, "All that I can significantly mean by 'true' is the degree to which my predictions are borne out." Truth, then, is a matter of degree which varies according to the predictive success or failure of a particular hypothesis or guess. If, for example, I predict that yonder chair is sufficiently stout to support a five-hundred-pound box of books, and I place such a box upon it without its breaking, then my belief turns out to be true. Now this *pragmatic* or *predictive* test seems eminently reasonable. But we must note that it too operates within restricted circumstances; namely, where simple predictably observable conditions are possible. If the correlations between my hypothesis and any experienceable consequences are indirect or tenuous, or where no condition would clearly be able to falsify the hypothesis, the pragmatic test can only indicate some degree of confirmation or disconfirmation. Normally hypotheses are devised to account for some previously unexplained phenomenon (as for example, when the Bohr atom was devised to explain certain breaks in the spectrum) and then they are checked further by trying to devise some predictably observable situation (such as the measured positions of the lines in the spectrum as predicted by Bohr's hypothesis). If the further predicted observation is found to be accurate, then the hypothesis has received a further degree of confirmation. It is, of course, not "proved." We can only say that the more direct or clearly correlated is the relation between hypothesis and possible observable consequences, the more useful is the pragmatic test.

From another area of our knowledge comes another favorite check. This is the rule of *coherence* or *consistency,* largely adapted from deductive systems, such as we find in logic and mathematics, where demonstrating noncontradictoriness of postulates among themselves is important. Similarly, if a new hypothesis can be shown to be logically consistent with other hypotheses which we are prone to accept, then we tend to trust it. Mutual support among hypotheses, however, is no conclusive assurance of factual truth, for an entire fabric of well-constructed propositions may still be only a fiction. Nevertheless, in areas beyond sense impressions where neither direct evidence nor correlated indirect evidence is available, our best reliance is on the test of consistency.

In addition to the tests of sensory comparison, pragmatic prediction, and consistency among hypotheses, we often depend upon *agreement with other persons* as a truth check. If I am uncertain about an idea or theory in my own mind, I am very apt to ask someone else what he thinks; and if I find that individuals whose judgments I respect are in agreement with me, I gain confidence in the truth of my belief. However, it is well known from past experiences that groups of people have wholeheartedly agreed on what later turned out to be pretty silly ideas. So we must beware of placing overmuch faith upon agreement among people as a test for truth. A lot depends upon the competence and understanding of the person whose judgment we accept.

Our four means of checking on the truth of an opinion or hypothesis (sensory comparison, pragmatic prediction, consistency, and agreement with others) are all of some use under the appropriate circumstances and with the proper cautions. But we must also notice that ascribing truth is in part the result of a feeling of confidence. If we have confidence in a belief—if we really regard it as trustworthy—we are inclined to call it "true," otherwise not. Some beliefs engulf us with a feeling of rightness which we cannot lightly set aside. Some of us are gullible and willing to believe whatever we are told. Others are "from Missouri" and have to be shown. Some of us rely more upon sense impressions ("seeing is believing"). Others, like Descartes, prefer the concepts which are illuminated by the "natural light of reason." Yet others find in their nonrational inner feelings—aesthetic, moral, or religious— a basis for ultimate commitment which is stronger than any other ground for belief. In any of these cases the strength of the commitment may vary from extreme dubiousness and tentativeness to fanatic espousal.

It would be very helpful if the psychological factor of the feeling of conviction could be carefully isolated from the question of the criteria for checking truth. This is possible if we concentrate our attention upon the criteria and hold our feelings to a minimum. Then the criteria as applied will determine whatever feeling of confidence may arise in regard to any particular belief. Yet it is important to realize that the term "truth" as it is most frequently used is more apt to be an indication of the degree of feeling of confidence than of the application of some well-considered and carefully applied criteria. Moreover, wherever truth is concerned, the feeling of confidence will undoubtedly be present to some degree. The important thing is that we know as clearly as possible upon what conditions and standards this feeling rests. We must never be guilty of prejudging any issue before examining all the alternatives that we can imagine or discover. To accept dogmatically any belief or set of beliefs, whether religious, moral, aesthetic, or scientific, without critical examination of its truth claims is to stultify imagination and to put blinders on our understanding.

SUGGESTED READINGS

Kant, *Prolegomena to Any Future Metaphysics,* Preamble, Sections 1-2 (on the notion of the synthetic a priori) .

Mill, J. S., *A System of Logic,* especially Bk. III. (Note especially Ch. 8 on Mill's "four methods" for inferring probable causal connection.)

Peirce, C. S. *Collected Papers,* Vol. I, especially Ch. 2, Section 10 (on kinds of reasoning) and Vol. V, Bk. II, No. 4 (on "The Fixation of Belief").

James, William, *Pragmatism, Lecture VI* ("Pragmatism's Conception of Truth") .

Cohen, M. R., *A Preface to Logic,* Chs. 6-7 ("On Probability" and "The Statistical View of Nature") .

Reichenbach, Hans, *Experience and Prediction.*

CHAPTER XIV

Systematizing

What is the goal of philosophical thinking?

WE HAVE STUDIED some basic thought processes and something of the way in which they are put to use in clarifying ideas and making inferences. Is this the end of the journey? For many of us, no doubt, it is enough. For others, who are strongly imbued with Oriental skepticisms toward typical Western modes of thought, we have already gone too far and should counterbalance our love of clarity and system with at least an equal devotion to a Hindu bliss that transcends all pattern or to a Chinese world of continuous flow, rising and ebbing like an endless tide but never caught in rigid structures. Nevertheless, we Westerners are the experts on system, and this has been our glory; for it includes our science in its scope. The least we can do, then, is to examine our efforts toward systematization and then evaluate them.

First, let us inquire into the urge toward system. Why is it that in philosophy, for example, the stages of critical examination, logical exploration, and justification have not been enough? (See Chapter IX, pp. 224-27.) Perhaps it is that we feel an incompleteness about fragmentary insights and unrelated developments of ideas, just as we would about the parts of a building that are lying around waiting to be assembled. Meaning, after all, grows by discovering interrelationships between fragments; and the larger the body of such interrelationships, the more the particular fragment is understood.

The drive for systematization is not limited to philosophy; it is present in all our sciences. Yet in the sciences it encounters some well-recognized hazards and limitations. A scientific *theory*, for example, is designed to coordinate hypotheses, and a large theory more than a small theory. But the larger the theory, the more difficult it is to substantiate; and so the sciences have learned to regard larger theories with greater suspicion and greater tentativeness than they regard the smaller theories and the hypotheses for which confirmation is easier. The very large theories, which may be called *world views,* are usually turned over to the philosophers; or if some scientist propounds one, he is regarded by his colleagues as something of a philosopher himself. The implication is that these larger and more "philosophical" theories must be even more hazardous than the lesser ones. Is this really the case? Is a philosophical system really such a gamble in regard to its value? An answer to this question must be deferred until we have examined more closely the character of philosophical systems.

What are the characteristics of a philosophical system?

In the construction of philosophical systems, there are many stages from unrelated, aphoristic utterances at one end to the supremely coordinated system of a Spinoza at the other. Aphorisms, like the Golden Sayings of Pythagoras or the Analects of Confucius, constitute the bare beginnings of a philosophy. These are the raw materials of philosophical systems which the systematizer must correlate. To do this he ferrets out some underlying patterns and some unifying ideas around which his system will be built.

He might attempt an organization akin to the deductive system of Euclidean geometry, where a few definitions and a few major assumptions (*postulates*) which one hopes are self-evident (*axiomatic*) entail a large number of *theorems* (propositions that can be rigorously inferred). Spinoza, for example, used this model in his great metaphysical compendium, which he entitled *Ethics* or more fully and in Latin, *Ethica ordine geometrico demonstrata*. But whereas this model works fairly well when one is dealing with the refined abstractions of mathematics or formal logic, it is scarcely adequate for the fuller-bodied ideas of most philosophical insights. Here the key ideas seem more like seeds* which grow in repeated motifs. To see more clearly how a philosophical system is built around a few key ideas and basic insights, let us look at some examples. We can do no better than to start with Plato and Aristotle.

Plato's philosophy is not easy to reconstruct, not only because, like any philosophical system, it involves a great many facets, but even more because he wrote mostly in dialogue form (i.e., conversational discussion), and one is never quite sure whether he is putting forth his own views or those of one of his characters. But we normally assume that most of the views presented (at least those presented in a favorable light) are the ones to which Plato himself adhered. A further consideration with any philosopher, of course, is whether he developed his ideas in a consistent direction throughout his life or was forced at some point to change them. In the case of Plato, both views have been maintained. In spite of all these difficulties, the key ideas of Platonism are fairly clear.

The first and most important fulcrum upon which to rest his philosophy is assuredly for Plato the idea of FORM. Plato seems to have assumed that there are supreme, perfect, and unchanging forms for all the experienceable objects and aspects—even the subtle aspects of human relations which we call virtues. If one's intellectual appetite is strong enough and if one is endowed with philosophic vision, one may win his way closer to an understanding of these supreme forms. If you wish to know what it is to be just or wise or good, you must inquire into the *nature of* justice and wisdom and goodness. If you want to know how the oneness of the universe turns up as a multiplicity of things in human experience, you must inquire into the nature of the one and the many. With these assumptions, Plato correlates a belief in a SOUL

---

* It is interesting that biological metaphors seem preferable to mechanical ones here, whereas the mechanical ones appear appropriate to logical systems. Stephen C. Pepper, for example, has aptly coined the expression "root metaphor" for the basic orientational ideas of a philosophy. See his *World Hypotheses*.

element which ideally strives for wisdom, and a BODY element which all too often stands in the way. The procedure, then, should be that of freeing one's mind from bodily concerns, of concentrating upon the formal natures of things and events, and of constantly striving to discover the harmonies and symmetries which are imperfectly copied in the world as we experience it. Knowledge is achieved through a nurturing of one's innate structural sense, so that it can come to penetrate deeper and deeper into the underlying structural realities.

This very sketchy, minimal statement of Platonism may yet suffice to allow us to observe the main characteristics of a philosophical system. Here are the key orientational ideas (forms, soul, body), and here are the suggestions for a philosophical procedure (concentrate on clarity of idea and turn away from bodily disruptions), which incidentally turn out to be good ethical advice. One must seek above all to understand the Good; and through the poetic language which Plato uses in regard to the Good, one glimpses the fundamental idealization of order, harmony, and symmetry. What does this mean as a guide to human behavior? It means that a dignified, stately, and well-regulated manner of life is preferable to any which might be termed erratic or wayward. It means at least that one should behave in harmony with one's fellowmen and with the universe. It means that man should seek the sober and enduring pleasures, especially those of intellectual pursuits. It means that man must seek the common good and avoid greedy or selfish action. It means that the intellectual visionary should be ruler, the philosopher should be king. And it suggests, as correlate, that there is a God who is seeking to instill the love of order into man, even though God may only partially succeed. All these ideas form a system in the sense that they are at least consistent with the basic insights and the key ideas of Platonism.

Thus in Platonism a few key concepts suggest a whole set of correlated ideas in every area of philosophical interest. But how did Plato reach his key concepts? This is indeed a difficult question, and one upon which much depends; for the difference between the great philosopher and the amateur, among other things, can be discovered in the vitality of the key concepts. Certainly Plato's notion of FORM was a highly vital idea; for it not only went to the heart of a profound insight that the Greek thinkers had been seeking to elucidate during at least a century and a half before Plato, but it also led to a world of interesting and useful implications, both for Platonism and for Western philosophy in general.

Platonism, then, is a philosophical system oriented around some basic insights: what is real is unchanging; perfect forms are not subject to change, and are the ultimate realities. The key concepts involved in these insights are primarily those of FORMS (Platonic "Ideas"), the GOOD (order, harmony), and the power of INTELLECTUAL VISION in the SOUL.

As a major contrast to Platonism, let us look briefly at the philosophy of Plato's disciple Aristotle. Aristotle's dominating philosophical orientation led him to reject Plato's perfect archetypes as ultimate realities and to focus instead upon the various kinds of objects in the world that we experience. These objects are regarded as the primary realities or SUBSTANCES, composed of both matter and form; so that form does not need to be relegated to Plato's ideal status. For Aristotle, each kind of thing has its NATURE, which can be known by examining the characteristic attributes and behavior of the various substances. Each kind of thing, moreover, acts naturally to fulfill an ideal behavioral norm, even though for the most part there is a falling short. Thus, the various plants and animals follow a formal and functional pattern for each species; and all else likewise, from a cooking pot to the universe as a whole, has its appropriate form and function.

Aristotle's basic insight incorporates many of Plato's key concepts (form, essence, ideal norm), but in a new setting. We start with the here and now; for the world as we observe it is real enough and is capable of being understood through the intelligent use of sense perception combined with reason. In fact, Aristotle not only accommodates these concepts, but repeats and adopts many of the basic insights of earlier Greek philosophers, such as that everything must come from something, and that all activity must have a causal force. This latter notion, combined with a rejection of all endless series (infinite regresses) as being naturally impossible, led him to posit an ultimate causal force, or Prime Mover, which he equated with God.

In the realm of value, Aristotle claims simply that the "good is that at which all things aim." The good or value, that is, is determined by being a goal for the functioning of some kind of substance. Each kind of thing, including man, has its own best end which is discoverable by examining its nature. Thus for man, the rational animal, a rational activity is best, especially when this rational activity dominates his physical and social behavior; for he is also a physical and a social being.

Aristotle's total philosophy is a highly involved and very complex affair which contains quantities of particular items, many of them only distantly capable of being correlated with the system. Inevitably there are such items among the ideas of all great philosophers; but the aim of the systematizer is to bring these items into the general scheme whenever possible. For example, Aristotle, like many another, grappled with the problem of *chance*. Should chance be considered a special kind of cause? Or is it rather the absence or lack of cause? Perhaps it is only ignorance of cause. At least some people would say so. But Aristotle notices in his system that among the functions of substances there are those which are necessary and "essential" to bring about natural ends, and then there are events which are only incidental or "accidental." So, he reasons, why not consider the accidental events responsible for what appears to be chance?* And in this way, the nature of chance is correlated with another part of his system.

In Aristotle's system, then, we find a dominating orientation: that the world as we experience it contains the primary realities (substances). We also find a number of basic insights (e.g., that substances are arranged in kinds, each with its own guiding nature; that they are endowed with form and matter, and are also activated by causal forces to move in accordance with natural goals). The key ideas in Aristotle's thought are indeed numerous (SUBSTANCE, FORM, MATTER, CAUSE, NATURE, GOAL) and many others that we have not mentioned here; for Aristotle was able to fit into his developing system most of the key concepts of his predecessors. This very richness, together with its common-sense orientation, accounts in some measure for the continuing appeal of Aristotelianism.

In contrast to the philosophies of Plato and of Aristotle, one might glance at the basic orientation of Saint Augustine (354-

* See Aristotle, *Physics*, II, 4-6.

430). Augustine, after exploring several philosophical viewpoints, including Neoplatonism, became the central thinker in the formulating of a philosophy for Christianity. His mature system is, as we might expect, fundamentally God-oriented, so that man is seen as one product of the DIVINE WILL to create, and the various characteristics of man and of the universe must be interpreted in the light of a theory of creation. God is necessarily all-good, all-wise, and all-powerful; so the creation must be oriented toward the good. Each type of thing in the world has a good "nature" which determines what it ought to be, even though because of its imperfections it may fall short. So man, to be good, must be God-oriented and must strive for an understanding of God. A simple faith in Divine love is the essential prelude to full understanding; and knowledge is thus the result of Divine illumination flowing directly to man's thought. God, for Augustine, is the supreme power, the inspiration of all those actions in which natures are being fulfilled. Here the dominating key idea is not only that of the Divinity Himself, but of the tremendous power of DIVINE GRACE, which can bring about salvation. The sense of motivation or will within and behind all intelligible activity is central to the thought of Augustine. All reality is value- or goal-oriented; and human moral evil is due simply to the failure of the will of man to orient itself toward the Divine purpose. With the gift of grace, the will becomes able to turn freely toward these goals.

In Augustinianism we find a consistent philosophical system, carried out in the face of one of the most perplexing dilemmas for a monotheistic world view: the problem of evil. Augustine's basic orientation turns around the key ideas of a loving God, whose ethical values have been revealed to man and are recorded in the Scriptures. In the midst of the universe is man, a noble and high-born creature, endowed with a free will, without which he would be but an ignoble robot. Yet man's fall from grace and struggle for redemption in no way detract from the perfection of God or from the basic goodness of creation.

We could continue with our examples of philosophical systems; but the foregoing will have to suffice. The major point to be made is only that these systems are all based on some few fundamental orientations and insights which involve a number of key ideas. The rest of the system is not deduced from these;

it is only a set of correlated propositions that answer the larger philosophical questions of reality, knowledge, and value in a way that is consistent with the primary insights.

What are the limits of philosophical systematizing?

Philosophical systems, we saw, are built around some basic orientations and insights which involve a number of key concepts. Through the history of Western philosophy the dominant concepts recur again and again, but often with different insights to change their orientations. There have been efforts to seek superorientations which might overcome the previous differences. Such efforts have resulted in higher syntheses, or systems of systems. For example, the philosophy of St. Thomas Aquinas (1225-1274) represents a remarkable achievement in this direction. His methodical and persistent efforts to resolve previous points of disagreement aimed in each case at a reasonable compromise which would preserve what in his view were the stronger insights of his predecessors and eliminate their errors. The extensiveness and balance of this philosophy has placed Thomism in an unusually strong position among those systems which have sought to correlate their basic insights and key ideas with the dogmas of Christianity.

A later and different type of synthesis was that of Hegel, who developed the logic of polarity (Chapter VII) as a means for creating a synthesis of philosophical systems. For Hegel, all key concepts (e.g., Being and Nonbeing) could be worked into his scheme of polar opposites. Moreover, each pair of opposites reveals implicitly a higher "dialectical" synthesis which is fuller and more concrete than either opposite category by itself (Chapter X). Thus, by working through a large number of earlier key ideas, Hegel sought to develop a system in which all other philosophies would have their place.

Thomism and Hegelianism are two important examples of synthesizing philosophical systems. But each in turn may be charged with its own overemphasis from the point of view of some other system. Thomism to many has appeared too much a categorial and static defense of Christian theology, and not sufficiently all-encompassing in its syntheses. Hegel, on the other hand, allowed his dialectical pattern to become so all-engulfing and so dominating an idea that to many his philosophy is simply another philosophical system of its own based on the key concept of this particular pattern.*

Nevertheless, the notion of polarity continues to play an important role in the work of synthetic philosophers. W. H. Sheldon, for example in a recent volume, *God and Polarity: A Synthesis of Philosophies,* has taken up again the principle of opposites, such as the mental and the physical, the existential and the essential, the static and the dynamic, structure and process, and the like, and has utilized this principle as a guide for integrating philosophical systems. Thus idealism and materialism are for Sheldon but overstatements of two necessary and complementary views. Likewise the stability of Thomism, he says, must be supplemented with the dynamism of modern process philosophies, such as that of Whitehead. The emerging overall philosophy is one in which a cooperative spirit, motivated by love of the best— that is of the most inclusive—will succeed in realizing the many possibilities that exist in the philosophical matrix.

Another recent attempt to use the idea of polarity as the basis for including all positive philosophical positions in one comprehensive scheme is the organicism of A. J. Bahm,† in which a varying emphasis on any key concept (e.g., spirit) can be graded from the exclusiveness of that key concept at one pole to that of its opposite (e.g., matter) at the other pole, passing through a middle position in which each opposite concept receives equal weight, either as independent hypostatized realities or as aspects of another reality. It is Bahm's thesis that there is some merit to all possible positions, at least to the degree that they involve positive assertions. With this scheme, any pair of properly paired and properly defined key concepts can be given meaning and truth in one's total philosophy.

In contrast to those who believe that synthetic philosophical

---

* As Richard McKeon has aptly put it: "The existing values on which philosophy is based as a form of expression and as a means of communication are therefore transmuted by the values expressed and communicated, and philosophy even in its most sober and scientific form is a kind of conversion which turns attention from principles in operation to principles recommended for acceptance"—Philosophy and Method, *The Journal of Philosophy,* Vol. 48, No. 22, p. 657.

† *Philosophy, an Introduction,* Ch. 20.

systems are possible, most contemporary philosophers prefer a more limited goal. Stephen C. Pepper, as noted above, has proposed the view that each philosophical system is built around a major "root metaphor," and that to attempt a supersynthesis would in some measure violate the basic insights and vitality of each root metaphor. Instead, he prefers a number of "maxims," or judgments about all philosophical systems, such as "A world hypothesis is determined by its root metaphor"; "Each world hypothesis is autonomous"; "Eclecticism [selecting some from this and some from that] is confusing"; "Concepts which have lost contact with their root metaphors are empty abstractions." What he wishes to do in lieu of working toward an overall synthesis is "to squeeze out all the cognitive values that can be found in the world theories we have and to supply a receptacle in which their juices may be collected, so that they will not dry up from dogmatism, or be wasted over the ground through the indiscriminate pecking of marauding birds." * One should add that the "marauding birds" of which Pepper is afraid are probably not the supersystematizers so much as the supercritics of philosophical systems. His own concept of a root metaphor has much virtue; for the basic insights of philosophical systems (such as Plato's insight of the permanence of form and harmony) do become the roots from which a system grows by a kind of metaphorical extension of this insight.

So strong is the current temper against system building that several of the most popular current philosophies reject the effort toward systematizing, either in whole or in part. Positivism, for example, rejects any utilization of the older metaphysical categories (God, ultimate substance, first cause, and the like) and restricts its attention to matters that can have scientific verification together with a purely formal logico-mathematical type of systematizing. Analysis, a recent British movement, has turned to the exploration of ordinary linguistic usages and their many specialized meanings in various contexts. Insights may be derived in this way with regard to complexity of relationships, which other philosophies had taken as rather simple and readily classifiable. Thus one comes to avoid the pitfall of the oversimplified view, too often present in philosophical systems, and one which

* *World Hypotheses,* pp. 86-87.

the tendency to systematize has itself nurtured. If any systematizing is to be done by the analyst, it is simply that of discovering under what conditions a given meaning is allowable, or "makes sense."

Existentialism too rejects systematizing. Its key insight is that of each individual's consciousness, challenged and shocked into a fuller self-awareness by the very unintelligibility of external objects, by the necessity of choice, or by the prospect of one's own future nothingness; until the self, thus vitalized, is seen to be the basic or "authentic" reality, the creator of morality, the sensitive appreciator or disparager of human efforts, even the challenger of the transcendent and unknowable. There are many versions of the existentialist theme, some leading to a greater closeness with God, some avowedly atheistic. But they have in common the insight of man's ultimate reality for himself, a reality which would be violated by any effort to impose a philosophical system.

It is no wonder, then, that some philosophers are directly concerned with the question of the limits of philosophical system building. Nathan Rotenstreich, for example,* proclaims that it is an error to attempt to combine an epistemological procedure or methodological system with systems in the other spheres of philosophy (e.g., ethics, aesthetics, religion). He concludes that one cannot transgress the various "inviolable" spheres of intellectual activity by attempting to create some more encompassing system, as philosophical systems have normally attempted to do. System building, however, is still permitted within the various spheres.

Let us not judge hastily about the limits of system building. We have seen good reasons for the tendency toward system. We should also beware of the frequent habit of easy disillusionment and violent reaction, which normally leads to an opposite and equally disillusioning viewpoint. A saner approach lies in a willingness to explore any path and a willingness to use the results of one's explorations without allowing oneself to become infatuated with any extreme position. This is a judgment which we ought to apply to the question of favoring or disfavoring philosophical systems.

* "On Constructing a Philosophical System," *Logique et Analyse*, N.S., 21-24 (1963), pp. 179-194.

What is the purpose of philosophical systems?

We have reviewed something of the nature of philosophical systems and something of the drives and doubts which accompany them. We may also observe that philosophical systems from all ages and lands are studied and restudied, compared and debated; and we may think it strange that the earlier ones are not relegated to the limbo of error and inadequacy as in the case of earlier scientific theories. Indeed, if philosophy like science were simply a continuing search for better knowledge based on superior techniques of investigation, then our puzzlement would be justified. But there is a basic difference between the goal of science and the goal of philosophy. Let us note what it is.

Both philosophy and science are concerned with the search for knowledge, but in different ways. The scientist extends his investigations into new areas and devises better instruments and techniques for doing the job; but his standards of careful methodical observation and of formulating testable hypotheses of varying degrees of generality he simply accepts. The philosopher, on the other hand, is concerned with the standards themselves and with what they mean. His theories aim in the direction of clarifying a set of ultimate presuppositions which would or would not explain and justify scientific knowledge, or any other knowledge which may use a different approach, such as the knowledge of the mystic or the religious dogmatist. The philosopher, then, is concerned not just with the nature and structure of man and the universe, but rather with the criteria for knowing and with the basic perspectives and attitudes which emerge from any coordinated and systematized set of presuppositions. Moreover, his job is to explore all varieties of presuppositions—not only those concerned with knowing, but also those concerned with the nature of reality and with the nature of valuing. Clearly these questions go beyond and underlie the enterprise of the scientist.

Granted this difference in goal, our next question may challenge the philosopher with his accomplishments. In the course of scientific investigation the results seem clear. New knowledge is gained by the continuing work of generations of scientists. Modifications of hypotheses continually flow from the requirements imposed by new data. One beholds an enterprise in which the boundaries of knowledge are steadily being pushed on. But obviously this image of progress is not appropriate to the philosophical endeavor where one seemingly encounters continuous debates and endless reviews of certain traditional positions. So when one turns to philosophy with the image of scientific progress as his criterion for accomplishment, he may well conclude that he is entering a field devoted to the futile repetition of outworn ideas. This view, however, is based on a fundamental error, and it is in answering this error that we can also answer the challenge to philosophical accomplishment.

If, as stated above, philosophy explores the basic assumptions or presuppositions of all our knowledge and seeks to correlate and systematize these assumptions, then the estimate of success or failure must be measured in terms of this kind of enterprise and not in terms of some other. Success here lies in the increased understanding and in the improved and more comprehensive perspective which we as individuals gain from such explorations. Following the leads of others, we may find what we need for our own philosophy at any place throughout the whole history of human cogitation. We may observe the consequences—desirable or undesirable from our point of view—in what others have explored before us. The entire gamut of previous philosophy is grist for our mill; for one never knows where a much-needed link may be found. So, in the realm of philosophical study, all previous philosophy is our primary data, and the measure of success is our personal understanding.

Moreover it would be a mistake to conclude that there has been no progress in philosophy. But progress here is made with respect to a different content and method from that to be found in the sciences. If the primary data of philosophy are the previous philosophical explorations and systematizations, then when a certain pathway has been competently explored by a philosopher, that job is done. We need not repeat it. We can pick up where our predecessor left off. But which path we select to follow, or how far and in what direction, is going to be a matter of personal need, inclination, and taste. For this reason, philosophy is not susceptible to the kind of teamwork that one finds in the sciences. Cooperation in philosophy comes rather from the open discussion and mutual criticism of the basic concepts which each of us is using in his own explorations and constructions. The discussion is the laboratory of the philosopher.

Philosophy traditionally is the search for "wisdom." Wisdom has a connotation of something wider and deeper than knowledge and may suggest that more than simply being a knowing about, it also involves a way of life. When philosophy does contribute to wisdom, it can clarify and shape our basic attitudes which in turn affect our way of life. Persons of a critical and analytic temperament, for example, tend to live in a framework of cautious and critical attitudes. Persons who are sensitive to the qualities of feelings and emotions prefer an attitude toward life strengthened by a philosophy which recognizes and places feelings in a significant position. This is not to say that we are unable to consider or even hold to a philosophical view which is inconsistent with our inner predilections; and certainly it does not mean that our philosophies are simply the product of our various temperaments. There is good evidence that the study and development of a philosophy has great influence upon our attitudes. But this is to say again that a philosophy is ultimately a personal creation, shaped partly by our own preferences and tastes, partly by our observations and insights, and partly by the studies we make in the philosophies of others. The measure of success will lie in the reward to understanding contributed by the coordinating of all these sources.

SUGGESTED READINGS

Pepper, Stephen C., *World Hypotheses,* especially Ch. 1.
Passmore, John, *Philosophical Reasoning,* especially Ch. 1.
Marías, Julián, *History of Philosophy,* especially sections on Plato, Aristotle, Augustine, English-Language Philosophy, and Heidegger's Existential Philosophy.
Passmore, John, *A Hundred Years of Philosophy,* especially Ch. 16 (on Logical Positivism) , Ch. 18 (on Wittgenstein and Ordinary Language Philosophy) , and Ch. 19 (on Existentialism and Phenomenology) .

Bibliography

The principal purpose of this bibliography is to offer a list of the published volumes in which the Readings and other works referred to in the text may be found. Where possible, the editions and publishers listed are those now available.

AARON, R. I.
  The Theory of Universals, Oxford University Press, 1952.
ADAMS, GEORGE P., and WILLIAM P. MONTAGUE, eds.
  Contemporary American Philosophy, 2 vols., Russell and Russell, Inc., New York.
ALEXANDER, H. G.
  Meaning in Language, Scott, Foresman and Co., Glenview, Ill., 1967.
ALSTON, W. P.
  Philosophy of Language, Prentice-Hall, Inc., Englewood Cliffs, N.J., 1964.
AQUINAS, ST. THOMAS
  Concerning Being and Essence, George G. Leckie, tr., D. Appleton-Century Co., New York, 1937.
ARISTOTLE
  Basic Works, Richard P. McKeon, ed., Random House, Inc., New York. Includes all works referred to in this text.
  The Works of Aristotle, Great Books of the Western World, Vols. 8 and 9. Encyclopaedia Britannica, Inc., Chicago. Includes all works referred to in this text.
  Categories, On Interpretation, and Prior Analytics, Loeb Classical Library, 325. Harvard University Press, Cambridge, Mass.
  Metaphysics, Loeb Classical Library, Vol. Nos. 271 and 287. Harvard University Press, Cambridge, Mass.

Physics, Loeb Classical Library, Vol. Nos. 228 and 255. Harvard University Press, Cambridge, Mass.

Posterior Analytics and Topics, Loeb Classical Library, Vol. No. 391. Harvard University Press, Cambridge, Mass.

Metaphysics, Richard Hope, tr., Ann Arbor Paperbacks, AA-42. University of Michigan Press, Ann Arbor.

Physics, Richard Hope, tr., Bison Books, BB-122. University of Nebraska Press, Lincoln.

AUGUSTINE, ST.

Basic Writings of Saint Augustine, Whitney J. Oates, ed., 2 vols. Random House, Inc., New York. Vol. I includes the Confessions.

Confessions, City of God, On Christian Doctrine, Great Books of the Western World, Vol. 18. Encyclopaedia Britannica, Inc., Chicago.

Confessions, Modern Library College Editions, T-72. Random House, Inc., New York.

Confessions, R. S. Pine-Coffin, tr., Penguin Books, Inc., Baltimore, L-114.

Confessions, Rex Warner, tr., Mentor Books, MT-490. New American Library, New York.

AUSTIN, JOHN L.

How to do things with Words, Oxford University Press, 1962.

Philosophical Papers, Oxford University Press, 1961.

BACON, FRANCIS

The New Organon, Great Books of the Western World, Vol. 30. Encyclopaedia Britannica, Inc., Chicago.

The New Organon, Fulton H. Anderson, ed., Liberal Arts Press, LLA-97. Bobbs-Merrill Co., Indianapolis. For Bacon's "idols," see *New Organon,* Book First, Sections 39 ff.

BAHM, ARCHIE J.

Philosophy: An Introduction, Asia Publishing House, Bombay, India, 1964. Orig. John Wiley and Sons, Inc., New York, 1953.

Polarity, Dialectic, and Organicity, Charles C. Thomas, Publisher, Springfield, Ill., 1970.

BEARDSLEY, MONROE

Practical Logic, Prentice-Hall, Inc., Englewood Cliffs, N.J., 1950.

Thinking Straight, Prentice-Hall, Inc., Englewood Cliffs, N.J., 1950; 2nd ed., 1956.

BERGSON, HENRI

Creative Evolution, Modern Library, 231. Random House, Inc., New York.

BERKELEY, GEORGE

Principles of Human Knowledge, Great Books of the Western World, Vol. 35. Encyclopaedia Britannica, Inc., Chicago.

Principles of Human Knowledge, Thomas J. McCormack, ed., Open Court Publishing Co., La Salle, Ill., P-49.

Principles of Human Knowledge and *Three Dialogues between Hylas*

and Philonous, intro. by G. J. Warnock, Meridian Books, M-150. World Publishing Co., Cleveland.
Principles, Dialogues, and Philosophical Correspondence with Johnson, Colin M. Turbayne, ed., Liberal Arts Press, LLA-228. Bobbs-Merrill Co., Indianapolis.
Berkeley's Philosophical Writings, David M. Armstrong, ed., Collier Books, New York, No. 06417.

BLACK, MAX
Language and Philosophy: Studies in Method, Cornell University Press, Ithaca, N.Y., 1949.
Models and Metaphors: Studies in Language and Philosophy. Cornell University Press, Ithaca, N.Y., 1962.

BLANSHARD, BRAND
The Nature of Thought, 2 vols., Humanities Press, New York, 1964.
Reason and Analysis, Open Court Publishing Co., La Salle, Ill., 1962.

BOAZ, FRANZ
The Handbook of American Indian Languages, Smithsonian Institution, Bureau of American Ethnology, Bulletin 40, Part I, 1911; Part II, 1922.

BOORSE, HENRY A., and LLOYD MOTZ, eds.
The World of the Atom, 2 vols., Basic Books, Inc., New York, 1966.

BOWMAN, ARCHIBALD A.
A Sacramental Universe, Princeton University Press, Princeton, N.J., 1939.

BROWN, HARCOURT, ed.
Science and the Creative Spirit, University of Toronto Press, Toronto, 1958.

BRYANT, MARGARET M., and JANET R. AIKEN
Psychology of English, Frederick Ungar Publishing Co., New York.

CALIFORNIA ASSOCIATES
Knowledge and Society, D. Appleton-Century Co., 1938. Out of print.

CARROLL, LEWIS (CHARLES LUTWIDGE DODGSON)
Complete Works, Modern Library, G-28. Random House, Inc., Chicago.
Alice's Adventures in Wonderland and Through the Looking Glass, illus. by John Tenniel, Airmont Publishing Co., Cl-79.
Alice in Wonderland and Through the Looking Glass, intro. by Louis Untermeyer, Collier Books, 04235, New York.

CASSIRER, ERNST
An Essay on Man, Yale University Press, New Haven, Conn., 1944. Also Yale Paperbound, Y-52.

CHASE, STUART
The Power of Words, Harcourt, Brace and Co., New York, 1954.

CHOMSKY, NOAM
Aspects of the Theory of Syntax, The M.I.T. Press, Cambridge, Mass., 1965.

Cartesian Linguistics, Harper and Row, New York, 1966.

COHEN, MORRIS R.

A Preface to Logic, Peter Smith, Publisher, Gloucester, Mass. Also Meridian Books, M-32. World Publishing Co., Cleveland.

DAMPIER, WILLIAM C.

History of Science and its Relations with Philosophy and Religion, Cambridge University Press, 1930.

DESCARTES, RENÉ

Philosophical Works, E. S. Haldane and G. R. T. Ross, trs., 2 vols., Peter Smith, Publisher, Gloucester, Mass.

Rules for the Direction of the Mind, Discourse on the Method, Meditations on First Philosophy, etc., Great Books of the Western World, Vol. 31. Encyclopaedia Britannica, Inc., Chicago.

Discourse on Method and Meditations, Laurence J. Lafleur, tr., Liberal Arts Press, LLA-89. Bobbs-Merrill Co., Indianapolis.

Discourse on Method, John Veitch, tr., Open Court Publishing Co., La Salle, Ill., P-38.

Meditations and Selections from the Principles of Philosophy, Open Court Publishing Co., La Salle, Ill., P-51.

DIXON, ROBERT M. W.

What is Language? Longmans, Green and Co. Ltd., London, 1965.

EPPERSON, GORDON

The Musical Symbol, Iowa State University Press, Ames, Ia., 1967.

FINGESTEN, PETER

The Eclipse of Symbolism, University of South Carolina Press, Columbia, S.C., 1970.

FRYE, ALBERT M., and ALBERT WILLIAM LEVI

Rational Belief: An Introduction to Logic, Harcourt, Brace and Co., 1941.

GARNETT, A. C.

The Perceptual Process, University of Wisconsin Press, Madison, Wis., 1965.

GHISELIN, BREWSTER, ed.

The Creative Process, Mentor Books, MP-383. New American Library.

GRAFF, WILLEM L.

Language and Languages, Russell and Russell, Inc. New York.

HALL, ADELAIDE SUSAN

A Glossary of Important Symbols, Bates and Guild, Co., Boston, 1912. Out of print. A similar work, though not so complete, is Rudolf Koch, *The Book of Signs,* Dover Publications, Inc., New York.

HEGEL, GEORG WILHELM FRIEDRICH

Encyclopedia of Philosophy, Gustav E. Mueller, tr., Philosophical Library, New York, 1959. Out of print.

HEMPEL, CARL G.

Fundamentals of Concept Formation in Empirical Science, International Encyclopedia of Unified Science, Vol. II, No. 7, University of Chicago Press, Chicago.

HENLE, PAUL, ed.
Language, Thought, and Culture, University of Michigan Press, Ann Arbor, 1958. Also Ann Arbor Paperbacks, AA-97.

HUME, DAVID
A Treatise of Human Nature, Everyman's Library, 548-549. E. P. Dutton and Co., New York.
A Treatise of Human Nature, D. G. C. McNabb, ed., Meridian Books, M-139. World Publishing Co., Cleveland.

JAMES, WILLIAM
Pragmatism, Longmans, Green and Co., New York, 1907.
Pragmatism and Other Essays, Meridian Books, M-16. World Publishing Co., New York.
Some Problems of Philosophy, Longmans, Green, and Co., New York, 1911. Out of print.

KANT, IMMANUEL
Critique of Pure Reason, Norman Kemp Smith, tr. (abridged and unabridged editions), St. Martin's Press, New York.
Critique of Pure Reason, J. M. D. Meiklejohn, tr., Great Books of the Western World, Vol. 42. Encyclopaedia Britannica, Inc., Chicago.
Critique of Pure Reason, Modern Library, No. 297. Random House, Inc., New York.
Prolegomena to Any Future Metaphysics, Paul Carus, tr., Open Court Publishing Co., La Salle, Ill., P-53.
Prolegomena to Any Future Metaphysics, Mahaffy-Carus, tr., Liberal Arts Press, LLA-27. Bobbs-Merrill Co., Indianapolis.

KATZ, JERROLD J.
The Philosophy of Language, Harper and Row, New York, 1966.

KIRK, G. S., and J. E. RAVEN
The Presocratic Philosophers, Cambridge University Press, London and New York, 1957. Also Cambridge Paperbacks, 356.

KOESTLER, ARTHUR
The Act of Creation, Dell Publishing Co., New York, 1967.

KORZYBSKI, ALFRED
Science and Sanity, Institute of General Semantics, Lakeville, Conn.

LANGER, SUSANNE K.
Feeling and Form, Charles Scribner's Sons, New York, 1953. Also Scribner's Library, paperbound, SL-122.
Philosophy in a New Key, Harvard University Press, Cambridge, Mass. Books, MT-365. New American Library, New York.

LEACH, MARIA, and JEROME FREID, eds.
Dictionary of Folklore, Mythology and Legend, 2 vols., Funk and Wagnalls Co., New York.

LEE, HAROLD N.
Symbolic Logic, Random House, Inc., New York, 1961.

LEFF, GORDON

Medieval Thought, Penguin Books, Inc., Baltimore, A-424.

LEWIS, CLARENCE I.

Analysis of Knowledge and Valuation, Open Court Publishing Co,. La Salle, Ill., 1946; and paperback, P-99.

Mind and the World Order, Charles Scribner's Sons, New York, 1929.

LEWIS, M. M.

Infant Speech, Humanities Press, New York, 1951. Out of print.

LOCKE, JOHN

An Essay Concerning Human Understanding, Alexander Campbell Fraser, ed., 2 vols., Peter Smith, Gloucester, Mass. Also Dover Publications, Inc., New York.

An Essay Concerning Human Understanding, Great Books of the Western World, Vol. 35. Encyclopaedia Britannica, Inc., Chicago.

An Essay Concerning Human Understanding. A. S. Pringle-Pattison, ed. Oxford University Press, 1924.

An Essay Concerning Human Understanding, 2 vols., Everyman's Library, 332, 984. E. P. Dutton and Co., New York.

An Essay Concerning Human Understanding, Books 2 and 4, Mary W. Calkins, ed., Open Court Publishing Co., La Salle, Ill., P-58.

An Essay Concerning Human Understanding. A. D. Woozley, ed., Meridian Books, M-182. World Publishing Co., Cleveland.

LYONS, JOHN

Introduction to Theoretical Linguistics, Cambridge University Press, 1968.

MACKAYE, JAMES

The Logic of Language, Russell and Russell, Inc., New York, 1965.

MARÍAS, JULIÁN

History of Philosophy, Appelbaum and Strowbridge, tr., Dover Publications, Inc., New York, 1967.

MILL, J. S.

A System of Logic, University of Toronto Press, Toronto.

On Bentham and Coleridge, Peter Smith, Gloucester, Mass. Also Harper's Torchbooks, TB-1070, Harper and Row, New York.

Utilitarianism, LLA-1, Bobbs-Merrill Co., Inc., Indianapolis, Ind.

MILLER, GEORGE A.

Language and Communication, McGraw-Hill Book Co., New York. Also McGraw-Hill Paperback Series, 42001.

MOORE, GEORGE EDWARD

Principia Ethica, Cambridge University Press, 1903.

MORRIS, CHARLES W.

Foundations of the Theory of Signs, International Encyclopedia of Unified Science, Vol. I, No. 2. University of Chicago Press, Chicago.

Signs, Language, and Behavior, George Braziller, Inc., New York.

MYERS, EDWARD D.

The Foundations of English, The Macmillan Co., New York, 1940. Out of print.

OGDEN, C. K., and I. A. RICHARDS
The Meaning of Meaning, Harvest Books, HB-29. Harcourt, Brace and World, Inc., New York.

OSGOOD, CHARLES E.
Measurement of Meaning, University of Illinois Press, Urbana, 1957.

OSGOOD, CHARLES E. and THOMAS A. SEBEOK, eds.
Psycholinguistics, University of Indiana Press, Bloomington, 1965.

PASSMORE, JOHN
A Hundred Years of Philosophy, Penguin Books, Inc., Baltimore, Md., 1968.
Philosophical Reasoning, Charles Scribner's Sons, New York, 1962.

PEI, MARIO
The Story of Language, J. B. Lippincott Co., Philadelphia, rev. ed., 1965. Also Mentor Books, MQ-492. New American Library, New York.

PEIRCE, CHARLES SANDERS
Collected Papers, 8 vols. Harvard University Press, Cambridge, Mass. The essays, "The Fixation of Belief" and "How to Make Our Ideas Clear" appear in Vol. 5 of the *Collected Papers.* These essays also appear in the following paperbound collections of Peirce's writings.
Essays in the Philosophy of Science, Vincent Thomas, ed., Liberal Arts Press, AHS-17. Bobbs-Merrill Co., Indianapolis.
Philosophical Writings of Peirce, Justus Buchler, ed., Dover Publications, New York.
Values in a Universe of Chance, Philip Wiener, ed., Anchor Books, A-126. Doubleday and Co., New York.

PEPPER, STEPHEN C.
World Hypotheses, Peter Smith, Gloucester, Mass. Also California Paperbounds, CAL-45. University of California Press, Berkeley.

PIAGET, JEAN
Judgment and Reasoning in the Child, Humanities Press, Inc., New York, 1947.
Language and Thought of the Child, Humanities Press, Inc., New York, 1955. Also, Meridian Books, M-10, World Publishing Co., New York.
Origins of Intelligence in Children, International Universities Press, New York, 1966.

PLATO
Dialogues, Jowett, tr., intro. by Raphael Demos, 2 vols., Random House, Inc., Chicago. Includes all works referred to in this text.
Dialogues, Jowett, tr., Great Books of the Western World, Vol. 7. Encyclopaedia Britannica, Inc., Chicago. Includes all works referred to in this text.
The Euthyphro, Apology, and Crito, F. M. Stawell, tr., G. P. Putnam's Sons and J. M. Dent and Co., New York and London, 1906. Out of print.
Euthyphro, F. J. Church, tr., Liberal Arts Press, LLA-4. Bobbs-Merrill Co., Indianapolis.

Meno, Jowett, tr., Liberal Arts Press, LLA-12. Bobbs-Merrill Co., Indianapolis. Also W. H. D. Rouse, tr., in Mentor Books, MT-302. New American Library, New York.

Phaedo, F. J. Church, tr., Liberal Arts Press, LLA-30. Bobbs-Merrill Co., Indianapolis. Also W. H. D. Rouse, tr. in Mentor Books, MT-302. New American Library, New York.

Phaedrus, W. C. Helmbold and W. G. Rabinowitz, trs., Liberal Arts Press, LLA-40. Bobbs-Merrill Co., Indianapolis.

RIDDELL, JAMES
Animal Lore and Disorder, Harper and Brothers, New York, 1948.

ROBINSON, RICHARD
Definition, Oxford University Press, New York, 1950.

RUBY, LIONEL
The Art of Making Sense, Keystone Books, KB-15. J. B. Lippincott Co., Philadelphia.

SAPIR, EDWARD
Language: An Introduction to the Study of Speech, Harvest Books, HB-7. Harcourt, Brace and World, Inc., New York.
Selected Writings of Edward Sapir in Language, Culture, and Personality, David Mandelbaum, ed., University of California Press, Berkeley and Los Angeles, 1949.

SARTRE, JEAN-PAUL
Being and Nothingness, Hazel Barnes, tr., The Citadel Press, New York, C-156.

SAUNDERS, A. N. W.
Imagination All Compact: Understanding the Arts, Methuen and Co., Ltd., London, 1967.

SHANNON, CLAUDE E., and WARREN WEAVER
The Mathematical Theory of Communication, University of Illinois Press, Urbana, 1949. Also paperbound IB-13, University of Illinois Press.

SHELDON, WILMON H.
God and Polarity, Yale University Press, New Haven, Conn., 1954.

SWIFT, JONATHAN
Gulliver's Travels, Great Books of the Western World, Vol. 36, Encyclopaedia Britannica, Inc., Chicago. Also, Modern Library, T-92, Random House, Inc., New York.

TSANOFF, RADOSLAV A.
The Great Philosophers, Harper and Row, New York, 2nd ed. 1964.
The Ways of Genius, Harper and Brothers, New York, 1949. Out of print.

TWAIN, MARK (SAMUEL L. CLEMENS)
A Tramp Abroad, Harper and Brothers, 1899.

TYNDALL, JOHN
Fragments of Science, 2 vols., D. Appleton Co., New York, 1897.

URBAN, WILBUR MARSHALL
Language and Reality, The Macmillan Co., New York, 1939.

VON FRISCH, KARL
"The Language of Bees," in *Smithsonian Annual Report,* 1938.
Bees, Their Vision, Chemical Senses, and Language, Cornell University Press, Ithaca, N.Y., 1950.
The Dancing Bees, Harvest Books, HB-40. Harcourt, Brace and World, Inc., New York.

VYGOTSKY, LEV S.
Thought and Language, Eugenia Hanfmann and Gertrude Vaker, trs., The M.I.T. Press, Cambridge, Mass., 1962. Also paperbound, MIT-29.

WERKMEISTER, W. H.
The Basis and Structure of Knowledge, Harper and Brothers Publishers, New York, 1949. Also, Greenwood Press, Inc., Westport, Conn., 1968.

WEINBERG, JULIUS R.
Abstraction, Relation, and Induction, University of Wisconsin Press, Madison, 1965.

WHFELWRIGHT, PHILIP
A Critical Introduction to Ethics, Odyssey Press, Inc., New York, 3rd ed., 1959.
Metaphor and Reality, Indiana University Press, Bloomington, 1962.

WHITEHEAD, ALFRED NORTH
The Concept of Nature, Cambridge University Press, London and New York. Also Cambridge Paperbacks, 245.
An Introduction to Mathematics, Galaxy Books, GB-18. Oxford University Press, New York.
Process and Reality, Torchbooks, TB-1033. Harper and Row, New York.
Science and the Modern World, The Macmillan Co., 1925. Also Mentor Books, MP-538, New American Library, New York.
Symbolism, Cambridge University Press, London, 1928. Also Capricorn Books, CAP-13. G. P. Putnam's Sons, New York.

WHORF, BENJAMIN LEE
Language, Thought, and Reality, John B. Carroll, ed. The M.I.T. Press, Cambridge, Mass., 1956. Also paperbound, MIT-5.

WITTENGSTEIN, LUDWIG
Philosophical Investigations, G. E. M. Anscombe, tr., The Macmillan Co., New York, 1953. 2nd ed., Blackwell, Oxford, 1958.

ZELLER, EDUARD
Outlines of the History of Greek Philosophy. The Humanities Press, Inc. Also Meridian Books, M-9. World Publishing Co., Cleveland.

Index

For information about works cited, see the Bibliography, pp. 341 ff.

abbreviations, 66
absolute, in Chinese, 39; zero, 139 f., 140, 255; and universals, 255
abstract, and concrete, 107, 111 ff., 147; generalizations, 122, 234 ff.; terms defined, 266, 287 ff.; extensions, 289
abstractable similarities, 87, 118, 233
abstracting, 107-29; a process of thought, 105; as focusing attention, 107 ff.; levels of, 110; applicable to concepts, referents, and symbols, 115 ff.; not generalizing, 118; and reality, 120; importance of, 127
abstractions, simple and altered, 108; residue, 109 f.; part and aspect, 113 ff.; errors regarding, 118 ff.; expressed in language, 124 ff.; quality, relation, and function as, 125, 129, 153, 177; taken from immediate experience, 129; generalized, 234; concreted, 237
accidental qualities, 131 ff.
action, sentences 43 ff.; included under function, 178
active, and passive order, 54, 190 ff.; dimension of meaning, 83 f.

adjectives, 40 ff., 124 ff., 149 ff., 195
admission into a class tent, 88, 133
adverbs, 40 ff., 124 ff., 149 f., 192
affixes (including prefixes and suffixes), 39 f., 125 f., 149 f., 206
agreement, as a truth check, 325 f.
algebraic statements, 194
Algonquian languages, 39
ambiguity, of metaphor, 1; and vagueness, 97 f.; to be avoided in defining, 272, 274, 296 ff.; futility of arguing from, 280
American Indian, languages, 14, 52; symbols, 62 f.; mythology, 319
analogy, reasoning by, 302 ff.
analytic propositions, 312 ff.
Anaximander, notion of opposites, 155; notion of the boundless, 206; on eclipses, 319
aphasia, 37
aphorisms, 328
a priori, 165
arbitrary symbols, 65
Aristotle, and Plato, 4 f., 121; definition of man, 13, 102; logic of, 46, 50 f., 54, 85, 100 f., 216, 246, 310; essence and accident, 132: classification, 132; substances as primary realities, 147, 158, 161,

178, 249 f., 331 ff.; four kinds of change, 180 f.; philosophical system of, 331 f.; *De Interpretatione,* 5 n, 54 n, 246 n; *Topics,* 102 n, 261; *Metaphysics,* 132 n, 180 n, 246 n; *Physics,* 180 n, 332 n; *Nicomachean Ethics,* 271 n; *Posterior Analytics,* 277 n

Aristotelian universal, 246 ff.

Art, and symbols, 69; role of imagination in, 222 ff.; definition of, 277

articles (parts of speech), 40, 47, 150

aspect, and part abstractions, 113 ff.; simple, 129; clusters, 147; in relations, 152

assumptions, examined in philosophy, 225, 338 ff.

atoms, concept of, 134, 218 ff.; defining, 271, 277

attitudinal (emotive) failures in communication, 23 f., 29 f.

attribute-substance relation, 157 ff., 170

attributive sentences, 43 ff., 158, 189 ff.

Augustine, Saint, philosophical system of, 332 ff.

Austin, John L., 77 f.; *How to Do Things with Words,* 77 n, 78

axiology, 76

background experience, in communication, 15 ff., 33

Bacon, Francis, 5, *Novum Organum,* 5 n

Bahm, Archie J., vii, 335

Bentham, Jeremy, 145

Bergson, Henri, 167, 177

Berkeley, George, subjective idealism of, 117, 160; on abstract ideas, 121 ff., 250; on primary and secondary qualities, 135 f.; *A Treatise Concerning the Principles of Human Knowledge,* 122 n, 136 n, 250 n

biological and social relations, 169

blue, as a quality, 150; defining as an abstract concept, 288

Boas, Franz, *Handbook of American Indian Languages,* 98 n

Bohr, Niels, 220

borderline cases, in defining, 285; *see* variable extension

bound elements, in language, 39

Bowman, Archibald, *A Sacramental Universe,* 194 n

Bridgman, Percy, 270 n

British analysis, 336; *see also* ordinary language philosophy

broadening extensional meaning, 96

California Associates, *Knowledge and Society,* 237 n

Carroll, Lewis, *Through the Looking Glass,* 66 f.; *Alice in Wonderland,* 120 f., 209

Cartesian system of coordinates, 214

Cassirer, Ernst, interest in language, 5 f.; on importance of symbols, 34, 59; *Essay on Man,* 34 n, 59 n

cause, and condition, 162; and effect, 162 ff.; arbitrarily separated from effect, 164; expressed by verbs, 170, 191 f.; associated with action, 178; indicated by correlated functions, 186; in defining, 276

Celtic, an Indo-European language, 42

ceremonial discourse, 75 ff.

change, included in function, 177; emphasizes frame of reference, 179; proportional, 179; as creation, negation, substitution, and variation, 181 f.; as before-and-after aspect, 189

changing factor in extrapolation, 305

Chase, Stuart, *The Power of Words, The Tyranny of Words,* 11 n

checks, on communication, 29 ff.; on truth, 323 ff.

Cheshire cat, 120 f.

Chinese, typewriters, 14; language, 14, 39 f.; symbols, 63; world view, 327

Chomsky, Noam, 53, 200

circularity, to be avoided in defining, 272, 274

class, logic, 50 f., 100 ff., 212, 215; and individual, 86; relations and extensional variability, 100 ff.; as a refined concept, 101; generalizations, 230 ff.; two ways of forming, 236 f.

classification, in languages, 50, 98 ff.; precision of, 102, 132 ff.; needs similarity and difference, 153; ideal, 244

class-inclusion relation, 50 ff., 100 ff., 198 f., 231 f.; test for, 156 n, 242 f., 285

coherence as a check for truth, 325

collective, generalization, 232; universal, 247 f.; terms defined, 266, 287

communicatee, 15 ff.

communication, 11-32; among insects, 13 n; successful, 17; failures of, 18 ff.; checks on, 29 ff.

communicator, 15 ff.

complementative sentences, 45

conative discourse, 70 ff., 83

conceiving, failures in, 19 ff.; habits of, 26 f.

concepts (ideas), in communication, 15 ff.; adequate, 30; included in terms, 83; basic or "key," 225, 329 ff.

concreta, 112

concrete, and abstract, 111 ff.; whole, 112; not specific or particular, 119; and quality, 147 f.; and abstract generalizations, 234; terms defined, 266, 282 ff.; extensions, 289 f.

concreted abstractions, 237

concreting, 112

concretionistic philosophies, 112, 247

condition, and cause, 162; necessary and sufficient, 162, 273 f.

confirmation, desire for by children, 71 f.; of hypotheses, 321 ff.

Confucius, 328

conjunctions (parts of speech), 40 f., 124 ff., 173 ff.; defined contextually, 269 f.

connotation and intension, 85, 87

connotational, overtones, 99, 278; differences between synonyms, 263, 267

constant, ratios, 185; search for in science, 188; and universals, 255

context, in classification of symbols, 66; as aid to meaning, 91; primary (literal) and metaphorical (nonliteral), 99 ff.

contextual definitions, 269 ff., 283

continguity, and similarity, 62 f.

conventional, symbols, 66 f., 266; definitions, 264, 266

conversion, a logical operation, 173, 310

core, meanings, 91, 99; example (paradigm case), 282, 284; meaning used in implication, 294

Coughlin, W. J., 11, 11 n

Cranston, Julius, Jr., vii

Cratylus, 5, 180

creation, as type of change, 181; imaginative, 206

credentials for admission into a class tent, 88 f., 283

critical examination, in philosophy, 225, 327

cultural differences, a handicap in communication, 21 ff.

Dali, Salvador, The Persistence of Memory, 207

Dalton, John, 218

Dampier, William C., *A History of Science,* 219 n

De Broglie, Louis, 220

deceiving, in communication, 25, 28

decoding, 16 ff.

deductions, inverted, 314; cautions regarding, 316 f.; relevant, 320

deductive, definitions, 281 n; inference, 308 ff.; system, 328 f.

definiendum, and definiens, 261 ff.; 272 ff.

defining, 259-78; ways of, 266 ff.; ideals of, 272 ff.; cautions regarding, 275 ff.; concrete terms, 282 ff.; collective terms, 287; abstract terms, 287 ff.; imaginary terms, 292 ff.; limits of, 298 f.

definitional implication, 309

definitions, importance of, 259; nature and purpose of, 261 f.; equivalence in, 263; types of, 266 ff.; and hypotheses, 271, 277; tests of, 272 ff.; cautions regarding, 275 ff.; formulating one's own, 279 ff.

degree and kind, 137 ff.

democracy, 291, 295 f.

Democritus, theory of atoms, 134, 218

denotation and extension, 85 ff.

Descartes, René, on primary and secondary qualities, 135; dualism of, 225; ideal of clarity and distinctness, 263; natural light of reason, 326; *Meditations*, 135 n

descriptive definitions, 264, 266

difference, of kind and degree, 137 ff.; and similarity, 153 f.

differentia, and genus definition, 268 f.; finding the, 283, 285 f.

discourse, types of, 70 ff.

discursive symbols, 67, 69 n

dualism, 225

dyadic relations, 171

eclecticism, 336

eclipses, theories of, 319 f.

effect, *see* cause

Einstein, Albert, 179

either-or thinking, 146

El Greco, 222

emotive, causes of failure in communication, 29 f.; meaning, 82 f.

Empedocles, 206

empiricism, 135, 147, 216, 250

encoding, 16 ff.

English, language, 37 ff.; 40 ff.; 42 ff., 50 ff.

enumeration, a quantitative relation, 168 f.; and imagination, 209; of subclasses in defining, 267

epistēmē, 24

epistemic, errors, 24 ff.; factors, 33

Epperson, Gordon, *The Musical Symbol,* 69 n

equivalence, in attributive sentences, 51; in defining, 261 f.

Eskimo, notion of trees, 21 ff., 29; language, 52, 200 f.; words for snow, 98; explanation of eclipses, 319

esse and *essentia,* 132 n

essence, and intension, 88; and accident, 131 ff.; as Platonic universal, 246; search for in defining, 260 ff., 282

essential qualities, 131 ff.

Euclidean geometry, 216, 328

evaluative discourse, 70 ff.

Evans, Melbourne G., vii

event function, 183, 197

excluded middle, proper use of, 146

existentialism, 6, 337

explanation, contrasted with definition, 276

exploration, logical in philosophy, 225, 327; of meanings, 280

expressive discourse, 70 ff., 75

extended generalizations, 231

extension, and denotation, 85 f.; variable, 89 f., 98, 100 ff.; 118, 262, 267, 275, 282 ff.; and intension vary inversely, 90 f.; core, 91, 99; literal and metaphorical, 91 ff.; broadening, narrowing, and transferring, 95 ff.; and kind, 138; built in imagination, 231; abstract and concrete, 234; changed in overgeneralizing, 240 f.; universal, 246; equivalent in definitions, 261 ff., 272

extensional meaning, 85 f.

external and internal relations, 153, 171

extrapolation, 216 ff., 292 f.; and interpolation, 304 f.

family resemblances, 91, 119 n, 242, 275

feelings, as ground for belief, 326

Fichte, Johann Gottlieb, 160 f.

forming definitions, 279-99

Frye and Levi, *Rational Belief,* 75 n

functions, 177-201; of parts of speech, 40 ff.; expressed in language, 47; as an aspect of abstraction, 113; change or action, 130 f.; expressed in symbols, 151, 194 ff.; compared with quality and relation, 177; defined, 182 f.; as events, 183, 197; qualifying, 184, 188 f., 197; related, 184 f., 188 f., 197; expressed in propositional form, 188, 194 ff.; used in creative imagination, 204, 207 f.

gatekeeper, for term tents, 88
general, and specific meaning, 90 f.; extension, 91; terms, 230 f.; propositions, 232
generality, expressed by article, 150
generalization, not abstraction, 118; levels of, 119; types of, 231 ff.; concrete or abstract, 233 ff.; hasty, 243, 314
generalizing, 230-56; as a process of thought, 105; distinguished from abstracting, 118, 233 ff.; and imagination, 212, 238 ff.; concrete and abstract particulars, 235; abstractions vs. concreted abstractions, 237; cautions regarding, 240 ff.
Genesis, Book of, 206
genos, 138
genus, and species, 97, 232; meaning of, 138, 230; finding a proper, 156 n, 242, 285; and differentia in defining, 267 f., 283, 285; eliminated in contextual definitions, 270
German, language, 42, 99; idealism, 160
gossip, 71
Graff, Willem L., 52, 200; *Language and Languages,* 52 n
grammar, as patterns of language, 37 f.; and logic, 41 f.; generative and transformational, 43, 53; and clear thinking, 55 ff.; and types of discourse, 74

Hegel, Georg Wilhelm Friedrich, concretionistic philosophy of, 112, 247; opposites in dialectic of, 156, 161, 247, 334 f.; logic of, 216
Hegelian universal, 247 ff.

Heidegger, Martin, *An Introduction to Metaphysics,* 6 n
Helmholtz, H. L. F. von, 219
Hempel, Carl G., 270; *Fundamentals of Concept Formation in Empirical Science,* 270 n
Hendel, Charles W., vii
Heraclitus, 177, 180
Hindu philosophy, 205, 327
Hobbes, Thomas, on primary and secondary qualities, 135
human, community, 11, 13; touchiness, 12 f.
Hume, David, idea of similarity and contiguity, 64 n; on primary and secondary qualities, 136; on substance, 136, 147 f., 158; on causal connection, 163 ff.; on abstract general ideas, 250 f.; *A Treatise of Human Nature,* 164 n, 250 n
humor, etymology of, 95 f.
hypostatizing, akin to fallacy of misplaced concreteness, 121, 123; due to nominalizing in language, 150
hypotheses, formulating, 217 ff., 307 f., 318 ff.; and definitions, 271, 277 n; checking on, 321 ff.; coordinating in philosophy, 328
hypothetical models, 217 ff., 221 f., 271, 307 f.

ideal and actual meanings, 295 f.
idealism, as a type of philosophy, 117, 160, 225
ideas, *see* concepts
identity, extreme similarity, 154 f.
illocutionary acts, 78, 83
imaginary, referents, 20; concepts, 108, 204 ff.; numbers, 216; terms defined, 292 ff.
imagination, as altering of abstractions, 108; recollective and creative, 203; levels of, 210 ff.; and truth, 227 f.; involved in inference, 300 f.; controlled, 316; in observing, 318
imagining, 202-29; as a process of thought, 105; and inferring, 300 f.

imitative symbols, 63
immediate inference, 310
implication, in logic, 49 f., 300 ff.; from terms, 308 f.; from propositions, 310
Indo-European languages, 40, 42, 49 ff.
induction, 302 ff.; mathematical, 306 n; statistical, 306 f.; cautions regarding, 314 ff.
inductive, definition, 281 n; generalization, 302; inference, 302 ff.; analogy, 303; extrapolation and interpolation, 304 f.; construction of hypothetical models, 307 f.; leap, 315
inertia, idea of, 178
inference, 7, 49 f., 300 ff.
inferential indicators, in language, 309, 316 f.
inferring, 300-326
infinitesimal, concept of, 213 f.
informative discourse, 71 ff.
insights, basic in philosophy, 329 ff.
intension, and extension, 85 f.; and connotation, 87; and intention, 87 n.; and essence, 88; varies inversely with extension, 90; and kind, 138; changed by overgeneralizing, 241; universal, 246; in definitions, 263 ff., 272; implied by terms, 309
intensional meaning, 85 ff.
intention, 81, 84; and intension, 87 n; and creative imagination, 204
internal and external relations, 153, 171
interrogative-explanatory discourse, 71 ff.
intransitive, see transitive
irrelevant reasoning, 315

jargon, 1, 25
James, William, on flux of percepts, 148; Some Problems of Philosophy, 148 n
justification, in philosophy, 226

Kant, Immanuel, and modal logic, 46; answer to Hume on substance and self, 136; on self and other, 160; answer to Hume on

causalty, 165; on analytic and synthetic propositions, 313 f.; antinomies of, 322 n; Critique of Pure Reason, 164 n, 165 n, 322 n; Prolegomena to Any Future Metaphysics, 165 n, 313 n, 314 n, 322 n
katholou, 246
Kelvin, William Thomson, Lord, 219
Kepler, Johann, second law of planetary motion, 185 f., 197, 210
key concepts (ideas) in philosophy, 225, 329 ff.
kind, and degree, 137 ff.; as extension or intension, 138; originally "tribe," 230
Kirk and Raven, The Presocratic Philosophers, 134 n
Korzybski, Alfred, Science and Sanity, 116 n

Latin, suffixes in English, 41; an Indo-European language, 42
Leach and Fried (eds.), Dictionary of Folklore, Mythology, and Legend, 319 n
Leucippus and Democritus, 134, 218
Lewis, Clarence I., An Analysis of Knowledge and Valuation, 87 n
Lewis, M. M., Infant Speech, 35 n, 71 n
lexical definition, 264, 266
literal and metaphorical meaning, 91 ff.
literary and rhetorical forms of discourse, 73 ff.
literature, imagination in, 222 f.
Locke, John, on language, 5; on primary and secondary qualities, 135; An Essay Concerning Human Understanding, 5 n, 135 n
locutionary acts, 78
logic, Aristotelian, 46, 50 f., 54, 85, 100 f., 216, 246, 310; modal, 46; defined, 49; and language, 49 ff.; class, 50 ff.; substitute symbols in, 67; refined concepts in, 101; propositional forms in, 194 ff.; imagination in, 215 ff.
logical discourse, 75; symbols, 151,

172, 175 f., 194 ff.; conversion, 173, 310; forms for sentence types, 193 ff.; quantifiers, 198 f.; obversion, 310

Lyons, John, 53; *Introduction to Theoretical Linguistics,* 53 n

MacKaye, James, 297; *The Logic of Language,* 297 n

malapropisms, 25

materialism, in early Greek philosophy, 178, 249; as a philosophical system, 225 f.

mathematical, relations, 168 f.; induction, 306 n

mathematics, substitute symbols in, 67; refined concepts in, 101, 213 f.; and the search for measurement, 145 f.; concept of variable in, 186 f.; imagination in, 209; extrapolation and interpolation in, 305 f.

McKeon, Richard, "Philosophy and Method," 335 n

meaning, 81-103; ranges, 49; intentional (purposive), 81; referential, 81, 85 ff., 261; emotive, 82 f.; active, 83 f.; extensional and intensional, 85 ff.; specific and general, 90 f.; core, 91, 99; literal and metaphorical, 91 ff.; changes in, 95 ff.; actual and ideal, 294 ff.

measurement, in cases of degree, 145 f.; a quantitative relation, 167 f.; and imagination, 209 f.

mechanical failures, in communication, 27 f.

mediate inference, 310

member-of relation, 51

metaphor, in philosophical language, 1 ff.; meaning of, 91 ff.; analogy in, 93; limits of, 95; trite, 97; not to be defined, 265

metonymy, 97

Mill, John Stuart, criticism of Bentham, 145; *Utilitarianism,* 145 n

Miller, George A., *Language and Communication,* 16 n

misplaced concreteness, fallacy of, 121

modal, sentences, 46; logic, 46; concepts expressed in verbs, 191

Mohammed, 4

monadic relations, 171 f.

Moore, George E., 137

moral ideals, problem of defining, 294 ff.

More, Sir Thomas, 295

Morris, Charles W., *Foundation of the Theory of Signs,* 24 n; *Signs, Language, and Behavior,* 24 n, 76 n

Moses, 4

movement, included in function, 177

music, as a language, 35; symbols in, 69; imagination in, 222

Myers, Edward D., *The Foundations of English,* 39 n

Nagaoka, 220

names, proper, 86, 154, 265 f.

naming, by children, 35

narrowing extensional meaning, 96

natural, symbol-referent relations, 62 f.; divisions, 98 f., 132 ff., 283 f.

necessary, conditions, 162, 273 f., 283; conclusions, 311

negation, as a type of change, 181; imaginative, 205; expressed in language, 206; in philosophy, 206

Neoplatonists, on good and evil, 146; and Saint Augustine, 333

neurological failures in communication, 27 f.

Newton, Sir Isaac, universal of gravitation, 255

nominalism, 249 f.

noun, formed from other parts of speech, 38, 125 f.; functions of, 40 ff.; and verb languages, 47; primary and derived, 124; used to express qualities, 150; defining of, 268 f.

object, and event level of experience, 112; as aspect clusters, 147; and subject relation, 161

objectlike status of qualities, 150

observing, 317 ff.

obversion, a logical operation, 310

Ogden and Richards, 81; *The Meaning of Meaning,* 81 n

one-quality ideas, 139 ff.
opaque symbols, 68
operational definitions, 270
operationalism, 270
oratorical and political discourse, 26, 70 f.
ordinary language philosophy, 6; *see also* British analysis
Osgood, C. E., et al., "Phonetic Symbolism in Natural Languages," 64 n
ostensive definition, 266 f., 271
Ostwald, Wilhelm, 218
other-to-self relation, 160 ff.
ousia, 132 n
ownership relation, 159

part, abstractions, 108, 113 ff., 125; as unit of relations, 152; whole relation, 156 ff., 170; imaginatively used in substitution, 207
particular, distinguished from concrete, 119; expressed by the article, 150; typical, 232; opposite of universal, 246; special meaning of in Aristotelian logic, 198 f., 246 n; extension of, 265 f.
parts of speech, as functions, 40; four primary, 47, 124; defined by contextual definitions, 269 f.
passive and active order, 54, 190 ff.
Peirce, Charles S., interest in language, 5
Pepper, Stephen C., 336; *World Hypotheses,* 329 n, 336 n
perception and communication, 20 f., 33
perfection, notion of, 140; due to imagination, 215 f.; ideal of logical, 274
performatives, 77, 83
perlocutionary force, 78, 83
phenomenal and physical objects, 117
phenomenalism, 117
philosophical discourse, 1 f., 26; *see also* logical discourse
philosophy, goal of rational explanation in, 2; born in ancient Greece, 2; method in, 9, 224 ff., 328 ff.; imagination in, 224 ff.; and science, 227, 257, 328, 338

ff.; and the problem of truth, 228; aphoristic stage of, 328; errors concerning, 339 f.
phonetic, range, 35 f.; component, 49
physical objects, 117
physiological failures in communication, 27 f.
Plato, 2 ff.; and Aristotle, 4 f., 121; on writing, 18; dialogue form, 72; doctrine of forms, 121, 131, 144, 188, 214, 246 f., 249 f.; and Socrates, 259 ff.; philosophical system of, 329 ff.; *Cratylus,* 5; *Sophist,* 5; *Phaedrus,* 18 n; *Phaedo,* 131, 144 n; *Euthyphro,* 260
Platonic universal, 246 f., 249 f.
Platonism, 3 f., 188, 249 f., 329 ff.
Platonists, 121, 169
poetic discourse, 1 f., 26, 74 ff., 82
polarity (bipolarity), models of, 139 ff.; as a relation, 155 f.
political discourse, 26
positivism, logical, 6, 336
possession, relation of, 159
postulates, 328
practical discourse, 75 f.
pragmatic check of truth, 324 f.
pragmatics, 24 n
predicate, and subject, 35, 55 f.; adjective and noun, 45
predication, expressed by verb, 191
prefixes, 39 f.; negative, 206
prejudices and predispositions, in communication, 23 f., 28
prepositions, 40, 47, 124 ff., 173 f.
prescriptive (stipulative) definitions, 264, 266
presentational symbols, 69 n
primary and secondary qualities, 134 ff.
probable conclusions, 311
Procrustes, bed of, 209
pronouns, 36, 40, 47, 68, 127, 174
proper names, 86 f., 154, 265 f.
propositional, forms, 151, 188, 194 ff.; implications, 310
propositions, general, 232 f.; analytic and synthetic, 312 f.
Pueblo Indian, cloud symbol, 63
Pythagoras, 2, 328

qualifying functions, 184, 188 f., 197

qualities, 129-51; expressed in language, 47, 124 f.; as an aspect abstraction, 113; as a unitary aspect, 129; compared with relation and function, 130 f., 152 f., 177; and Platonic Ideas, 131; essential and accidental, 131 ff.; primary and secondary, 134 ff.; tertiary, 137; in kind and degree, 137 ff.; one and two quality models, 139 ff.; as abstractions, 147; expressed in language, 149 ff.; expressed in logical symbols, 151; substitution of in imagination, 207

quantifiers, logical, 198 f.

quantitative relations, 167 ff.; correlated with variables, 187; imaginatively altered, 209 f.

questions, by children, 71 f.

Raju, P. T., "The Principle of Four-Cornered Negation in Indian Philosophy," 205 n

realism, common-sense, 117; Platonic, 249 f.

reality, and abstraction, 119 f.

reasoning, human, 13; relational analysis as key to, 153; inductive, 302 ff.; deductive, 308 ff.; progressive and regressive, 314 n; irrelevant, 315

receivers, and transmitters, 15, 18, 27 f.

reductionism, 130, 271

referent, related to symbol and concept, 15, 62 ff.; wrong, 19; perceivable and imaginary, 19 ff.; 82 n, 87 n, 261 n; correct, 29; abstract and concrete, 116

referential meaning, 81, 85 ff.; changes in, 95 ff.; in definitions, 261

refined (logically idealized) abstractions, 101, 146, 169, 214, 293 f., 296, 329

reflexive relations, 172 f.

relata, 153

related (correlated) functions, 185, 188 f., 197

relations, 152-76; in attributive sentences, 45; in parts of speech, 47; part-whole, 97, 156 f.; species-genus, 97, 232; link between parts and/or qualities, 130, 152 f.; abstract to concrete, 147 f.; expressed in logical symbols, 151, 172 f., 176; major types of, 152 ff.; analysis and clarification of, 171 ff.; monadic, dyadic, and triadic, 171 f.; reflexive, symmetrical, and transitive, 172 ff.; progressive, 175; contrasted with function, 177; functioning, 193; substitution of in imagination, 207 f.

religion, according to Whitehead, 26; a complex notion, 30

resemblances, family, 91, 119 n, 242, 275; in causal relations, 164

rhetorical and literary forms of discourse, 73 ff.

Riddell, James, *Animal Lore and Disorder, Hit or Myth,* 207 n

root metaphor, 225, 329 n, 336

Rotenstreich, Nathan, 337; "On Constructing a Philosophical System," 337 n

Russell, Bertrand, *Principia Mathematica,* 6

Rutherford, Ernest, 220

Sanskrit, an Indo-European language, 42

Sartre, Jean-Paul, *Being and Nothingness,* 6 n

Schmidt, Paul, "Truth in Physics," 271 n

Schopenhauer, Arthur, 161

Schrödinger, Edwin, 221

science, role of imagination in, 217 ff.; and philosophy compared, 227, 257, 328, 338 f.

scientific, imagination, 217 ff.; method, 317; system, 328

secondary qualities, 134 ff.

secondhand information, 315

self-other relation, 160 ff.

semantic, errors, 24 ff.; factors, 33 ff.; relations, 85

semantics, meaning of, 24 n; and symbolism, 59

semiotic, 24 n
sense impressions compared, as a truth check, 323 f.
sentence, as unit of thought, 40; types in English, 42 ff.
sentential forms, *see* propositional forms
Shannon and Weaver, *The Mathematical Theory of Communication*, 16 n
Sheldon, Wilmon H., *God and Polarity: A Synthesis of Philosophies*, 335
sign, language, 14, 34; Greek word for, 24; compared with signal and symbol, 59 ff., 62; uses of, 70 ff.
signal, 60, 62
similarity, and contiguity, 62 ff.; in classes, 87, 118, 233, 275; and difference, 153 ff.; in causal relations, 163 f.
Slavic, an Indo-European language, 42
slang, 25
society, communication necessary for, 13
Socrates, 2 f., 259 ff., 275
solar system, Ptolemaic and Copernican notions of, 320
solipsism, 160
sorites, 175
Spanish language, 54 f.
spatial relations, 166
species and genus, 97, 232
specific, and general meaning, 90 f.; not same as concrete, 119
speech, defects, 27; forms of, 34; response to, 35
Spinoza, 328 f.
statistical statements, 306 f.
stimuli, vs. symbols, 82
stipulative definitions, 264, 266, 283
structure sense, in backgrounds of understanding, 33; need for, 228, 313
subclasses, and extension, 86; and kinds, 137 f.; in part-whole relation, 157; as species, 232; in defining by enumeration, 267
subject, and predicate, 35; need for clarity in expressing, 55 f.

subject-object relation, 160 ff.
substance, according to Hume, 136, 147 f.; according to Aristotle, 147 f.
substance-attribute relation, 157 ff.
substitute symbols, 67 f.
substitution, as a type of change, 181 f.; in imagination, 207 f.
successive definition, method of, 299
sufficient conditions, 162, 273 f., 283
suffixes, more and less dominant, 38; lacking in Chinese, 39 f.; nominalizing, 125 f.; with various functions, 149 f.; ambiguous, 297 f.
sui generis, 138
Swadesh, Morris, *Conversational Chinese for Beginners*, 170 n
syllogism, 175 f., 242, 310 f.
symbolic, meaning, 81 ff.; sentential forms, 151, 172 ff., 194 ff.; overtones in the arts, 223
symbolizing, a mental process, 58, 317
symbols, 58-80; pictorial and ideographic, 14; related to referent and concept, 15 ff.; appropriate and inappropriate, 25, 64 f.; knowledge of, 25 ff., 30; influence on concept formation, 26 f.; importance of, 34 f., 58; definition of, 60 f.; functions of, 61 f.; natural objects as, 62, 66; artificial, 63, 66; arbitrary, 65 f.; conventional, 66 f.; discursive, 67, 69 n; substitute, 67, 264; esoteric, 68; opaque and transparent, 68; internal (expansive) and external, 69; presentational, 69 n; uses of, 70 ff.
symmetrical relations, 172 ff.; and conjunctions, 173
synecdoche, 97, 157
synesthesia, 64
synonyms, connotational differences between, 263 f., 267; defining by, 267, 272
syntactics, 24 n
syntax, 49 f.
synthetic, languages, 39; proposi-

tions, 312 ff.; philosophies, 334
system, in philosophy, 226 f., 327
ff.; in science, 328, 338
systematizing, 327-40

taste, in art and science, 224; in philosophy, 227
temperature, notions of, 138 ff.
temporal, aspects in language, 46, 191; relations, 166 f.
tent diagrams, 85, 88, 92, 93, 96, 98, 231, 232, 262, 267, 269, 273
terminological quibbles, 24 n, 80
terms, include both symbol and concept, 85; as a tent, 86; general, 231 f., 265; definition of, 261 ff., 280, 282 ff.; implications from, 308 ff.
tertiary qualities, 137
testa and *tete,* 97
Thales, 205 f.
theorems, 328
Thomas Aquinas, Saint, 250, 334
Thomas, Dylan, 48; *The Collected Poems of Dylan Thomas,* 48 n
Thomson, Joseph J., 219, 222
touchiness, human, 12 f.
transferring extensional meaning, 91 ff., 96
transitional sentences, 46
transitive, verbs, 44, 189 ff.; relations, 172 f., 175 ff.
translatability, 99
transmitters, 14 f., 18, 27 f.
transparent symbols, 68
triadic relations, 171
trite metaphor, 97
true, as a quality, 150; not applicable to definitions, 277; problem of defining, 288 ff.
truth, of imaginary ideas, 227 ff.; synonym of reliability, 277, 290; and validity, 311; formal and factual, 311; tests for, 323 ff.
Twain, Mark, *A Tramp Abroad,* 99 n
two-quality ideas, 139 ff.

unbound linguistic units, 39
uniqueness, concept of, 130, 140
universal, conditions of thought (Kant), 136; and particular

propositions, 198 f.; and particular classes, 246; collective and particular typical, 248; beliefs vs. natural aspects, 254
universals, nature of, 245 ff.; Aristotelian, Platonic, and Hegelian, 246 f.; existential status of, 249 ff.; limited, 254 f.; and absolutes, 255; and constants, 255
Urban, Wilbur M., *Language and Reality,* 69 n
Ussher, Archbishop, chronology of, 315
utopia, 295

vagueness, and ambiguity, 97 f.; not in abstractions as such, 118; decreased in defining, 275; futility of arguing from, 280
validity, and truth, 311
valuometer, 145
variable, extension, 89, 98, 100, 118, 262, 267, 275, 282 f.; independent and dependent, 186; in propositional forms, 194 n
variation, of extension and intension, 89 f.; continuous, 138 f.; as change, 181 f.; direct and inverse, 188; imaginative, 208 ff.
verb, regular and irregular, 36; a traditional part of speech, 40 ff., 47, 124 ff.; transitive and intransitive, 44, 191 ff.; temporal aspect and modality shown in, 46, 191; expresses idea of function, 124 f., 191; tense, predication, and causality shown in, 191
verifiability, and falsifiability, 271, 289; and confirmation, 322
vocabulary, limitation of in children, 36
von Frisch, Karl, *The Language of Bees,* 13 n
Vygotsky, Lev S., *Thought and Language,* 119 n

Whitehead, Alfred N., on religion, 26; on abstracting, 107, 123; on the fallacy of misplaced concreteness, 121; on difficulty of describing key concepts, 159 n; on minimal and inclusive events, 165;

process philosophy of, 335; *Principia Mathematica,* 6; *Process and Reality,* 26 n, 121 n, 159 n, 165 n; *Science and the Modern World,* 197 n, 121 n

Whorf, Benjamin Lee, 26 f., 52 f., 200; *Language, Thought, and Reality,* 26 n, 52 n

Wittgenstein, Ludwig, 91, 251 f., 275; *Philosophical Investigations,* 91 n

word, formation and function, 39 ff.; and term, 85

writing, the story of, 14; in cultures, 19; as one form of linguistic expression, 34; learning of, 36 f.; advantage of, 56

Zeno the Eleatic, 214, 218